AF239068

Additional Praise

"*Punk Spirit!*, with its unique blend of anarchic counterculture and classic psychoanalytical theory, makes for a most compelling read. From incarnation to oral history, the power of punk compels you!" **—Steven Blush, author and filmmaker,** ***American Hardcore***

"I devoured *Punk Spirit!* in two sittings. It was pure enjoyment to read—pure exhilaration! Crack open *Punk Spirit!* and behold a 'volatile church' where the lifeblood of a rich, complex, and passionately punk spirituality surges through every page. Incited by John Malkin's galvanizing questions, the collective voices of his interlocutors raise up a kaleidoscopic vision of punk spirit that is as vibrantly alive as it is full of surprises." **—Glenn Wallis, guitarist for Ruin, author of** ***An Anarchist's Manifesto***

"*Punk Spirit!* is an affirming and varied testimony to the significance of punk music and spirit in the library of humanity and existence. Explore! The Spirit of Punk reflects how, in our extreme punk expression of letting go of societal norms and indoctrination, we find liberation and peace in reaching for and manifesting another state of being and its possibilities." **—Yaotl Mazahua, Iconoclast, Aztlan Underground (aka Anahuak Underground)**

"A skilled interviewer, John Malkin is one of a handful of punk mavens willing to explore its deep, spiritual intimations. This is a monumental collection of conversations, offering anyone with a reasonable curiosity about punk rock and spirituality the opportunity to understand their amorphous, vibrant, and sometimes revolutionary entanglements. If God is dead, punk is not dead, and the anti-establishment postures and rebellious spirit captured in Malkin's book lives on!" **—Ken Chitwood, religion scholar, journalist, and theologian**

"Punk is far from dead; it is getting richer and richer. We are lucky to have John Malkin look at a very specific aspect of that world. With gems from more than 150 interviews conducted over the course of a quarter century, *Punk Spirit!* is an important contribution to the ever-growing oral history of one of the world's most compelling subcultures." **—Gabriel Kuhn, author of** ***Sober Living for the Revolution: Hardcore Punk, Straight Edge, and Radical Politics***

PUNK SPIRIT!

AN ORAL HISTORY OF PUNK ROCK, SPIRITUALITY, AND LIBERATION

JOHN MALKIN
FOREWORD BY PENNY RIMBAUD

BLOOMSBURY ACADEMIC
NEW YORK · LONDON · OXFORD · NEW DELHI · SYDNEY

BLOOMSBURY ACADEMIC
Bloomsbury Publishing Inc, 1359 Broadway, New York, NY 10018, USA
Bloomsbury Publishing Plc, 50 Bedford Square, London, WC1B 3DP, UK
Bloomsbury Publishing Ireland, 29 Earlsfort Terrace, Dublin 2, D02 AY28, Ireland

BLOOMSBURY, BLOOMSBURY ACADEMIC and the Diana logo are trademarks of Bloomsbury Publishing Plc

First published in the United States of America 2026

Cover design: Sally Rinehart and John Malkin
Cover photos:
By John Malkin: Lenny Kaye (Patti Smith Group), "Masha" Alyokhina (Pussy Riot), Ray Cappo (Shelter)
Photo by Ed Colver: Jello Biafra (Dead Kennedys)
Photo by Matt Fitt: H.R. (Bad Brains)
Photo by Julaire Scott: Klee, Jeneda & Clayson Benally (Blackfire)
Photo by Tom Potisit: Kyaw Kyaw Thu Win (Rebel Riot)

Library of Congress Cataloging-in-Publication Data
Names: Malkin, John, interviewer. | Rimbaud, Penny, 1943- writer of foreword.
Title: Punk spirit! : an oral history of punk rock, spirituality, and liberation / [interviews by] John Malkin ; foreword by Penny Rimbaud.
Description: Lanham : Bloomsbury Publishing, 2025. | Includes bibliographical references and index.
Identifiers: LCCN 2025015157 (print) | LCCN 2025015158 (ebook) | ISBN 9798881802714 (hardback) | ISBN 9798765155950 (pdf) | ISBN 9798881802721 (epub)
Subjects: LCSH: Punk rock music—Religious aspects. | Music and spirituality. | Punk rock musicians—Interviews. | Liberty. | LCGFT: Interviews | Oral histories
Classification: LCC ML3921.8.R63 P86 2025 (print) | LCC ML3921.8.R63 (ebook) | DDC 781.66/112—dc23/eng/20250401
LC record available at https://lccn.loc.gov/2025015157
LC ebook record available at https://lccn.loc.gov/2025015158

ISBN: HB: 979-8-8818-0271-4
ePub: 979-8-8818-0272-1
ePDF: 979-8-7651-5595-0

Typeset by Deanta Global Publishing Services, Chennai, India
Printed and bound in the United States of America

For product safety related questions contact productsafety@bloomsbury.com.

To find out more about our authors and books visit www.bloomsbury.com and sign up for our newsletters.

Figure 0.1 John Malkin interviews H.R. on the Bad Brains tour bus before their 2010 concert in Santa Cruz, California. Photo by Matt Fitt.

CONTENTS

CONTENTS

CONTENTS

FOREWORD

BENEATH THE MASK

Religion is dogma rather than faith or, conversely, religion is faith in dogma; much the same applies to politics. The crows fly wild with not a shadow to part them. Hush, winds blow.

Whoosh, spiritual identity is an oxymoron. Likewise, spiritualism is not an alternative to materialism, rather it is an extension of its egotistic vanities. Our natural-born entity becomes mutated by the vulgarities of Freud's "id" which, coupled with Cartesian vagaries, becomes the "I am" of the consumerist individual where, truly, "we are not." Buy now, tomorrow never arrives. Meanwhile, beneath this materialist mask, there is nothing but eternal emptiness bound to an immovable "isness." Spirit cannot be worn; we stand alone, naked in body and mind. So yes, know thyself, but first accept that your self is not the self you might like to think it is. There is no question: identity falsifies entity. Id? I think not.

All things are sentient: animal, vegetable, and mineral, the breath and the breather. This is both being and non-being, not a path, but a universe dancing its dance, an ever-changing yet static symbiosis. One foot before the other we walk, always mindful, traveling nowhere. The "middle way"? There is no way. Journeys are nothing but reflections in a static pool. Quantum infinities and Blake's grain of sand prove the void: no Gods, no masters. Only silence.

We are prisoners of consciousness, which is in itself self-deluding. Fly, then, fly if you must, but know that transcendence is but a flight of fancy. There is nothing above, nothing below, nowhere to run, nothing to know. Never again, but how could it be otherwise? Each is its own unrepeatable moment. We are alone in this, yet we are also profoundly together. Each move and every moment is both multidirectional and multidimensional in its entirety. Neither here nor there, the symbiosis is beyond delusions of time and space. In short, it has no body. As much as we drift forward, so we fall backward. Attempts to harbor these forces merely compound the poisonous nature of the materialist narrative. The boat has pulled anchor. The ocean consumes. The tides turn.

Harmony versus friction; being essentially divisive, ideologies lead to conflict. No doubt. Mind the gap. Are you joking? It takes a stone a lifetime to walk, two to talk. Then what might it have to say, and where might it feel free to say it? The Piper has long since crested the brow of the hill, Nietzsche lies defeated in the valley, and Moses avalanches to rest as mere moraine. Thou shalt if thou choose to, yet the inexplicable has no voice. Silence is a language. The lotus is simple transference, matter from mud which is also matter. Then where the this and the that of it? Where the division? I am thou as thou art I. Then why the pain? Pain is in attachment. No exception. The manacles are an abacus. Count me out. If you think you're meditating, you're not. Prostration is flagellation. Remorse is a form of self-hatred. Hatred is a form of failed love. Love is all, or love is not at all.

In breathless skies, the crows drift unmeasured, clouds also. No contradictory song to sing, no horizon that is not other. Sentience is in and of all things, all matter. Now is an eternity. There is no escape. We are the never of forever. In the nanoseconds between an event and our perception of it, anything could happen. Thus the indefinable passes us by, describing greater universes than ever we might imagine. Beware, for ism is schism. Left or right, the lake is frozen. Illusion is delusion casting blame. Nothing is happening because there is nothing to happen. We live; we die. Spot the difference. The fusion is entire. If you think you've got the answer, you didn't hear the question.

Penny Rimbaud, January 2025

BE PUNK NOW

We gotta *Be Punk Now*. Here in the twenty-first century, to attain the pure raw state of punk is just a dream. We would have to tear off a mile-thick layer of saturation advertising, artificial intelligence, and mountains encrusted with pixels. It's time to whip up the force of a new honesty, a no-bullshit counter-invasion against corporate virtual consumer culture that is making mass extinction at the present moment.

John Malkin's view of punk comes from the far side of the Rock barrage, from the world against which Americans in particular have battlements of neuroses. We erase the Spirit with stark raving fear. It's in the roots, the loving gentleness, and the hit-and-run visions that held together the ecosystem of punk. And still holds it together. Punk lives. But we have to find it again.

Debra White Plume, the Oglala prophet, believed that the Earth would rise up to cleanse and balance and do what had to be done to make life survive, and that the Earth would reach out to human beings and invite our participation in this work. And Debra White Plume went on to say that some humans would immediately respond to the Earth and work with her. Others would hesitate and disappear.

We still might have time. We need to enter the fire and flood and walk among the ruins after the disaster has passed; the Spirit of punk is there. It is the spiritual life in direct experience. No sneaky product placements, view-counts, reputational consultations . . . A rock 'n' roll scream for Earth justice could rise from the rubble of a thousand tornadoes. It was just as strange in the late 1970s and early 1980s. The same Spirit moved through kamikaze artists who walked into the lies with a loud sound.

The Spirit moves farther into actualized experience with punk because punk self-enforces directness. But in today's all-bullshit-all-the-time culture, locating the punk is like diving for pearls. The Earth is today's great punk—an honest, fearless comeback at the lies. That's the Sixth Extinction. A punk rock hit that goes on for decades. As life after life leaves us, and finally we leave too . . . Will we be able to duet with that world-scale fuck you? I'm sure some of us will go down with our rock screaming like 200 mph wind. Earthalujah!

Rev. Billy Talen—The Church of Stop Shopping
February 2025

INTRODUCTION

THE MUSIC OF NO MUSIC

Are you ready to be liberated?

—"The Young Crazed Peeling" by The Distillers (2002)

The mercy of the West has been social revolution; the mercy of the East has been individual insight into the basic self/void. We need both.

—"Buddhist Anarchism" by Gary Snyder (1961)

Things are not as they seem. Nor are they otherwise.

—Buddhist Lankavatara Sutra

The reason I'm not a Buddhist is because Buddha wasn't a Buddhist! He was just a bloke sitting on his ass with ideas and insights. I'm the same.

—Penny Rimbaud (Crass)

No Gods, No Masters.

—Anarchist slogan

Life gets intense / Just like rock and roll.

—"I Live in The City" by The Humans (1979)

Everything is connected with everything else.

—Sign on studio wall at end of video for "Failed Imagineer"
by *Propagandhi* (2017)

I discovered punk rock and Buddhism around the same time when I was seventeen years young in 1979. Both appealed to my rebellious side that intuitively sensed what I'd learned about the world from adults was, at best, incomplete. Punk rock pushed me toward anarchism, high-energy music, and questioning authority. Buddhist meditation practices grounded my journey and revealed truths about interconnection, impermanence, and liberation. Punk and spirituality both create energy that connects people through self-expression, emotional release, and creative responses like music, writing, film, art, and direct social action. Punk rock has sometimes been an attempt to take music beyond the confines of music, thereby manifesting the *music of no music*. This sentiment easily coalesces with Alan Watts' 1951 philosophy book *The Wisdom of Insecurity* where he describes Buddhism as "The religion of no religion."

Punk and spirituality harmonize toward liberation and living free, and this surprising combination has kept me company during my adult life. Naturally, people have asked, "Punk is loud and angry while spirituality is calm and compassionate. How do those go together?" *Punk Spirit!* is partly an attempt to answer that, plus deeper questions like: What makes music a spiritual, transcendent experience? What's the difference between religion and spirituality? Is personal and collective liberation possible? Why has the power of punk rock been combined with spiritual and religious traditions? Do social and personal liberation happen through creating or destroying? Or both? How have punk musicians been affected emotionally by their music? What's the use of anger and other intense emotions? How best to transcend suffering? The voices in *Punk Spirit!* offer insights into liberation, living free, and how to respond creatively to injustice. They describe the importance of community and also criticize the hypocrisy of religions used for control and permanent war. They practice authentic self-expression and revolutionary love through words, music, and direct actions.

2025 marks sixty years since proto-punk band Los Saicos (Peru) released the song "Demolición" in 1964, and forty-nine years since the Ramones' self-titled debut album was released (April 23, 1976). It's forty-eight years since the release of *Damned, Damned, Damned* (February 18, 1977) and *Never Mind the Bollocks, Here's The Sex Pistols* (October 28, 1977), which the Pistols will perform live on July 4, 2025 (with Frank Carter instead of John Lydon). Patti Smith is seventy-eight years old and celebrating the fiftieth anniversary of her album *Horses* with a 2025 Europe/US tour. Iggy Pop is seventy-seven. Final tours were announced in 2024 by Gang of Four, Devo, and X while 69-year-old H. R. (Bad Brains) is on a Spring 2025 US tour with Dead Kennedys. On January 1, 2025, Au Pairs singer/guitarist Lesley Woods released her first new music since 1982: *In The Fade* with "Say Peace" and "Let it Go." Propagandhi announced the May 2, 2025 release of their eighth studio album with Chris Hannah singing on the title song; "I am at peace these days, give or take a fit of blinding rage."

Last year, Klee Benally, of Diné punk band Blackfire passed away at the age of forty-eight, just after contributing the foreword to the first book in this series, *Punk Revolution!* and producing his own book, *No Spiritual Surrender: Indigenous Anarchy in Defense of the Sacred*, and an anti-colonial board game called *Burn the Fort*. I had an interview scheduled on May 7, 2024, with Gary Floyd, singer with the Dicks, Sister Double Happiness, and Black Kali Ma and on May 3 Floyd passed away surrounded by loved ones in San Francisco. Nick Cave would've fit very nicely in these discussions of punk and spirituality, but my attempts to contact him were unsuccessful. His 2022 book, *Faith, Hope and Carnage*, and 2024 album, *Wild God* express spirited emotional connections to loss and beauty, grief and gratitude, longing and empathy. Maybe I'll catch up with Cave for my next book.

> *"People always talk shit about religious people and spirituality," says Cruz, like "Oh, you believe in a man in the sky." But then the same people come up to me and look to me like I, or my songs, have the answers to their questions. Because everyone's looking for something, everybody needs something. Sometimes, as a dad and as a husband, I wish I could call my dad or somebody and just ask "What the fuck do I do here?" Everybody needs a Northern star. So, while those two lines kind of contradict each other, at the same time they lend to each other that we're all just looking for something and we all put our belief in something, no matter how ridiculous or superstitious it is. And those things can let you down, but they also can rise you up.*

Jason Cruz of Strung Out; April 2024 press release for album *Dead Rebellion* (Fat Wreck Chords)

GRATITUDE AND ACKNOWLEDGMENTS

Deep gratitude to my son Bodhi for being an inspiring artist and to my wife Alison for her loving support. Thanks to Holger Roessler, Lutz Helmke, and Henni Rottstock for translating interviews. Thanks to Key Pankonin for helping me make contact with a wider group in Berlin, and much gratitude to everyone who did interviews with me for this project. Thanks to Beth Nauman-Montana for the great index for both *Punk Revolution!* and *Punk Spirit!*

Punk Spirit! is the second in a trilogy of books between *Punk Revolution!* (2023) and the forthcoming *Punk Roots!* Thanks to Michael Tan and Rowman & Littlefield / Bloomsbury for supporting my dream of creating this expansive series on punk rock, spirituality, and social change. All of these interviews were originally broadcast on Free Radio Santa Cruz (1997–2016), San Francisco Liberation Radio (1999–2000), and KZSC 88.1 FM / kzsc.org at the University of California, Santa Cruz (2016–2025). I'm very grateful to everyone who helped sustain Free Radio Santa Cruz for thirty years; it was a dynamic anarchist, punk rock experiment. Special gratitude to Uncle Dennis. Some of the interviews in *Punk Spirit!* were previously published in print in *Z Magazine*, *Razorcake*, *Punk Planet*, *Spirituality & Health*, *Lion's Roar*, *In These Times*, *The Santa Cruz Sentinel*, and *The Santa Cruz Good Times*. I have made considerable effort to contact copyright owners of images and seek permission from interviewees. Should any rights owners come forth, I shall include permissions in future printings of *Punk Spirit!* My interviews with Henry Rollins are not included in this book and are available online at kzsc.org. I have capitalized the word "god" only when it seemed the interviewee was doing that in their speech, and I've chosen not to capitalize the word "capitalism," to put it in its place.

PUNK AND SPIRITUALITY
DIRECT CONNECTION/MEANING AND PURPOSE/IN THE FLOW

Spirituality is very much about doing what you believe in and being aware of other sources of information. Every person has got their own percentage of how much spirituality they think they need to take notice of.

—Dick Lucas (Subhumans)

Music has that ability to make you lose track of time and be so fully mentally and physically engaged that that's all you can do.

—John Doe (X)

I had a spiritual experience listening to it.

—Flea on hearing the Germs album *GI* ("The Spiritual Punk Record That Changed Flea's Life Forever" by Aimee Ferrer, Far Out Magazine, June 1, 2023)

Punk rock is commonly associated with anarchy, slam dancing, spikey hair, self-published zines, social change activism, and DIY record production. Spirituality is not often linked to the world of punk rock, and organized religion has been passionately criticized in many punk songs. In the meantime, punks have embraced self-expression and living free by developing cooperative communities, creating art and music in response to injustice, feeding the homeless, opposing cultures of domination, experimenting with emotional authenticity, and aiming for personal and social liberation—realms and actions that might be called spiritual.

While organized religions and other authoritarian institutions serve as controlling gatekeepers between humans and nature, many spiritual traditions embrace life-enhancing practices that throw open the door to anyone who would like direct and full participation in their own life, without a middle person. Where organized religion relies on judgment, coercion, and laws, spiritual mystics are process-oriented and thrive on living free. Mystics embrace mystery and paradox and aim for joyful community through music, poetry, and dance. Indeed, punk rock might be called the *modern mystical arm of rock and roll*. As Ian MacKaye told me, "I celebrate the journey rather than the goal."

Punk rock signified a return to the radical roots of the unholy trinity of amplified guitar, bass, and drums. From anarcho-punk to straight edge to Krishnacore, punks have experimented with rebellious, creative responses to injustice and suffering. The slam dancing and sonic blast of punk rock may seem far from spiritual practices like meditation and compassion, but the alternate reality created inside a punk basement concert has a surprisingly similar intensity to that of Indigenous American sweat lodge ceremonies. Or Victor Sanchez's recapitulation box, primal scream therapy, holotropic breathing, whirling Sufi dervishes, Tibetan Buddhist cymbals and chanting, or Osho's wild dancing meditations. The idea is to be fully present to life's experiences, express emotions creatively, and contribute to the world. Punk is a process.

VOLATILE CHURCH

LENNY KAYE (Patti Smith Group): Punk rock is music of the human spirit. All music, including punk rock, is spiritual. Music doesn't speak to our rational, conscious mind. It speaks to our unconscious mind. To connect with that is beyond all genre and style of music. All music reaches inside your soul. Punk rock is, in its own way, a variant of the greater music. Just like there's different people in the world but we're all reflecting the eye of God. If you can reach that with any music then you're in the realm of being blessed.

JM: I imagine you'd say there are particular things about punk that facilitate that.

LENNY KAYE (Patti Smith Group): It doesn't make a difference what route you use to get there, as long as you get there. On the other hand, it's interesting to look at the scenery on whatever road you've chosen. Punk rock, with its emphasis on a confrontational energy and a sense of making things move just a little bit faster and a sense of aggression and, in some ways, sensuality; it's a way to connect with your core. It's loud. It has a lot of the things that all great spiritual gatherings have; a sense of trance and rhythm and communal energy. It really works well in a social setting. You look at especially the more extreme forms of punk rock with the mosh pit and people surfing on top of each other, where the audience is as much a part of the band as the band themselves, leaping up on the stage, leaping off the stage. It's a very volatile church.

JONATHAN RICHMAN (Modern Lovers): Music with feeling is spiritual. It's music with heart and soul. When music affects you in your guts, then it's got spirit. I think that all sound is spiritual. The sound of voices and instruments is spiritual—*just* the sound. The colors that sound makes are from the spirit.

JM: Sometimes I have a hard time using words to define what spirituality means.

JONATHAN RICHMAN (Modern Lovers): I would! I'm just saying, "heart and soul." To me, if you don't feel it, it ain't there. Music is spiritual because it's talking about feeling. That's what the spiritual part of music is. You're feeling. That's it. Whenever young groups ask me; "Hey, we're going into the studio, what should we do?" I always say the same thing; "Sing and play what you feel. And *don't* sing and play what you *don't* feel." They say, "That's it?" I say, "That's it."

MARK ANDERSEN (*Dance of Days* / Positive Force DC): To this day I will argue with anyone who tells me that punk rock is about music. Or it's a style of dress or it's about tattoos and piercings. I'll admit that certain aspects of those signifiers are identified with punk, but the essence of punk is something that can't be contained by any of those things. It is a spirit that is seeking the truth and is willing to challenge the world, and yourself, in that process. What I've just described is the spiritual search. If people don't like certain terms, that's fine. But let us agree that not just punk, but all art is part of a spiritual journey, to the extent that it is about seeking truth and striving toward authentic expression. The only reason we think they're opposed (punk and spirituality) is because we've bought into concepts that are actual blasphemy against love, beauty or truth.

PETER CASE (The Nerves / Plimsouls): Usually, spirituality is about trying to be good to people. To find a place where you belong and where you're centered and happy simply with being alive, within your spiritual self. Often finding that place doesn't come through buying things. It's something you find within yourself.

PENNY RIMBAUD (Crass): One of the great spiritual masters was John Coltrane. He hardly ever said a word, but he said everything that is. And sometimes it was uncomfortable because it *is* uncomfortable. Sometimes he was profoundly beautiful because it *is* profoundly beautiful. He didn't need the words to give us light. It was in his very being and his progression through "Love Supreme" and then into his *come with me or suffer the consequences*. Like a good Zen master. It's a violent world and you've got to go along with it. If you resist, you're going to get hurt.

YAOTL MAZAHUA (Iconoclast / Aztlan Underground aka Anahuak Underground): Music saved my life. Especially punk and hip-hop. Music is a medicine as it heals by validating and empowering. I do music for that same reason, in order to lift spirits and provide medicine. It literally uplifted me in times of darkness just like spirituality does, therefore it is spiritual. Indigenous culture values songs as medicine, so it's about intention, purpose and wellness. Both bands are committed to this intention and therefore are prayers to the universe. Whether angry, introspective or analytical, it is all inspired by love.

CELINE BELLI (Rotten Ruckus): Starting a band and being in the punk music scene saved my life when I was sixteen. I tried to commit suicide and I came back from it. The only thing that kept me going was music. I think it would be fascist to say punk is a religion in itself but I think the spirit of punk saved me. Our Oxford dictionary defines spirituality as "elevating principle." That's the spirit of punk. I know a lot of punk people from a pagan background who celebrate deities and gods. I come from a Buddhist background and everything I grew up with makes me appreciate punk for what it is. People can be hard-line (straight edge), Christian, Muslim or whatever and if you understand the element of punk, it doesn't really matter what religion you're from. That's just the freedom of spirit. It's not attached to a belief or religion; it's about freedom. The band Bane from America were straight edge, but they remained positive. They were always open to fans who weren't straight edge. I went to see them twice in Kuala Lumpur and Manchester. There are still people out there who have their own ideas and ethics, but they don't impose on people.

MATT CLEAVER (Stalin's War): Even if punk is not primarily spiritual it may be secondary in many ways because it can help people get on a positive track with their lives. Because they listen to a song and relate to the whole vibe, it really can mean a lot. It meant a lot to me.

TWO PATHS: SELF-DEFENSE AND BLESSING WAY

CLAYSON BENALLY (Blackfire / Sihasin): In the Navajo culture and spiritual practices there's a belief that there's two paths within each of us. On one hand we have our arrowhead, 'Anaa'jí, the enemy way. This is self-defense, protection.

It's the way of our Naabaahí warrior society. And then on the other hand, we have our corn pollen, Tádídíín; the things that give life. That's Hózóónjí, the blessing way. We have these two powerful ways to navigate through life. We have our prayer, but we also have our self-defense or protection and we learn how to navigate both of those worlds.

Every weekend we'd be going to ceremonies with my dad. (Jones Benally) I'd be helping him out or hiking up to the mountain tops, being with nature. I felt more comfortable in solitude or in a spiritual, ceremonial setting where I was helping out at various ceremonies with my uncles, my dad's relatives. That process definitely started to help me identify this spiritual path that we have. That was part of my foundation.

On the other hand, when we were starting to tour and perform as a punk rock band (Blackfire) I found that there was almost equal solace in a mosh pit. You'd go into a show where it was like a sweat lodge. You'd be with tons of other youth releasing so much pent-up frustration and anger, identifying with the music. And that song might be talking about a particular political or social issue. A lot of punk genres at that time were more politically oriented and talking about issues that were pertinent, that you could see but had zero control over. But when you'd listen to these songs, you'd get into this mosh pit and vent and release and it felt like something maybe on a higher level may have been contacted. This is a process of coping, learning to release and at the end of that punk rock show, the weight of the world has been released and you feel human again. It's such a very unique feeling. Now when you go to a music show and you don't get to dance and you're seated, you don't allow all of your senses to fully connect. It's such a different experience going to a concert today (2024) versus a punk rock show back in the 1980s or 1990s or '2000s. There was a transference of energy that you used to be able to feel and connect with more.

JENEDA BENALLY (Blackfire / Sihasin): No one goes into a mosh pit to look pretty! You go into a mosh pit to let go of yourself and learn how to go with a flow and the faith that you put in others around you. You bounce off people, fall down, hit the ground, but people pick you up. It's having that faith, "Hey, I'm going to be okay at the end of it all." It's the same with life. I might come out with some scars, bumps and scrapes, but I'm going to be okay.

I also want to go back to the concept of punk rock and spirituality. I feel like a lot of people have this kind of illusion of *punks not caring*. But I feel it's the opposite. It's that we care so passionately, that it's not only about what is here and now. At least for me, it's about what is the past and what is the future? And what can I do to honor the past but also ensure a better future? Going back to what we were talking about earlier; you can't buy your way to spirituality. You can't bomb your way to spirituality. Yes, you can find religion. It's a book, a great guide into spirituality. But you have to find your own way and that's kind of the punk in all of this; you have to find your own sense of spirituality. Where do you sit within yourself? Where do you sit within this world? How are you connected to your community? It's not about the disconnection, but rather about the connection. And how do we then connect with each other to attain the better world? It's not even about attaining spirituality, but about reconnection. When you gravitate toward what you are, then you know you're becoming your authentic self. Even though I'm a punk musician, I am traditional Diné and I resonate with that spiritual connection with the Earth, with my relationship with plants, people, animals, the water and I recognize how our relationship is to be in harmony, in balance.

CLAYSON BENALLY (Blackfire / Sihasin): When you think of self-sacrifice in a lot of indigenous philosophies or practices, you'll have things like the sweat lodge. Or some of the Plains tribes do a fast that is a four-day process of testing one's limits within the physical form. Punk rock is like this. As Jeneda was saying, it's about finding that true, authentic element within yourself and being free. A lot of people view punk rock as dangerous. And it's there when you look at traditional indigenous ceremonies like the Sundance where there's flesh offerings or piercings. When somebody is trying to obtain a spiritual kind of understanding with the universe and looking for guidance, there's a journey and oftentimes it's not going to be comfortable. You're going to be self-sacrificing. But it's the process.

JOHN ROBB (The Membranes / *Punk Rock: An Oral History*): Punk and spirituality is a really interesting angle. Obviously, you've got Krishnacore and also Christian and Muslim punks. You could argue that a lot of time, pop culture is people seeking—maybe not so much spirituality—but trying to make sense of the world in a way that spirituality would have done two hundred years ago.

RAY CAPPO (Youth of Today / Shelter): I took a lot of hell for being in a punk band that was singing spiritual lyrics! People said, "Hey, you can't do that. You went from straight edge into spirituality? That doesn't belong here! This is punk rock." And I said, "Well, what does punk rock mean?" They said, "It means no God." I said, "Well, it means there are no rules." So, when you live in a world of no rules, we said, "We're going to bring spirit back into music." Music can be a vehicle for hate and political angst. Or for messages of unity. I was always interested in how to bring people together. Jesus wasn't trying to create Christians. Buddha wasn't trying to create Buddhists. There's universal spiritual truths and those truths have a lot in common. We're already spiritual beings; we just forgot.

Many will argue that spirituality is the origin of music. Music was originally an homage, prayer or praise to a higher power, spirits and energies. So, to kick God or spirit out of music—that's the bastardization of music!

ROB FISH (108 / Resurrection / Judas Factor): The thing that's always hard for the punk scene to digest is seeing the difference between religion and spirituality. I'm fairly anti-religious. I think that goes back to the root that it always runs deeper than the external allows you to see. Spirituality and punk rock are one and the same in the sense that both are striving to understand things more deeply than they seem on the surface. Whether people are atheists or into religion, a large majority in this world feel they need to know something that other people don't know; that they have truth at their beck and call. Whether *there is no truth* or *this old man rules the world* or *this woman is the most supreme deity*; everybody seems to feel they have something that other people just don't have. To me, it's kind of silly. All we have are our experiences and things that touch us.

RIKKI VANDERPOL (Dying for It): I've come into this stage of my life where I'm seeking—I don't want to say spirituality—but, looking for something more meaningful. The normal Christianity isn't for me. Joe (Clements) from the Deathless recorded my second band (Dance for Destruction) and he was telling me about choosing the dharma. So, I've been exploring that realm of spirituality.

JOHN STOCKBERGER (Sense Field): There was a crossover between punk and spirituality in 1980's hardcore and that became part of the scene. My own interest in spirituality and self-discovery happened during the same time I got into punk rock. I was already into the Sex Pistols but when hardcore hit it was the same time I got interested in Buddhism. For me it's always been connected. I gravitated to Buddhism because there was a lot of baggage with the concept of God, churches and religions. I was in a comparative religion class in eighth grade and the teacher got to Buddhism and told us the Buddha had said, "Life is suffering." Of course, at that age you're like, "Yeah! That sounds right!" (*laugh*) I got really interested in Buddhism from that point forward. I was already into punk rock. A lot of punk rock people were devout atheists, and I tended more toward that. There has to be more going on in reality and on the spiritual level than we were being presented. It's like we were being short-changed on some level.

GLENN WALLIS (Ruin / *An Anarchist's Manifesto*): Ruin was spiritual in the sense that we valued practices that led to self-overcoming. In the earliest days we would plaster the city (Philadelphia) with flyers that combined a shocking image with a provocative statement. I remember one that had an image of a starving child in Biafra with stomach distended with the statement, "A monstrosity born of decaying humanity." At the bottom right-hand corner was the Ruin logo. No show dates, no album for sale. We were careful to paste them not only in the usually gritty spots where punks hung out, but also where morning commuters from the suburbs would see them. That is a kind of punk spiritual sermon! We wanted people to leave our shows feeling uplifted. The times were grim. Darkness and despair were even *fashionable* in certain punk circles. I love darkness and melancholy more than practically anyone, but we didn't want to be dragged down by our subculture. The "spiritual" in this case might be the uplifting with clear eyes.

Most people generally get along. It takes effort to bring people into the dogma of political and religious regimes who want power, which is politics and not God. They are the ones who divide us and create conflict. Spirituality is an answer against that. Punk rock was an answer toward liberation. We said, "No! We want freedom." We want freedom spiritually, emotionally, physically, mentally and expressively; all these types of freedom.

DAVE DICTOR (MDC): The band came out of a frustration of us not wanting to be part of the world and not wanting to be passive. At the same time, we weren't so armed with a spiritual sense of how to go about confronting it. So, it became a very physical and visceral performance. I'm multidimensional and if we have to go for a label to define ourselves, which people seem to love to do, then people can just hold *that* label: multidimensional!

JONNY WICKERSHAM (Social Distortion): Music is such a spiritual thing for me because it's such a release. Whether it's through the lyrics of a song or the music or both together. Music really is *the* thing that has moved me more than anything else in my whole life. And there's been many shows that were really spiritual in nature. You walk off the stage and you're drained after giving everything you've got. It's very satisfying.

STEVEN LEE BEEBER (*The Heebie-Jeebie's at CBGB's: A Secret History of Jewish Punk*): Spirituality to me is not limited to religion; the ritual and dogma. I think of music as a kind of spiritual expression. Similar to the ideals of a lot of the lefties in New York of the 1930s who created collectives, this sort of idealism of a better world has aspects of spirituality and there is a lot of that in punk.

REVEREND BILLY TALEN (The Church of Stop Shopping): It's part of the DIY nature of spirituality that our side of activism—the earth spirit program—is less developed and less sure of itself than formal religions that have the patriarch in charge. In formal religions the marketing and theological end are very well developed. For us in the Church of Stop Shopping it's experimental. All of us are in recovery from our grandparents' religious fundamentalism! We're activists who sing. I was raised by right-wing Christians from Holland, Michigan. They were Dutch Reformed Christians, creators of apartheid. Part of my wearing the polyester suit as the Elvis-impersonating-late-night-televangelist character Reverend Billy is my own self-appropriation of my right-wing caste. I defend myself against it by making fun of it. But the people in the thirty-five-voice choir have backgrounds in Hinduism, Islam, Catholicism and Judaism. We're all kinds of fundamentalists!

CONNECTED TO EVERYTHING ELSE

JM: What's your view on spirituality and how it fits, or doesn't, with the punk approach?

AMY RAY (Indigo Girls): It depends on where you live. In the South, we're pretty steeped in spirituality. Most of the musicians I grew up with, I would consider them extremely religious. It didn't seem like a weird idea to me to combine the two and to have it all affect each other. Even Ian MacKaye and the Dischord set in D.C. had a sense of a power that was mysterious and greater than themselves. And some sense of something; I don't know what. You can feel it when they talk about what they did. For me it's like this; the creator is this omnipresent sort of thing and the world is all invested with a spirit and so you live engaged with all that. Punk is about community and it can't really exist without that network of the web of intermingling and looking at things as being invested with some kind of power in your community. My spirituality is not about an authority figure. It's about something that's within me and it can manifest itself and do greater things than I can do by myself because it gets connected to everything else. That's the kind of religion I have.

Any fundamentalist or orthodox religion, including fundamentalist Christianity, has an authority and often it's a male figure that is angry and has rules and walls. A lot of people resist it and I can understand why. They don't want to be affiliated with it. I don't even want to be! That's what rebellion is about: questioning authority. Emily (Saliers) works a lot with the reconciliation movement within the church and it's hard for her. It's hard to say, "I go to a Christian church, I'm Christian," because there are so many bad connotations. A lot of my friends that are activists—not in the native community, but in white communities—are more secular. It's always hard for me because I'm used to: *you pray before you do things*. That's why I'm so comfortable working in the indigenous communities because it's the same thing. A lot of the punk bands that I grew up with around Atlanta, and people on Daemon (Ray's record label) like Danielle Howl, she's a total punk rocker and so gospel-oriented and all about Jesus. It's just in you. You can't help it. Even if you're pagan, it's in you.

STEWART EBERSOLE (*Barred for Life*): Whatever gets me closer to transcendence is a great thing. Each person has a different switch to get them to break down certain barriers. Punk did that for me. It changed me from a kid that was probably destined to become a redneck construction worker to a person that broke down every political and social barrier in his own head and began to make his own decisions. I'm not only thankful for that; I will eternally owe it back to that scene. How do you pay it back? Punk doesn't have temples and shrines. You can't really make offerings anywhere.

MITA SCHAMAL (Namenlos): Spirituality and punk rock are liberation. Music is a small part of punk. Music is wonderful; it's a very good gift. You can play with the vibrations. But for me, the point is not just to make music, it's also to dance or write. And draw, paint, play theater, make jokes, kiss each other, touch each other, have relationships; all this is punk for me. But especially punk means to liberate ourselves from all the prisons and cages we get from the outside and the inside, from your trauma and desires. To liberate ourselves is punk.

HIDÉ FUJIWARA (Ultra Bidé): Music is attached to everything; music is attached to the universe. The Black African woman Lucy was the first punk rocker. A long time ago she played music, she ate, had sex, looked at the sky. That means the first musician—Lucy—was attached to everything. That means every subject is for musicians.

ROB FISH (108): You've got to change yourself internally, change how you view yourself and others, for anything to change on a wide scale. Politics isn't outside. I might chant "Hare Krishna" and the guy next to me might chant "Hare Krishna" but he might be a pro-life, right-wing piece of garbage. It's not just about doing some activity or believing in something that's going to all of a sudden make things right. If it were that easy, we'd already be there. It's a combination of having some sort of spiritual understanding of yourself and the world around you and not being lazy in terms of applying that to how you live your life politically and socially. Many people say, "I'm not into politics. I don't really care." That's bullshit. It's a cop-out. If you're into spirituality, how can you *not* think that politics is important? Not that you become a political activist and go live in the woods, but there should be some part of you that looks at your life from a political standpoint like, "I'm not going to shop at Walmart. I'm not going to wear Nikes. I look at their labor practices and how it affects the world around me." If someone is spiritual, there should be a sense of political thought in how they live.

You cannot change anyone in the world / The only one you can change is yourself.

—"Ten Thousand Ways to Rebel and Fight" by SMZB

JM: What comes first, personal liberation or social liberation?

WU WEI (SMZB): Personal liberation is first and foremost, but personal liberation must also be accompanied by self-discipline, although this is not easy to achieve. There is no absolute freedom, which is the difference between humans and animals. Let me calm down first. I can express my emotions through punk music. It is not meditation or martial arts. Understanding and knowing myself is also part of the content of thinking. This song is to say that everyone is an individual, with their own ideas and way of life, and they should not interfere with others, and should not be interfered with by others.

JM: Do you view yourself as a spiritual person?

ISHAY BERGER (Useless ID): Not at all, but it *is* funny, because I may be more spiritual than what I might view myself. Does that make sense?

GABRIEL KUHN (*Sober for the Revolution: Hardcore Punk, Straight Edge and Radical Politics*): One of the main difficulties in talking about spirituality is terminology. If you associate spirituality closely with religion or esoteric trends it often has negative connotations. Gustav Landauer (1870–1919) saw a strong spiritual dimension in his anarchism. He means that in order to change society you need to change your spirit, *yourself*. This means changing the way you perceive the world and this leads to affecting the way you interact with other human beings and other forms of life that you encounter in your daily existence. A lot of straight-edge folks would say that it allows them to relate to the world around them in ways they perceive as more compassionate. Parts of straight edge have made the link to spirituality very explicitly. Krishna straight edge bands picked a very specific kind of spirituality, which is Krishna culture. This may appeal to some people yet others view it as dogmatic or ideological. I think these are very conflicting issues that one has to confront personally.

DICK LUCAS (Subhumans / Citizenfish): Spirituality is very much about doing what you believe in and being aware of other sources of information. Spiritualness is hard to pin down, really. Every person has got their own percentage of how much spirituality they need to take notice of. You've got to function in everyday life. It's not like we're all sitting in caves being very spiritual, because we don't have the time or will to do that. Why should we? We only live once and there's a lot of things to do and people to interact with. Spirituality is a far more subtle thing than can be described in words. It's a resonance between people that fires people up.

JORDAN COOPER (Revelation Records): With punk rock the biggest thing that can be called spiritual is the whole idea of doing something different from getting on the treadmill and doing what the herd is doing. In the human brain, that's what spirituality and all of those feelings are triggered by. The thing that drives people to be spiritual is the same feeling that drives them to listen to punk or try to understand what's going on in the world. It's about expanding their mind and understanding of the world and hopefully trying to do something about the things they think are wrong. Punk and spirituality connect primarily because some people use spirituality to get to that place.

JM: I like Shelter and the lyrics blew me away in songs like "Appreciation" and "Empathy." Isn't it a bit ironic to have such intense music that talks about compassion?

JORDAN COOPER (Revelation Records): It makes no sense. I agree! My mom was one of the first people to point it out to me because she read Youth of Today's lyrics and said, "Jordan, the lyrics are so positive but the music is so angry. I don't understand!" That's pretty true! Youth of Today is a special case because Ray (Cappo) wanted to have this positive message in his music and he had a hard time actually being a positive person. The youth culture of the Northeast (United States) is probably not too different than it is anywhere and everything we did was to belittle each other. That didn't go away when Youth of Today started but they wanted to be positive. There is a conflict there. They were an anomaly in punk. Shelter was pretty much only talking about Hare Krishna and the things Ray picked up from that. I'm sure if anybody read the lyrics—even Ray himself—we'd find contradictions in the lyrics. Like belittling someone who doesn't express compassion is not really compassionate.

SPIRITUAL SEARCH

PENELOPE SPHEERIS (*The Decline of Western Civilization / Wayne's World*): The reason I've been through this spiritual search is because I got dosed with ecstasy at a Burning Man festival and everything changed since then. I really almost OD'd. If you've ever been out to Burning Man, there ain't no fucking doctors around. I was pitching a tent, drinking a beer and these girls came by and I think they put something in my beer. I was tripping big time. I stayed in the van that I rented and I wouldn't let anyone talk to me. That's when the whole devil thing started! (*laugh*) I was sure they were all working with the devil. I wouldn't let any of my friends in the van and I kept throwing up out the door and looking around and seeing these naked people drive by on bicycles with beanies on their heads spinning around. I thought, "Jesus! I am in hell!"

JM: This would not be a good ad for Burning Man. Sounds scary.

PENELOPE SPHEERIS (*The Decline of Western Civilization / Wayne's World*): It was the most frightening thing in my life! I thought I had died and gone to hell. I was used to waking up really early and I knew what time the sun comes up and the sun didn't come up when it was supposed to. That was a big red flag right there, you know? (*laugh*) I looked up on this mountain—and dig it, there ain't no mountains there, it's on a dry lake bed—I look up on this mountain and there were neon signs and all these naked people up there fucking in public! "Okay, I'm in hell." Finally, the sun came up. When you're more north, it comes up later. I didn't realize that. Anyway, I busted the hell out of there, left all my friends and just took off. I drove back to the airport and said I had to get away. After that I think my brain flipped around. Just the fact that I lived through it was a pretty big miracle. It probably should've killed me. I was never so sick and crazy in my life. It was almost like being re-born. They call it mind-expanding for a reason. Now, please children, do not take ecstasy. That stuff is too dangerous. People are probably going, "Hey, man I'm on ecstasy right now, what are you talking about?"

JM: People have different reactions to things.

PENELOPE SPHEERIS (*The Decline of Western Civilization / Wayne's World*): I think I'm allergic to it! I took a shitload of acid back in the day. I've been strung out on every drug there is. But I came off of them. They say that cigarette smoking is the hardest thing to quit. For me it was cocaine, even harder than heroin.

JACK GRISHAM (TSOL): Buddhists, Christians, Muslims—there's parts of all of those things that have been my truth. I realize that no one has *my* truth. No one. I've sat with some unbelievably heavy spiritual cats, guys that are known worldwide. I've hung out with them on a friend level and realized that *this guy is as fucked up as I am, man.* Unbelievable! I went to this monastery one time and I was sitting with these monks, talking. We were visiting with them and we started talking and the first thing out of this one monk's mouth was, "Fuck Brother Ted! He ain't doing his chores!" (*laugh*) He was pissed off! It was funny. People make pilgrimages to these guys and we're just sitting there laughing about it!

JOHN DOE EXPERIENCE—PUNK AND SPIRITUALITY

I've sometimes felt uncomfortable asking punk musicians about spirituality. I've wondered if they might think I'm trying to convert them to some religion or that I'm so dopey I don't realize that punk rock is robustly anti-authoritarian and anti-organized religion. So, here I am waiting to say hello to John Doe before a show with his band John Doe Experience. I introduce myself and inquire, "I'd like to do an interview with you for a book about punk and spirituality." Despite my fears, this query usually opens interesting conversations. But this time I get what I deserve when John Doe responds:

> *Punk rock and spirituality have absolutely nothing to do with each other.*

> —John Doe (X)

I quickly and awkwardly try to explain that I don't necessarily mean "religion" when I say "spirituality" and that I want to hear how he thinks punk has affected him and the world. But check this out; a few months later, Doe was back in town doing a show with X and I spoke with him backstage, and he immediately remembered our earlier conversation and humbly offered a new take. "I was being flip with you last time we spoke," Doe offered. "I'll do an interview with you about punk and spirituality. I may not have the same ideas as other people, but I'll talk with you." We ended up having a great conversation.

JOHN DOE (X): I'm not a traditional spiritual person. I'm not religious or anything like that. I do believe in a life force. If you're engaged and aware and in the moment, then I guess you're spiritual. If you're part of the world and you're not just living in the future or living in the past; that to me is spiritual.

JM: A year ago I told you I was working on this project about punk rock and spirituality and you said, "Punk rock and spirituality have absolutely nothing to do with each other."

JOHN DOE (X): When I responded to that—it depends on your definition of spirituality. And I'm not sure what your definition is. As far as being at one with the world, being whatever they call it; in the flow, losing track of time because you're so engaged with what it is you're doing, whether it's surfing or skiing, playing music, meditating, gardening or whatever it might be. All those are the same. Whether it's punk rock, singer/songwriter, new age; music has that ability to make you lose track of time and be so fully mentally and physically engaged that

that's all you can do. When you have one of those transcendental performances all of those things are happening. You're also drawing on the past and seeing a connection between what the song was written about and what's going on presently and you're sort of experiencing all of those elements simultaneously. In addition to singing and playing a song! That's certainly something! I don't know what it is. I guess that's spiritual.

JM: It's amazing what we human beings are capable of doing simultaneously.

JOHN DOE (X): I don't know if it's *simultaneous*. I heard that your brain is so fluid and facile that it can switch from one thing to another. You're not actually multi-tasking, you're switching and focusing on completely different things.

JM: It's just very, very fast.

JOHN DOE (X): Yes. Seemingly simultaneous.

JM: There are huge realms of religion that are about authority and rules. Punk rock often sings out against that. When I spoke with you before, what did you understand by *spiritual?*

JOHN DOE (X): Something that is meditative in a quiet sense. Not active. Spirituality can't get away from religion. But religion is rules and tradition and all these things that have been built up over the years. Certainly, punk rock and religion are *not* similar because the origins of music and especially punk rock, are inclusive—well, parts of it are inclusive. You can be who you want to be. And religion is exclusive. You have to be with that one group.

BILLY ZOOM (X): Music in general, if it's done correctly, comes from the heart. Playing music is a spiritual experience. If you can tune in, or tune out—however you want to look at it—the music just flows from your subconscious. At risk of sounding too arty—I don't like to sound arty—when it's good, that's how it happens, it just flows. It's sort of a spiritual thing. You don't really know where it comes from. It just keeps coming. I've only recently gotten to the point where I can say the word "art" without getting a tone of sarcasm in my voice. I didn't like being called an artist for a lot of years. I've kind of accepted it now.

JM: Why didn't you enjoy being called an artist?

BILLY ZOOM (X): To me, art was when you made it sound bad on purpose because you couldn't really play. If you could really play then you didn't call it art. As Keith Richards said, "Art is short for Arthur."

IAN MACKAYE (Minor Threat / Fugazi): I think it's a reach to bring in the spirituality aspect of it. I kind of know what you mean by it. A twenty-one-year-old girl said to me the other day, "It's like everything's just gotten thrown into a blender lately." That is so true. People are trying to explain life and are just mixing in all these different elements. I find it inspiring to see people who have spiritual practices; I'm interested in what people get out of it.

A FOOL TO LIKE SUFFERING

JM: I hear in some of your lyrics, ideas that address suffering. What do you think about suffering?

DAVID THOMAS (Rocket From the Tombs / Pere Ubu): It is best not to! (*laugh*) Go on with your question.

JM: I like that answer, though.

DAVID THOMAS (Rocket From the Tombs / Pere Ubu): Well, that is the most obvious answer there is! You'd be a fool to like suffering. But we live in times and worlds where there is a lot of pain. My pain isn't anywhere near the same pain as some starving, dying child somewhere in Africa or Asia. It is a different sort of pain. But I don't think that you can get away without talking about pain. I am not going to pretend that I understand that person's pain. But pain is pain. And how you deal with it is how you deal with it.

JM: It's ironic but tragic that some of the ways that people try to get away from suffering cause more suffering.

DAVID THOMAS (Rocket From the Tombs / Pere Ubu): That is the general human condition. Whatever you try to solve, you usually end up screwing up more. That is pretty standard stuff at this point. In the end, we are all individuals. You—Me. We are all separate islands. You reach out and that is part of what art is supposed to be. It is the attempt to reach out beyond the prison of words and pictures and sign language or whatever else. Music works with the same elements that human consciousness works with. So, you try to achieve some kind of communion with other human beings at a deep, deep level. And that level has to be beyond words because words are images and concepts. Human beings are a weird combination of physicality and spirituality, as music is.

ANDY GILL (Gang of Four): You get into a very complicated situation trying to decide what "spiritual" means. There would be an argument to explore that word and see it in a very wide context. There's something about Gang of Four—the music, lyrics, the performance and the whole thing—which slightly connects with the Blues in a very non-obvious way. There is something in our music about the universal human condition and it's a Humanist argument. In that sense Gang of Four does connect with spirituality. Initially I would say, "Spiritual? What? That's not on the agenda." But on the other hand, if you consider it in a very wide context than I suppose it is.

JM: Do you have a sense that Earth is paradise and oftentimes we're just not seeing it? Or is there something missing, that would make it paradise?

DAVE ALLEN (Gang of Four / Shriekback): It goes back to what's spiritual and what's not. It even goes back to the, "We Live as We Dream Alone" idea. I don't know what we're missing. Perhaps we are, but I'm not that spiritual a person. I feel you are. And that's fine with me but it could be a long, drawn-out discussion!

ROB FISH (108): The stronger people will always take advantage of the weaker people. I don't believe in this spiritual utopia where everybody is so spiritually or psychologically advanced that they're always helping the person next to them. Political movements are just like religious movements. You have a theology or philosophy and then you have the popular understanding or acceptance of a dynamic within that philosophy that then defines the movement. Sometimes you'll have splinter groups that come out with a different dynamic. I wish it was as easy as pre-packaging the truth to ensure there is no pain and suffering.

In the punk rock scene, the shows I've played lately (2007) there is really no sense of political, social or spiritual context. Maybe it's the bands we're playing with. We played with a few bands that at least have some sort of political or social message around vegetarianism. If you go to a show, it's all about dancing, stage diving and scene unity. And not as much give and take about spiritual or political topics. In the late 1980s hardcore scene everyone was straight edge or vegetarian. A few years later in the early 1990s there started to be a lot more ideas around politics and social issues and the whole spirituality thing came to the forefront. I think it's cyclical and it'll come around.

TAKE GOD OUT OF THE CHURCH AND INTO NATURE

JIM LINDBERG (Pennywise / *Punk Rock Dad*): Right as the band was starting, I was finishing up at UCLA (University of California, Los Angeles). I was an English major and luckily had a great teacher for American literature who turned me on to Henry David Thoreau and Ralph Waldo Emerson. For me, growing up listening to punk rock was like finding your patron saint. If you read most of Emerson's essays it's like a punk rock Bible! There is so much information in his works about self-reliance; look at yourself for the answers. About being a non-conformist and not looking to other people about how to behave. Not falling into tradition, but making your own way in life.

I'm simplifying it but the Transcendentalists were one of the first movements to try and take God out of the church and bring it out into nature. To truly understand the divine, you need to experience nature. Without expressing it directly, they were starting to mistrust organized religion and how it can be corrupted. Thoreau was a student of Emerson and put it into practice by building a cabin out in the woods in Walden, and tried to put the principles to work. It was great for me to absorb and definitely it found its place in our lyrics and songs. It's something that people have responded to; I hear from people around the world that they get the message.

JOHN DOE (X): Living in Los Angeles, I don't think I could do it anymore because it's so difficult to get from one place to another. Bakersfield is a lot lower impact. On the other hand, living in the country, it's really difficult to complete things. If you need to get your kids to school or go to the grocery store, you have to drive for ten miles. The round trip takes forty minutes. It's always something. It just depends on how you deal with that something. So, does that something really get you down? The interference between what you *want* and what you *can* do: How do you deal with that? Most people are happier when they have less interference and less stress.

JOHNETTE NAPOLITANO (Concrete Blonde): I don't think people are aware of their need for stillness and solitude. Some people aren't comfortable with peace and quiet! Or it could be a raging forty mile-per-hour wind slamming my shutters to splinters any given night just as easily. I'm pretty conscious of time and believe in reflecting every once in a while. Am I where I thought I would be in life? It helped me to remove myself from a certain amount of influence, a lot of noise, static. Physically just shoving oneself through the population is a hell of a chore. I trust the sense of perspective I have when I'm out here in the desert.

JOE CORRÉ (*Burn Punk London* / Malcolm McLaren's son): On a personal level, I've always felt very connected with the Earth, nature and all the fantastic things in the wild and that energy that we get from the Earth we live on. That is very spiritual to me. That's all the spirituality that I need. I get so much pleasure, energy and clarity of thought from connecting with nature. First and foremost, we need to respect our habitat and not destroy it. If you really feel that in your heart, then that's all the spirituality you need. By respecting the Earth, you respect other people, creatures, animals, plants and water and everything we live on.

PATTI PATTEX (Cut My Skin): Feeling your existence is spirituality. Connection with nature, one's self and all other living beings. Gardening is spiritual, and revolutionary nowadays. Everything that triggers joie de vivre is spirituality; music or helping to redress grievances, showing solidarity, doing the right thing even at risk of being in danger. The true spirit of punk is integrity. We wanted to abolish injustice, disrespect and violence so that no one rules over others. Anarchy! The key word to happiness. Not only in the political sense, but the freedom to listen to the inner voice—it is a spiritual experience. My personal spiritual healing happens when I'm near the ocean; the vastness of the sea opens my soul.

2

"WHAT WE ALL WANT"

SELF-EXPRESSION/AUTHENTICITY/ LIBERATION AND LIVING FREE

People forgot what so-called real punk came from, which was just a form of self-expression.

—Ari Up (The Slits)

Authenticity is about being alive. It's what makes great rock, funk and pop music. Utterly thrilling.

—Jon King (Gang of Four)

While relearning to trust my mind / I recognized I still knew sincerity.

—"Spiritual Level of Gang Shit" by Soul Glo
(*Diaspora Problems* 2022)

HEART OF PUNK IS SELF-EXPRESSION

NADYA OSTROFF (The Slits / The Home Office): The heart of punk rock is the need for self-expression. If you're deprived of self-expression, you're deprived of your identity. You're deprived of your sexuality, your physicality. That's what was happening maybe in America in the '70s, but definitely in the UK. There was so much oppression on so many people from different angles. They all came together and had to fight to find an artistic justice and justify what they thought about their oppression.

ARI UP (The Slits): There's a way you barricade yourself and put limits on yourself. That's what is different about The Slits. They're not politically correct. They just move with the flow and humor and it's a balance of having fun and still being expressive and serious about topics that affect people, affect us as women. When people put a label, then you limit yourself and you don't fully become what you can be. I just say Punky Reggae now because I don't know what else to say anymore! People need labels all the time. People forget what so-called real punk came from, which was just a form of self-expression. People forgot, so now I remind them! Because most bands, though they say they're punk, they're really a rock band that's just influenced by punk. But they're not really punk so-called, even though I don't like using that term, even. But I have to use it now because people have strayed from the real shit.

NADYA OSTROFF (The Slits / The Home Office): Every generation needs to have a kind of reassessment. It's a coming-of-age thing. Sometimes I think people don't come of age until they're fifty! I don't think it needs to be only a youth thing. I find that really patronizing. It's an evolving process and that's what the Slits is about. You're always learning and growing. Ari hasn't finished—she's just started! She's always just starting because she's always learning, always thinking. It's the same for all of us.

JM: There's an ongoing process that's never completed.

NADYA OSTROFF (The Slits): I think that has a lot to do with spirituality. I've made some wrong turns in my life. I didn't grow up in a stable atmosphere. What it does teach you is that from a negative, there is always a positive. I know this idea is overused, but it taught me to be really independent and that nobody takes care of me except myself. That was the most important thing I learned in life from a very early age; I'm responsible for myself right now and for the future.

GLENN WALLIS (Ruin / *An Anarchist's Manifesto*): I will risk sounding like an old romantic, but I feel like self-expression is the whole point. Get working on creative projects you deem valuable! I feel unmoored unless I'm working on a project. I don't do this under the capitalist compulsion to produce. I do it in the spirit of self-overcoming and generosity.

KID CONGO POWERS (Gun Club / Nick Cave and the Bad Seeds / The Pink Monkey Birds): I came out of the freedom of the glam rock scene. David Bowie had liberated all of us! And given us hope and an example to identify with, whether he was really bisexual or not. If he was really an alien or not. Punk rock was also quite liberating because I was able to dress up and prance around and be obnoxious, but free. At least within that world. That didn't make me free in the rest of my life and with my parents. Punk rock was perfect because so many people I met were queer. There were already trans people in punk rock then. So, it was a great gathering spot. I'd go between Los Angeles, San Francisco and New York and meet my tribe. There was a definite openness with people about freedom of sexual expression.

CONEY ISLAND OF THE MIND

LYDIA LUNCH (Teenage Jesus and the Jerks / Big Sexy Noise): I want to spread pleasure to other people. And who are those people going to be but *other people* who have also had an incredible amount of anger, hatred or torture in their lives? So, you want to go in there as some kind of a healer, which is why I collaborate with a lot of people who are pretty intense. With art I want to create a sacred space where there is no fucking bullshit. You can be exactly like you are to the nth degree.

In my nights I want to create a private opium den of the mind—a *Coney Island of the Mind*—where you let that all go and you claim what is rightfully yours. Which is the absolutely phantasmagorical experience of being fucking alive on this planet! It is so fucking amazing and so outrageous. *People aside.* If you don't appreciate the most minor things, you're not going to appreciate the bigger things. If you gluttonize on everything and you still feel that it is not enough, you better reduce it to really open your fucking eyes and see how glorious so much of every day is. If you don't, you're denying yourself. I've never denied myself. I want other people to see themselves as they are and I want to give them an opportunity to create something that would not be created without this sacred space. I'm feeling much better than I've ever felt and I just find a way to not be driven by the madness that was put upon me. Not only to use it to the best of my ability, but get back to the origins of my essence before the contamination of life hit me. So, that's my spiritual journey.

MITA SCHAMAL (Namenlos): We don't need to think there is something missing. If we're able to open our hearts, then we can touch each other without any violence and war. There's so much possibility to live in freedom, to enjoy all the richness in the world. But even in a country where you have a lot of money and food, people are unhappy. They're too busy. They are busy so they don't have to feel their feelings. They didn't learn that the feelings they have are the best you can feel. If you learn to really feel feelings, and then see that every feeling passes and then there will come a new feeling. It's the same with thoughts.

DANNY ELFMAN (Oingo Boingo / film composer): Students today ask me, "How did I get started?" I say, "I can tell you how I got started, but I wouldn't recommend that. Because that kind of attitude will most likely end your career in two seconds!" But I didn't give a shit! I didn't care if I had a career or not. I didn't care if the film studios liked my music. I really didn't care about anything except that I was having fun and my director was buying into it and allowing me to do it. The rest of the world, I could just give a shit. Over the years I realized that was from the punk influence of just not caring what the establishment or the people at the party that I was crashing into, what they cared. And the fact that they hated me inspired me more! It all tied together in a weird way; that ability to take fuel from hostility definitely comes from that punk thing of "Spit on me, throw shoes at me. I don't give a shit!" The more you do that, the more I'm just going to throw it back in your face. It's an attitude. It's not necessarily a healthy attitude, but fortunately it worked for me.

JM: There's a promotional video for your mantra-based album *Wilder Shores* (2017) where you're discussing with Simrit Kaur your own history with the Germs and the Go-Go's, and you say, "Discovering mantra music was like discovering punk rock all over again." What's the common ground between punk and mantra music as you've experienced those?

BELINDA CARLISLE (The Germs / The Go-Go's / Black Randy and the Metrosquad): My musical beginnings came out of the garage and that early music was always a real expression of where I was at inside. It wasn't necessarily angry, but it was a complete anything-goes form of self-expression. And mantra is pretty much the same thing. It's kind of hard to put into words. Both are forms of self-expression, especially with combining the two genres. I've been doing this for forty years and anything I've ever done has always been a true expression of where I'm at in my life at that time. That is the similarity between my beginnings and now. It all makes complete sense. My last album came out of living in France for twenty-four years. That French album (*Voila*) was a reflection of my love of French pop. Every album I've done has made sense in reflecting where I've been at that time. My early days with the Germs and the early Go-Go's and Black Randy and the Metrosquad is very similar to *Wilder Shores*. It's just hard to put into words.

CECI BASTIDA (Tijuana No!) As a teenager, I used to think that people should talk about political issues in their lyrics. I'd think, "Why aren't you talking about poverty and corruption in Mexico?" But people express art in their own way, and it doesn't have to be political. It can be whatever you want and that's what's great about the arts and music. There are other ways of being involved with social issues. I know many people that make music and don't talk about anything political but they're active in their personal lives, participating in events that benefit certain groups or donating time with different organizations that are doing great work.

IT'S THERAPY, REALLY

DARIUS KOSKI (Swingin' Utters): The songs I write are extremely personal. Sometimes it's not what *I* am but what I see in other people or what I've learned through the years. It's super personal. It's therapy, really. If I wrote these songs and had them lying around it wouldn't work as well as the lucky situation I'm in now, where I have a couple of bands and somebody's willing to put out our records. So, someone can hear my ideas! Because you want someone to listen to you! Really, to me it's like therapy. Just getting it out there is huge for me; it's a massive burden lifted off of me!

STEWART EBERSOLE (*Barred for Life: How Black Flag's Iconic Logo Became Punk Rock's Secret Handshake*): Can you imagine a more awesome life? You're open to things and free. We're all empowered by a totally different force. Punks were closer to the spirit, closer to the nature of the soul. We were operating from an *I want to make my own decisions* standpoint. I want to express what the creator put into me and what the universe endowed me to do. Was that to work at a crummy job that somebody else invented? Or go to third world countries and help people feed themselves? Why did the universe put me on this tiny piece of rock? You're in better harmony with your own soul than someone who says, "I've got this job because this is the job that will get me the house, car and husband I deserve."

RAMSEY KANAAN (AK Press / Political Asylum): All music contains within it an instinct for freedom, or *rhythm* of freedom, shall we say. Music is one of those wonderful things like words and ideas, which can and ought to be unfettered. Like the broad river of life which we both drink from and we also contribute back to.

JM: What was the best part of playing drums with Crass?

PENNY RIMBAUD (Crass): The packing up and going home part of it! (*laugh*) I'm not a performer. I now do a lot of performing of my poetry. I don't enjoy it. I don't enjoy being on stage. I never have.

JM: You played pretty fast drums in Crass.

PENNY RIMBAUD (Crass): Yeah, I wanted to get off stage! (*big laugh*) I used to get a lot of complaints particularly from Steve (Ignorant) and Eve (Libertine) because when we rehearsed I'd play much slower. But on stage, I just went fast. It was me thinking, "Get out of this bloody place! Double the tempo on this one and you're out five minutes early!"

JM: Do you still play drums?

PENNY RIMBAUD (Crass): No. There's one poet I'm very fond of, about my age, called Hugh Metcalfe. Respected for his insane renditions of rubbish poems. He's the only person I work for. I do about six gigs a year with him of anti-drumming. If I start making a rhythm, then I fuck it up. It's fun. I enjoy it in a funny, sort of painful way. A lot of his work is very painful. He's a very gentle, quiet, lovable, beautiful man, but on stage he's liable to be self-destructive, explosive and totally unpredictable. I love that. I don't see my job, when I play with him, as accompaniment. I see it as protection. I try to create a wall around him which saves him from hurt. Sometimes I do it by walking around him with bells, sometimes I do it just by diversion. And sometimes I do it by doing absolutely nothing at all. Apart from that I don't and I won't. None of my friends come to see me because they all think it's dreadful.

LIZ LAMERE (Alan Vega [Suicide]'s widow / creative collaborator Alan Vega solo / solo recording artist / SSNUB / Backward Flying Indians): In part of the punk movement, there was a little bit of, "This is how it should be done." Ironically, right? Because there was supposed to be no rules! That's one of the reasons Alan (Vega) used to joke about Suicide—"We're so punk even the punks hate us!" Because they weren't following the rule book of guitar-driven three chords and play fast. They were exploring different nuances.

A big part of that was freedom. Not being afraid to be, as Lydia (Lunch) said, in the isolation and loneliness that comes with that. Alan used to think that all the time, "Am I crazy? I really like what I'm doing. Are we the only ones who hear it?" That's one of the key things Alan imparted on me: If you like it and it's genuine and you're expressing something you're feeling, that's all that matters. I always wanted other people to hear what he was doing. He could have been perfectly happy being the research scientist in the basement and never releasing anything. I was the one who'd say, "Hello! This is really good. I want to release this music. Can we put this out?" But if I hadn't done that, who knows? We might be discovering all these works decades later. He only released a small percentage of what he created. But the freedom to create without any constraints is rare.

HARDY FOX (The Residents) The Residents are not based in music. They based their existence on ideas. They were never, "You're the drummer, I'm the bass player." It was, "Who's got an idea? What would be fun?" Everything came out of a very intellectual approach. They thought the first thing they need is to make up the rules and framework. If you're going to do this group thing, you can't have people running around helter-skelter doing whatever they want. The rules included things like: there can't be any names and faces. It has to have the identity of a group, with a group result. It's not about "me."

STRATEGIES OF JOY

IAN MACKAYE (Minor Threat / Fugazi): I often feel that people's ideas of happiness have less to do with what they actually feel and rather what they've been conditioned to think is happiness. Consumption! There is this idea that you can be happy by buying things constantly. There is this constant collection of crap that people engage in. It apparently brings them so much joy. I think that so much of that approach is really conditioning. As a child I used to think a lot about all the things I wanted. I wished my family had more money so that I could get a swimming pool. Looking through comic books, magazines or watching television, those images brought up these fantasies that you could have anything you wanted. At some point I realized it does not bring happiness at all—it's just a diversion.

I don't think about the strategies of joy. Rather, I think of the simplicity of it. The people who are most at peace with their lives are people who are not contemplating strategies but are waking up and living. I don't know what the root of happiness is. We should be happy. But it is not the sole goal. I think *to be engaged* is our purpose. That is the point of life and sometimes that engagement may be something extremely removed from happiness. I want to be engaged and feel everything. The most distressing times in my life are when I become a bit numb and I'm not feeling. I have never quite figured out what is responsible for that. I think it's perhaps something like a virus, in a way. Something that has gone unchecked in my life revisits and then I start to become numb and it sends me into a place where I feel low because I am feeling disconnected. I don't want to feel disconnected. I want to feel alive. It's not always about happiness; it's a matter of connection.

JM: There's a Propagandhi song where you sing about the sacred qualities of music. Tell me about your enjoyment of music and what comes through you when you're making music.

CHRIS HANNAH (Propagandhi): Contrary to this tour—where you get in a van and you travel around and set up your equipment in a different venue at a particular time, and you're told to be on stage at a certain time and despite how you're feeling, you perform a set of songs for a crowd that's paid money and will assess what you're doing—I enjoy playing music with Jord (Samolesky) and Todd (Kowalski) in the basement and that's about it. I am not a performer. I'm not a musician. I'm not an artist. I am a music enthusiast and I think music is most true when you're making it with other people and not having it assessed by others, especially people who have paid. It is the life I am currently in, but it is something I grapple with all of the time and I'm very confused about all of the time. Touring for me can be a very unhappy time. We travel from one Kentucky-fried city to the next and it just isn't how I think music should be, for me personally. I go to shows. I like to see a band come through town, but it's not how I want to make music, really.

PENELOPE SPHEERIS (*The Decline of Western Civilization* / *Wayne's World*): Since I got to know the punk philosophy and lifestyle, I have become a more spiritual person. As opposed to being a case for getting into punk, it's more a result of *having been* into punk. But I'm at a point where—I guess you could call it spiritual. It's not like I go to a church or have this traditional definition of God or religion that I live by. But I do have my own rules. To a degree they've actually made it very difficult for me to navigate, especially lately, in the film business. Because there are some underhanded slimeballs out there, man! When I run across them, I fight them and I won't deal with them. And you kind of have to if you want to get anywhere in the film business. You have to suck up to those creeps. And I just can't do it! That's okay, because in the big picture *I'll be dead and gone and what have you got left?* You have your pride and that you think you did the right thing. That's what you've got left. It ain't about money.

JM: In the new age realm there's the idea that, "Everything is fine." But pretending things are fine doesn't work.

PENELOPE SPHEERIS (*The Decline of Western Civilization* / *Wayne's World*): It does for a while. That's why there's so many people doing it! There's this whole movement of, "If I just create it in my mind, it will be there." I think that works short term. I don't know what works long term. What I've been noticing is that there's a lot of people walking around with blinders on.

JM: I have the idea you're interested in studying the brain and thinking.

PENELOPE SPHEERIS (*The Decline of Western Civilization* / *Wayne's World*): Back in the day there weren't film schools. I studied art at Long Beach State College (California, USA) and realized later it was the same time Spielberg was there. But I got to a point with the people who were in the art school where they just seemed like a bunch of phony-poseur-losers and I didn't like them. So, I flipped around 180 degrees and went to U.C. Irvine that had just opened and studied Psycho-Biology. When I was at Long Beach State, me and Chuck (Dukowski) from Black Flag studied the same thing, trying to understand life through chemistry and physics. I did pretty well. There I was with a couple of years of art education behind me and natural sciences and then I was standing on a hill—I remember the moment—when someone said there was a film school at UCLA. Later I realized that film is the perfect combination of art and science. I fit right in there.

PAUL TRYNKA (*Iggy Pop: Open Up and Bleed*): Many people in the magazine industry will tell you that Iggy is an intelligent guy and very good fun. He is basically up for anything. We went down to the Lower East Side in New York for a photo shoot and it was a very hot summer, 104 degrees. We started photographing him and at one point we came across a lot of kids who were playing with a broken fire hydrant, splashing themselves with water. The photographer says, "Hey Iggy, can you stand over there and splash yourself with water?" And he's like, "Yep, okay. No problem." He goes over and splashes himself with water.

Meanwhile, this being New York and people in the street seeing this weird guy in jeans and no shirt splashing himself with water and a bunch of weird English guys photographing him, they looked over and thought, "This guy splashing himself with water—we'll help him." I remember watching and photographing all of this; I've got images of Iggy splashing himself with water from a fire hydrant and meanwhile behind him are two big, fat guys filling up a huge bucket of water, walking up behind our hero and emptying the bucket of water right over his head! I've got a photo of Iggy completely drenched, turning around at the guys and laughing his head off.

That's what made me think, "You know, I love you," in a way. Every other pop star I've interviewed, at that point they would have walked off and said, "That's it. I'm upset. How could you do that to me?" Here's a guy who just responded to people around him, having fun. He actually enjoyed the chaos around him and had a laugh. At the end of it all, what can any of us do with life when weird things turn up, but just enjoy them for the comedy of it all. That's what Iggy was doing. I appreciated that and loved it in its own way. That is the attitude we all need to have to put up with life's chaos; just enjoy it!

JAMES WILLIAMSON (Iggy & The Stooges): Our band was just very determined to do our own thing and to do it in a way that was experiential and would impact people in our performances. One of the things about us that was not commercially viable was that we never would play the same music. You would never hear a Stooges set twice. We would always be creating new stuff as we went along, even on the road. No one ever learned our songs. We wouldn't play the album or anything. Even though we wanted to be commercially successful, *believe* me, we did! We didn't know how to, basically. There was nothing about us that was commercially viable. It was wonderful. You're young making sort of a living at it. A lot of girls, everything's happening. You're going to different towns. It was a lot of fun. But in terms of being professional or making a living at the music business, we were pretty marginal. But we were very creative.

JORDAN PUNDIK (New Found Glory): I enjoy being on stage, when people can relate to what we're singing about and look up to you as an inspiration. That's one of my favorite things about being the singer in the band. To play in different places and hear stories, especially overseas in different countries, that's the best thing about the band. I like playing in Santa Cruz (California). Often, we save it for the end of the tour, like the light at the end of the tunnel.

JON KING (Gang of Four): None of us want to do *nothing*; we want to be active in the world. When it came to writing the music, the lyrics were only one part of the thing that Andy (Gill) and I put together. We were trying to take away camouflage in some of the songs. The songs themselves had this funny structure or element to them. "What We All Want" doesn't actually have any verses or choruses as such. "To Hell with Poverty" doesn't have verses and choruses. In fact, it's only got three notes in it! We sometimes tried to take away even the elements of reverberation. I think there were parallels, which I wasn't aware of at the time, with those movements of photographers who took photographs and never allowed their pictures to be cropped. Or filmmakers who showed *everything* they filmed. There was the idea that you're trying to have authenticity. Authenticity is about being alive. It's what makes great rock, funk and pop music. Utterly thrilling.

I've listened my entire life—and still do more or less once every couple of weeks—to "Voodoo Child (Slight Return)" by Jimi Hendrix. I just come back and listen and I hear him doing his thing. You sense that it's an epiphany. It's all in the moment of itself. It has its own purity, joy and brilliance and this wonderful man is playing this wonderful tune and each decision is kind of a decision of, "Am I going to be alive or not?" When it grinds to a kind of *cu-chunk* in the middle you think, "It's all running out," and you hear his buddies shouting in the background and then he starts all over again because he can't quite get it up. Those things are what we have to get to. I'm sure that's what people like about the music they love the most. They love its inevitability.

JM: Gang of Four have a song called "Colour From the Tube" (1991) where you sing, "If the times don't fit, you can't go look for another, use the color from the tube, there is nothing else that you can do." What is the *tube*?

JON KING (Gang of Four): Tube of paint. It's about authenticity, when you just use it straight and go for the unmediated experience. Don't try and water it down. Just go for the bravery of it. Now, the most half-assed, talentless loser can sing half decent with loads of technology. I'm not by any means a particularly good singer. Things being like they are is really valuable. So, guitars sounding like guitars is quite an interesting concept! But now guitars sound like pianos, and pianos sound like guitars. Back in the late 1970s and early 1980s the idea that *things are what they are* was quite a revolutionary concept.

There was a great film *The Deer Hunter*. It has a fantastic scene which I thought was one of the best moments of scriptwriting. When DeNiro is up in the woods with that guy and he holds the bullet up and starts shouting at him. He's 'gotta be a method actor! He's holding up the bullet in his hand and screaming "This is this!" It's a brilliant piece of writing because it's trying to get over to the guy that sometimes things are what they are. Sometimes things aren't other things; you've just got to focus wherever you are exactly.

You mentioned meditation; those moments of absolute clarity that you know that something is what it is, the absolute clarity. Miles Davis is playing something which has total meaning for that moment and you're taken aback by it. These are the songs you listen to your whole life. Me and ten million other people still get an amazing feeling listening to Robert Johnson tracks from 1937. This young African-American who met the devil at the crossroads and had this amazing incandescent life and wrote twenty-nine songs and then was murdered and it's a perfect life. There's something incredible. It connects you to that existence in a brilliant way. *This is this.* Don't water things down. That was "Colour From the Tube."

JON LANGFORD (The Mekons): There is a sort of osmosis that happens when we write songs; what's going on immediately around us ends up in the songs. That's what we always thought was the importance of what we were doing through the years. We were trying to describe and reflect the world that we live in. Yeah, we do live in a post-factual democracy and here's some songs.

STEWART EBERSOLE (*Barred for Life*): I became a Quaker in the last three years (2010—2013). It's all about consensus and collective decision-making. It's something I'm very proud of. Becoming a Quaker was brought on by me being a punk. I was an atheist for a while and then agnostic. I needed to find the perfect fit and I found it in becoming a Quaker. I'm not the perfect Quaker but it provides a spiritual foundation for me. We talk a lot about the idea of *freedom*. Freedom is something where you do not impinge on someone else's pursuits of freedom. Unless they're doing something so terribly wrong that you must morally intervene. If a friend has a slave, for example, you're not going to let that shit go. But if your friend is having a difficult time with his relationship you're not going to butt in and say, "This is how you should do things." Let people figure things out on their own—that's freedom.

My Boy Scout troop was affiliated with my church and when I hit eighteen my pastor called me in and said, "I want to know how you see your life going." I said, "Don't take this wrong but I don't see the church being a part of my life." I was very sad and may have been teary-eyed. I said, "I want to leave the church. I have to figure out what the fuck's going on. I don't want to be here unless I made the decision to be here." He couldn't believe that I'd thought about it this deeply. I stepped away for twenty-five years. I never missed Christianity. That is a part of the whole freedom equation. You go out and make a complete and total honest decision to discover what you truly need in life. I was forty-one when I fell into the Quaker thing.

PENELOPE HOUSTON (The Avengers): There is an honesty to punk rock. The pursuit of that honesty is pure and is, in that way, almost spiritual. The emotions I expressed when I was in the Avengers when I was younger were a pure energy. There was anger in there but there were also ideas and feelings. We did the song "Corpus Christi" which I wrote with Brad Kent. It was one of our later songs and I've done it throughout my career, both in a punk style and acoustically. People were always a little confused about that. They thought it must mean I was Christian or religious. The song is more a condemnation of organized religion and people being sheep and not thinking for themselves. My mantra was that people should be individuals and express themselves and try to live their lives outside of a box. I don't know if you'd find much of it (spirituality) in the Avengers but I've written a lot of songs since then that touch on spirituality. But back then my main voice was of righteousness and anger and organized religion was definitely one of the things that needed to be spotlighted.

LESLEY WOODS (Au Pairs): As a musician you have to be there for the music and believe in what you believe, but don't try to push it on other people. The moment you do that, the music is lost and it becomes a whole different thing. You have to allow people to interpret it as they want and not dictate what that should be. I do think famous musicians have a duty to speak out against things like war and torture. Music and politics are very intrinsically bound up. Musicians sing of the times they're living in; they're the poets of the times. Donald Trump has been elected again (2024). That says a lot about Americans. It means that a lot of people in America, somehow their consciousness hasn't been raised.

MARK REEDER (Die Unbekannten): The creation of punk brought hope. It cried out for attention and got it. The punk attitude of not caring also created a platform that showed that anyone with an idea or an ounce of creativity could do it. Kids would spend their dole money on cheap guitars and hope that was the way out. There was a possibility that you might even make some money out of it, or at least travel about and who knows, even get a shag. And if you were good enough maybe you'd get signed by a record label. The legacy of punk is that it has managed to survive. Admittedly, the visual image is a bit dated now, but the idea and attitude behind it is still there, infiltrating these days into other musical genres.

MARK MOTHERSBAUGH (Devo): We thought of ourselves as conceptualists and artists. There were things we were questioning and some of it overlapped with punk. And some of it didn't. A lot of punk music was just nihilistic and stupid. And then some of it was more thoughtful. The energy came from the gut and it allowed people to go crazy and to be able to celebrate that part of their humanity. That's what was interesting to me about punk.

GERALD CASALE (Devo): Cooler punks were questioning authority, and it was certainly necessary to challenge an illegitimate authority at that time. And it's never really changed, has it? We're right back where we were. But also, like Mark said, we were anti-stupid. Devo were more like a *punk scientist*. We didn't adhere to some orthodoxy like, "white T-shirt, black skinny tie, black jeans, three chords." That wasn't Devo.

BRAD LOGAN (Leftöver Crack / Rats in the Walls): If you want to live together you have to compromise because people are different and they believe in different things. If you want to live in a world where we're not fucking killing each other all the time, we have to allow the other person to believe in what they want to believe and they allow us to believe in what we want to believe. Freedom is the bottom line of what all of these punk songs are! We want to be fucking free.

3

"WHAT'S SO FUNNY ABOUT PEACE, LOVE, AND UNDERSTANDING?"

REVOLUTIONARY LOVE AND COMPASSION/ FROM DIY TO DO IT TOGETHER/BEYOND EGO

Initially the punk thing started out with destruction because it was such a depressive age in England. The system needed to have some destruction. We still carry that. The balance of love and destruction is in there. We don't love the system but we're going to kill 'em with love!

—Ari Up (The Slits)

When you've been really hurt you either become more caring or you become a criminal. Most punks have chosen to become more caring.

—Penelope Spheeris *(The Decline of Western Civilization)*

Compassion is the foundation of most religions . . . Yet religion is used as an excuse to create enemies . . . George Bush's final excuse for going to Iraq was God told me to do it.

—Dick Lucas (Subhumans)

Peace will come, Peace will come, in time.

—"Spinning Song" by Nick Cave & The Bad Seeds
(*Ghosteen*—2019)

THERE IS NO AUTHORITY BUT YOURSELF

Many punk musicians have embraced this powerful idea: "Think for yourself." Or as the Buddha reportedly said, "Be a lamp unto yourself." Consider this further common ground between punk, spirituality and compassionate activism; many punks have engaged in direct actions to end suffering caused by sociopolitical systems that maintain poverty, food insecurity, incarceration, slavery, environmental destruction and war. Punk musicians and activists have created community-based mutual aid projects like Rock Against Racism in Britain, Positive Force in Washington DC, the Táala Hooghan Infoshop in Kinlani, Arizona and Food Not Bombs internationally. Punks have also generated support to free US political prisoners like Mumia Abul-Jamar, The West Memphis Three, Geronimo Pratt and Leonard Peltier.

JM: In your book with Greg Graffin (Bad Religion) you write, "There is a drive in my mind toward loving." This reminds me of Che Guevara's famous quote, "The true revolutionary is guided by a great feeling of love." Tell me about compassion.

PRESTON JONES (*Is God Good, Bad or Irrelevant? A Professor and a Punk Rocker Discuss Science, Religion, Naturalism and Christianity*): What is the evolutionary value of me loving my children? A rational evolutionary answer can be given to that question; I pass on my genetic code for the next generation. But I got an email this morning about a student of mine whose father was struck by a driver who had a heart attack and died in the accident. I felt this heaviness come over me and I prayed for this man and this student, his father and family. What would be the evolutionary explanation for that? Why should I care about people who have no connection to me? I think that would be hard to explain in terms of evolution. I don't think you can deal with that question in a scientific way. That's the kind of question you deal with at the theological, spiritual level. What's going on in this world that human beings feel compassion for each other, even for complete strangers?

PENNY RIMBAUD (Crass): We're all just the same matter. There isn't anything between us. I've got great love and belief in human spirit. I don't believe there is any such thing as human nature because we are just *deep nature*. We are simply nature and we act in accord with it; we can't do otherwise. If we can't breathe, we move to where there is air. We are it. We can't separate ourselves from our own deep nature. Neither can we separate from our own deep nature through death.

Within a Buddhist framework I could possibly suggest that what I was doing with Crass was presenting dharma in an extraordinarily contorted way. The first and most essential question in all Buddhist, Taoist or Zen teachings is, "Who are you?" Basically speaking, that's what I was trying to ask in Crass. "There is no authority but yourself" is another way of saying the same thing. "What is the self?" We were nudging people into asking these questions because we weren't going to give answers. There is no answer to, "There is no authority but yourself" but to accept it and get on with it. There was all the time this jingle-jangle going on, particularly in my part within Crass. I've never been far from attempting, through one route or another, to take a revolutionary cultural position. I can't say I thought of it that way at the time, but looking back over the years I see a cultural activism right back to when I was a kid. It's why I love the Beatles' "All You Need is Love." That's another way of saying the same thing.

RAY CAPPO (Youth of Today / Shelter): The real principle is *loving people* and being concerned about people's welfare. And doing it in a super-loving way and not, "I'm better than them. Why won't you just be like me and my God?" It's so ugly and obvious. Like, "My team is better than your team." It's important to say, "I choose to disagree," and it's not like I'm going to kill you because of it. I might even still like you if we don't agree.

It's supposed to be a progressive world but we're going backward. If religion doesn't serve us then it's not worth it. I've seen it happen with Hare Krishnas. I see people caught up in details of philosophy and not the principles. They miss out on the whole picture, the whole relationship with God. I'm convinced that to lead a spiritual life you have to be loving and understanding. You've got to throw away that criticism. I don't think it works with loving God to be a real critic. For example, my mom; she's not straight edge. She's not a vegan. But she's super-loving. Doesn't she get any points for that?

BILLY BRAGG: Individualism is just one aspect of humanity. A much greater aspect is how we help one another. The thing about the (Covid-19) lockdown is that we have to be responsible not just for our own health, but for the health of our neighbors, our loved ones and people in our community. In some ways the coronavirus is like a tide that has gone out and the people that are still standing are really crucial to us being able to live our ordinary lives. They are the health workers and the people keeping us connected, safe and fed. These are the people who are really important in society, rather than those people who get the headlines and the money. The lesson that comes from this is one of the importance of social solidarity.

TOM MORELLO (Rage Against the Machine / Prophets of Rage): The beginning of a radicalization of a person often stems from compassion. It comes from an empathy for others. And then the indignation that one feels when you see yourself being wronged, or your family or community. Or people around the globe you see being maltreated. The impulse to instigate change will often come up. I agree that there is a spiritually compassionate core at the center of all great revolutionaries.

MARK ANDERSEN (Positive Force DC / *Dance of Days*): Punk rock was the bridge from the struggle for personal identity and purpose to seeing how that required me to step out of simply being concerned with myself to a broader engagement. Underneath it all I now see that I was on a spiritual journey before punk, and punk became the vehicle to expand and fulfill that journey. Punk is still part of that spiritual journey today.

DAVE WAKELING (English Beat): The Buddha said that there was no evil, just ego. The ego makes you feel that you're separate and that's the first step toward being able to hurt someone else, because you view them as different or separate from you. I would've thought those photos from space, "Look at them lot! They're all one, aren't they? (*laugh*) Whether they like it or not!" I've always felt that intuitively. You just do the best you can. If you fuck up then that's what you were meant to learn. And don't beat yourself up. Someone else will do it if it's required. That's the worst bit of it, the constant self-denigrating thought.

JELLO BIAFRA (Dead Kennedys / Guantanamo School of Medicine): There's only so much time in the day. When I get up, I don't look in the mirror and see this great person who everybody should be patting on the head or bowing down to. I see all these songs that never got finished and it would be *so* fucking cool if they got recorded! That's a good way to put the ego back in its cobra basket!

DICK LUCAS (Subhumans / Citizenfish): Compassion is the foundation of most religions. That is the ironic thing! Most religion is founded on being nice to other people. If you take the worship of god out of it, the rest of it is based on being nice to other people and don't fuck each other over. Yet religion is used as an excuse to create enemies: *my* God versus *your* God. George Bush's final excuse for going to Iraq was *God told me to do it.* Whoa! We are dealing with a fundamentalist lunatic! Fundamentalists are partially running the government in America. It's very dangerous.

MARJANE SATRAPI (*Persepolis*): I try to be kinder to everyone I know. If I can be a better person, then maybe I can change something. We want the world to change but none of us wants to change, really. The change has to come from us. But changing everything in a global way all together; I tried it and I don't think it works at all. We are imperfect human beings. With us being this imperfect, how can we make a perfect world?

STAN LEE (The Dickies): I try not to let emotion overtake me. It could happen for a second but then I realize I don't need to go there. It might be fun to jump up and down for a minute, but really at the bottom line of it, all of life is a comedy and not a drama. Once you have that figured out it takes a lot of the heat off of everything. It's all just a fucking comedy. Sometimes you get the bear and sometimes the bear gets you.

SARA MARCUS (*Girls to The Front: The True Story of the Riot Grrrl Revolution*): It's very hard to pursue the work of changing any part of the world from a space of feeling isolated and unsupported. So, building communities that can home us can be a really important element in a larger attempt to affect greater systems. It's not always easy. . . . That's an understatement! It's almost *never* easy. It was Archimedes who said, "I can move the world with a lever if you show me where to place it." To a certain level, having self-understanding so that one isn't behaving in an entirely reactive way that will both burn one out and potentially lead to unskillful actions, isn't necessarily counter-revolutionary.

LESLEY WOODS (Au Pairs): Punk let you out to meet people of your own mindset. That was the most wonderful thing for me! Punk opened a door. It was a way out of the quagmire which was to get married, have kids and follow religion. Punk gave you a way out, and that was a way into freedom and yourself and your people. Everyone wants freedom and space to be themselves.

DAVID LESTER (Mecca Normal / Horde of Two): I believe that people favor working together and doing things for the greater good of their communities. We see that even in very conservative political areas, where they band together to help each other but they just don't see it as part of a larger, inclusive environment. I think the human tendency is toward this anarchist idea of mutual aid. It's just that people are so in their own silos, they aren't seeing the connections. This isolation is very destructive in trying to progress and be a more democratic, freer and more inclusive society. The human tendency is to be cooperative but the capitalist system is built on competition and works against this cooperative impulse. But remember, capitalism is a relatively recent adventure going back only three hundred years. So, we shouldn't allow our lives to be dominated by that as the only mode of society.

STEWART EBERSOLE (*Barred for Life*): I do believe in the revolution that punk presents to individual people. It offers choices in a spectrum that they didn't know existed before. That's one of the most awesome things about punk rock music and culture. It offered people like me—total freaks and losers who wanted to kill themselves over and over—a place to go. I thought, "I'm not the only one who feels this way!" What you did with that following the revelation—coming into your own political and spiritual consciousness—that was your thing. It brought together people who had the same fears and desires and wanted to make changes. A lot of them went on to make changes and some went on to do some stupid stuff, too. That's human existence.

KARMIC YOGA: A LIFE OF SERVICE

PENNY RIMBAUD (Crass): In my own case, it all came from the Hindu principle of karmic yoga. A life of service, which I met when I was in my mid-teens. I read something about karmic yoga and thought, "Wow, that's a meaning to life. Helping people!" That's easy. You don't need a deep philosophy to help people, even when they don't want helping! (*laugh*) Most communes—which this isn't (Dial House)—operate on some sort of abiding principle: Buddhism, Christianity, Marxism or whatever. This place doesn't have any *whatever*. It could have, if I imposed my own specific feelings. But people are going to see a lot of it just in the stuff that lies around here. If they're into label making, they're going to see a lot more hippie than they are punk if they come to visit.

PENELOPE SPHEERIS (*The Decline of Western Civilization*): You know Greg Ginn? (Black Flag) He has a rescue for cats. I was trying to give him money for licensing a part of *The Decline* and he said, "Send it to the cat rescue." Isn't that cool? Who would ever've thought?

JM: One might think of punk rock people as tough and angry, who . . . don't rescue cats.

PENELOPE SPHEERIS (*The Decline of Western Civilization*): When you've been really hurt you either become more caring or you become a criminal. Most punks have chosen to become more caring. They're good people in general. That's why I like 'em.

JAY BENTLEY (Bad Religion): Any time that religion comes into play with us as a band we identify ourselves as individuals. We don't have a collective agenda against, or for, a specific religion. I myself have a leaning toward a mix of Western and Eastern philosophies. I take the good stuff without the fire and brimstone and the spiteful God. I immediately remove the Santa Claus looking figure and say that's not going to happen either! Greg (Graffin) is a scientist. He says, "Prove it to me and I'll gladly accept it. But until you do that, I won't." Brett (Gurewitz) on the other hand *wants* to believe it but just can't! It's all about the jump (into spirituality). He always asks me, "How did you do it?" I go, "I just don't care." You build up the wall. I said Greg was agnostic, which is not true. He's just an atheist! Brett would be agnostic, but not the Agnostic Front! (*laugh*)

JM: Where does compassion and kindness come into this?

JAY BENTLEY (Bad Religion): Random acts of kindness. When you do something nice and just walk away and don't tell anybody you did it, it's one of the strongest things you can ever do for yourself. You live with that goodness inside you. The minute you tell somebody, then you're bragging about it and it diminishes. Sometimes I get depressed; it's when I feel I'm not doing enough around me. I have a wife and two kids and everything I do is for them. And then it's one step out; my neighbor's got cancer now and it's just one phone call. Or I walk over and ask, "Are you alright? Need anything?"—"No, I'm alright."—"That's cool." That's all it takes. Every now and then I might not do that for a couple days 'cause I'm busy fixing the lawnmower and I think, "I'd better go call them 'cause I haven't called in a couple days." Sometimes I think I'm starting to be a bad friend because I don't call my friends and tell them how much I appreciate them.

JM: I think all of this comes through Bad Religion; compassion to self and others.

JAY BENTLEY (Bad Religion): I think, "Be kind to yourself" comes through more than, "Be kind to others." We try to say that, but you can't expect people to do anything they don't want to do. More than saying, "Be kind to yourself" it's more along the lines of "educate yourself." That's what will make you happy. What makes you unhappy is fear. You become afraid of things because you don't understand them. People are not dumb. There's so much information and it's so hard to filter the truth out that you end up not accepting any of it or just accepting the one you hear the most.

RON REYES (Black Flag): I certainly don't have any regrets. I've always been really proud of whatever I've done. It's very interesting to hear people say, "It's your music that got me through something." I have to take that with a grain of salt because the Black Flag stuff was written by Greg (Ginn). I performed it, but it was primarily written by Greg. But there was something about the performance as well—an actor in a movie is what moves people. Last night we played at this tiny house party in Sacramento and there's these kids that are anywhere from eighteen to their thirties and people said, "Wow, your music got me through some hard times. And particularly *your* stuff." For some people I'm their favorite Black Flag singer. Not for everyone, but for some people. *My* favorite Black Flag singer is Henry.

*We're starting to destroy ourselves with pollution, war, and
greed / You need support to keep you alive / us fish must swim
together!*
> —*"Us Fish Must Swim Together" by Subhumans*

JM: I enjoyed some things you mentioned from the stage tonight. You spoke
about lyrics from a song about noticing when you're thinking of people being
higher or lower than you. This is a spiritual practice that transforms judgment.
Thinking of people as lower or higher and having this sort of moral judgment
toward others is perhaps a form of subtle violence. I think it's what leads to the
possibility of killing people.

DICK LUCAS (Subhumans / Citizenfish): That's an interesting thought. I would say
it was less internal *violence* as internalized *fear*. Those who perceive themselves
to be higher are fearful of being mocked for their heights. Although you're right
in some situations; if they think they're higher in terms of power, they will be
able to use force and violence through controlling other people to do their jobs
for them.

It's all about self-perception. Those who perceive themselves as lower are
quite a lot of people. The height set by advertising is to be a bronzed, macho-
plastic, feminine person of so-called beauty. People who feel themselves to be
lower than that tend to get depressed and perhaps drunk and violent. People
who think they're outside of this and think it's all ironic and they're above
it, they tend to think of themselves as more intelligent than people who don't
realize it. But that is setting themselves apart and everyone ends up being apart.
Whether you think you're higher or lower, you are separating yourself. The
point is, there is no higher or lower because if you *can do this* better than that
person, that person can do something else better. The whole point is to share
each other's talents and possibilities. The song is called, "Us Fish Must Swim
Together."

DAVE DICTOR (Millions of Dead Christians): In punk rock, through the decades,
people have gotten away from wanting to make judgments about others. It was
very easy for us when we were in our twenties to say, "Racism is bad and the meat
industry is bad." Then you find yourself making judgments on people; "That
person is bad." When you're twenty–something and self-righteous, it seems okay.
But looking back, there's something about making a judgment about somebody
else that turns you into an asshole. It makes you full of yourself! I find myself not
wanting to do that! It would be easy to tell people, "I don't eat meat, I don't eat
meat!" We have a song called "Chicken Squawk." It's about dancing with your

farm animals and setting your chickens free. I approach the ideas that way, as opposed to a more condemning style, or a song about the angst of vivisection or something like that. That's where my own personal songwriting style is heading at this point in my life.

JM: My sense is that people don't listen if you're judging them. They listen if you're being empathetic about where they're coming from.

DAVE DICTOR (MDC): That's very true. You get noted as a stick in the mud, full of yourself. People come to your music from all sorts of different lifestyles, backgrounds and different parts of the evolution of where they're going as people. In certain situations, I feel more comfortable sharing that and putting it out there. In Portland we played at the anarchist bookstore. It's a very enlightened crowd. It can be very young but you can share with them about veganism and they get it. Some other times we're playing, for lack of a better word—less evolved—crowds where they'll dance to "Chicken Squawk" and "Corporate Death Burger" and they'll be eating a roast beef sandwich right next to you, breathing it on you ten minutes later. And not really make that connection!

DON'T BE VIOLENT

JM: I see that not harming other beings is a fundamental part of your philosophy, and that comes through your lyrics and music.

DICK LUCAS (Subhumans): It is absolutely fundamental. At no point during your life are you taught that you have to hurt other people. At worst, or best—whatever it is—it's called self-defense if somebody attacks you and you fight back. Gandhi would've said *don't fight back*. Don't imitate your oppressor or eventually oppression will become the status quo of existence and you will have to tow along with that and be oppressive to other people. The most painful, but the best way, to stand up to your oppressors is not so much lying down and taking it, but to use words, imagination and logic and the truth of who you are. This way has to win out in the end. This must sound a whole bunch of hippie bullshit! I don't mean that it will win out next week or next year. It might not happen unless you pass it on to your kids, for another couple of generations. But hope has to spring eternally in all these situations when you face things like McDonald's selling billions of burgers. Or facing nasty skinheads fucking up your shows or other people's headspace. When we face any sort of violence or police violence you just have to stick to these principles, roughly: *don't be violent*. Be good to animals. Be

41

good to other people. Don't get exploited by other people just because they seem tougher than you. Stick up for that despite everything.

CLEM BURKE (Blondie): There's a lot of hate in the world. I try to be positive, but not in any religious way. Modern-day pop culture role models are not fulfilling what's needed. When you think about people like John Lennon in the 60s, they were preaching peace and love. Punk rock has nihilism but it got a lot of people where they needed to get in life. People that came out of punk rock are true survivors. Punk rock helped people to get on with their lives in a positive way. I'm optimistic for the future but I don't know if everything's going to get resolved in my lifetime. All of this about Bernie (Sanders) like "Socialist" is such a bad word. It's ridiculous! We'll have to see what happens with the election. (2020)

JM: You were just on stage saying to the audience, "Are the Slits violent?" And each of the band members replied "No!" There's lots of violence in the world and people have come up with all kinds of ideas about how to stop it, mostly through more violence. Nonviolence isn't being studied deeply.

ARI UP (The Slits): It was always a mistaken idea, in the early days when there was this punk revolution that we had going on, that *punk* meant *violent*. We were actually the least violent! There were all these other sects of people like skinheads—not the good ones, the evil ones—and all these other movements like Teddy Boy revival, Mods, Slickers, disco freaks, and Yuppies and Hippies. There were these different people who were more violent than we were! But it was easy to hate us because we were standing up against injustice, which is what Reggae and Rasta people did as well. We were standing up for justice. When you feel persecuted, it comes across as violent, but it's not violent; it's just standing up for your rights. There's a difference between being spiritually aggressive and violent.

JACK GRISHAM (TSOL / *An American Demon*): One of the main things for me is that when I seek to *get*, it's never enough and I will never be satisfied. When I seek to *give*, I'm always satisfied. Right away. It's almost a real selfish trip 'cause it's a very easily attainable goal. Just stick a hand out and make somebody's day easy. A lot of people think that spirituality is this great big thing. I try to explain to them—*just be kind*. Stick a hand out and smile. Open a door for someone. Lighten that person's day. It's a very spiritual move. Anytime that you step out of yourself, you're doing it.

JM: The Dalai Lama has said, "Compassion is the radicalism of this age," and the one who first receives the benefit from compassion is the person *being* compassionate. He calls it *wise selfishness*.

JACK GRISHAM (TSOL): Yes, it is! It solves an unbelievable amount of problems right away. You would be shocked to find out how many problems are solved when you stop doing the majority of your actions based on self. Unbelievable! It stops. The bottom line is that the more self-centered you are, the less spiritual you are. If you look at spirituality it's basically *God-centered* instead of *ego-centered*. The opposite of the spiritual would be the temporal. Anything that's serving *me* is not spiritual.

A simple spiritual act is picking up a piece of trash when you walk down the street. It has no real immediate benefit to you. But to the next guy coming down the street, the street looks nicer. It sounds ridiculous but it's a very simple spiritual act. The self-centeredness is the trip. We're sitting here talking about spirituality and punk. I think it's a great question. To me the essence of spirituality is caring for others; to step out of the temporal and into the spiritual. The fact that we don't care about our own people is disgusting. We have a government that talks about how God-loving and God-fearing and what believers they all are and they're not willing to stick a hand out.

You mentioned your John Doe (X) quote about how spirituality and punk rock don't mix. ("Punk rock and spirituality have absolutely nothing to do with each other.") I hate to say that I really agree with him! The trouble is that the essence of punk rock was to do whatever you wanted regardless of how it affects anyone else. The punk rock thing, for me at least, was really a self-centered trip. It hurt a lot of people. I never cared once how this was going to affect someone else. It was all about self-satisfaction and glorification. It was about self, self, self! I treated people like crap. I never thought of how my actions were going to harm someone else.

The essence of spirituality is the complete opposite. We talk about self-will. *I'm* going to do this. *I'm* going to do that. The first sin of Christian mythology was will. God said, "Don't eat of it," and Adam said, "Fuck you! I'm in." Total punk rock move! (*laugh*) That's what I was constantly doing and not caring about others. To me, the essence of spirituality is to care about others. Some people did say, "Thank you. You helped me, you reached out." There were small bits of spirituality in what I did that affected people, but for the most part on my end—*worthless*. Other than the fact that my actions completely broke me down. I had run my self-centered actions so far into the ground that I realized there was nothing left and I had to look in a completely different direction. All of the searching, meditation—anything I do—is all a side note to *serving*. All of that is what I do part-time when I'm not serving somebody.

JM: Was punk rock part of that new direction for you, or something completely different?

JACK GRISHAM (TSOL): The music came later. At the end of my old life—and it basically was a completely different life—every single thing in this world had failed me. People couldn't adore me *enough*, there wasn't enough money, there wasn't enough power and love. There wasn't enough of anything. I was blocked up; it was like a stagnant pond. I had run every single option into the ground. I destroyed everyone that I came in contact with. There wasn't one person happy with me at the end of my past life. They were upset, concerned and angry. Not one of them said, "Jack's doing a great job." Not one. At the end, everything just ended up tasting like sand. No pleasure from any of it anymore.

JM: When was that?

JACK GRISHAM (TSOL): 1988 or 89. I was twenty-six years old. What's really funny is I always noticed all of these big rock guys always die around twenty-seven. Basically, I died also. But it was a different death. My spiritual death was in those years.

JM: Sounds like at some point you realized selfishness was causing you a lot of suffering and to serve others was going to be a new way to live. How did that play out for you?

JACK GRISHAM (TSOL): It took a long time and it was very painful. I stopped the drugs and alcohol. That was the first thing. I had to stop and get my head clear; little by little, waking up and getting a look at my life. When I woke up and got a look at myself it was frightening! I was suicidal for four years. Seriously swimming out in the ocean with my clothes on to die. I wanted to swim out far enough to just go to sleep so that I couldn't make it back to shore. I was done. I was devastated. I woke up to the fact that I'd left a trail of destruction. I had a daughter that I wasn't seeing. I owed back child support. I had a father whose death I was blamed for; estranged relationships with all of my family. My friends were afraid of me. I lived at my mom's. I'd run every business and school opportunity I had into the ground. It's not a good place to be, man. It's pretty ugly and it took a long time of reading and learning. Every single belief I had in God had to be completely shattered. All of my beliefs in spirituality were shattered. It's a very frightening place.

JM: When the ground that you trust isn't there anymore?

JACK GRISHAM: Completely. Anything that you reach out for is gone. It's a great place to be—though not at the time—but afterward it is.

JM: You realized it was a transformational point. But when you were in it, it was frightening.

JACK GRISHAM: Frightening. And I deal with guys in this all of the time. I'm not going to say that I help them; I attract people like that to me, who seek that kind of help.

JM: Because you've been on that path you know firsthand what it's like and you can maybe give people an idea of what's to come?

JACK GRISHAM (TSOL): Right. A little understanding. It's one thing to go to school and learn psychology or therapy to treat people. But it's different to have gone through it yourself. Other than that, all you're talking is theory. Swimming theory is useless when you get thrown into the ocean! (*laugh*) Who gives a shit! Know what I mean?

SCORPION AND FROG

JACK GRISHAM (TSOL): Some people are just fucked up. They're just punks. It could've been punk rock or you could've thrown *whatever* name on it you wanted. People used to get mad at me and they'd say, "Well, that's punk rock!" And I'd say, "Yeah, it's punk rock. But it's *not* punk rock." It's a certain type of person; that craziness that comes out. I used to tell people, "How come these guys say they're punks and they go to work?" I *couldn't* show up—I could *never* show up. There was no way that I was going to be successful—it just wasn't going to happen, man. The minute you said something against what I believed in, "Fuck you! I'm out of here." Or I'm throwing something at you or hitting you or just lying, ripping you off. My nature was evil.

There is a little story about the scorpion and the frog. They're standing at a river and the scorpion says, "Give me a ride across." The frog says, "No, you'll sting me!" The scorpion says, "Why would I do that? We'd both die." So, the frog says, "Okay, get on." And when they get in the middle of the river, the scorpion stings him. The frog says, "Why did you do that?" The scorpion answers, "It's my nature." That was *my* nature. These people would invite my band to do shows and the place would get wrecked and they'd be upset about it. It's like, "Dude, you bring in a wild animal and then you're mad that it shits on the carpet? *You're* the crazy one!" This is what I am—this is my nature. "*You* were the fool for believing that I was something other than what I was."

JM: So, for you, punk rock that talks about compassion is not really punk rock?

JACK GRISHAM (TSOL): Yes. I'm going to have to go with that. The essence of punk rock is, "*Fuck you, I do what I want.*" The essence of compassion and spirituality is, "*I love you, what do you need?*" It's completely two different things. Maybe it has that punk rock sound or whatever, but it's not the ethic that I believe punk rock started with.

JM: Often reincarnation is thought of as across many lifetimes. But some think of reincarnation as occurring during one lifetime, where different periods of experience feel like distinct lifetimes during this one life. You've been talking about your life that way, with one life ending and a new life beginning. Does reincarnation make sense to you in this way?

JACK GRISHAM (TSOL): As in this life, yeah. But a lot of people never change. A lot of people drift this whole life. I got lucky to be able to step into a different life. It's unbelievable to know what it's like to constantly be trying to be satisfied; to take, take, take. There's a basic futility to that existence. And then waking up and seeing something completely different. It's unbelievable. I'll never be able to appreciate life the way someone that is blind would be. If a man was blind half his life and all of a sudden, the lights came on and he could see he'd say, "Don't you see this! Look, it's a couch!" You'd say, "Fuck, what do you mean it's a couch? I sit on the couch every day!" To appreciate the littlest things. When you're so destroyed you can't appreciate anything and everything tastes like sand. Everything is worthless. Nothing is good anymore. Not sex, drugs, money. And then to wake up and all of a sudden, "Look at this!"

I remember I was walking down the street and it was pretty early on and I sat for an hour and looked at a flower. I just stood there and looked at it through the fence. I remember exactly what it looked like through the fence. It was a rose. It was pink and it was kind of darker red on the inside. The flower was pink and red. The leaves were really green. And the fence it was growing through was a black rod iron fence next to an old apartment building. I just sat there staring at it. It was like it was the first time I'd ever seen a flower! It was great. I had a life before and I didn't appreciate one bit of it. So, appreciation's been huge.

JM: It sounds like a lot has shifted for you by transforming how you view the world, rather than trying to change the world around you to fit your desires.

JACK GRISHAM (TSOL): *Nothing's* changed! That's just it. Nothing in *the world* has changed. Which is great! (*laugh*) Know what I'm saying? *Nothing* has changed. It's my perception of *what is* that has completely changed. But the sad thing is, man, we can't make people see that. You can't make people wake up, no matter what you do. You can't make them wake up. I get opportunities to talk to a lot of people and all I have to do is sit back and wait and see if they wake up. I don't tell them they're asleep. I just watch and one day all of a sudden, they're having problems. They're starting to wake up a little bit and stuff's not okay. Stuff they've done their whole life is all of sudden starting to become unacceptable. And they start to wake up. They start realizing their self-reliance is failing. It's cool.

JACK GRISHAM—HE'S HUGE. I'M FIVE FOOT FOUR

LYDIA LUNCH (Teenage Jesus & The Jerks / Big Sexy Noise): Have you read Jack Grisham's book? (*An American Demon*—2011) It's horrifying—what a fucker! I put him on a bill about three years ago in L.A. and I had never met him before. I'm certainly not part of that scene or interested. I've never heard his band. But I really liked what he was reading. He posted—somebody told me this, cause I'm not on Facebook—that he was scared of me. I think he was just kidding. He's huge. I'm five foot four.

I was very nice to him. I'm always nice to people. I put him on the bill and I wanted him to be reading. I just thought his reaction was weird. I thought, "God, is he really scared?" Whether he's scared of me or not, I loved that he said it. So, it didn't matter. But his reading was great. I mean, you have to admit your asshole-isms sometimes. I also understand, which is why I'm glad I inhabit the body that I do—which is as male, macho, butch and violent as I am. That's why I need so many vehicles to get it out. And which is why I explore what the nature of violence is. I can understand the passing down of traditional generational hormonal insanity. What I don't understand is that we haven't figured out a better way. Even those that channel it sometimes are still beating the shit out of people. On a global level, what if we could figure out how to really channel all the hatred, which is basically fear?

SELF-HELP GURU

JM: I read in the New York Times about workshops you're doing. The journalist called you a self-help guru. ("Finding Inner Peace with the Angriest Punk of 70s New York" by Ada Calhoun—December 20, 2013)

LYDIA LUNCH (Big Sexy Noise / Teenage Jesus and the Jerks): That's such crap. I've *always* been helping the individual. That's what my music and my work *does*. I like doing workshops especially for women only, to encourage them to lose their inhibitions. We don't have sports and we don't have war. We might as well have a fucking meeting and talk about writing. I can impart to them ways to improve spoken word. To me, there's still not enough spoken word. It's still a very important format.

You need to read your shit out loud! There are certain tricks to make it easier to do. That's what my workshops are about. I just think it's good for women to be together in a very uninhibited format. I just taught at Naropa University, the Jack Kerouac School of Disembodied Poets, under Anne Waldman. Thurston

Moore was there. I'm a cattle prodder; I always have been. I've curated a lot of shows in a lot of cities: at the Knitting Factory, The Parlor and various other places. Doing it in a workshop is great because it's a very intimate experience and you just want to give people the power of their own voice.

I didn't like that article very much. I thought she was kind of idiotic and didn't really get it. I'll continue to do workshops. It's important to have somebody saying, "Go ahead, experiment. Let's hear how that sounds. Let me read it to you." Not that you have to read it like me; just hear your words. "Now, what do you have to do?" I really like doing that. It's very satisfying for me and everybody that goes to them. It's really just about encouraging the individual to find their voice and do something with it.

MARK ANDERSEN (Dance of Days / Positive Force DC): It's obvious the world changes. Not always for the better, but sometimes. The other side of that is if you believe that the world and people are so malleable that they can change overnight. Probably none of us who have engaged in transformation or justice work didn't at some point feel, "Okay, it's going to change quickly." Sometimes it *does* happen like that. You reach a tipping point where the forces in the universe shift and the people who, for example, believed that slavery was divinely justified suddenly shift and believe that it's an abomination. How long ago was it that we believed all kinds of crazy things about what women couldn't do and now it's like *how could we have ever believed that?* It was in my lifetime when the majority opinion felt a different way about the capabilities of women.

The folks who say, "Nothing's ever going to change" have a mirror image in the folks who are saying, "It's going to change *now.*" The key thing is living in the paradox. I believe that people have the power to change the world and change themselves. I think Karl Marx dealt with this in saying, "People make history but they don't make it just as they will." We're dealing with something that is beyond our comprehension, beyond the tools that we have at hand. You could argue that this is a Marxist way of dealing with paradox. The different ideas and forces contend with one another and then what emerges out of them—the thesis versus the antithesis creating a synthesis—is stronger and more true. That's one of the ways change happens in our world. I also think that's partly how we advance spiritually.

JAMES SPOONER (*Afro-Punk*): I was talking to my wife because we're struggling to come up with a name for our daughter and one thing a lot of people say is, "If you're going to have a name that is unique, it should really have meaning." I'm thinking to myself, "Who is it that actually means something to me, that I would want to pass on to my daughter?" A lot of people will name their kids after family members or artists. I couldn't really think of anybody because all of the punk icons I've ever loved as a kid and grown up to meet, I was always really disappointed. They turned out to be assholes or just bitter or didn't live up to who they presented on their records. All of them except for Ian MacKaye. I really thought long and hard about possibly naming our daughter MacKaye. He's the only person who has all the punk rock ideals that I've always believed in and, now probably nearing fifty, still is that way. He's been successful and I really have respect for him. I don't think we're going to go that way, but it was telling to me because I don't believe in God but I do believe in Ian MacKaye! (*laugh*) That's the closest I can get to talking about spirituality. I have a belief in what punk rock can be. It's up to the individual how close they want to bring it to their heart and how much they believe in it to make it be their life.

PENNY RIMBAUD (Crass): This place (Dial House) is my greatest commitment, more than my creative work or any relationship I might have. I live in a shed in the garden, which is where I am at the moment. It's very beautiful. It is like Eden here, but there's also an undercurrent which is incredibly hard for a lot of people to exist within for very long because you're left on your own. The principle I apply to myself is to not impose ideas, unless asked. Not to engage, unless asked. Gee (Vaucher) has lived here not as long as I have; she moved here three years after it was established as an open house. She acknowledges things in my attitude she doesn't agree with. She has the right to act according to her own principles within the house. So, that leads to conflicts when you have two people trying to apply principles to a situation. You're going to have arguments. There's only been one or two occasions where that's gone too far. Even there I won't interject unless I'm asked. It's not my business to intervene. It's rather like when the band (Crass) smashed up. I could've intervened and doused the flames, but I didn't. It actually led to me being on my own here again, as I had been before the band.

CHRIS HANNAH (Propagandhi): People should think about self-reliance. Do what you can to be self-reliant, do what you can to organize yourselves. Because things are going to come to a point where we are all going to have to take care of ourselves. Things are fucking going down the toilet and we are on the edge of a near extinction if we're not careful and people are going to have to know how to take care of themselves cooperatively.

AUTHENTIC ME—REVOLUTIONARY WE

MARK ANDERSEN (*All the Power: Revolution Without Illusion*): Community itself is a fundamentally important concept. The idea of community—that we're all bound together in this deep and mysterious but very profound and precious way—is really essential to my political/spiritual approach. A lot of my politics were about my personal affirmation and trying to oppose conformity and speak the truth. In *All the Power* I call it a kind of existential politics. But if punk was saying; *I'm not like everybody else* and *don't dictate to me,* that's an essential place to start from. But it's not really an ending point. Again, we're emphasizing the journey.

If we're talking about community or revolution, then you can't just stay with the *me*. The *authentic me* is connected to what I would call the *revolutionary we*. But it's not a simple connection and there is a certain degree of tension between the two. Human beings are social animals and we need one another. However much I may be at odds with society, I don't believe that human life is possible outside of that connection to other people. What it requires from us is actually to reflect on not simply what feels good or what is important to us, but to try to connect with what *actually* touches other people and is meaningful for them.

JM: How did you get interested in punk rock, Buddhism and Taoism? In 1979 I came across *The Wisdom of Insecurity* by Alan Watts, at about the same time I encountered punk rock.

CHINA MARTENS (*Future Generation: The Zine-Book for Subculture Parents, Kids, Friends and Others*): It started when I was a month pregnant. I was at my parents' house, and I walked by the bookshelf and this book fell off. So funny! It fell on the ground. It was *The Way of Zen* by Alan Watts. I could apply it to myself and it gave me a bigger strength. It felt like a good thing in my life. Alan Watts helps you think without words. When you're young everything around you is one way and it doesn't feel good and you don't know it can be another way. There's a lot of hierarchy in our Western dominating binary system and these Eastern religions were a really good counterbalance to all that crap. This Buddhist guy introduced the concept to me that sometimes what's more important than truth and justice is compassion! We don't want to create a new form of oppression. It's important to understand that sometimes people are hurting inside and that's why they hurt others.

DAVE WAKELING (The English Beat): Unless most everybody on stage is *in the moment* it doesn't click. Once everybody on stage is in the moment you can move effortlessly with the crowd. They sense it and they start to be in the moment as well. Sometimes we'll see it flash over the crowd like a flame, almost. They're not aware of it but we spot it before they do, and the crowd is actually dancing in step with each other, but they don't know it yet. In a couple of songs, they will! "Whoa! We're a thousand-footed creature!"

JM: You once thought about becoming a Buddhist monk?

DAVE WAKELING (The English Beat): Yeah, that was the choice when I was going to join The Beat. In fact, we'd started saving up money for about six months. The choice was either I was going to be in a group or I was going to join Greenpeace and hang myself off chains in front of mammals of some sort. Vaguely. Or I was going to be a Buddhist monk. I'll admit it; *Lobsang Rampa* (*The Third Eye*) was the first one I read when I was twelve. It affected me. I bought a second-hand paperback copy of Jack Kerouac's *Dharma Bums* and I was attracted to it because it had this big golden Buddha on the front, which I'd never seen before. I thought, "Whoa, what's that? I've got to have that!" That actually led me into the Beat writers and ended up with me calling my group The Beat. (*laugh*) That was really the start of it. I've been a follower—I've been limping along ever since.

Me and my mate Dave were saving up money to travel East. As I started saving up the money I started having loads and loads of dreams about girls and motorbikes—girls on motorbikes, me lying on girls on motorbikes, girls lying by the sides of motorbikes—all that. I started to realize, "You know, there's very little point going and shaving your head and sitting on an orange towel in Thailand and thinking about girls on motorbikes. You may need to get this out of your system." So, I thought, "Well, be in a group then." That's what being in a band looks like, really—girls and motorbikes with a bit of singing in the evening! (*laugh*) Unfortunately I got stuck there!

I did get to work with Greenpeace for about five years when I took some time off from singing. I still dream rather less now, but I always expected that I was going to retire and go to a monastery. I don't think I'll be able to do it in this lifetime. I don't want to leave the people who like me; family and friends. I don't know if I could leave them just to better myself. Might be a bit of doing dharma yoga. I might just be doing that this time around. I've been told that I was a monk before. I must have done some terrible things—who did I shag in the monastery? (*laugh*) "You will do thirty years of girls and motorbikes and singing "Tears of a Clown." No! No that! Please abbot, not that!"

I got an invite to go to Tibet for two weeks with Mike Peters from The Alarm. He's been struggling against an illness that he's just beaten and they're going to do some documentary about his challenges and it's going to be expressed as a ten-mile hike up to the base camp of Mount Everest. He wants to do it with two friends who play guitar and sing. He invited me last week. (2007) I've always dreamed of going to Tibet. What a brilliant chance! There's a lot of Buddhism cropping up in the (English Beat) songs now. Tons of it.

JAMES WILLIAMSON (Iggy & The Stooges): We were like a family. We all knew each other for years and years. These guys were my closest friends. We spent all of our time together. It was a group of people who moved around together everywhere and our reality was our own and it had very little to do with anybody else's. It was kind of like a little cult, if you will. As most bands do, we fell out eventually and so once that magic is gone, it's gone. But during the times when the magic was there, it was very good. We're still—I wouldn't say close—but we still know each other quite well. It's quite easy to pick up the phone and talk.

CHUCK D (Public Enemy / Prophets of Rage): I say, "Revolution means change, don't look at me strange." The spiritual part of revolution is balancing out the world and taking the powers to be at task to say, "You guys have to understand that the world is to be shared." This whole mentality of making a killing with capitalism is the thing that is diametrically opposed to making a living. Revolution in that regard means how you actually get more power to the people. Also, how you get people food, shelter and clothing when it's necessary. That has to bite at capitalism's tail. Music does a good job of that. That's not always an easy call because a lot of times musicians get caught up with the whole capitalist program—so much that they can't bite back at it. *The human family is the most important thing.* The beautiful thing about culture is that it brings human beings together for our similarities and knocks aside the differences. That's a beautiful thing about music and culture. Being able to enjoy the human family together and go forward in a proactive way.

ISHAY BERGER (Useless ID): Life is short and I've found that my purpose, and what I will leave behind, is punk music. If you take music out of life, it's just working, eating and sleeping. So, this is mega-crucial for me to keep writing, recording and doing shows. We bring people together by making music. Maybe we didn't buy a house or quit our day jobs but hell, seems like we *did* do something. And I will keep doing it!

PENELOPE SPHEERIS (*The Decline of Western Civilization*): I was watching a TV show last night—"Wife Swap"—and this woman who is a right-wing, God-loving freak says to this liberal, hippie kid, "Why are you trying to promote peace? There's *never* been peace in the world." I thought, "She's absolutely right." Never in the history of the world has there been peace. Where the hell did this concept come from? Doesn't mean it won't happen someday, but it doesn't seem very likely. It keeps getting worse and worse.

JM: Do you think peace is possible?

PENELOPE SPHEERIS (*Wayne's World*): Do I think there will ever be world peace? Maybe if we all sit around and hold hands and sing "Kumbaya." (*laugh*)

JM: Maybe there's always a dynamic tension?

PENELOPE SPHEERIS (*The Decline of Western Civilization*): Yeah! It's just part of the life force and that's just the way it is. The code of my life is that *no good deed goes unpunished*. Every time I try to do something good for anybody, I swear to God it backfires! Like when I was working for Sharon and Ozzy (Osbourne) for free for four and a half years! And I've been working for free on this Janis Joplin movie for four years and where's it at? Nowhere! I swear to God, the last ten years of my movie-making life has sucked big weenies! (*laugh*)

JM: I heard that maybe you'll make a movie about John Lydon.

PENELOPE SPHEERIS (*The Decline of Western Civilization*): I've been talking to John (Lydon) about it for five years. We've got a good script and hopefully that will happen. These things almost have this organic natural life of their own.

"ANGER IS AN ENERGY"

The Buddha said 2500 years ago that if you're angry you're just exercising your angry muscle. The more you exercise it, the more able it is to be angry.

—Dave Wakeling (English Beat)

That energy—that negative energy—had to be released.

—Jack Grisham (TSOL)

Everyone has a side that needs to be totally unhinged for a while. Punk rock provided that safety valve for a lot of people.

—Jim Lindberg (Pennywise)

When punk was born all of a sudden it was okay if you showed your anger. So, that was cool. As long as there were rules to the anger: you don't hurt anybody else.

—Penelope Spheeris (*The Decline of Western Civilization*)

Is the whole thing a healthy release of tension or yet another disturbing sign of the escalating violence in society?

—Robert Hilburn, Los Angeles Times, January 23, 1981
"Stagehoppers Flit, Flail but Black Flag Plays On" review

of show at Santa Monica Civic (California) with Black Flag,
D.O.A., The Adolescents and opening band The Minutemen.

It's a calm spring afternoon in 2006. I'm sitting on a meditation cushion, relaxed and focused. I'm at a Buddhist center near San Diego, California, called Deer Park Monastery, established by Vietnamese Buddhist teacher/activist Thich Nhat Hanh. A large bell is struck and the simple, extended sound resounds. During meals, we're invited to eat in silence and bring full awareness to our eating. (All of this is in great contrast to the thrashing and booming at the Bad Religion show I was at the week before.)

Thich Nhat Hanh speaks about mindfulness, concentration, and the nature of reality, and emphasizes how important it is to notice when seeds of anger are watered inside of us, and how to stop them from growing. He suggests bringing compassionate awareness to our anger and then watering a different set of seeds: those of understanding and mindfulness. He says that anger is a state of mind that clouds judgment and that actions we take while under the influence of anger cause harm. Thay, as many of his followers call him, then said clearly: "Anger is an energy." Naturally, John Lydon's voice comes into my head, singing those very same words—"Anger is an energy"—on the 1986 song "Rise" from the Public Image Limited album titled *Album*. Some music critics have identified the song as being about the racism and violence of the apartheid system of South Africa, a human rights issue that took center stage among students and activists in the 1980s.

ANGER IS AN ENERGY

JM: "Anger is an energy"—what does this line mean to you now? (2019)

JOHN LYDON (Sex Pistols / PiL): That refers back to having meningitis, when I was trying to recover my memories to know anything about myself. My mum and dad told me that the doctors advised that they keep me angry and through that I might get my memory back quicker than just being molly-coddled. Well, it worked because my memory did come back. It took a few years to do that. That was my energy—anger. They did not pamper me at all. I wasn't allowed to be institutionalized or pampered. Which could've been two very vicious weapons turned against me. And there you go. *Anger is an energy*. I had to learn the hard way, and on the receiving end of it. But, my god, do I not love my mum and dad for that. And that must have been very, very hard for them. Because the temptation I suppose; you see a little baby monkey injured, is to go and hug and cuddle.

Well, that's the wrong move, isn't it? Life is a series of hard knocks and without them we wouldn't be what we are.

BRAD LOGAN (Leftöver Crack): Anger is a thing we're born with. It has its purposes. How I've used it, or how it's used me, has shifted since when I was a kid. It's definitely a motivation. You don't like your job? "Damn, I can do better than this!" And you start your own thing. That's one positive use. Or someone is attacking you and your family and you fucking defend yourself. That's another way it can be used in a constructive way. Or, "I don't like this fucking music I'm being forced to listen to, so I'm going to write my own shit." Same kind of thing.

But it's not something to dwell on all the time because it loses its effect. When I was a kid I thought differently—fucking twenty angry songs in a row? Awesome! As I got older, you gotta have some variety, so tap into some other emotions. You can't live in that all the time. You're going to have a heart attack or go insane. I've seen that happen; people go insane behind their anger and unwillingness to accept things and tap into other emotions.

IAN MACKAYE (Fugazi / Minor Threat): I came from a background of chaos, anger and insanity. All of a sudden there was a way that I could fit in with other people that were just as wacked.

JM: A lot of punk rock musicians and fans have said that punk concerts were a venue for creating community and also for releasing anger. Henry Rollins has said, "Anger is what motivates me." What's your view on how you deal with anger? Is your music part of that?

JELLO BIAFRA (Dead Kennedys): Anger is one of my motivations. I can't deny that was one of the underlying driving forces getting me to leave Boulder, Colorado and go to San Francisco and push myself to come out of my shell and immerse myself in punk rock and meet people and try to create something myself. One underlying motive was getting revenge on all the people back home who told me I was a loser and I'd never amount to anything—school, family, you name it. I think that's what creating punk and hardcore music means to a lot of the younger people who started it. It's the first thing they ever made on their own. *It was the first really tough project they actually finished without some school deadline or a parent or coach telling them to do it.* They made it themselves.

Even if the first thing they shot off to Alternative Tentacles was a cassette of totally generic hardcore, I have to remind myself that the first Dead Kennedys demo was kind of generic, too. The only way to find your own sound is to keep doing it. But it's no surprise how many influential bands got started either coming to Ramones or Dead Kennedys shows and/or being in a forgettable punk or hardcore band who end up making something really *unforgettable* later.

Apparently even Moby is an ex-member of that Connecticut hardcore band The Vatican Commandos. They not only had a great name, up there with Leftöver Crack, but they put out a couple of seven inches, too.

Let's go back to the original thing about Henry (Rollins). Anger is part of it but I've just been shocked to see myself being written up from time to time that, "Jello felt so bad about the condition of the world that he started Dead Kennedys." How far down an academic rabbit hole are these people? Jesus Christ! You don't start a band because you feel bad—you start a band because you want to feel good! You want to get on stage, you want to rock! It's positive stuff. And in my case, let's not forget *humor*. I think Henry would say the same thing, that the most important band when we were young was The Stooges. With me there was also Hawkwind, Magma, Sparks and The Sonics. But let's not forget people like Frank Zappa. I mix all of that stuff into what I do. Maybe my lyrical style is closer to vintage Sparks than anything else. If you read the words to *Indescreet* (1975) or *Propaganda* (1974) or *Kimono My House* (1974), there's layer upon layer of well-sharpened sarcasm. At the same time they're really fucking funny! That's part of what this culture should be.

JM: What do you think about anger?

STEVE IGNORANT (Crass): Personally, I think it's brilliant.

JM: Eastern spirituality like Buddhism suggests anger is something that gets in the way. While in punk, anger is seen as a positive force for motivating action. The Clash sang about this: "Let fury have the hour / anger can be power / you know that you can use it."

STEVE IGNORANT (Crass): That's what's fired me all of these years; anger. I've been angry most of my life. I'm angry at the injustice I've seen through these tired eyes and still it goes on. Of course, I'm angry. But I channel the anger, hopefully, into what I do. Musically and lyrically. I know what you mean about the Eastern and Buddhist perspective on anger. When I was getting into Zen a little bit, that made sense. On the other end, "What shall I do then?" Fuck off and sit in a cave and sort of meditate to myself for the rest of my life? Or hope to change the world with a cup of tea? Or do I wake up to the fact that anger is just as justifiable an emotion as love, sorrow, jealousy and all the rest of them. Anger is something that every person feels. And rather than punch someone in the face, I channel it in a different way. But I don't think it's anything to be afraid, or ashamed, of. If it wasn't for those twats in power—so-called power—perhaps we wouldn't be so angry.

AMY RAY (Indigo Girls): I used to subscribe to the John Lydon "Anger is an Energy" PiL song; "I may be wrong and I may be right." I really believed in that. I still do, but I believe anger is an impetus but it does need to be transcended. If it's not, you just end up bitter. To have compassion and to really work within the world, your anger has to be transcended. You can't accomplish anything if you're not listening.

It reminds me of talking to my dad. When I get really angry I don't hear anything he says, so I don't really learn how to dialogue with him and disagree and change his mind. But now I can do that more because I really listen to what he says and I realize, "This is his perspective." I feel that we activists can sometimes be alienating to people and elitist even. There's a lot of people who are active in a different way, who are engaged in their life in a way that's suitable for them. We can sometimes be classist in North America with our activism. Sometimes anger can get in the way of breaking down those kinds of walls.

JELLO BIAFRA (Dead Kennedys): There's been plenty of people that I got so mad at over the years—I'll mention no names—that I feel like fucking shooting their ass. "The world would be better off without them!" But that's all the more reason for me *never, ever* to own a gun. Or even carry a knife. When you get cornered and you're unarmed you're more likely to be able to talk your way out of a fight and diffuse the thing because it's the only tactic you have available. Otherwise, if I'd gone crazy with a gun, I might still be sitting in prison over some useless fuck I got pissed off at in the '80s!

JM: I agree. People do get angry and if you have a gun—not a good combination.

JELLO BIAFRA (Guantanamo School of Medicine): Yeah. It was already a little out of hand when you had all the switchblade action going on in the '50s and early '60s. Of course, those people are mostly still alive. But once those same kind of people—at the same age, with the same amount of poverty and anger—get handed guns instead; it's way worse. Not just more people getting killed, but more people getting permanently injured or paralyzed.

TURN THE KNIFE OUTWARD

Hate and anger, for anyone that's been traumatized, is far more productive than depression and suicidal thoughts. I've always turned the knife outward but I've always wanted to enjoy myself at the end of the fucking day.

—Lydia Lunch (Teenage Jesus & The Jerks)

LYDIA LUNCH (Teenage Jesus & The Jerks): The other night I had a show with Weasel Walter and I really didn't want to do the show. And I *always* want to perform! I just didn't want to go. I didn't even know what it was. I went there and we did the show. I didn't like my part of the show. Whatever, a lot of young girls came up to me that had never seen me. They *loved* it. It was about death. But even for me it was aggressive in a way I should know how to finesse at this point. And after it, I was so incredibly raging with violence, which is something we never hear women talk about because most of them haven't learned to turn the knife outward. I was so burning with hatred and rage and violence and I'm like, "Oh my God—I used to live in this corrosion, for decades. Fuck! Wow!"

What's interesting about spoken word is that I and Exene and Biafra and Rollins all came up pretty much at the same time and we were all pretty political at that point. Some of us still are and Biafra still does what he does. Everyone still does what they do but even I see some of my early spoken word shows and I'm like, "My God. You are truly fucking insane!" What I am is just incredibly fucking passionate! And if I didn't have that vehicle—I *had* to have that vehicle. And all the other vehicles.

So, one night every few years I go into a spasm of chemically imbalanced hormonal rage that makes me feel like an unrepentant serial killer looking for anything to destroy! Although I can reel it in because I have a bit more control than the average man and besides that, I love to occasionally puppeteer the psychos. It was kind of shocking to realize I used to burn with that all the fucking time. I wasn't kidding and I'm not fucking kidding now.

JM: Henry Rollins told me that anger drives his creativity. I'm guessing that thirty-five years of being motivated by anger must be tiring.

LYDIA LUNCH (Teenage Jesus & The Jerks): Fuck *yeah*!

RIKKI VANDERPOL (Dying For It): I'm a pretty angry person in general. It's really therapeutic for me to be on stage and be angry as a front person in a band. In the scene it can be taken two ways; it can be really powerful for other women. It's cathartic for me and it's really empowering for other women to see that. But at the same time, it can be intimidating for men. Because we're not used to seeing that. Women are typically taught not to be angry. When you see a woman so angry, your mind may go to, "She's a pissed off feminist, an angry bitch." Knife inward and outward; I haven't ever thought of it that way, but I see that.

ANGER CREATES MORE ANGER

MICHELLE CRUZ GONZALES (Spitboy): I agree that anger creates more anger. We have to be careful to be very mindful. Speaking of *mindful* in terms of spirituality, I'm not a Goddess type but I think of the female deities in my own culture like the Catholic female indigenous deities. If I were ever to fall on my knees, I would pray to "La Virgen." But I do think that if there were a real spirituality, it would be mindfulness practice around things like anger and trying to be mindful of using anger as a motivator and not allowing it to consume you and take over.

CRIS KIRKWOOD (Meat Puppets): It comes down to this: are emotions merely chemical reactions because we're conglomerates of goo put together by evolution or God or however we came? "Caspar the Unfriendly Ghost." Emotion is something that we all experience, like hunger or pain. Sometimes when you're making music it's strange. That's what I like about it. It's very mysterious. Occasionally emotions will come into it. So will your bowels. So will the food you've eaten or the amount of sleep you've had over the last few days. Or the weather. We bring some of those elements into it, too.

As far as expressing anger, I don't think you could find a much angrier band than The Meat Puppets. We're terrible people! If you haven't been getting that in our music then you're obviously playing the records at the wrong speed! (*laugh*) The Meat Puppets are fucking hateful! We're despicable, wretched people! We deserve the lot that we have scraped off of the decaying corpse of the Earth's crust for ourselves. We have a new record coming out in March (2009) and there's a song called "Love Mountain." It's only about hate!

JM: Have you experimented with different ways of dealing with anger?

CRIS KIRKWOOD (Meat Puppets): Yes, there's lashing out at others, lashing out at myself . . . I definitely have tried to sift through the rubble of my mind and find some sort of alignment occasionally and tend to my body's demands. I have found that I'm not really good at it, as a lot of people have found. In the words of the delightful Hank Williams, "No matter how you struggle and drive, it all winds up in the same place." That is freedom to me. Depending on what you're willing to put up with, you can vent any particular feeling that you care to vent. If you share the wrong feelings with some people, they will share them back in ways that you may not like. But if you're willing to put up with that, you're free to do that.

JM: You were shot in 2003 in Phoenix, Arizona.

CRIS KIRKWOOD (Meat Puppets): It was my fault. If you're me—a little too sensitive and free-wheelin'—there are known and well-defined ways to allow your life to go completely out of control. I did a lot of that. After years of having treated myself very poorly, I stumbled into a stupid situation at the post office and I wound up having a scuffle with a security guard who decided that to end the scuffle he would shoot me. I had already decided that the scuffle was over and I was trying to trundle away and he shot me in the back. Then the Feds took it upon themselves to incarcerate me for a while because I had had fisticuffs with the gentleman. That's my sordid story. I managed to pull myself out of it, which is amazing. I think I'm a testimony to the strength and endurability of the human spirit. I've put myself through some awful stuff. Ultimately it was my fault and it didn't need to happen. I'm very pleased that the world allowed me to get beyond it.

RAMSEY KANAAN (Political Asylum / AK Press): I was attracted to punk because it was angry. Well, all kinds of people are angry. Many right-wing reactionaries are angry. They're just angry about different things. Anger in itself is not necessarily a positive or attractive quality. Most forms of music tend to be associated with young people. And young people tend to be associated with rebellion. Young people have more energy and get up and go. As a political person who's involved in certain counterculture, other than just enjoying the music and having a good time, I wanted to inject some politics into it and expand the radical elements that are already there. I would posit that in all aspects of my life. Culture is neither positive or negative, radical or reactionary. It's what we make of culture. Politics also is neither reactionary nor radical. It's what you make of it. My interest happens to be in music, reading and ideas so I'm going to inject some politics into it. I don't mean that it's a vacuum with no politics, but I'm going to try to accentuate and exaggerate further what I consider the better, more radical elements within punk.

"IN GOD WE TRUST"

There are videos on YouTube of the young Dead Kennedys at recording sessions for their 1981 *In God We Trust, Inc* EP. The video opens with a close-up of a sticker on an amp, "If you love God burn a church." As they begin playing, Klaus Flouride says with a sarcastic grin, eyebrows lifted, "I'm really angry!" When I spoke with Klaus about this he commented; "I was making fun of the punk stereotype in mainstream media that presents anger and punk as synonymous."

KLAUS FLOURIDE (Dead Kennedys): There's that bumper sticker that says, "If you're not angry then you're not paying attention." I think it should be *outrage* more than anger. There's a difference. Being righteously outraged and being angry to a point of blindness are two different things. Anger to the point of blindness turns you into a terrorist. Being outraged and trying to do something constructive about it is a totally different thing. When we were doing that recording and I said, "Oh, I'm angry," that was taking the piss out of the whole concept that, "We're punk rock and we're supposed to be angry all the time!"

KIM FOWLEY (The Runaways, producer): Maybe the anger of punk is digestible Vaseline for the ears or the senses. The musicians say, "Oh, it's anger." But then you listen to the words and it's not very angry at all. It's kind of informative.

TIM MCKEE ("How Punk Rock Saved My Life"): When I think of slamdancing I think of how much I liked it and how cathartic it was. It was about being physical and rough, but to music. There was an intention not to get hurt and not to hurt other people. That container was just what I needed. I felt tough when I did it. I also felt like maybe some of the anger that I was feeling would dissolve a little bit into that container.

Punk was a coming-of-age ritual for a young person who is instructed in what the container is and who has some elders helping them understand it. I would read about slam dancing in punk zines and listen to some of the live show recordings. I listened to people like Ian MacKaye berating people who didn't get this. There was a code of respect. It wasn't about hurting people. I would encounter people who did not understand that code and the ritual would get compromised a bit. There was that dark side because there were some people who couldn't tap into that anger respectfully.

> *Let fury have the hour / anger can be power / You know that you can use it.*
>
> —"Clampdown" by the Clash

JM: I often think of the line from the Clash song "Clampdown." I know a lot of punk rock folks and social change activists believe that anger is a power. There's this bumper sticker, "If you're not angry, then you're not paying attention."

EXENE CERVENKA (X): Well, anger will destroy you before you get any work done. Anger is an extremely negative force that has no value whatsoever. I believe more in people like Martin Luther King Jr. and Gandhi. I just don't believe in negative energy. I don't think that it can do any good. I know so many people that are so extremely angry about the Bush administration and the war that they are blinded to everything else. You can't have a conversation without it always reverting back to George Bush. I don't think there's any point in hating George Bush. I think there is a point in ending the war and doing a lot of things to make society better and to someday have a better government. But I don't think being angry is going to make George Bush and his policies go away. I just don't believe in it. I'm too old to believe in anger. It doesn't work.

Anger is like intolerance. It's dismissive of someone else's point of view. When George Bush stole the election (2000) a lot of people were angry at the middle of the country, and the average person, for voting for him. But there's no point in being angry at someone because they voted for George Bush. It doesn't matter that he might be the worst president in the history of the country! I'm not saying that he isn't. I'm not supporting him in any way. I'm just saying that being angry isn't going to make anything better. That's a hard thing for people to hear because they feel that if you're not angry then you're not doing something right. I've seen too many people just become angry all the time about everything. It's a waste.

PRIMAL SCREAM

D. J. BONEBRAKE (X): I know that there was a cathartic result from this music. Like you said, it's loud and it's primitive. Anyone can do it, to an extent. Although it's not as easy as some people think. I've had people say, "It helped me get through tough parts in my life." Maybe it's like the primal scream. Maybe you need to just get that out. Part of society can be so uptight and so structured. But as a person going through it you realize that you can't just do that all of the time. There's more than one emotion. So, there's a transformation there where you say, "I want to do something beyond this scream or one chord song."

BRIAN BRANNON (Jodie Foster's Army): Sometimes we have anger in our songs and when we're done, it's cathartic and we share that with the crowd.

DON REDONDO (JFA): I've taken yoga with my wife and I find that very calming. And I surf. And at the same time playing a forty-minute hardcore set with Brian, I have so much fun playing that I don't even remember that I did it. Because you're so in the moment and you're so hitting the chord changes and the velocity. It's funny because both those things shut my brain down completely and it's really nice. Right? To let it go for a minute. And they're both so different. You think of a yoga person playing a punk rock set! But both bring you into the moment. It's a good thing. It's a new day.

RAY CAPPO (Youth of Today / Shelter): I felt it was cathartic to release anger. Our songs were anthems of transformation. One of the songs people sang along to was, "Break Down the Walls." It's an anthem you sing with great ferocity and we'd be singing it together, almost as a family.

CHUCK WILD (Missing Persons): I'm openly gay—I came out in 1976. I joined ACT UP LA. We'd go with cans of red spray paint in front of city hall and lay down in the drawing of the body. Ronald Reagan never mentioned the word AIDS. Now it's called HIV. There was little movement by the government to let people know it was a sexually transmitted disease. I had over fifty-five friends die. There was this zeitgeist of anger. We were feeling that we had to do something and make a difference. There was also a feeling of helplessness, especially when you're in your twenties or thirties and everybody you know dies. It's not only tragic, it shakes the foundations of who you are. There was a real feeling that society could be changed. I think it was some hangover from the 70s. I'm glad I had an outlet for all that energy. It was quite an interesting time. I still live in Hollywood but since then I've never experienced anything like that window from 1979 to 1986. It was an experience.

MIKE NESS (Social Distortion): It's okay to be agitated and moved. I watch public broadcasting TV to learn the truth about history and all it takes for me is to watch a show on white supremacy and my blood boils. But it's not healthy. It's better to ignore your enemies and use agitation positively. Education and information are the most powerful tools; finding awareness and then sharing it with people. I agree that anger or fear can be counterproductive.

JIM LINDBERG (Pennywise): We play music that's aggressive—it's loud and fast. On stage we're raging and having a good time, going pretty crazy while we're performing. At the same time, we look at that as a righteous way to let off steam. Everyone has something inside them, a side that needs to be totally unhinged for a while. Punk rock provided that safety valve for a lot of people. I've often thought that sometimes some of these bands should be given credit because you see a lot of these guys at these shows in the slam pit going crazy and it's a very healthy way for guys with a lot of testosterone to go out and release some energy and frustration without getting arrested for it.

DARIUS KOSKI (Swingin' Utters): My songs are the equivalent of a journal entry for me. It drives me crazy after awhile if I don't sit down and write. Most of my songs seem to be not dark, but pessimistic. I'm sort of a pessimist but it's really a way of letting my frustration out. It's the only outlet I have. I don't want to go around beating people up. I really don't know what I'd do if I wasn't allowed to write songs. It's the only thing that grounds me. None of my stuff is overtly political; you probably have to look for it. I look at song lyrics as being more like poetry than anything else. All the lyricists that I admire, I could read their lyrics as if they were poetry. A lot of people like Tom Waits, Shane McGowan or Elvis Costello are really underrated as far as their writing goes because they're rock stars.

LIZ LAMERE (Alan Vega [Suicide]'s widow / creative collaborator Alan Vega solo / solo recording artist / SSNUB / Backward Flying Indians): Alan (Vega) was genuine, honest and empathetic. Just a very caring human being who felt deeply. Could he be reactive at times? Absolutely. But he never held a grudge. He could freely vent his feelings and then let it go. Letting that out during his performances was actually very healthy because he'd get off the stage and be absolutely the nicest person that you'd want to meet.

GLENN BRANCA (Theoretical Girls): Anger has a lot to do with punk music—you'd have to agree with me about that! My opinion about the punk approach was that we took the anger and frustration and we didn't go out into the streets and shoot people. We went up on stage and we took it out there. It was like Artaud's *Theatre of Cruelty* and we allowed the audience to participate in getting all of this out of ourselves. We're not some super beings! We're animals. We have all of those instincts. We have that lizard back brain. It's all part of our makeup. We have all of those feelings. As ugly as they may be, every one of us has those feelings. I think that's a lot of what punk was about. It was what hardcore would become and eventually the various movements that came after that. It's a way of expressing ourselves without hurting anyone. That's a lot of what my music is about. It's about dealing with both the animal and intellectual aspects of our nature. They're real and part of what we are. So, why deny it? Being in denial about it is far more dangerous than expressing it.

JM: That's one of the things that excited me about punk when I first heard it. Pop music had songs about loss and frustration but they didn't *sound* upset. Punk came along and the music and lyrics sounded authentic in their emotional expression.

GLENN BRANCA (Theoretical Girls): Right. That is a lot of what I was trying to do. I was more interested in the sound and the intensity of it than the poetry and lyrics. I love poetry and great lyrics. Like I said, I love Lennon and Dylan but I wanted to find a way of communicating something without using words, without being literal. I wanted to get at something that wasn't necessarily conscious. I wanted to get into that part of you that can't be articulated, that can just be felt. That was what I was thinking about when I started doing this kind of music. And it still is. It's still what I'm doing.

JUSTIN SANE (Anti-Flag): Punk rock is something that is aggressive and usually angry. I think that's a good thing. Those are expressions of emotion that can motivate people. There can be a positive way to express your frustration and your anger. That was one of the things I really loved about punk rock when I first heard it. I didn't feel like taking the route of some of the jerks in my high school who wanted to bully and intimidate other people. They seemed to take out all of their frustration and their problems on weaker people and beating people up.

That didn't make any sense to me. What I loved about punk rock as a teenager, and even to this very day; I have frustrations at times and I might be angry at times, but I can focus that anger or frustration in a positive way. I can actually create something positive with it and maybe create an expression that others can relate to.

All emotions can be used as a motivating factor. I don't think the idea of pretending that you're not feeling a certain way is a good idea. To deny your feelings is not productive. You can embrace those feelings and turn them into something positive. Just because you're feeling angry or aggressive doesn't mean you have to injure another human being. You can find other ways to focus that energy. Unfortunately, people seem to need to be desperate before they're willing to take action. Maybe people need to hurt a little bit more. It's sad. Especially with the kind of corporate media control that is out there and the information people hear is so slanted.

> *Anger is a response to violations against love.*
>
> —Chris Hannah (Propagandhi)

JM: I hear in some of your lyrics a sense of despair, anger and frustration with the state of the world. Can you say more about what helps you move beyond that?

CHRIS HANNAH (Propagandhi): Move beyond anger or despair? I'm not sure that I have moved beyond despair or anger. I think anger is a very important state of mind to have. I think it is often dismissed too easily as being reactionary. People talk about this aesthetically, that loud angry music is not going to be heard. That you have to be quiet for people to listen. I understand that people are compelled by different forms of art, but I think that dismissing anger, loud music or angry manifestations of how you assess the world is a mistake. Anger is a response to violations against love. That's what it is. What's more righteous than anger? I don't really try to get beyond anger if it is actually what compels me to get involved and do things. I have no problem with it because I know where it comes from. It comes from the same place that quieter music or poetry comes from; it comes from the same place. With despair, I am not there yet. I do feel despair. Partially, because I know myself, and I imagine that most people aren't too different than me. And like I said, I don't do nearly enough. There are a lot of distractions. It's a very comfortable Western lifestyle that I am involved in and it's very easy to sink into a sofa and watch television. That's haunting.

TOM MORELLO (Rage Against the Machine / Prophets of Rage): When you see the harsh realities of a cold, capitalist world causing great harm to the environment and to persons, that is when one creates changes. You should be angry! You can either retreat into a world of escapism—video games or computer screen or television—or you can engage the world and try to funnel that anger into doing the right thing. That is what my heroes have always done. Whether they be in music or in the world of activism and politics, it is those who have channeled their anger into fighting for justice.

IAN MACKAYE (Minor Threat / Fugazi): I would say that I'm a pretty angry person. What I'm angry about is just how close everybody is to being well, how able the world is to be well. If I'm angry it's really because of this frustration of seeing possibilities and then all of these other things leaping up in the way. There are distractions and diversions, illusions. So, my anger is mostly connected to that. Obviously, I get angry when someone is rude to me but that's like having an itch. You scratch it and it's fine. Maybe you've eaten some ice cream and you get a cold headache. You have to wait a second and it will pass. That is just everyday. But anger in a larger sense can be something that motivates you to work because you think, "God, we are so close. Let's keep pushing!" One thing about me, I don't believe that everything *will* be fixed. I believe that everything *can* be fixed. Do you see the distinction? I'm not operating under any idea that if we go off and protest that the war will stop.

LENNY KAYE (Patti Smith Group): Punk rock is art! That's the thing. It's art! You're not out there hitting anybody. You're making your instruments speak for you. That's what it's about. It doesn't mean that if you're singing about nonviolence you have to have some kind of airy-fairy music with tinkling harpsichords. That's not what it's about. You want to play music to get this violence—of which we're biologically capable—of getting it out of you so that it doesn't harm somebody. When I'm hitting my guitar at the end of the show and making it howl, that doesn't mean I'm gonna put that down and go out to an audience member and start strangling them. That's the point of it; to get this out of your system. I feel very lucky that I've been able to pick up a guitar and speak with it.

PENELOPE SPHEERIS (*The Decline of Western Civilization / Suburbia*): When I was doing *The Decline* I remember that even back then anger was the issue that I was addressing. Not only in myself but in the subjects of the film. I remember saying to Phranc, the lesbian folk singer girl, "Why are you so angry?" She kept saying, "I'm *not* angry." I wanted her to admit that she was angry so we could get a story out of her. She kept saying, "I'm not angry!" She probably wasn't. It was probably me that was angry!

I noticed back then that there really was a lot of anger. When punk was born all of a sudden it was okay if you showed your anger. So, that was cool. As long as there were rules to the anger: you don't hurt anybody else. That's what I've noticed about punks. I don't go along with the punk and violence thing. There's crazy people in any group; you take any section of society and you'll get your evangelists and your criminals. For the most part punk is not a violent movement in my opinion. It was an angry movement that sort of made it okay for you to express your anger. I really liked that about heavy metal, too. I was angry and I wanted *not* to hurt anybody. I always said I should've either ended up in jail or dead. But I didn't. I ended up this filmmaker! The thing about anger that I was fascinated with is that I came to notice that you could either be angry or depressed but you couldn't be both at the same time. These are manifestations of the same emotions. People that are depressed, they're really angry and they're really suffering in it. Have you ever seen an angry depressed person? That doesn't happen. It's the *same* thing.

That's why I wasn't ever on board with that whole grunge movement in Seattle. They were just depressing! "Stop whining!" If you're pissed, be pissed and don't hurt anybody. That was my take on it. I think it is a terrible thing that people are so afraid of their anger. It causes a lot of problems. That's what I love about punk—it's okay if you're pissed. As a matter of fact, they turned it into being cool and sexy. See some chick walking around in big army boots, a short plaid skirt with her hair in a mohawk and she is just pissed.

What I've noticed is that sometimes punks would rather hurt themselves rather than other people. Most punks are very intelligent and are usually very educated, kind and socially aware people. They're good people. They don't look so great by normal standards. They look great to me. But by establishment America they look kind of scary, especially back then. The first comment I got after the first screening of *The Decline* at the Writers Guild Theatre, this woman said, "How dare you glorify these heathens!" I thought, "Oh my God, have I made a mistake by documenting these people?" Now I realize that I've come to define myself as a filmmaker and artist and I don't think I made a mistake, but that's what I had to deal with back then. I got that kind of criticism for even recognizing the movement.

PENELOPE SPHEERIS (*The Decline of Western Civilization / Suburbia*): Let's say you have a rough childhood like I did. I had seven stepfathers and they were all drunks. My mother was either bipolar or schizophrenic or both. But she was a genius! (*laugh*) I clubbed one of my stepfathers over the head with a lamp when he was passed out drunk. He had hurt me before he passed out. As I said, I could've been either dead or in jail by now. I could've killed that guy right then. At the time I wished I would've. Bad choice.

You're at a point in life at that age when you're so damn pissed. So, there was punk rock. Even though I was older when I first came in contact with it, I could so totally relate to it, even to this day. Psychologists say that human beings are totally formed psychologically by the time they are six or seven years old. By that time, it's all over with and you're just dealing with the shit that already happened.

I'm this really, really angry person. I think the only reason I was successful in making films is because, "Fuck 'em, I was going to show 'em!" That was my attitude. And I did. But after awhile—this is where your spirituality thing comes in—after awhile, that anger can play against you. There's an expression: *when you get old, you get the face you deserve.* If you look at old people, you can see that some of them are saturated with anger that they never got rid of. You see other people that are eighty years old and they look like blossoms on a tree. They look beautiful! I believe it's how they handle their anger. Some people were raised in nice environments and didn't need to be angry. I was actually beaten. I had the shit kicked out of me when I was a kid. You get pissed off when that happens. Well, first you get depressed. And then you get pissed off. Like I said, it's the same thing. I'm telling you all the secrets here. (pause)

Hold on. My dog is drinking out of the pool and it's got chlorine. *"Darby! Stop it!"* My dog is named Darby. I don't want him drinking chlorine—even my dog is trying to kill himself! (*laugh*) I should've never named him Darby! I didn't name him that, someone else did, but whatever . . . Where was I? You get to a point in life where you kind of have to give up that anger. Not give it up, because it is your core. But you need to address it and understand why it's there and how to handle it. I'm not like a flower child and I never fit into that whole hippie movement, believe me!

SPIT IT OUT ON STAGE

DICK LUCAS (Subhumans): There has to be an element of anger in real protest on the streets and not being too soft about it. The hippies were seen as a generation that had all this potential but by the mid-70s they'd all become small business-men—or big businessmen—exploiting other people. A lot of it got sold out. The ideas got retained in the heads of people who didn't have the power to spread it further than their own local community.

Personally, when I'm angry I write it down and spit it out on stage. It's a great exorcism. An *exercise* in *exorcism*, perhaps. Other people bottle it up until it explodes in bad directions like violence, drinking, self-abuse, craziness. It's a case of sharing it with other people. Being angry *with* other people. It's quite a happy thing to do. It can make you happy to be angry with other people, a catharsis of getting it out. And it's not all about shouting and throwing bottles. It's about writing it down as well; self-expression in one way or another.

DAVE DICTOR (Millions of Dead Christians): Punk is a way to verbalize the anger, in singing a song like "No War / No KKK / No Fascist USA." ("Born to Die") There are lyrics that are very strong and make you very angry and yet on the other hand make it so that you don't have to carry that anger around with you on a 24/7 basis.

You have to work with anger. Here we are—MDC—doing it twenty-seven years. I don't want to carry anger around with me 365 days a year. If I'm at a demonstration or if I'm playing a rally where that feeling is part of the energy, I'll go with it. We played Rock Against Reagan's. We recently played celebrations of the Tompkins Square Park riots about seventeen years ago in New York City. We might play a show with a band like Leftöver Crack and there will be three thousand kids and four hundred cops in the background, all literally gripping their nightsticks. We might play a Food Not Bombs rally and all of a sudden there's police there and there's tension and you just don't know where it's going to end up sometimes. I find myself trying not to be the bomb thrower. I try to work with the energy to not let it go somewhere where it's going to be violent. I'd rather diffuse situations. I want people to be conscious of what the facts are but my days of trying to lead people into physical confrontation with police, I withdraw from. As far as carrying the angst, it's sometimes part of the show and how I feel at a certain point. Then I find myself wanting to get away from that once that show is over. So, I will go back and try to relax. It's an ongoing process.

You can be conscious that there is global warming and oppression but for us to carry around the moment-to-moment anger, day in day out, is going to cause stress and early death. We were in front of up to five thousand people with the Dead Kennedys at the Lincoln Memorial playing with ten bands and there'd be thousands of people. We were part of a movement that did capture the anger and frustration. Time went on and I went from being a man in my twenties to a man in my thirties. I still had the frustration but I didn't want to carry this anger. Punk is a lot of things to a lot of people. That's what it was for us when we started. Now I try to share those thoughts but not have people be so angst ridden where they're going to leave my show and throw rocks at the cops.

NADYA OSTROFF (The Slits): I don't think anger is necessarily a negative thing. But you have to channel it correctly. A lot of people say they're spiritual and they chant and do this and that. But then they turn around and say something that you can't believe! It doesn't really mean much. A lot of punk imitated this kind of force for social or personal change. Then this Oi punk became what stood for punk. Punk became destruction and anger, hating, spitting and throwing bottles. That wasn't the musicians, it was a kind of outside force. The reason that all ignited was because people felt so much energy and had nowhere to express it. They had no money. They couldn't go and buy the kind of clothes they wanted. The schools were terrible so many people couldn't hardly read and write. Many people could think so much more intelligently when they could express themselves, so they either picked up a guitar or threw a beer bottle at a guitarist because they were so envious of those people.

BILLY ZOOM (X): I've never been angry. A couple times for a few minutes, but I've never wanted to play about it. I always thought it was fun playing. I never thought Elvis or Jerry Lee Lewis were angry either.

JM: What do you make of this idea that anger can be a motivating force to make change in your life or in the world?

BILLY ZOOM (X): I don't know. If you're angry you're probably not being very effective in whatever you're trying to do. You should probably calm down, deal with it and concentrate a little harder. I didn't get the hardcore violence and anger thing. The Ramones were happy! They were happy pop music with a sarcasm and dark humor to what they were doing. But it wasn't angry. I get a little frustrated now and then, but I'm not really an angry person. I'm a pretty happy guy. I just like the way music sounds. I like when you play notes and it sounds cool.

C. J. RAMONE (The Ramones): The frustration and anger that builds when you realize how unjust the world is, is what leads good causes and people to become violent. When you see basic stuff like genocide in the world it is frustrating. In my head I think, "How long can we sit back and just watch it?" Some people think, "We've got to get in there and kill these dudes who are committing this genocide!" *Then* what happens is *their* kids grow up to hate us and then they want to come and kill *us!* It's complicated and I don't have the answers. The only thing I'm one hundred percent sure of is that *that's* our biggest problem in the world. It all stems from a cycle of violence that's been going since we were put on this planet or started walking upright, however you want to look at it. We're caught in a cycle of violence and we just can't break it.

CAMILLE ROSE GARCIA (The Real Minx / *Tragic Kingdom*): Anything that young men are involved with that involves anger and frustration leads to violence at some point because the capacity for having a mature reaction to those things isn't there. That's why punk rock is the realm of the young, in a way. For me

71

personally, violence is not something I believe changes anything. I come from more of a Buddhist Vedic point of view. I know that sounds like Berkeley Hippie kind of stuff! (*laugh*) But there is a lot of overlap, too!

DARIUS KOSKI (Swingin' Utters): There's almost always violence at punk shows, unfortunately. For the most part it's a bunch of young dudes and they're excited and it's fast, loud and aggressive music. We just stop playing (violence at gigs). It's not a rule, but an unspoken thing we've done for years. We used to have a lot more violence at our shows in the early 90s. But if a fight breaks out and anybody in the band sees it, we just stop playing. We tell them to stop fighting and we'll wait until it's dealt with and then we start playing again. The whole way I look at it is that I don't want to be somebody's soundtrack to their weird violence. I don't want some guy to beat another guy's head in while the Swinging Utters are playing. That's just disgusting to me.

5

"BLEED FOR ME"
SELF-HARM IN PUNK ROCK

They say that Quang Duc's heart survived the flames unscarred / A righteous calling card left on the palace gates for the invertebrates.

> —"Cop Just Out of Frame" by Propagandhi
> (*Victory Lap*—2017)

Burn, burn, yes, you're gonna burn!

> —"Bombtrack" by *Rage Against the Machine*

We live in violent times and sometimes people try to use violent methods to not only wake up those around them but to wake themselves up.

> —Lenny Kaye (Patti Smith Group)

The cover art for the 1992 debut album from Rage Against the Machine is an image of a Buddhist monk sitting calmly in a meditation posture. He's cross-legged in the middle of a street in Saigon, Vietnam and has just set himself on fire. It's June 11, 1963 and this direct action is meant to bring attention to the persecution of Buddhists by the South Vietnamese government. The monk is Thich Quang Duc and this image came to represent the growing anti-war, pro-peace sentiment of the time. The photo was taken by Associated Press journalist Malcolm Browne and has been featured in books, films and on the poster that came with the Dead Kennedys' first album *Fresh Fruit for Rotting Vegetables* (1979).

The intensity of punk rock doesn't quite reach that of actual flames, but provocative images of war and poverty are sometimes used by punk bands to represent revolutionary ideals that confront state violence, like the image of police cars in flames on the album cover of the Dead Kennedys' first album. Conversely, images depicting poverty and war have sometimes been commodified to sell products and ideas, a practice that's been criticized by some punks. The 1986 debut album from anarcho-punk band Chumbawamba was titled *Pictures of Starving Children Sell Records: Starvation, Charity and Rock and Roll Lies and Traditions* and was a direct response to the controversial July, 1985 Live Aid African charity concert organized by early punks Bob Geldof (Boomtown Rats) and Midge Ure (Rich Kids / Ultravox).

Many spiritual and religious traditions have incorporated initiations or practices that push and test human endurance as a method of expanding physical, emotional, and spiritual awareness. Worldwide, indigenous practices have involved self-inflicted wounds, scarification, and body piercings including the Sun Dance of Plains Indians where the chest is pierced with hooks and practitioners are lifted off the ground to hang for a period of hours or days.

Historically, Christianity and Islam have included controversial rituals of "self-flagellation" and "mortification of the flesh" with practitioners aiming to move past attachment to physical needs and pleasures. Many monastic traditions limit food, water or sexual activity. According to stories of the Buddha's enlightenment, he practiced a form of asceticism with a group of forest-dwelling monks who focused on meditation and fasting and became very thin and weak. Siddhartha was then offered milk and rice by a kind woman and had the realization that a healthy, peaceful way of life is the result of relaxing the extreme views of both attachment and aversion. Buddha used a musical metaphor to describe this middle path; if the strings of a lute are too loose, they will not vibrate when plucked and if tightened too much, they will break.

Punk rock musicians have sometimes featured violence and self-harm as aspects of performance to express anger and despair, encourage political awareness and, in some cases, to simply survive. Henry Rollins speaks of the post-traumatic stress he still endures from being attacked on stage as singer with Black Flag because fans disapproved of the music or the length of his hair. Iggy Pop also received taunts and physical projectiles from audiences and responded with dramatic self-harm by cutting himself and bleeding on stage. As punk rock evolved, performer violence spread to audience violence where hardcore shows sometimes became gang fights in places like Orange

County, California. In the 1981 film *The Decline of Western Civilization* director Penelope Spheeris asks Germs singer Darby Crash, "How is it that you're always getting hurt?" Darby replies, "At first I did it on purpose, to keep from being bored."

JM: The cover of Rage Against the Machine's first album is a very dramatic photo of a Buddhist monk named Thich Quang Duc immolating himself in Saigon in 1963. What is the significance of that photo for you and the band?

TOM MORELLO (Rage Against the Machine / Prophets of Rage): We thought that image signified an absolutely uncompromising adherence to principle. That is the same kind of uncompromising adherence to principle that we were going for in our band and in our music. So, it seemed like an appropriate symbol to put on the cover.

LENNY KAYE (Patti Smith Group): A big part of punk rock is smashing your guitar. Self-destruction is a response to the brutality of this world. Let's face it. Let's not mince words here. We live in violent times and sometimes people try to use violent methods to not only wake up those around them but to wake themselves up. I'm not into that, personally. To me art was created so that you don't have to do that. You have to bare your soul, which is perhaps harder than taking a drumstick and scratching your chest.

But the whole point of art is to express all these raw human emotions—in conflict or not, but usually in conflict—because when people write from great pleasure, they don't find the necessary tensions that create art. For better or worse. Art is there to take it out of you, to make an artifact and remove the pain. To help you transcend your emotions and make you understand and reflect who you are. The Stooges at their best certainly did that. They held up a mirror to their audience and their audience sometimes reacted badly and sometimes embraced them. They are quite a bedrock group of the music that would define itself as punk in the later '70s.

> *The sound was often ragged, the singing just a shout, much of the music simplistic aural thuggery, but the real performance was in Iggy's incessant insulting of the audience. The banter was drawn out, and any odd projectile—a coin, ice cubes, an egg—launched in his direction served only to prolong his speeches.*
>
> —*Iggy Pop: Open Up and Bleed* by Paul Trynka (page 176)

JM: In popular media, punk rock is often portrayed as violent. Iggy Pop was famous for inflicting violence upon himself on stage. What was your experience of that at the time?

JAMES WILLIAMSON (Iggy & The Stooges): I hated that. We were very assertive and very involved with the audience. We created a lot of the audience interplay, but it stopped short of any violence. At the very end, that last job that we did at Michigan Palace, with the bottle. (February 9, 1974) Well, the biker thing before that and then the bottles and all of the stuff getting thrown. That was really the beginning of when this violence started coming into the picture. And later the head banging and pogo dancing; that stuff was not around when I was involved. I don't like it. He (Iggy) was a very strong exhibitionist and he is still. He would always take it to the limit. There was no plan there. There was never a plan. We improvised. We would have a basic idea of what we were going to do and then we let it rip.

I was at that show and one thing led to another. Something got broken on him and he got cut and he started cutting a little more. Those cuts weren't deep, but they made a lot of blood. He was all about trying to explore the situation, for the show. And he still is—*more so* now. Now he's a lot older (60 in 2007) and he's trying to make some money at it, so there's a little bit more of an act involved. But in those days, it wasn't any act.

JM: I wonder how much you think Iggy's playing music and being expressive helped his mental health?

JAMES WILLIAMSON (Iggy & The Stooges): I don't know. I can't really project on what his well-being was all about. But he (Iggy) did go through some cycles where he would certainly spiral down. Largely that was around the times when he wasn't playing music. He seems to be happy now—he's still doing it.

JM: You've written about Iggy Pop harming himself as theater and how this originated from his fear of not being loved by audiences.

PAUL TRYNKA (*Iggy Pop: Open Up and Bleed*): Iggy, with his band The Stooges, was making something unique. He was on the edge. He was committing himself. That requires a special sort of dedication that few have. If you imagine what it's like to commit yourself as utterly as he did and then be faced with not even rejection, but a kind of indifference. That's very soul-destroying. A lot of what he went through was like, "Damn you—I'm going to make you react! If *this* doesn't work then I'm going to do something else." It was ultimately very harmful to him. But it was an expression of his absolute commitment to his music and art.

All that self-abuse wasn't stupidity. It wasn't him being incapable of expressing himself. It wasn't like a Sid Vicious who hurt himself because he didn't have access to other forms of communication. With Iggy this was another form of his communication. He was going to show us his pain and share it with us. He was in a very extreme place, artistically. In a way those silly, stupid or harmful acts do have meaning, though many people would condemn the guy for it. I don't at all. I think it points out that this was very real. It's something much bigger than just show business.

Bands like The Jesus and Mary Chain were faced with audience riots and people throwing stuff. The set would fall apart or dissolve into feedback. With the generation of post-punk bands like the Damned or the Dead Boys there'd be a lot of audience violence. I was around at the time. I was a kid when suddenly people would start spitting at bands. I remember going to concerts myself with punk bands I didn't like and bringing a water pistol and squirting them. *(laugh)* There was always this edge of violence and chaos.

Performers who do play with risk, it's generally done within a kind of show-business framework. You might go and see U2 or Coldplay and they'll be produced by somebody like (Brian) Eno who is trying to keep them on the edge. They may introduce a little frisson of risk. Maybe if things fall apart, they'll look silly. The thing about The Stooges; it wasn't just their reputation or credibility that was at stake. It was almost their lives that were at stake. That's how important it was to them. They'd given themselves up to this completely. When Iggy crashed and burned it wasn't just, "Here's Iggy. He isn't going to make a living from show business anymore." People thought he would *die*. The stakes were so much higher. That's what made the music so much more intense. It wasn't so much about show business, it was life or death.

RENDERING THE STATE POWERLESS

JON KING (Gang of Four): The first band I ever saw was The Stooges. It was Iggy having a go at himself with bottles. Self-harm is often a function of abuse. Abused people harm themselves. Violence is a very interesting thing. I'm not at all a violent person. I don't think it's a good thing. But the state always monopolizes violence and will use violence intentionally against people who try to usurp that role. Punk rock teased around the edge of that. A lot of punk rock, when it started, was about that self-harm thing. It was saying, "Okay, we'll damage ourselves." Like Sid Vicious cutting his arm up with a bottle. It was, "There's nothing you can do to me that I can't do to myself." It's an interesting way of rendering the state powerless.

JM: It's some sort of expression of freedom?

JON KING (Gang of Four): It's some sort of expression of freedom, but only for a period of time. If it's not really real and authentic, it becomes a bit of showbiz. It *has* become a part of the showbiz of punk rock. The last twenty years or so of punk rock, it's got certain devices about it. It's not really saying to the state, "You are powerless to exercise violence against me because I can do it myself." It's become, "This is what you do when you do punk rock." It becomes part of the dominant/sub-dominant/tonic chord progression thing. Do songs like *this* and at the same time do yourself a bit of harm with a broken bottle. Or have a fight.

Fighting has always been a part of rock and roll. That brilliant song of the 1950s "Wang Dang Doodle"—"We're gonna kick in all of the windows and smash down all of the doors, we're gonna have a helluva time, wang dang doodle all night long!" (Willie Dixon) Have a good fight, go to a good party and then get laid—It's a fantastic evening! These things get sort of fossilized. Violence is a funny thing. In the US those who exercise the most violence are the states that are the most likely to be formed of religious extremists. The American Midwest states are the most violent. The majority of people believe in a really strange, cruel, Old Testament kind of thing. This means that, weirdly, they live in a much more cruel environment. The blue bits (Democrats) of America are much less violent, statistically.

GORAN "MAX" MARIĆ (Bjesovi): Those manifestations of self-destruction are consequences of a strong feeling of social deprivation and probably the lack of love in everyday life. It is some kind of primal scream for love and attention. The whole punk thing is one loud primal scream, in my opinion. When you are in the process of soul-searching, and if you resolve to find some answers, one of the possible results can be to find the answer in the theological way of comprehending the universe and the meaning of existence. If art pervades your soul-searching, that is maybe the most likely outcome. I did it through my band Bjesovi and I am so glad that I had that opportunity. Music is like the air I breath. I think that real creativity is not dead, despite the all-corporate approach in modern pop culture. You can't stop the people who have something important to say.

JM: Do you have any insights about performers who harm themselves on stage?

JOHN LYDON (Sex Pistols / PiL): There was one wasn't there? I can't remember his name; the Suicide bloke? (Alan Vega) When I was young, I used to love going to London to all-night concerts. There'd be one at Kings Cross, which is where I seen Iggy; it was a mess but it was hilarious! And that's the point! There was great humor in it. He was running around, threatening to slash himself up. It was deeply funny! Kind of like Jerry Lewis. Comedy! It really struck me that way.

That's a good thing. I loved Alice Cooper, too, because I thought there was great comedy in it. Not too deadpan serious.

It was an issue I had with poor old Sid (Vicious). Because Sid was born not one of the brightest sparks on the planet, he had a penchant for copying when he'd run out of ideas. So, Sid would cut himself on stage. It was like, "You can't be like that, mate. You have to have respect for what it is we're doing here." Animosity is what that led to, really, when I'd see Sid behave so second-rate. I think he let us down in a serious way. It's not that he could help it either, so again there's empathy for him. The sad, sad person. It was very difficult for him because his mother was a registered heroin addict. So, you can imagine what his Christmas presents were.

All of that serious flagellation! Oh gosh, there's some really serious one's out there for that! It's somewhat screaming for help, even if they're faking it. These people need help! And there's no help offered. They're being laughed at, really. And then they seem to get addicted to being laughed at! The self-pity trail is a dreadful one. Now, what am I personally supposed to do about that? Over the years I've talked to many people that way inclined and I give them any advice I can but ultimately, you're facing resentment for daring to challenge them on their originality of slow, but deliberate, pathetic suicide. It's a very difficult world we live in. All you can do is lead by example, and not lead deliberately.

LIZ LAMERE (Alan Vega [Suicide]'s widow / creative collaborator Alan Vega solo / solo recording artist / SSNUB / Backward Flying Indians): Alan (Vega) couldn't have been more of a gentle, sweet person. But he allowed all these feelings and emotions to run through him. It was almost like he was the vessel and he became these things on stage and that can be very scary for people who weren't connecting with that. People tried to run away. There were instances where he literally was chaining the doors at Max's Kansas City so you had to go through the room where Suicide was playing, to go see the New York Dolls or other more popular bands. People would be afraid and try to leave! He had a bicycle chain, he's swinging around. When people were throwing things at him, he's breaking bottles and cutting open his own face saying, "You think you can scare me? I'll do more damage to myself than you could ever do." It wasn't out of being a masochist, or trying to hurt people. It was this idea of trying to awaken in them, and make them aware, that life is no joke.

Alan was well-versed in Antonin Artaud's *Theatre of Cruelty*. There was something about breaking down the barrier between the performer and the audience that really appealed to him. The first time he saw Iggy Pop perform really underscored this breaking down of that barrier. Alan was constantly challenging himself and putting himself into situations which are uncomfortable, because that forces you to go beyond the boundaries that you might otherwise set for yourself, and you find new ground that way. It became part of his DNA to constantly set himself up in difficult situations.

The band Suicide was a two-man entity with no live drums or guitar. When they went on tour with The Clash and Elvis Costello, their music was so radically different with these two guys making this crazy sound! They were literally attacked. There were instances where switchblades, hammers and an axe were thrown and Alan was almost killed on a number of occasions. But they felt so strongly about what they were doing that he was willing to put himself in harm's way and put his life on the line. They believed so strongly that they were creating this sound that was the future. And as history has now shown, it really became the future.

Suicide performances could be very scary because Alan was so deeply immersed in the emotions that he was experiencing on stage. When he got on stage, he became the character in the song. Not only did he write about characters that were really slice of life, he started as a kid by drawing Bowery bums in the street. If you look at his portrait drawings, you can see the full range of human emotion and the energy just leaps off the page. He had the same kind of ability to channel these intense emotions when he got on stage.

PATTI PATTEX (Cut My Skin): Our band name came from The Gits song: "Cut my skin, it makes me human." I can understand this feeling. I was doing little rituals with blood brothership, cutting a bit of skin to press it together for unity. Never on stage. In our song "I Hate Them All" there's a part when the music builds up tension. You only hear the bass drum and that's my heart; I hit my heart with the mic to the beat—boom, boom. It hurts every time. I often had bruises. Later, when I got heart rhythm problems, I stopped this and did it on my leg instead. I wrapped barbed wire around our wrists with a friend as a ritual for bonding. It hurt and I bled and I felt very alive. Through pain you can feel yourself in the here and now. When the outside world crushes you with its demands and dangers, oppression and violence, it can be very liberating. Like the catharsis of a tattoo; I would never have the area numbed. I want to go through the pain, which then passes over into the symbolic power of my tattoo. That creates awareness.

JM: I'm imagining you saw the Germs.

EXENE CERVENKA (X): Many times, all the time.

JM: What was your impression of Darby Crash and others who self-inflicted harm on stage?

EXENE CERVENKA (X): It was done for theatrical effect, credibility and for catharsis. Like people that cut themselves. Because when you bang your head against the wall it feels so good when you stop! I think it's not one-dimensional. But I think that a lot of that stuff is sensationalism. It has a lot to do with the same sensationalism that we have now with our over-sexualized society. I wasn't into hurting myself on stage. I was trying *not* to get hurt as much as possible. It wasn't my thing. I was trying to avoid beer bottles and falling off chairs and hitting my head falling off the stage and getting beat up in the crowd. I didn't want to come up on stage with a bloody nose.

DICK LUCAS (Subhumans): (Long pause) I can't even express how that must have felt, to cut yourself up on stage. That is beyond showing off. That's actually doing something to yourself that you need to, inside. I went through a small phase of cutting my arm up with a safety pin at parties. Was it to show off or was it to feel something more realistic than being drunk? I don't know. It was a long time ago. People do that sort of thing. People do it on stage regularly; perhaps it's just for shock. Maybe it's because they *can* do it.

PETER CASE (The Nerves / The Plimsouls): I think the desire to hurt yourself has something to do with wanting to create vulnerability and thinking that's the only way you can move people and yourself. I think it's also a spur-of-the-moment, intense kind of thing. If you read *I Need More* by Iggy (1997) he talks about it. I've hurt myself and bled playing music and wounded myself on stage and just let it go. I never did it as an artistic statement. I've done it as a suicidal act, like being drunk out of my mind and I tried to cut my arms open. One of the reasons I quit drinking and taking drugs was because I was out of my mind. I suppose it was an expression, but it wasn't an artistic expression. It was a self-destructive expression.

To me the body is holy. It's a temple. I'm from an older generation that look at it like that. I don't believe in cutting up your body because cutting up your body is like cutting up your mind. It's the same thing. I'm sad that people don't see that. There are certain aspects of self-adornment that have a tribal African influence and that does *not* fall into that same area. But the actual cutting yourself with glass on stage and all that shit? Do you know who Chris Burden is?

JM: No.

PETER CASE (The Nerves): He's a performance artist who had himself shot. He had a guy shoot him! There's a whole world of artists that do that kind of stuff. It's shocking. I suppose it's a reaction to some sort of numbness. I do think that LSD was the thing that took the place of that in the '60s. LSD was for people that were all tied up in materialism—you take LSD and all of a sudden you realize that the world *is* a spiritual place. *The physical world is a container for the infinite.* It blows your mind! On some level, people cutting themselves is a version of trying to get that across to yourself, or to someone else. It was the version of the '70s with Iggy. But it doesn't seem like that road really goes through. In a sense, even the LSD road doesn't go through. It's a form of trying to deal with alienation that is violent. Maybe those aren't the best ways to do things. I understand it, but I don't subscribe to it.

The period when The Plimsouls were biggest, which would've been, "A Million Miles Away," was really just a complete rejection. "I'm a million miles away"—people take it different ways but for me it always meant complete *alienation*. It is a certain kind of stance in relation to politics. It's not empowered in any way. We were just singing the Blues. Then I went solo and all of a sudden, I tapped back into the political side. On my first solo record, I've got a song "I Shook His Hand." It was about the fact that they killed John F. Kennedy, Martin Luther King, and Bobby Kennedy as a wound on everybody. It's a combination of spiritual and political ideas that was the way I came back into having any sort of awareness.

PAIN BRINGS US CLOSER

MIKE NESS (Social Distortion): A friend told me that pain is good and *extreme* pain is *extremely* good. You have to realize that for most people pain usually brings us closer to our God and therefore makes us stronger in the long run. At a certain point I was able to take life's experiences and turn them into positive. When Dennis (Danell) died, the first thing I thought was, "We need to just stop the band." It only took a couple days of reflection to realize that he and I started this band. This is our dream. Rather than quitting I was able to turn it around. I thought, "We need to continue in honor of him." For lack of a better analogy, the firemen who lose a friend in a fire—it hurts but they have to keep going because their job is to protect people. Definitely I've been finding love and other purposes in life. I used to think that my purpose in life was my career. As I've gotten older, I've realized that's just one part of my life; I'm also a husband and father. I find myself wanting to be part of the community and make the world a better place. It all goes back to my perception of what punk was. Here we were, this revolution that was against the status quo.

JARBOE (Swans / Neurosis): The body is viewed as part of the performance for quite a few musicians. When I first went on the Swans tour of 1984, I was lugging around gear. I was very straight edge, clean cut and wholesome; a boxer and a vegan and everything else! *(laugh)* And I entered this debauchery of guys that chain-smoked and drank and they were all over the place! I was drawn to the physicality of the lyrics and I saw it as a metaphor. I saw it as an art project. I understood that the words were a metaphor for this state of being, of being a slave of the body, a slave of this life.

I will always remember visually, even when I started touring in the group, like you said about Iggy; Michael (Gira) was literally throwing his body around the stage. He'd slam it down to the ground and throw it around. He would be very violent with his body as part of the performance and it really fit the music we were doing at the time. To counter that, when I started singing (Swans) in 1985 or '86 I would be almost like a Madonna statue, very poised. Not moving my body around. It was this juxtaposition of the body as an instrument. When I started doing solo performances, I had a feeling of not only wanting to break-down a barrier between audience and performer, but *no stage*. The band would be on stage but I was performing in the audience. I went through a whole phase of this idea of being a complete sacrifice; putting myself in total vulnerability to the audience.

A performance artist that's done this to the extreme would be Marina Abramovich. She's done work where she's offered the people coming to see the performance a table full of knives, a loaded gun and everything else. What would *I* do to her? She's standing there vulnerable. ("Rhythm 0" by Marina Abramovich—1979) With some of these performers rolling around in glass and all of that; I understand that was part of punk, but at the same time when you think about it, that *too* is a form of hostile confrontation to the viewer. Perhaps I don't want to see that kind of pain being inflicted on your body! You have to think about the other person and not just yourself, when using your body in a performance.

PENNY RIMBAUD (Crass): There was a time I was massively self-destructive when performing. It was a bad choice, but I was sort of taking the line of, "I'll die for you here. I'll do anything for you if you could just, for a moment—*stop*." That was the sort of thing that was going on in my mind. I sometimes had to think, "No, don't do it Penny." I would do crazy, damaging things to myself. I didn't start cutting myself up. I remember on one occasion really having to fight the desire—and it wasn't just a fancy—of throwing myself through the window of the club I was in. You know, just doing a bomb through it. It was a genuine thought and it was real, but I managed to think, "What's going on here?" I want people to recognize the fact that I love them, in the deep sense of the word love. "For fuck's sake, listen! I love you!" *(laugh)* And if you manifest that in an audience, you're talking to the universal. Finding that unity. We all know it; that's why we're on

Earth. Because we are a unified mass. And I get desperate when people refuse to recognize that. It's so simple. Nothing more than that. We're here and this is it.

DARBY'S LAST GIG

PETER CASE: (The Nerves / The Plimsouls): I saw Darby hurt himself. I wrote "A Million Miles Away" on the way home from a Germs concert. It might have been Darby's last gig, at the Starwood. Actually, it was The Darby Crash Band, now that I think about it. I was seeing Darby play and there were people jumping from the balcony. It's someone else's thing, it's never been mine. Not that I haven't hurt myself. I did it inadvertently or drunkenly. And I've done it on purpose, too. I'm as crazy as anyone else. But I don't really subscribe to it. I love words, man. Violence doesn't help. A cry of despair remains a cry of despair. The Blues aren't a cry of despair. The Blues are a cry of triumph! When Lightnin' Hopkins is singing the Blues, man, he's got power. He's got a way of soothing his soul and keeping himself together to the next stop. But pure despair? It's a lesson you learn as you go along in music.

I don't see Iggy doing that stuff anymore. And poor Darby did himself in. I used to talk to him all the time. When I first started talking to him his name was Bobby Pin. He'd call me up and we'd talk late at night on the telephone, back when I was in The Nerves. He was just a kid that was trying to get his band going. He was kind of a cool kid. You read the stories now and he was such a Charles Manson figure or something. But I didn't really see it like that at the time.

JM: Penelope Spheeris said that Darby told her, "I'm going to be in a band for five years and then I'm going to kill myself."

PETER CASE (The Nerves / The Plimsouls): I don't think he killed himself on purpose. I think he overdosed on drugs. The dope was super powerful and he got tricked. He went out with the tide. A lot of people could sit around and say, "I'm going to be a star for five years and then kill myself." I used to say shit like that! I'd say, "Before I kill myself, you'll see me do this, this, and this. You'll be seeing me try a lot of radical things. So, if you see that, it might be a lead-up to me killing myself." *(laugh)* I was a complete atheist and really in a dark place in the '70s. It's a struggle to live like that.

D. J. BONEBRAKE (X): Darby Crash obviously wanted to commit suicide. I don't know if it's unanimous that his heroin overdose was a suicide, but I think he was on that track, from the little I knew him. My wife knew him pretty well. I guess that it's a good way to get attention. I wouldn't want to do it, but I used to see Darby jump on bottles and he would cut his feet and his chest. What can I say about that? I wouldn't want to do that.

PENELOPE SPHEERIS (*The Decline of Western Civilization*): I don't think Darby should be used as a representative. Why make a hero out of a guy that said, in the beginning, that he was going to be in a band for five years and then he was going to kill himself? That was his goal. Is that a hero? Fucking face up to life, man! It ain't easy for any of us. Let's pull up our boots and kick ass instead of planning on checking out because you can't take it. (pause) That was nasty! (During our telephone interview Penelope Spheeris calls out to her dog who I can hear barking in the background; "Darby! Darby!")

JM: I would love to hear more about your experiences being the drummer in the Germs. I wonder what you thought about Darby Crash harming himself on stage?

BELINDA CARLISLE (The Germs / The Go-Go's): I have a whole different view on that now than I did back then. Back then it was considered kind of cool. At the time I was seventeen years old and I didn't think, "He must really have a lot of self-loathing to do that." Because now my reaction would be, "Oh my gosh, how can you do that to yourself? You must really have some issues!" But back then it was all about expressing anger. I think for the most part a lot of those L.A. punks—speaking for myself—I didn't have a whole lot to be angry about growing up in Southern California. If you were growing up in the UK at that time in the '70's there was a lot to be angry about. And maybe in New York there was more to be angry about, but growing up in Southern California, for the most part there just wasn't.

Obviously, Darby had issues. Being a drug addict, you usually do. Myself having a history of addiction, I can say that. But at that time, it was just like a cool thing to do. I went from being the drummer in the Germs—the drummer that never played because I came down with mononucleosis, the kissing disease, and had to go home to my parents in Thousand Oaks and recuperate for a few months. So, one of my schoolmates Donna (Rhia) took over and then of course Don Bolles took over. But I would actually hand Darby broken glasses. And salad dressing and peanut butter. I became the Germs spokesperson and I didn't have any problem with that. I have a Germs burn, which I'm looking at right now. If you were a part of the Germs crowd you would be burned by Darby with his cigarette.

KIM FOWLEY (The Runaways producer): That's part of the cutter-culture. Why do people cut themselves? To prove to indifferent people that they can bleed. It's a form of self-mutilation and automatic crucifixion. It goes along with the inability to be noticed; like a ten-month-old kid screaming in a supermarket. He doesn't want to be there and he yells incoherently, to everyone but him! "I don't want to be here! Maybe if I disrupt this place, they'll take me outside so I don't have to be here!" Maybe cutting yourself is a way of saying, "I don't want to be here."

Now we're living in an oppressive century where the average person doesn't have any way out of their pain so they get high, drunk, they do porn, fight, puke, they sleep. But I'm different. I think the streets are paved with gold and money grows on trees. There are tremendous opportunities if you're willing to work hard. Every time someone says "No," I get excited! And when they say "Yes," I'm already on to the next thing anyway. Last year: ten movies, seven books, six albums I contributed to. Nobody cared about any of this stuff but I did it anyway. I'm actually musically gifted and I'm conceptually brilliant. I'm a jerk but I do amazing work so I couldn't care less about anything.

JM: What do you mean you're a jerk?

KIM FOWLEY (The Runaways): I'm not very nice. I'm not trying to be your friend.

RON REYES (Black Flag): I'm not equipped to diagnose people and their issues but I'm sure there are people who would say Darby had some issues. Probably he needed a little bit of help and didn't get it. And maybe if he did, things would've been different. And maybe if he did, we wouldn't have that awesome album. There's a lot of different ways to look at it. I don't really know his motivation for doing those things but it was definitely part of the package, the self-abuse and self-destruction. The self-destructive nature of it was glamorized by guys like Sid Vicious. "Wow, he sure did look good!" It's not the part I like. I fortunately didn't get involved in the drug culture of that scene. I drank like a fish, but that was it.

JONNY WICKERSHAM (Social Distortion): It's nothing I've ever done. I've been self-destructive in other ways. But, as a kid, I remember trying to cut up myself a little bit. When I did see people doing it on stage I thought, "Wow, shit, look at that!" I saw Stiv Bators (Dead Boys), Iggy and Darby doing that. At the time I thought, "That's punk rock!"

TAIT REED (Junk Sick Dawn / Noise Clinic): Rock and roll is fundamentally dangerous, right? There is that edge about it and I think my own art contains a measurable degree of confrontationalism. It might not be necessary to have confrontationalism in your music, art or poetry but it's something I've embraced. It's about not wanting to follow the normal things that people find acceptable musically or in as far as your conduct goes, how you dress or what you say.

JOHNETTE NAPOLITANO (Concrete Blonde): Pure adrenaline. You get so damn amped-out, you don't feel it. Pure adrenaline and some good street drugs. Everybody trying to "out punk" each other.

JM: Darby Crash and Iggy Pop were famous for hurting themselves on stage.

STAN LEE (The Dickies): I don't know if they really hurt themselves. A little candle wax or cutting their chest. Wrestlers do that! Darby was kind of for real. It was reckless abandonment. If there was a bottle, he'd crack it on his head. I stood right there; it was real. I don't know why he'd do that sort of thing, but he did. The scene was so little and there was really no big Germs thing, but as the years went by he's become some sort of a poet. It's bizarre. At the time, it was not what was happening.

THEY BRANDED ME

CLAYSON BENALLY (Blackfire / Sihasin): Here in America, there is so much racism. Going to schools, I ended up getting branded in the locker room from racism by people that don't respect indigenous cultures. They tell you to keep your views and identity on the reservation. That's part of the reason I identified with punk rock. I was a social outcast and misfit, just to have my cultural identity and have my long hair up in the traditional Navajo way with the hair in a bun, a tsiiyééł. I was different. In order to find the group that respected and valued me as an individual, naturally, that's where punk rock came in.

JM: You just said that at school you were branded. You don't mean physically?

CLAYSON BENALLY (Blackfire / Sihasin): Kids called me a TROG, which means Total Reject of God. I was held down in the locker room and they took a lighter and held it upside down until it was nice and hot and then held it to my stomach and they branded me. I still have the scar. I carry that with me.

JM: I'm sorry that happened. Something I want to ask you about is oddly related to that—the violence that began to permeate the punk rock scene. I did an interview recently with Belinda Carlisle, singer for the Go-Go's who was also the first drummer for the Germs in Los Angeles. During the interview she said, "I'm looking at my body now and see the scar from my Germs burn." Darby Crash had burned people in the Germs circle with a lit cigarette. We all engage in self-harm to some degree and in the punk scene there have been people like Darby and Iggy Pop who infamously hurt themselves. I'm guessing that's something you wouldn't want to incorporate in your music.

CLAYSON BENALLY (Blackfire / Sihasin): As an indigenous person coming from a history of colonization and five hundred years of violence against our people, I did not see the need to harm myself. It was actually the complete opposite response where we were trying to uplift and bring our youth out of that self-harm, out of the dark paths of vicious cycles of violence, where you have some of the worst of it from that oppression. It's first taught to us by colonizers and then it becomes a learned behavior. It was this vicious cycle that we would see happening in our own families; our uncles and relatives using violence against our own people. We are fortunate to have a strong cultural foundation and our traditional songs and healing ceremonies that helped us become, in our community, a strength and a pillar. We started putting our traditional songs into our music to try and empower and uplift so that people wouldn't feel that self-pity or hatred toward themselves. I hate the word pride, but to feel that there is some sort of identity that they could grasp onto that would help them find their way.

JM: In the documentary *Taqwacore: The Birth of Punk Islam* (2009) you go on tour with a group of Muslim punk bands and there's a scene of a ritual with a group of men who are very intensely slapping their chests and you join in and everyone is bleeding. I'm curious about self-harm in spiritual practices and its parallel in punk rock. There are also stories of your wrestling that included throwing yourself onto a bed of thumbtacks and barbed wire. What's at the core of self-inflicted harm for you?

MICHAEL MUHAMMAD KNIGHT (*The Taqwacores*): It was a Shia practice. It's about the grief for those families of the prophet, commemorating the martyrdom and sacrifice of the prophet's family. I think these things often get mixed up: punk self-harm, Shia self-harm and wrestling. I've done a lot of wrestling with barbed wire and thumbtacks. That's a performative, theatrical kind of violence but I have real cuts on my body from it. I don't know what's going on inside of me with all of that. I think they all intersect with a kind of performance of masculinity.

I don't necessarily see a meaningful resonance between what was going on at that Shia site versus GG Allin. People who are doing these things have different meanings in mind. I can't say there is a meaning that is outside of what the people themselves say it is. I don't think GG Allin or Iggy Pop, or anyone who cuts themselves on stage, have the same intention that Shia practitioners would identify with their practice

I'm personally a mix-up of strange ingredients. I can compare the wrestling self-harm to the performative punk self-harm because in both cases it's an individual at the center of attention doing it for an audience. When I get thrown into barbed wire, that's a performative choice. When I'm bleeding in front of people, that's a choice I'm making to put on a show. The audience gets what it gets out of it, in both the wrestling and the punk context. When a person on stage is really bleeding, there is something deep going on there. I think that GG Allin and Mick Foley (wrestler) could have a conversation with each other. But I don't know that GG Allin and Mick Foley and the guy whose chest is bleeding at a Shia site can all have a meaningful conversation. It looks similar to the outside observer, but not to the people who do it. It's easy for us to sit back and say, "Here's a person who's bleeding and another person who's bleeding. There must be something in common." Maybe I'm an intersection of these different things but that's more about me then these things themselves.

REID CHANCELLOR (*Hardcore Anxiety: A Graphic Guide to Punk Rock and Mental Health*): Self-harm is such an odd thing, because the intention and context changes everything. I can watch a video of Iggy Pop cutting his chest with a broken bottle and respond, "Hell yes!" But if the same thing happened in seclusion, it would be heartbreaking. You can read about countless performers including self-harm as part of the performance, and I think for a lot of them that's all it is. When punk first began it sometimes had the intention of shocking people. It told all authorities, "We aren't like you!" For a while it was just that, an expression of being indifferent to all rules and social norms. However, self-harm comes in all sorts of different forms: substance abuse, cutting, self-negligence, anorexia. Self-harm is a way of expressing an apathy toward living. It represents not caring to be alive.

"ALL RELIGIONS MAKE ME SICK"
ATHEISM/ANTI-AUTHORITARIAN/ANTI-WAR

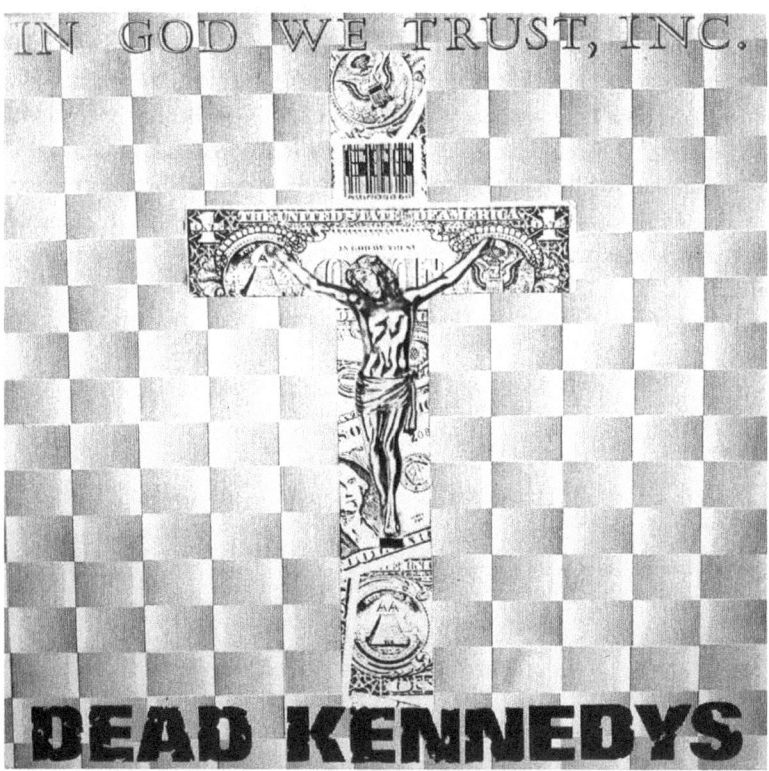

Figure 6.1 Dead Kennedys' 1981 EP In God We Trust, Inc. cover depicts Jesus on a cross of dollar bills. Includes songs like "Religious Vomit" and "Moral Majority" with Jello Biafra singing about authoritarian Christian evangelists and politicians: "God must be dead if you're alive." Contributed: GoldState Music.

Most religions have the basic general tenets but the fundamentalist end of things can ruin anything, including something like punk rock.

—Klaus Flouride (Dead Kennedys)

Save me from the people who would save me from my sin /
They've got muscle for brains!

—"Muscle for Brains" by Gang of Four

When is a cult no longer a cult because there's too many people involved?

—Jello Biafra (Dead Kennedys)

JM: It's strange how religious philosophies that start out, "Love everyone, especially those who choose a different path" can evolve into, "Love your own group, but hurt other people."

JOHN DOE (X): It's even, "Kill those people!" or "Shun those people because they're not part of us." That's where all religion goes south for me. Most of it is really bad. There's a lot of strife behind religion. That's why I'm not religious in any traditional sense.

JOHN LYDON (Sex Pistols / PiL): All of these religions are too organized for me! That allows for corruption on an overwhelming scale, to dominate and dictate. One of the most repulsive Republican things is to want to bring religion back into school. (2019) I'm sorry, but state and religion are two absolutely separate things. Religion is choice, isn't it? You decide what you want to believe and that's up to you. But that doesn't mean the rest of us have to agree. Unfortunately, politics uses the bullying pulpit to their benefit and people just stand in line for it because it's easier than thinking. Maybe philosophy should be taught at school from a very early age. The art of the individual is surely the prime ambition of every philosopher.

JM: Obviously organized religion has often been combined with state violence. You've sung about that with Dead Kennedys. And there's another aspect of spirituality that is radical and connected to social change. The move to end slavery in this country was led in part by Quakers. The civil rights movement of the 60s was led by Christian preachers like M. L. K. Jr., and radical Catholic Worker activists went to Iraq to deliver food and medicine during the US embargo and wars. Overt spirituality has been combined with punk in Krishnacore and Christian punk. What do you think about punk rock and spirituality?

JELLO BIAFRA (Dead Kennedys): You're asking the wrong guy, my friend! (*laugh*) I'm a nonbeliever. There are certain areas that are interesting in some of these religions but not others. When is a cult no longer a cult because there's too many people involved? I would say I'm more of an agnostic than an atheist where I don't really believe in a higher power but I'm not closed to the possibility that it might exist. I have no scientific proof that it *doesn't* exist. It was great to see one night my dad and uncle arguing over this. My dad is more of an agnostic and was pretty much a Buddhist in his later years, while my uncle, the scientist, was a hardcore atheist. And they really went at each other. They both have the same kind of ego and temper that I do. I looked at my aunt and my mom and said, "Oh, my! Look who's going at it! Let's pour the lemonade and watch the fun!" So, maybe the closest thing I have to a higher power is music. It fills me with adrenaline and good energy and makes me want to go do stuff. Ideally. It's not the only art that does that.

KEN CHITWOOD (Dept. for the Study of Religion at Universität Bayreuth): I come from a place that was able to justify war and violence within the Christian tradition. I remember reading the primary documents around Just War Theory when I was studying for a theology degree. It just didn't jive with me. I found myself looking for some other tradition that might be able to offer a different interpretation of how religious people might approach violence. There's an anthropological concept—subaltern—that refers to people beneath the power structures that control this world, and they must use whatever "weapons" they have to resist. Those within the punk community that reject religion use this as a form of resistance against the power and hegemony that religion has been able to exert on culture, politics, music and art for thousands of years within the Western tradition.

ORGANIZED RELIGION IS DANGEROUS AND CONTROLLING

HUGO BURNHAM (Gang of Four): I abhor organized religion. I think it is dangerous and controlling. Yet I respect people's faith because faith is exactly what it is— you have to believe in something that you can't prove. I am a progressive-humanist. I don't like church and I don't like what it does to people. Do I believe in a higher power? No, I'm not in AA! Born-again pagan, that's me. Life after death? There is life after death, but strictly in terrestrial terms, in that if you do things either wonderfully or horribly you have life after death because people will keep talking about you after you're gone. That is all that life after death is; leave a legacy. Unfortunately, that doesn't always mean a good legacy. Proselytizing is something that I have no time for. That is invasive and it's just the first part of somebody ending up controlling somebody else.

LESLEY WOODS (Au Pairs): Do you believe in God? I don't. I believe we're all human beings and we're all composed of good and evil. I think those words have been transposed into "God" and "the devil" and in primitive times they just saw that people can be good and bad. I would never use religious terminology to define myself. There is a kind of emotionalism associated with punk but I'm not sure that it's what most people understand by the word spiritualism. It was motivating kids who had no future to express their spiritual feeling, which was a frustration with having nowhere to go, no one to be. Punk was an outcry against the confines of religion. The spirit of punk is anti-religion and for freedom. It's a way of breaking free of the normative systems that pervade people's lives whether it's a religion, family or government.

CELINE BELLI (Rotten Ruckus): I have ideas regarding religion and punk because I grew up in Malaysia where it's very Muslim. I'm not Muslim but all my friends were massively Muslim in the punk scene, and a lot of them were straight edge. They fasted, went to prayer, didn't drink or have tattoos. They were very good people and they really appreciated the ability to relax in the punk scene, to be themselves without parents, family or religious impositions. Being Muslim and punk together was never really a topic. They appreciated their culture, but they appreciated the music as well. People have certain ideas because of Islamophobia but there was absolutely none of that in Malaysia. I had girls with headscarves moshing with me. They would go home and fast and pray and then come and enjoy a gig. I think it was very freeing for a lot of them; it was beautiful to experience.

GLENN BRANCA (Theoretical Girls): I'm not religious in any way. I'm not interested in any organized religion. At the same time, I couldn't call myself an atheist either. I don't see it either way. For all I know, there is some kind of God who has a long gray beard who's up there in some kind of heaven. For all I know we live on a cartoon planet. I have no idea what reality is. I wouldn't have the audacity to think that I do. And why would I? The truth of reality may be amazingly mundane. But I certainly have no interest whatsoever in anything approximating organized religion.

YAOTL MAZAHUA (Iconoclast / Aztlan Underground aka Anahuak Underground): In the Western world, religion and empire go hand in hand as a force for control and power. There was no word for "freedom" because incarceration was not known. Not to romanticize indigenous culture, but it was understood that honoring the land is crucial to our sustenance and money did not exist. We honor the Mother Earth for her sustenance, and this is intrinsically connected to our spirituality. This is also the goal for the subversive punk movement; fuck society's dominant culture values.

PATTI PATTEX (Cut My Skin): The domination of the church over female bodies is the ultimate patriarchal oppression. The church was created by men and in every religion women are portrayed as subservient and inferior to men, so it is no wonder that men hold on to these power structures. Every religion praises its god as the only true god. Those who disagree are persecuted and murdered. This is how most wars start.

JM: Tell me about performing "Punk Prayer" at the Cathedral of Christ the Savior in Moscow. (February 21, 2012)

MARIA "MASHA" ALYOKHINA (Pussy Riot / *Riot Days*): It was just before elections when Putin decided to be president for the third term and Patriarch Kirill, the main guy in the Russian Orthodox Church, used the whole church and the main cathedral as a political stage for Putin. This was very wrong. He said things like, "All Christians should vote for Putin." Also, he owns a huge tobacco business and this particular cathedral he used for political parties. It's not actually a church in the classical meaning. It's a complex of different things and they don't pay taxes for all the things such as political parties. We made a song about that and performed it for forty seconds, just the first chorus and first verse. We made several songs before that and I think they started to somehow not like us after the Red Square performance where we sang, "Putin pissed himself." I believe that in any country—Russia or not Russia—it's totally wrong to use a church as a political platform for any president and it's stupid to put people in prison for criticizing this way of using church.

ISHAY BERGER (Useless ID): Atheist is a word I used to pull when I talked about these things but with time it feels a bit big. I've got no connection with any religion or tradition. I don't hate it or go against it—it's just not for me. No fun, ya know?

WE'LL CLOSE THE BOOKS

RAY MANZAREK (The Doors / X): Punks were leaving behind religion. We're coming to the end of the Piscean age; your little bumper sticker with a fish. That's the sign of the age of Pisces. We've come to the end of the age of Pisces that started two thousand years ago! It's not the sign of Jesus Christ; it's the fish. It's the end of the Piscean age. Do you know what the next astrological age is?

JM: Aquarius?

RAY MANZAREK (The Doors / X): That's right! The Age of Aquarius is an age when all the arts, philosophy and science all become one. We close the book. Right now, we're under the rule of religions of the book and we will close the books— the Christian Bible, Jewish Bible and The Koran. All three of them were in a drawer in my hotel room in Paris. I said, "Oh, look at that! All three of the books and they're closed in the bedside table. And that's where they'll stay." So, that's what's happening. We'll have to make due with our own hearts as our guiding factor. That is going to be terrifying but extremely exhilarating.

DAVE WAKELING (The English Beat): Christianity luckily has done itself in, so nobody has to bother anymore. All of the theist religions are showing themselves as being rather mean-spirited and ineffective. I sometimes despair of these Middle-Eastern cults—whether it's Christianity, Islam or Judaism. I feel like saying, "Go back to Palestine and sort it out and when you all can live together, come and tell me about it. Until then it's a load of bullocks. You can't even live next door to each other! So, don't come around the world telling us how to do it!" I just get irritated; it's so transparent and obvious. It's a load of old blokes with beards who don't know it's the Age of Aquarius! It's like, "Sorry! Did you not hear the musical? I know it was a crappy song but it was the truth. It *is* the Age of Aquarius." Or is it the age of Saint John in Christian mythology, the age of free-thinking Gnosticism? We've got the Internet, we've got consciences, education. We can find the truth ourselves now. We don't need any bloke with a long beard telling us what God said. He's probably the last one who knows. He's an anachronistic patriarch. Whether it's Osama Bin Laden or George Bush, it's the same act. "And thou shalt . . . "

GARY NUMAN (Tubeway Army): Looking at nature, if this is considered to be a God-given system, it's unbelievably cruel and savage. Most things eat other things to survive. How is that any kind of answer? I'm hardcore atheist. On the other hand, I remember when I was very young, a friend of my father's was killed in a car crash and his mother got a huge amount of comfort from her faith. She would go to church and pray. She genuinely believed she was communicating with her son and it made her life less painful. Her faith gave her a comfort. I have nothing but respect for that. If that's what you get from it, then good luck to you. It's the hypocrisy, the double standards that come with so much of it. Talking about loving your neighbor, at the same time you spit on your neighbor. People twist any sentence in the Bible to justify what they're doing and don't see the bullshit of that and still believe they're a good Christian person. Anyone with half a brain sees they're clearly nothing of the sort! Yet they feel righteous and that righteousness makes them look down on other people, which surely is the last thing any Christian should do! I have no time for any of it. I'm a good person because I know what being a good person means. Not because some fucking book tells you what the rules are!

EXENE CERVENKA (X): Churches haven't been able to obscure the beginnings of spirituality in the world. Unfortunately for them, the Catholic Church hasn't been able to erase enough of the scriptures. The followers of Jesus buried the Gnostic scriptures after his death and they weren't found until the 1950s. The scriptures mirror the New Testament in some places. Jesus is quoted saying things that are quoted in the Bible but instead of saying, "My *father* in heaven," he'll say, "My *mother and father* in heaven." His teachings were very feminine and Eastern; very reasonable, profound and hard to understand at times. He's talking about other life forms that were higher up than humans that came down from the sky.

They also have the book of Mary Magdalene. She's considered the most popular apostle and the one Jesus loved the most. The other ones are complaining about her. That was left out of the Bible. What Mary Magdalene had to say was really profound. *The Book of Thunder* is part of the Gnostic scriptures and is a very Eastern, philosophical, female, spiritual treatise. I recommend it. I find it to be very consoling. Having grown up Catholic and having believed in a lot of icons and saints and becoming pagan after that, it's a fantastic mixture of the two. There's a lot of mysterious things—life on other planets, life after-death, spirituality, astral projection, ESP. Amazing things we don't ever access because it's been cut off from us. I think the Gnostic scriptures are just one more glimpse into that world; that it does exist. There is a spirituality that's real and it's not just going to church on Sunday. The great teachers teach by example not by, "Come with me or else. Be like me or you're an idiot." They don't say that.

JOHNETTE NAPOLITANO (Concrete Blonde): Everybody's got their propaganda, that's for sure. People fear what they don't understand. The connections are basically human. To take the time to become familiar with someone's set of beliefs, whether you believe or not, simply shows respect. I went on a trip through Mexico with a couple friends. It really bothered me that they had contempt for religious people. My friends interpret religion as a sign of weakness or stupidity. I certainly do not and wasn't comfortable traveling with someone who didn't respect what the people believed. If you don't care about people, why travel?

People will anoint their saints whether or not their saints may wish to be anointed. People made the Beatles "bigger" than Jesus Christ! We'll find someone to worship on some level, for some reason, no matter what; Jesus, Oprah, Kurt . . . whoever. Collective consciousness plays a big part, water seeking its own level and all that. Some central galvanizing figure may emerge organically or not, like Dylan did, becoming the very reluctant "voice of his generation."

JM: One basic idea that all spiritual traditions have is to love other people even if they've chosen another path.

LENNY KAYE (Patti Smith Group): I know that's what they say, but Jesus! And he's really rolling over! It's nutty. It seems totally contrary to the entire drift of human evolution. But sometimes you gotta think that, no matter what people say, as we choose to interact, we're not that much different than primitive people's fighting over things. I'm curious; maybe we're very early in our history. Maybe we'll regard this particular era as 0 BC and that once the computer and all these things start tying our nervous systems together, who knows what mankind is going to evolve into? It seems ironic that all these religions that preach oneness-with-the-lord do it by *killing*. And I don't think there is a single religion that can be exempted from that. Or countries. America is built on genocide. These are things that fly in the face of our desire to live together as people.

PREACHING TO OURSELVES

JIM LINDBERG (Pennywise): We've tried to limit our sense of us preaching to our audience. We get accused of that sometimes. Any band that tries to put out a positive message gets accused of preaching. But a lot of it was preaching to ourselves in our lyrics. I've been through the gamut; I was brought up a strict Catholic. I was an altar boy and all that. I was a born-again Christian for a while. I studied Buddhism. In my college years I got into the transcendentalist movement with Emerson and Thoreau. I've always tried to take time for meditation and things like that. We've always tried to put out a message of self-reliance. Letting people make their own decisions about what is important. At the same time, it would be impossible for me not to mention that we lost our bass player to an alcohol-related accident. We've always warned people about the dangers of over-consumption and things that can happen if you let alcohol or drug use get out of control.

ETAY LEVY (Nekhei Naatza): I grew up around Judaism but it never quite sat well with me, even when I was a kid. The first class I ever got kicked out of was Bible class. We had Bible classes in Israel and I didn't think that was right. I was a kid in third grade, but I didn't want to be there. So, I was kicked out. I'm 110 percent atheist. I don't consider myself spiritual.

FEDERICO GOMEZ (Nekhei Naatza): I consider myself a spiritual person. Spirituality is very broad. Not in the sense of being something transcendental that is beyond human experience that we somehow can connect to. I got this hatred for organized religions because of the way it's used to divide and control people. Sometimes people are not only oppressive to people who don't belong to their own religious, but there is also intolerance for people inside their own religious communities who are willing to abandon it, or people that are not Orthodox.

I don't have anything against people being spiritual and believing in something—to each his own. But it's complex because it's not only about yourself. Usually, if you get into some sort of organized religion, you are going to be part of the oppression toward everybody that is unwilling to be inside that community. I'm very interested in theology, different sects and belief systems from a historical or philosophical point of view, but it's not something I want to have in my life.

JM: Does spirituality or the idea of a soul have any meaning to you?

DARIUS KOSKI (Swingin' Utters): My wife would be laughing now if she heard this because she thinks I'm completely void of spirituality. Which is a shame, because I don't think of myself in that way. For me the only sort of spiritual thing I can recognize really has to do with music. There's nothing else—aside from your kids— that gives you those physical chills. It's really spiritual to me. Writing songs is *completely* spiritual. I'm an atheist. My mother was born in Iran and my father was born in Finland. My father is technically a Christian, I guess. He's never been religious. Maybe my mother believes in God, she's not religious. She's Muslim, I guess. I've never believed in God and I still don't. As far as Swingin' Utters songs, whenever I mention any organized religion they're probably in a really nasty tone. Most of that stuff in our lyrics comes from Johnny who went to Catholic school. He's *not* religious. He had to go to Catholic school and seems pretty bitter about it.

DAN MCKEE (*Anarchist, Atheist, Punk Rock Teacher*): The biggest criticism of the (God) concept is the incoherency of positing a being beyond all human understanding and then claiming to understand it. The idea of omnipotence has long been questioned in the paradox of the stone; can God create a stone so heavy even God can't lift it? If God can lift the stone, then God isn't all-powerful. If God can't lift it, then God isn't all-powerful. And the idea of omniscience—God knowing everything—seems incompatible with the idea of free will, yet humans having free will is at the center of most religious ideas about right and wrong and the purpose of human life.

Free will is at the center of all theodicies attempting to solve the problem of evil, which is probably the most killer criticism of the concept of God. If God is all-knowing, all-powerful and loving, then God would know evil and suffering exist in the world, have the power to stop it, and love us enough to do so. Yet evil and suffering exist and God does not seem to stop it. Religions have been used to control behaviors and limit power into the hands of those who set the framework by claiming some sort of uniqueness to their own understanding of the divine. It's all just myth-making to give them power over others. Historically it has worked time and time again, in every part of the world.

PENELOPE SPHEERIS (*The Decline of Western Civilization*): I don't believe in the traditional definition of God. If you think about the brain capabilities that a dog has—a dog trying to do algebra or some sort of math; that is *not* going to happen. Think about the human brain trying to understand life or God. It's not going to happen. I don't think that we have within us the power, the ability, to understand it. You say that some people believe that science is going to answer all of the questions some day—I think that's hilarious! Every time we figure it out, we get thrown a curveball. Whoever it is up there, out there, wherever, is pretty fucking clever! They made it so we can't figure it out. Maybe that's me trying to figure it out! But that's okay because I know it ain't going to happen. I'm fine with that. All you can do is live every day the best you can. Do what you believe is right. Hopefully you're not hurting anybody or screwing anybody over. I love how you are really so earnestly trying to figure out life and understand it. A lot of people wade their way through and don't even think about this stuff. It's cool that you're trying to sort it out. I'm that kind of person, too. What I've concluded is that *we're never going to figure it out!*

JOHNETTE NAPOLITANO (Concrete Blonde): You may overestimate people. Most people would much rather be told what to do, and when, and how to live their lives. Then there's the mystery that is charisma. Jungle birds have wild colors painted on them to attract. And some humans just attract. They have that sort of drawing power, whether it's Hitler or Hendrix or John F. Kennedy, Charles Manson, Jim Jones—your own personal Jesus. Generally, something will make us feel connected to God, whether it's love for another person, the sound of music, nature, a hymn. Whatever that thing is, it becomes your gateway to your God and one may start to worship that in itself, whether it's a priest, rabbi, song, or a spectacular sunset.

Organized religion is also sitting around a fire in a drum circle. An essential part of the power of prayer, chant, song is the joining together in spirit with others. That by default is organized religion. Just like America is an organized society, but my government represents me as an American no more than the Vatican represents the interests and health of the Catholic people. Most thinking people who believe know they don't need anyone to speak to God on their behalf—the rest of them need approval for whatever reason. There is no human being on Earth who can judge, forgive or absolve another human.

SPIRITUALITY WITHOUT A GOD CONCEPT

JM: Do you see the idea of "God" as being inherently authoritarian? I did an interview many years ago with Howard Zinn after his play came out—"Marx in Soho"—where Marx shows up in today's NYC and tells people they've misunderstood his quote about "religion is the opiate of the masses." That he really meant that sometimes religion is useful, like a balm for suffering. "Religion is the opium of the people. It is the sigh of the oppressed creature, the heart of a heartless world, and the soul of our soulless conditions."

GLENN WALLIS (Ruin): It's true that that Marx quote is generally misunderstood. The rest of the passage in *Capital* has to do with *relief* for the poor and oppressed. Having said that, I think we need a spirituality without a God concept. I think a "punk spirituality" would also reject an authoritarian father-like conception of God. After my anarchism book came out (*An Anarchist's Manifesto* 2020) I was invited to many events with young anarchists and other lefties. I was repeatedly asked about the role of religion and spirituality in an anarchist formation. It was obvious that the younger generation did not want to reject religion out of hand like the older generations did. They *needed* something that only spirituality can give. Can't we imagine a world where the very *need* does not arise? My approach was not to give an answer. Rather, I would take the opportunity to work through the issue with people, and do a kind of thought experiment together. The reader of this book can do the same for a "punk spirituality." Given certain values and beliefs, roughly shared by the community of punks, what might a religious/spiritual practice and community look like? I can think of a lot of possibilities. But I can't see a place for a masterful, lordly, transcendent God.

PENNY RIMBAUD (Crass): I'm not a Buddhist but I've got time for Buddha. The reason I'm not a Buddhist is because Buddha wasn't a Buddhist! He was just a bloke sitting on his ass with ideas and insights. I'm the same. We are all Buddhas in that sense. It's all very well the Buddhists saying, "We're all Buddhas," but as long as they're using this guy as a figurehead, then they're *not* Buddhists.

Christ wasn't the same. Christ was dependent on followers. I don't believe Buddha sought any following. He might've got it, but he didn't seek it. And then it becomes modified as lesser people adopt the story. More than anyone, I think Krishnamurti represents that modern-day prophet. He'd take no shit on any level. Learning our own truth is exactly what Buddha was doing. Actually, that's what Jesus Christ was doing as well. I have to acknowledge that. That is essentially Bohemianism.

PENELOPE SPHEERIS (*The Decline of Western Civilization*): I do believe in karma. I got screwed over really bad by Sharon Osborne when I did the *We Sold Our Souls for Rock n' Roll* movie. I used to wake up every morning crying. I went out on tour with Sharon and Ozzy Osbourne and documented the Oz Fest. It's an awesome movie! I had Rob Zombie, Slipknot and Slayer. Awesome bands. Sharon told me she had the rights to the music and she didn't. So, the film couldn't be released. I worked on it for four and a half years! I worked on it through the early 90s thinking it was going to be released. A week before it was to be released, she had the lawyer call me and drop the bomb, "It can't be released. She was just kidding about having the rights!" Then she got cancer and I thought, "Huh! See, there you go! Karma!" Then she got better and she got to be a huge star that everybody thinks is such a wonderful person and then she got to be on the number one show *America's Got Talent*. Then it's like, "So, *is* there karma?" Well, let me just say, it's either in this life or the next life. She is hooked up with the devil and she could get back at me probably even if she's dead. (*laugh*)

JM: That's power!

PENELOPE SPHEERIS: That's power! I always say, "Early on everybody was thinking that Ozzy was possessed by the devil. Yeah, he was. It was Sharon!

LIZ LAMERE (Alan Vega (Suicide)'s widow / creative collaborator Alan Vega solo / solo recording artist / SSNUB / Backward Flying Indians): I wouldn't say Alan (Vega) was anti-religion. He was anti-organized religion and the structures and human beings who dictate our beliefs and how we should express our interest in a greater power. He believed in a greater power, a power beyond us. He believed that there was a lot that is unknown and he was fascinated by the unknown. That was something that really drove him because he was searching. He was seeking.

JORDAN COOPER (Revelation Records): The idea of organized religion and God are not very popular in punk rock and it's because so many kids have had bad experiences with religion, whether it was simply being made to go to church by mom and dad and realizing that maybe this wasn't for you. Being told you were a bad person because you didn't agree. Being forced to follow an ideology that didn't make any sense to you. I understand why a lot of people in punk rock shy away from organized religion and spirituality. Personally, I am a very spiritual person. I would never push my spirituality on anybody. I think everybody should make up their own mind about what they believe.

Religion and punk don't go together very well. Spirituality is separate from religion. A lot of people have a spiritual understanding of the world and punk fits into that. I was talking to someone in one of our bands in the late 80s the other day. I hadn't talked to him in fifteen years. He said, "I still play music. I'm not doing anything too serious but I've got to keep my head above the crap that's going on in the world." He was saying society is messed up and music helps him keep his head above it. That's where spirituality and punk connect. I've heard from a lot of people involved in political and social activism that if they didn't have spirituality in their lives, the struggles they're involved in would just burn them out to the point where they would just give up.

MARK ANDERSEN (*Dance of Days* / Positive Force DC): An old friend of mine, Tim Yohannen—who was actively anti-religious most of his life—said something like great liberation came to him one day when he started yelling obscenities against God, to the sky, and he *wasn't* struck down. You can blaspheme in the most egregious ways and not be held to account for it. For him that was very liberating. He felt like he was freeing himself from all of these concepts that were imprisoning and twisting people. If that's true and your blasphemy is actually against concepts, it's not against what might be called *the ground of being* or *universal love* or whatever you decide God might be. God is just a three-letter word which is used by people to point toward the things that are most powerful, beautiful and desirable—the highest ideals in our life—beauty, truth and love. God in that sense is the concept that gets in the way of the actual reality, which of course we can't express.

Actually, what my friend Tim was articulating might lead you away from an encounter with a false God into something that's more real. Which is to say that if punk is that spirit of raw rebellion—truth-telling, soul-searching—then what would be a more spiritual pursuit? Part of what you may learn at a certain point is that you may want to be a little more careful with how you use your own words because if you're not careful, your attack on other people's blinders can be your own blinder. Self-righteousness, for example.

PUNK IS A TRICKSTER—KICK THE DEITY

MICHAEL MEADE ("A Song is a Road" / mythologist): Mythologically there are elements of the trickster in punk. Early on at least, some of the torn clothing and ways of singing and almost attacking the instruments have some of the qualities of the trickster, which you see in Native American traditions and other cultures. One of the motions of trickster is to do things backward. I know some people find punk music distressing but there can be a great value in terms of changing things and creating a certain kind of awakening.

There are stories about this. I'm thinking of one in India about this fellow who keeps kicking the statue of the God Shiva. He's trying to prove to those people who are simply devoted, that you can even kick the deity to a certain degree and nothing really happens! In the story a big flood comes and everybody runs and leaves all the temples, statues and devotional practices and they all run away to save their lives. This guy stays and climbs in a tree and then, since he can't kick the statue which is now underwater, he takes nuts from the branches of the tree and throws them at the statue. Because that has become his kind of devotion. He is kind of a punk Shiva guy!

When the waters recede and everybody comes back, Shiva the God makes an appearance and everybody bows down. Shiva says, "You can do all the bowing you want because I know when the trouble comes you all leave. I only have one devotee here and that's this guy here who kept kicking me and throwing nuts at me. He paid attention even when the great flood of change came. This is my devotee." There is a quality of that in the punk scene. A lot of dramatic change can occur where the situation is conflicted and in stress. If people want to change a culture, what I suggest is go to the margins. And if people went to the margins all kinds of creative things can happen.

JACK GRISHAM (TSOL): The trouble is that a lot of knowledge is worthless. Because you can't match knowledge with service. I'll trade the answer on God for somebody sticking a hand out for someone that falls on the street. Any day. If you look in the New Testament in the book of James, there's an interesting part where James says, "You say you believe in God—so what? Even demons believe in God! It doesn't mean anything." How that translates is, "You say you have this knowledge and all of this belief? Who cares what you believe—show me! Show me through your actions." It's not what you think, it's what you do!

MIKE NESS (Social Distortion): I'm not a religious person. I don't go to church. However, I have gone into churches when no one is there. I choose to go alone. I've collected things that are symbolic, Catholic or Christian artifacts. To me they're symbolic of a God. I tend to always lean toward Eastern religions and philosophies. I do think that if you don't have some sort of spirituality in your life then you're kind of just existing. To believe in something and have faith has been crucial to my survival and consistency.

KLAUS FLOURIDE (Dead Kennedys): You can't preach to other people about how they should live unless you've examined how you live yourself. You shouldn't preach to people, in general. You can share your life a lot easier if you've examined it, easier than if you've just sat around watching TV all the time. There's a saying that Jack Perkins told me. He's a satirical graphic artist in the Winston Smith mode. He had a card that said, "Spirituality is like sex. The more people talk about it, generally the less they have."

I try to live and deal with spiritual aspects as just a matter, simply, from being a father and having relationships. As far as having anything to do with organized religion, that's a whole different ballpark. There are so many branches of organized religions that have nothing to do with spirituality as much as control. Most religions have the basic general tenets but the fundamentalist end of things can ruin anything, including something like punk rock. People say punk rock has to be this and this. They're crazy! They're missing the point!

RAMSEY KANAAN (Political Asylum / AK Press): Spirituality plays no part in my life. I've never been an adherent of any spiritual belief or practice. Arguably, music and anarchism could be considered as spiritual beliefs, in which case I'm guilty as charged. Personally, I think that punk rock that is Christian, Krishna or Buddhist is almost universally reactionary. I don't think it's great having born-again Christians who happen to like a certain genre of music. Or Krishnas, with beliefs and practices that are almost entirely reactionary, particularly when it comes to women. All the major religions are not good on women, among other things.

But there are many people who consider themselves to be Christians or Buddhist who do fantastic work and if that work is the result of their beliefs, then more power to them. I have a lot of time for Catholic Workers. They are anarchist Catholics. I have a lot of time for Quakers. There are aspects of what they believe that I don't believe. I could also say that I still have a lot of time for old Communist Party members as well. But I fundamentally disagree with the Communist Party and most of its actions in history.

CULT OF RELIGION

THURSTON MOORE (Sonic Youth): The spiritual has always been in music and art. We all have the spiritual because we're all sentient beings. Whether you have a belief system or you're atheist or agnostic, you're still a living sentient being who has to deal with concepts of metaphysics that may or may not have some definition for you as a being on this Earth. There will always be this analogous mystery. Whether you disregard it or are cynical about it, spirituality is a completely common thread with all living beings, with all life on Earth. The expression of spirituality is through art and music. That's what *it is*. Even Kraftwerk with their music that is really cold—where they send robots out to sort of do their tour, which was amazing—there is thought that goes into that, there are ideas there. That's spiritual exercise.

Getting involved with an organized cult of religion or a church; that's a choice that anybody can make. The idea of community that has its own rituals and regulations; this is something that's been going on long before we were here. I have a lot of respect for it as long as it deals with the common good of everybody. This is why I have a lot of respect for somebody like the Dalai Lama who says, "It's okay for you to be Buddhist and listen to me but if you're Roman Catholic or if you're Jewish and that's what you were born into, respect that. Be that. And know that they are all saying the same thing."

Of course we all have problems with anyone using religion for the sake of positioning in the world with borders. The Popes went to war in the old days. Or the factions of hardcore fundamentalist religions that goes on now. These factions that want to kill each other off using revenge tactics; it's a really weird violent minority that the rest of the world has to deal with and it gets really frightening. The violence has all this support from a weapons industry that's supported by the United States and other countries. It's ludicrous.

PETER CASE (The Nerves / The Plimsouls): If you look at the teachings of Jesus, it supposedly tells you what happens after you die. But the most valuable part of it is his description of these two commandments; you love God with all your being and then you love your fellow man. The whole thing boils down to that; that's what Jesus said. I can buy that. But what's God? Well, God is not just necessarily this really formal thing because the formal thing is just an interpretation. The religions are losing the facts of what they are trying to interpret. What you're trying to interpret is *where are we? What is life?* It doesn't seem realistic to me that there's this little moral code and if you violate some minor infraction that you're burned for all of eternity. In a loving universe—if it is indeed a loving universe—it seems like a contradiction that that would be true. So, I can't buy it.

JM: You mentioned reincarnation as being a possibility. Do you think it's part of reality?

PETER CASE (The Nerves / The Plimsouls): I think it's a possibility. I don't really know anything. I think every religion is some group's attempt to make an interpretation of what could be going on. Every religion is some approximate attempt to define something that really is undefinable. You can believe in reincarnation or in Jesus on different levels. For me, the religions themselves make the mistake of putting all their eggs in the basket of some sort of finite interpretation of what's going on. I always liked the line: "Whatever you think, it's bigger than that," by The Incredible String Band. Robin Williamson and Mike Heron. Everybody has the same facts, basically. Atheists make a decision based on the same facts available to right-wing Christians, left-wing Christians and Muslims, Buddhists and Hindus.

RUSS RANKIN (Good Riddance / Only Crime): The jury is still out on when exactly does a life as we know it start? Being a person who has gone through abortion to the extent that a guy can, I know it's a really horrible experience. I'm so upset with pro-life people who think that women who want to retain their reproductive freedoms only want to do it so they can have as many abortions as possible. As if it's something they enjoy. It's probably one of the toughest decisions a woman will ever have to make.

The Christian right's approach is making it worse. Other Western democracies that have a more pragmatic approach to this issue don't have the abortion rates that we do. To tell kids to just wait until they're married—that's bullshit! Who's going to do that? Nobody! Kids are going to go in the back of the car and they're going to fuck! The chances are better if you can offer some education. Give them options. They don't have any recourse to battle these hormones and they're scared to death to tell anybody because they'll be called sinners. They'll be cast out. One of the worst things about America is the line between church and state is so blurred. If the Canadian prime minister said he'd been talking to God, he'd be laughed out of office. Yet we have a US president who does just that and some people praise him for that. It's frightening!

JM: You recently performed acoustically at the Henry Miller Library in Big Sur. While introducing a song called "One More Hill," you said the song was about the hill of judgment and how, being in the punk rock world, you've dealt with a lot of judgment.

GREG GRAFFIN (Bad Religion): That song is interesting because a religious person lives their entire life knowing they are being judged every moment. I guess that's supposed to scare the little children into living a good life because god is always watching. But I live a very public life and with me it is not god watching, it's the punkers who are watching! (*laugh*) When I was younger, I cared a little bit more. Now I couldn't care less. It is strange how punk—probably just like vegetarianism or environmentalism—has factions of people who are so militant and righteous that they don't see beyond their own bathroom mirror. They think anything that exists outside of that mirror is not punk. That is very painful to people who want to enjoy punk music or a punk lifestyle, but they can't do it because they're so afraid of these punk police! That's why I found that song resonates with me as a punker. Because you can reach the top of the hill but the hill of judgment is still left to climb.

JAY BENTLEY (Bad Religion): I don't like what people do in the name of their religion. While I've felt a spiritual connection to something that helped me in times of feeling like nobody gives a shit, I never liked what people did to it. They would bend it to fit themselves. It always ended up in violence. "We're going to kill everybody who doesn't believe what we do." It's still happening now. None of us are perfect. That's why one of the things we say is *educate yourself*. We have a song that says, "Do what you want—just don't do it around me." I don't care what you do, just don't bring it into my party! (*laugh*)

MICAH ANDERSON (Ta'leef Collective): The conundrum we're up against is that the very thing that feeds our spirit for positive living can be used to control us. That can be democracy or organized religion. It's only a matter of time before a movement becomes about control. It took only a quick period of time for punk rock when people became excluded, "You're not in the club. You're from the wrong city and you don't know how to do it right." It's a slippery slope, right? The next thing you know it isn't a movement.

BRAD LOGAN (Leftöver Crack / Rats in the Walls): We all need to concentrate on accepting people that are different then us. I'm talking beyond sexual preference and religion. Let people believe what they want to fucking believe. And let me believe in what I want to believe and still be able to work together. I see a lot of that on social media; people condemning each other and maybe it's easier because it's not face-to-face. It's fucking bullshit. You have to start accepting each other. Or at least be willing to accept that you don't have the same opinion as me and that's cool. Maybe we have some common ground, like we all want to be free and we don't want to be living in an oppressed society. It doesn't matter who you pray to, so fine!

7

THE DISSENT OF MAN
BAD RELIGION AND GREG GRAFFIN/
RELIGION VS. SCIENCE

I became a punker long before I started thinking about myself as a naturalist, but the two worldviews actually have a lot in common.

—*Anarchy Evolution: Faith, Science and Bad Religion in a World Without God* by Greg Graffin (page 6)

You create your own reality / And leave mine to me.

—"Leave Mine to Me" by Bad Religion

It's August 20, 2006, and I'm at a live show outdoors amidst the towering redwoods at the Henry Miller Library in Big Sur, California. Greg Graffin is performing acoustic versions of Bad Religion songs, many of them about suffering: "Suffer," "Talk About Suffering" and "Sorrow." While introducing the song "One More Hill" to the small audience of about one hundred, Graffin explains, "This is a song about judgment. I'm very familiar with judgment. There is a lot of judgment in the punk rock world, unfortunately. It's a tragedy that it has become like that. This is a religious song about judgment that rings true for the punk world also."

Probably more than any other punk band on Earth, Bad Religion has focused on the contemporary tension between religion and science, two forces competing to be recognized as the superior model for illuminating truth and alleviating suffering. Greg Graffin has studied these realms deeply and intelligently and offers lyrics set to high-energy music that reflect his philosophical ideas. Bad Religion presents scholarships to young people to study anthropology and Graffin received a PhD in 2003 from Cornell University after writing a dissertation titled *Monism, Atheism and The Naturalist Worldview: Perspectives from Evolutionary Biology.*

JAY BENTLEY (Bad Religion): Graffin decided this year (2003) he's going to get his PhD instead of being a lifelong candidate. He has an August 16th date for delivery of his thesis. He's asked for the summer off so he can finish.

JM: Jay mentioned you're writing your PhD now. What's your dissertation about?

GREG GRAFFIN (Bad Religion): Evolution and religion, the tenets of the two bodies of knowledge and how they clash. I have spent half my life studying evolution and the other half of my life singing about religion. It was really a way to combine the two.

JM: I get feelings from your music about spirituality or precepts about how to treat other people, the environment, yourself, how to find truth.

GREG GRAFFIN (Bad Religion): *Morality* is what you're saying. Yeah, I'm a moral person. But I don't believe in god. My morality comes through naturalism. It's basically a belief in the reality of the universe and being able to find the truth through scientific pursuits. It's a very meaningful pursuit that leads to a very meaningful morality. I sent a poll to the National Academy of Sciences in twenty-two countries to survey the top brass in evolutionary biology, to see what their attitudes were toward religion. I found almost a complete denial of the truth of religion and a complete discounting of the tenets of religion and a complete atheism in all of their beliefs. And yet, I found a very moral and meaningful group of people who were very concerned about human welfare. It tells me that evolution might be a viable substitute for traditional religion. This is a very controversial conclusion—a lot of people are bummed about it. Too bad.

JM: You study and teach evolutionary biology at Cornell and sing about religion and science with Bad Religion. How do they serve each other?

GREG GRAFFIN (Bad Religion): One world definitely informs the other. I feel most productive writing music when I'm also doing academic work. I feel that if one were taken from me, it would be very lonely. I wouldn't feel like my life was whole. I wish there were more scientifically literate punks. And more punk-literate scientists! (*laugh*) The truth is that the two really keep to themselves and don't know much about the other. When I was teaching at UCLA and Cornell people would always ask, "Geez, aren't your students excited when you're teaching their class?" They thought that having me, the singer, teaching a class would be so exciting. But to be honest, most of those people didn't even know what Bad Religion was. I'm actually happy for that, that they didn't disrupt the class. The truth is that the issues I'm bringing up in Bad Religion's music, I always felt have a scientific foundation. That goes for the songs that Brett (Gurewitz) writes as well, because he's very scientifically literate. I think it would be nice if the music can be enjoyed as motivational, uplifting and inspiring for people to study more about the world they live in. As you know, there is now a big group of religious punkers. Christian punk is a whole genre. In fact, Bad Religion has a lot of Christian fans!

> *Graffin says his artistic side complements his scientific one, and both entail creativity.*

> —"Punk rocker becomes lecturer, preaching evolution"
> by Bethany Leibig,
> (Cornell Chronicle, November 30, 2011)

PRESTON JONES (*Is Belief in God Good, Bad or Irrelevant? A Professor and a Punk Rocker Discuss Science, Religion, Naturalism and Christianity*): Bad Religion did a song in the early '80s that I really liked. In the late '90s I really started paying more attention and got the *Stranger Than Fiction* cassette. At a high school where I taught, the headmaster was using a Bad Religion song in one of his classes. I contacted Greg Graffin in 2003 and asked him about his dissertation at Cornell University. It piqued his interest, that he got a note from a university professor. I was surprised to get his note back and then surprised to get another note from my response to that. And things just went that way for a few months.

JM: You teach at a Christian University, where you've played Bad Religion songs for your students.

PRESTON JONES (John Brown University): I've done it a couple of times. I once made the theme song for a class "Mediocre Minds." I was surprised to find later that it was a song that Greg didn't really like. In that case, the students were a little weirded out by it. They were expecting a normal Western Civ. lecture and I came in and blasted "Mediocre Minds." We looked at the lyrics. I guess they think it's a little unusual, especially at a Christian school in Arkansas, to be corresponding with the singer from a group whose symbol is the cross with a slash through it. But I haven't had negative comments and a lot of them think it's cool.

I don't listen to too much punk; I like to listen to smart people talk. I don't care where they come from politically, so long as they're smart. When I listen to Greg and read his lyrics I think, "Okay, here's a smart person." I also like the bass lines in Bad Religion. I play the bass. I like the music and the lyrics keep me there. When I listen to them, I think I'm in the presence of an intelligent person and I like that.

The only true messiah is ourselves / Sorrow no more!

—"Sorrow" by Bad Religion

PRESTON JONES (*Is Belief in God Good, Bad or Irrelevant?*): Greg (Graffin) and I have a lot in common. I think it's one reason we kept our correspondence going for a while. If you listen to Greg's lyrics, he spends a lot of time thinking about a question that people have been thinking about from the beginning and that is *why is there so much suffering in the world?* What's the point of so much pain? These questions go back to the epic of Gilgamesh, a few thousand years BC. At the heart of Christianity is an act of suffering, with Christ's crucifixion. The topic of suffering came up a lot in our correspondence. Greg and I talk about it in different ways and we come to different conclusions, but we have a common interest in this question.

JM: Scientists say their ideas are not based in faith, but on facts. Yet I sense that Greg and the scientists he interviewed have faith that science will figure out everything in the future. He's saying that the human desire for freedom is a phys-iological phenomenon that science will understand soon. In a way that requires a lot of faith, don't you think?

PRESTON JONES (*Is Belief in God Good, Bad or Irrelevant?*): I think there is faith there. It may be justified faith. Greg has a lot of faith that science will answer a lot of questions that aren't currently answered. *Are people really free?* Do they just *think* they're free? Maybe it's reasonable to have faith in science because science does have a good track record! I can fly from Arkansas to London in a day thanks to science. I can take a little white pill in the morning and it keeps my allergies at bay, thanks to science. I'm all for the scientific method. It makes our lives better. It complicates our lives, too. The atomic bomb was a scientific wonder; it worked. I'm not sure that's one we really needed to have as part of our experience, but there it is. "Tell me about natural history or DNA"—these are good questions to put to a scientist. Then to ask the question, "Why is there a world anyway?"

Greg calls himself an atheist. He's not obsessed, but he's very interested in this idea of God. I asked him, "Why have the overwhelming majority of people who have lived on this planet had the sense that there is more than this world?"

That's the kind of question I don't think you can take to a scientific lab. As a Christian, I think it's unfortunate that there's this idea that faith and science are at war with one another. Science answers the proper questions put to it. But there are different kinds of questions that are *not* scientific, but are metaphysical,

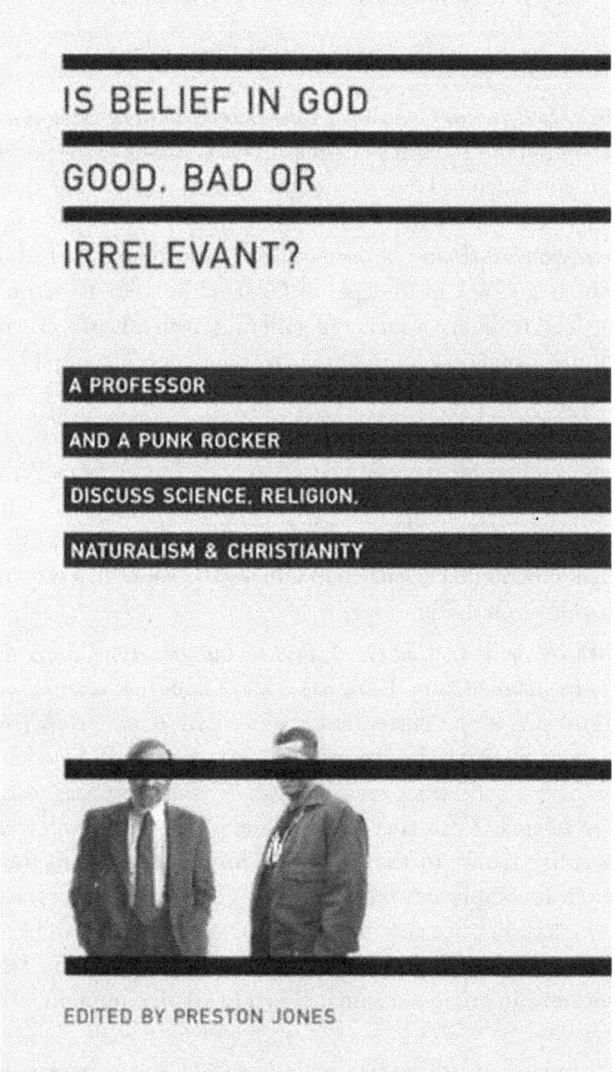

Figure 7.1 Is Belief in God Good, Bad or Irrelevant? *edited by Preston Jones (2006). Conversations with Greg Graffin, PhD, scientist and Bad Religion singer/ lyricist. Contributed: InterVarsity Press, Illinois.*

philosophical and spiritual questions. Greg is interested in those big questions but he wants to believe we can get answers purely through the scientific method. Faith is basic to life. To me the idea of faith isn't problematic. The idea of *blind* faith is problematic. I don't know anywhere in the Christian scriptures where people are told to accept things blindly. What I tell my students is that belief without doubt probably isn't good belief.

The reason there's violence in the world is because the world is inhabited by people. Violence pervades the natural world. I'm looking out over a big field and imagining that in this field there's all kinds of violence going on. Insects killing one another; birds are killing insects; parasites are getting the birds. Violence and suffering pervade the natural world. People are part of the natural world. We forget that because we live in this organized society.

LIFE IS ABSURD AND MEANINGFUL

JM: In your book, in an email to Greg Graffin you wrote, "Life is absurd and meaningful."

PRESTON JONES (*Is Belief in God Good, Bad or Irrelevant?*): Embracing paradox. That doesn't mean, "You have your truth and I have mine." It means we're in a complicated world. Each individual is complicated and then society is made up of all these complicated individuals. We have to simplify just to get through. It's always good to remember that it's a fascinating, scary and thrilling world we live in. It's a beautiful and ugly place. It's both. I think this view of the world is expressed very nicely in The Gospels. One reason I'm open to other ideas is that I have the sense that the more I learn about the world and science, and the way people work, the better I'll understand what it means to be a Christian.

> *The story of Jesus Christ does not apply to anyone's life anymore. Except in the most metaphorical way.*
>
> —Greg Graffin (Bad Religion)

JM: I see science and religion finding common ground where they didn't think that was possible previously. I think of Ken Wilber who wrote a book called *The Marriage of Sense and Soul*. And the Dalai Lama has been meeting with scientists for years.

GREG GRAFFIN (Bad Religion): Well, there are two kinds of people in the world: compatibilists and non-compatibilists. The compatibilists are people who believe we should have a dialogue between science and religion and understand one another. Whereas the non-compatibilists—most of them scientists, but some are hardcore creationists—they believe that, "No, the tenets of religion and science are completely mutually exclusive. We have got to figure out which one of these is explaining the right picture of the universe."

JM: Where do you lay in there?

GREG GRAFFIN (Bad Religion): I am a non-compatibilist, completely. I think religion is a joke these days. It doesn't explain anything. That's why we have so many lost people in the world. You wonder where all of this anxiety and tension comes from? It's because the symbols of religion have no meaning to these people in their daily lives anymore. The story of Jesus Christ does not apply to anyone's life anymore. Except in the most metaphorical way. And the people who are believers have to really have a deep metaphorical understanding of the story of Jesus to make it applicable *at all* to their lives. What most people have today is a little bit of a mix of spirituality—the story of Jesus—and a lot of scientific story about the origin of the universe. I think we need these scientists who are seen as atheists, baby-killers and cannibals—the most immoral people in the world—to come forth and say, "Look, we actually are humanists and are scientifically firm in our beliefs."

JM: I've heard Buddha described as a scientist who used his own experience and awareness as his grounds for scientific exploration.

GREG GRAFFIN (Bad Religion): I think science is generally a monistic pursuit and Buddhism is a monist worldview, and in that sense, I think that there are a lot of parallels. I think it's easier to be a Buddhist if you're a scientist than if you're a traditional Western person.

JM: Some people say that the huge problems of the world come down to a division between two camps of thought; those who view the world as material and scientifically definable. And another camp emphasizes that only what is experienced internally in the mind, body and soul is significant and that the material world is like an illusion. Any thoughts?

GREG GRAFFIN (Bad Religion): Well, that's a fundamental dichotomy that goes back to pre-classical times. What you're describing started with Thomas Aquinas and then finally became rock-solid doctrine with Descartes, who came up with mind/body dualism. And that dualism has plagued us ever since. I think you're right to identify it as one of the great tensions in the world. To put it into modern terms, basically the dualist believes in a natural and a supernatural, whereas the monist believes only in the natural. That's what I am: a monist and a naturalist. I don't think there are any grounds for belief in the supernatural.

Do I believe in the soul? I believe there is something that we call the soul, but it has a material basis. And in a very short amount of time—fifty years—neuroscientists are going to be able to identify that what we've been calling the soul all along, is really nothing more than a physiological process in our brain. I think that the soul exists, but it is not a supernatural entity. And do animals have a soul? Yes, they do. Animals have it as well as humans. Humans have it a little more developed, that's all.

JM: Do you think other living beings, besides animals, have souls or consciousness?

GREG GRAFFIN (Bad Religion): To varying degrees, what we would call the soul probably doesn't exist in any organisms other than mammals, birds and reptiles. I will leave it at that. Consciousness is another thing. I'm willing to say that there are varying degrees of consciousness in the mammals, birds and reptiles. There is a book called *The Universe of Consciousness: How Matter Becomes Imagination* (by Gerald Edelman—2008). It's the best modern theory of what consciousness is. It's a purely neuro-anatomical definition and I tend to favor that. By that definition there are very few organisms that have consciousness.

JM: We live in a country that says it's very important to separate church and state. In a way it's beneficial because religion can adversely affect politics and vice versa. But if you look at religion in it's best light, as being a support for cultivating compassionate culture and morality, we're now suffering because there is a separation between politics and morality.

GREG GRAFFIN (Bad Religion): Okay, there is a moral crisis in the world. It is particularly bad here in the United States. It's worse here than almost anywhere else. I agree with that. The reason we're having a moral crisis is precisely *because* of the church. *Not in spite of the church*. If the church were to vanish tomorrow, we would craft a new morality and it would be based on scientific data and information and it would, I believe, make a better society.

That is not to say that the church didn't have valuable morals to teach. They did. But it was based on lies. Lies that were uncovered progressively through the Enlightenment period until today. There is nothing that the church used to believe that it hasn't backpedaled on in order to remain relevant. We should just abandon the church as a teacher of a worldview and acknowledge the fact that it is not relevant anymore. The only way that it is relevant is that they scare the shit out of children, and those children grow up into a world where they can maintain the tenets of the church by prescription, not by observation. And not by any kind of empirical method, which I think is the key to forming a new morality. For instance, there is no way we would have any morality about preserving the rainforest had not scientists gone down there and actually studied the species' decline in the rainforests. To me, that is a direct indicator of morality coming from scientific research.

PARALLEL UNIVERSES

JIM LINDBERG (Pennywise): If it were up to me, I'd marry the two in the sense of *spirituality* and *science*. They're starting to find that common ground more and more. The more that's uncovered with string theory or various things about life, it's almost like they're uncovering more that we don't know and finding that the universe is much stranger and more complex than we ever thought it was. Multiple and parallel universes. The idea that you have spirituality and religion on one side and cold science on the other is false. The two can be intermingled. God and the universe represent a lot of ideas from, for example, Toltec wisdom and other ways to understand spirituality and a different kind of God.

There's a good movement in the Unitarian church; that's a great place for people to start. They accept people of all faiths and take teachings from different faiths and apply those to everyone. They're very accepting of all cultures. When you have something like that it does help you accept the discoveries made in science about the universe. Otherwise, you're like the creationists: "If it doesn't fit within our strict guidelines, then we won't believe it." It's much more important to teach our kids to have an open mind about things and to be tolerant, but still have a spiritual base as well so their lives can be meaningful.

ROB FISH (108): There is this whole debate about what's more real; science or spirituality. What's better? I don't know. When I look at science, there's a reason why every three or four years a science book that we use to educate children is completely updated and the old one is thrown away. It's an evolutionary process. What was science and fact fifty years ago is deemed ludicrous today. It's funny because people feel like you can't be spiritual and embrace science and vice versa. It's strange to me.

Spirituality to me is not that I have some answer that other people don't have. Do I know that there is a God? I have absolutely no clue. Do I care? No, I don't really care. All I know is that I've read these books, in terms of Radha Krishna, that really inspire me. They've become a part of how I aspire to view myself and the world around me. It's not a matter of right and wrong or fact and fiction. I can really care less. My spirituality is at four o'clock in the morning with my door locked and me sitting in my room, meditating on the things I aspire for, meditating on the person I aspire to be.

JOHNETTE NAPOLITANO (Concrete Blonde): Scientology pretty much has that *science as religion* thing down. Spirituality and science make total and complete sense; that's a no-brainer for me. I heard an interview with the first woman Episcopal Bishop, who is a marine biologist. (Katharine Jefferts Schori) She had no problem believing in creation as well as evolution; it made total sense. Also, no matter how much we know in the scientific sense, there is much more we don't, so I'll put my faith in the workings we *don't* see. Nikola Tesla is considered by many—myself included—to have been the greatest scientist that ever lived. His inventions came to him in dreams. That sums it up for me.

GOOD RELIGION

RON REYES (Black Flag): I love the fact that punk rock very actively takes on social aspects and things about nature and wanting to preserve the world we live in. That's fantastic. That enters into spirituality. It's all intertwined. Why try to put up dividing lines? Bad Religion is a great band name because there's a whole lot of bad religion in this world. But I think there's a whole lot of good religion in this world as well! The good religion is the religion that helps people, loves people and takes care of people, and creation and the world we live in. I don't think you can call that *bad* religion. Bring it on.

SEAN MUTTAQI (Vegan Reich): Religion and science are entirely compatible because science is nothing more than a process for understanding the miracle of life we see before us. From a spiritual or religious point of view, this is a physical creation that can be measured and studied. In Islam we have a *hadith* that says, to paraphrase, "God created the world because he was a hidden treasure that wished to be known." For us, creation itself is an *ayah* or "sign" and the revelatory experience known as prophecy is just a more nuanced expression, in human language, of a similar process; the divine unfolding and making itself known by way of signs. God, Allah and Yahweh are terms to signify a source for the material world that transcends matter. Although science could be close to measuring some ethereal essence within the body that one may call a soul it may only be one part of the picture, in terms of aspects that exist outside of our known dimension or in alternate planes of existence. Being a created aspect, the soul is a physical creation and could theoretically be measured.

JM: You have a song called, "In Defense of Reality" with the lyrics, "Today's modern science is your modern religion."

RAY CAPPO (Youth of Today / Shelter): The word *science* means *to know*. The fascinating thing is that if you study the Vedas, the first thing the teacher will teach you is that you can't know for sure unless things get directly revealed to you in your personal experience. You brought up Bad Religion and how science is the new religion. There's only one problem; scientists can never have objective reality. You can't have perfect knowledge with imperfect senses and humans don't like to admit they're imperfect. So, what good is science?

This whole idea of science versus faith—I've got news for them; the paradigm is crashing down upon them with quantum physics. We've realized there's more than three dimensions. Yogis have been talking about this for thousands of years! Yogis have a deeper understanding of reality than Christian fundamentalists. There are so many holes in scientific theory. We used to think the table was solid. The table is *not* solid. Sub-atomic particles could fly through that table!

We are like a frog living in a well; we think the whole world is a well. But outside the well are oceans, plants, forests, jungles and quicksand and other animals. A child can understand that, but some fundamentalist scientists cannot. These skeptics; why aren't they skeptics of their own doubt? Why do they have to have everything in hard stone? There can never be hard and fast rules to anything like this because spirituality is subtle. That doesn't mean we should throw away all discrimination. We shouldn't believe what anybody says just because they're a spiritual teacher. There are charlatans, bogus yogis and preachers. But I don't think we should throw away everything that we can't perceive as unreal. Or else we throw away radio waves and frequencies of sound.

JM: "Throw Away Your Brain" is your song about the limitations of the mind. Many people believe that science has replaced religion and will answer all questions about life and death.

YISHAI ROMANOFF (Moshiach Oi!): If you're an atheist, what you're relying on is science. People naturally want to have answers. Every atheist I've known treats science as the source of all their answers. That's silly because science is always changing and is theoretical. Nothing is solid. Rabbi Nachman teaches that there's only so much we can understand with our minds. In Judaism we believe in having faith. Faith applies to what we *don't* understand. What we do understand, we don't need to have faith in. I understand that the sun comes up in the morning and I don't need to have faith that it will happen tomorrow. Faith is when I don't understand something and I'm still going to believe in it anyway. "Throw Away Your Brain" is a song that was written by Mike (Wagner) our guitar player and is taken directly from Rabbi Nachman's teachings about faith, trust and following truly righteous people who have come to Earth to bring us closer to God.

On the flip side is the scientific and secular world of atheists who say that believing out of faith is delusional and crazy; "Faith is a thing of the past, from the ancient world. Now we should use our brains to reason and rationalize things." I understand the argument because I used to think that way, but I don't anymore. Just because people used faith many years ago doesn't mean it's something we should get rid of. I think if it was true back then, it's true now. You can't rationalize and reason everything.

DICK LUCAS (Subhumans / Citizenfish): We're not the same people. Our stomach lining gets replaced every five days because it just gets eaten away. Most of our genetic material belongs to bacteria that cover our body, all over. About 96% of our genetic material is bacterial and not human. There are something like 77,000 types of bacteria up your nose and we don't know what most of it does! What are we really? If you stretched out the DNA material from *one* cell it would go about twenty feet!

JM: Seems despite a lot of advances in science there's still a lot of unknowns.

DICK LUCAS (Subhumans): We don't know where we came from or where we're going. There are two types of pre-cellular entities—one begins with "p" and one with an "e"—and end in the syllable "yotes." (Eukaryotes and Prokaryotes) One was a smaller version of the other. The other evolved by devouring another and boosting itself. There was a few billion years of this before the basic cell was formed. On the one hand you've got religion being completely incredible and on the other hand you've got science which is more or less the same thing; you've got to take their word for it, right? They seem to have a lot of facts backing them up whereas religion doesn't have so many facts to back it up. One goes down the *philosophical faith* route and one goes down the *factual faith* route. But they both require quite a bit of faith. For some reason there's an unobtainable truth. People who believe the Bible is factual will say, "These are facts." In that sense it depends how much trust you've got in other people's faith in their own beliefs.

HE GAVE US FREE WILL

JM: What do you think about free will? It almost sounds like you think we don't have any choice. You write about this paradox in your dissertation and quote Smith from 1952 who says, "The most astonishing logical paradox ever to be cherished by man is that God in his omnipotence had predetermined the fate of every man and yet he never the less holds every man responsible for his actions."

GREG GRAFFIN (Bad Religion): I believe what Smith wrote. That's one of the most astonishing logical paradoxes that we ever came up with. But when he says "we" he need look no further than the early church fathers like Augustine Aquinas. They recognized before the year 1000 that the church doctrines were going to be contradictory, so they came up with this concept of *free will*. If you have a single god who is all-powerful and all-knowing, then how can we be expected to have any freedom if it's already written in the cards? Well, those are the guys who came up with this idea; because god loves us so much, he gave us free will. That is the justification for all of the punishment in the world today. The reason we punish people is because we say, "You are free to do what you want." That inner-city hoodlum who robbed the liquor store could have said no. But instead, he used his free will to commit an act of robbery and therefore he should be punished. I'm not saying that that is unreasonable. If someone robs me, I would want him to be thrown in jail. All I'm saying is that the circumstances leading up to the robbery have a lot more to do with the fact that he was uneducated, that he probably had children who couldn't feed themselves, and the fact that he was in an area where he could get handguns really easily.

I'm not saying that we don't make choices. Of course, we make choices! But we make choices the same way that a squirrel in my backyard makes a choice. When I throw an old corncob off the deck, he can decide whether he wants to eat an acorn or a piece of corn. Despite the fact there is an oak tree back there and thousands of acorns laying on the ground, he makes the choice for the corn. Now, do you think those church fathers would say that god also gave the squirrel free will? No way! *We* are god's favorite creatures. Squirrels are rodents. But the truth is that we are all vertebrates.

JM: In your dissertation, one of the many scientists you interviewed is Richard Lewontin. He says, "The only way to study things is by holding everything constant and you can't do that with organisms or consciousness." He's pointing to the difficulties of studying living things and processes like emotions that are constantly changing.

GREG GRAFFIN (Bad Religion): Science is definitely an exercise in creativity and imagination. The neat thing about science is that even though you acknowledge everything as always changing you can still come up with some pretty powerful predictions and understandings about the nature of objects. You can freeze them, even if it is for the briefest moment of time, and look at them. You're right; you always have to keep in mind that this is undergoing change. But if we can freeze it in a momentary frame, we can study it.

It's like trying to understand what a baseball is doing when a pitcher throws it. We can do some pretty powerful things with Newtonian physics, but you're right that it doesn't come close to capturing the essence of the ball in terms of quantum mechanics, but it can satisfy us to a great degree. It can make practical things understandable. Using modern technology, if we film the ball with a high-speed camera that is taken at a thousand frames per second, and we look at just one of those frames, we can look at the ball and understand its rotation from the angle we are looking at and we can extrapolate some useful things. Maybe if we look at it close enough to the release, we can understand how the pitcher's fingers were wrapped around it at the time. We can use our imagination, then, to think, "What if he moved his finger slightly this way or that way?" And that can be put into practice and we can see the results.

I wouldn't make too much of that quote by Dick Lewontin because he was making a different point. He wanted just to show that we can't be sure. In science, if you say that you are absolutely one hundred percent sure, you are lying to people. That is because science is probabilistic. It is perfectly reasonable to assume that I might fall right through the floor that I am standing on right now and our interview will be over. Of course, the likelihood of that is very, very low. I cannot be sure that it's not going to happen, but I feel reasonably sure enough about it that I don't mind pacing over the same old spot.

JM: I sense that seeking truth is something that motivates you. Einstein talked about truth as beauty and Gandhi spoke of God as truth. Tell me more about the quest for truth and how that has manifested in your scientific and punk rock life.

GREG GRAFFIN (Bad Religion): As I've gotten older the issue of truth has become a little bit more nebulous. There is wonderful triumph in being able to solve scientific problems. But the triumph comes from how it can be used to make life better for people. How it can be applied regardless of nationality, race or creed. The scientific puzzle that is solved can have wonderful practical benefits. The simplest example is penicillin. Vaccinations are another, as well as sanitation and avoidance of disease. When these puzzles are solved in the laboratory and then applied on a massive scale, it just makes everyone's life happier, so that the general happiness quotient in the world maybe can go up a little bit.

As for the physicists who are working in the realm of theory, especially nowadays, the frontiers in physics are really something that nobody can comprehend, except physicists. Those kinds of puzzles are imaginative and they still belong in science because they are experiments and repeatable. They are still based on the fundamental tenets of science. But whether or not wormholes exist is not going to increase the happiness quotient on the planet very much. I don't want to sound like I'm deriding those people who study those things because I'm not. Ultimately, I'm a naturalist historian who wants to know about how the world works. But if you ask me to interface that stuff with happiness and suffering, I'm going to focus on the biological sciences and on the way that people live their lives, the way the environment operates and the necessary things that it will take to maintain sustainability. And those things are not generally in the realm of theoretical physics.

JM: Your interest is in more practical, direct ways of making positive change?

GREG GRAFFIN (Bad Religion): I guess you would say that in Bad Religion that is true. It's what I sing about. My main interest is in understanding how the world works. And a lot of that is just pure exploratory discovery in natural science. Almost in the same spirit of Charles Darwin and the Victorian expeditions that went out collecting from all around the world because they didn't know what existed out there. That is what really gets me excited.

RELUCTANT ATHEIST

JM: Do you think science has replaced religion as a system for seeking truth and understanding?

JOSEPH OJO TAYLOR (Christian punk band from Orange County—Undercover): I have to be careful with that one. That's the claim that a lot of Christians make, that you've replaced one religion with another. I think that's patently false. I kind of agree with Greg (Graffin), that science will answer a lot of questions. I don't think there's any such thing as the human soul. Sam Harris is right; whatever happens to us in the human experience happens in our brain. That raises the question of consciousness and what is consciousness? And the meaning of identity and "Who am I?" Science gives us the best way, imperfect as it may be, of knowing the universe and our place in it. Religion used to be called the "Queen of Sciences" and it's had to retreat over hundreds of years. It's come to the point where religion is not really contributing anything to the discussion. We're not making new discoveries about the universe due to somebody's theology.

Having said that, I don't want to be overly dogmatic and I'll invoke my sociology background; some of these things are human constructs. The idea of love comes up often and for Christians this is a primary concept; "God is Love." If you ask almost any Christian, "Can you define what love is?" I don't mean give examples of love. I mean, "Give me an operative definition that I can take out into the field and measure." I think you'd come up flat, even how central that is to their religion. Yet, I think it's possible. There are ways in the social sciences to operationalize those human constructs such as love and justice, and even anarchy! Greg's an evolutionary biologist, if I remember correctly. Is that right?

JM: Yes.

JOSEPH OJO TAYLOR (Undercover): When I spoke at the *Freedom from Religion Foundation* (2012) I spoke right before Jerry Coyne. He's another one who thinks there's no reconciling religion and science. I'm on that side of things. I have discussions with religious people who say, "I'm a Christian and I accept completely whatever science has to say about the universe." And yet they accept things like a heaven and hell, or afterlife, or the existence of a human fall, or sin and the need to be redeemed. None of which have any evidence whatsoever. I'm a reluctant atheist. I'm an atheist because I don't have a workable god ideal. I'm using the definition of the world literally; I have renounced god! I'm also an agnostic; I'm not saying that there is no god. Just that nobody knows for sure. There might be. But if there is, we haven't glimpsed it yet and detected or measured it. Some would say, "The absence of evidence where there should be evidence is evidence of absence." These are not easy questions.

ADAM NIGH (Craig's Brother / Too Bad Eugene): This was the question that sent me into a theological education; *If there is a God, then we have no free will.* Then I studied some philosophy and realized that there are plenty of atheists and materialists who seem even more convinced that there is no such thing as free will. Greg Graffin, singer of Bad Religion and one of my musical heroes; I've read him articulate that position very clearly. Free will is incomprehensible, spiritual babbling. It means nothing. The world is all cause and effect. I hit that and I thought, "Oh, man." This was not necessarily just a theological question, it was philosophical in a larger context.

I did embrace a certain kind of fatalistic Christianity for years. I called myself Calvinist. I really did see there is a God and he is the author of this cosmic drama and we are just characters in it. Even that's too glorified! We are not even characters because characters are at least applying some skill. We are marionettes, just puppets. I became honest that I could not accept what I was saying. I think the experience of making a choice overwhelms that. Any kind of philosophical system that says there is no such thing as free will; I might say I believe it, but in the end I can't justify saying that I have no free will because I experience the reality of making choices all the time. We live in a universe that God is in control of, yet we have a similar potency. Though we are not God ourselves, we have a bit of his nature in the sense that; *as he is free, so we are free.* I've struggled with that quite a bit. It's made its way into lots of lyrics I've written.

For a person to encounter something that they think is true and then to encounter other truths; it's something Christians are very bad at. We tend to be, "No! Our God is right and our God will kick your God's butt." I don't want to use the word "exclusive" truth but I'm not sure of a better word to use. The reality of God and Christ—humility is bound into an authentic Christian spirituality. We are forbidden from going out into the world and telling everybody that they're wrong and we're right, even if we're convinced about that reality. I think we've seen enough of Christians going around telling people, "You have to experience God the exact way I have or you're going to hell."

GREG GRAFFIN (Bad Religion): You have to accept the fact that you, as a human being, are part of the natural world. That is the hardest point to get across to most people! (*laugh*) They don't want to believe that. They don't want to believe they're affected by the same laws and forces that are acting upon nature and the lowly squirrel in my backyard. But if we can get over that and accept that we are simply the product of all of the experiences and genetic influences that came before this moment in time, then we can say, "Okay, I'm thinking this way because of those influences."

Another major hurdle to overcome is the belief in free will. This is another hurdle that people have to get over before they can really accept this idea that we are simply the product of our experiences and genetic influence of our past. But if we can finally arrive at that point, then thinking becomes very paramount indeed. Then we can problem-solve and overcome the pretension that we are somehow exempt from the laws of nature. I think that it would force us to come up with solutions that are probabilistic in nature and not simply wishful thinking.

Obviously, I'm a big proponent of education. If we can educate people better, they will think better. They will then make better choices. And what does "better choices" mean? Well, it doesn't necessarily mean that they're going to save the environment. But it certainly gives them more of a *chance* to save the environment. And not in some psychological, dark place in their own mind, depressed out of their minds. Because they don't understand why their idea of free will or their will to succeed is not being matched by their success in life.

MUTUAL AID

> *If Charles Darwin were alive today, I think he would find something very attractive about punk rock.*
>
> —*Anarchy Evolution: Faith, Science and Bad Religion in a World Without God* by *Greg Graffin* (page 6)

JM: In your book *Population Wars* (2015) you write, "There is as much inter-dependence in the biosphere as violence." And also, "The natural world and the evolutionary processes are anarchic. There's no ultimate reason for our existence." And from this anarchy, "There is a great sophistication and beauty." I love your criticism of Darwin. I remember first discovering that Darwin actually argued *against* the popular understanding of his ideas. He warned people in his books, "Hey, I'm not saying "survival of the fittest" in the way you're understanding it." He actually identified empathy and cooperation as signifi-cant factors in evolution. I'm curious that you don't mention Peter Kropotkin. When I first was reading about Darwin, I came across Kropotkin's *Mutual Aid* which argues the side that you're arguing, it seems to me, that our evolu-tion is based more on cooperation than competition. Have you checked out Kropotkin?

GREG GRAFFIN (Bad Religion): Yeah. In many ways I did a modern restatement of Kropotkin. He has always been in my mind. His book was one of these books that came out right around the end of the nineteenth century. At that time there were so many ideas about evolution and how it worked that his book was sort of derided as pseudo-science. In many ways *Population Wars* is a restatement of an idea that he spent an entire book talking about. But we have much more science and data today. We have a hundred years of collecting biological data that I think makes it more robust.

Going back to another thing you said in your question; it's really interesting how the culture determines the shape of our beliefs. And that argues *against* free will. *We are not free to believe whatever we want.* The culture determines that. When Kropotkin's book came out it was seen as pseudo-science but today you can make the same statement in a scientific framework and that's because the current held view in the world is that we should actually paint our world view based on scientific, empirical information. Today we can make many more claims than they could a hundred years ago about cooperation and interdependence.

I won't call it *mutual aid.* As you pointed out, I avoided that word in the book because it's not really anarchism that I'm talking about. It's closer to a word that they do use in science: *co-evolution.* Organisms have an interde-pendence with one another but they're not necessarily eating each other to continue their existence. They simply evolve to a point of interdependence. Each chapter I try to show some of the scientific foundation for that worldview. I think as time goes on, hopefully my book will be seen as one of the earlier expressions of that idea in a scientific framework, where as Kropotkin's was not.

"NO SPIRITUAL SURRENDER"— INDIGENOUS PUNK ROCK

BLACKFIRE AND SIHASIN/OBSERVER SYNDROME/ ICONOCLAST AND ANAHUAK UNDERGROUND

Figure 8.1 Clayson, Jeneda, and Klee Benally of Diné (Navajo) bands Blackfire and Sihasin. Klee was forty-eight when he passed away on December 30, 2023. Photo by John Running.

She has brown skin and gold in her teeth, she's the baddest muthafucka that I have ever seen . . . Divine with beauty of defiantly breaking chains.

—"Nassissa" by 1876 featuring Kristen from Observer Syndrome. (*Pow Wow Punk Rock II—2021*)

854 million people suffer from hunger / 844 million people live without safe water / When will you stand against injustice / Liberation for all.

—"Liberation" by With War (2019)

The mohawk has been used by punk musicians like Joe Strummer, Jean Beauvoir, Wendy O. Williams, Annabella Lwin, Brody Dalle, Adam Ant, Darby Crash, Tim Armstrong, Lars Frederiksen, and others. Overall, we must take note that elements in punk scenes including the word itself "punk," and the very iconic mohawk hairstyle, have really been shaped by Indigenous peoples.

—Bergland, Jeff and Johnson, Jan and Lee, Kimberli editors; *Indigenous Pop: Native American Music from Jazz to Hip Hop*, Tucson, University of Arizona Press, 2016 (page 18)

SINGING IS HEALING

It's five o'clock in the morning on Indigenous People's Day, 2024. I join hundreds of bright-eyed people on a short ferry ride across the San Francisco Bay to Alcatraz Island, former prison and later "occupied" by Native American activists from 1969 to 1971. The sweet earthy aroma of burning sage permeates the air and a bonfire is the centerpiece for prayers, songs and dances as the sun rises. Clayson Benally and his father Jones, from Diné (Navajo) punk band Blackfire, offer a song of healing. Later at Yerba Buena Gardens they perform a hoop dance and Clayson sings the Sihasin song "Shine." He tells the audience, "We are all indigenous to somewhere. Today we honor indigenous people everywhere and celebrate that native people no longer get arrested for protesting Columbus Day, as so many have in the past." Yaotl Mazahua, vocalist with early '80s punk band Iconoclast and now singer in Anahuak Underground (formerly

Aztlan Underground) performed the song "My Blood is Red" and rapped about the current Palestinian struggle for survival.

CLAYSON BENALLY (Blackfire / Sihasin): I don't refer to our spirituality as religion because it's a traditional cultural-life way that's integrated with so much of our existence. The traditions that my father (Jones Benally) has carried on go back unaltered by colonization. He was blessed not to have gone to the boarding schools and have that removed from him at a young age. He went later in his twenties, after he'd been practicing the traditional Diné healing arts. He's a Hatáálii—a traditional singer, medicine practitioner.

If somebody is sick, they have a Hatáálii—a singer—come and identify; what is the root cause of the patient's particular ailment or imbalance and then try to figure out how to repair that. In the ceremonies, if somebody has a singing done to them it's all about healing. If you'll notice, I'm using the word "singing." That process of healing is incorporated with singing, for identifying the root cause. A Western hospital system looks at the symptom but is not getting to the root cause. For a lot of our traditional wisdom, we look at the root cause and go back, maybe before birth even.

JENEDA BENALLY (Blackfire / Sihasin): People are turning to indigenous ways because people connect with the concept of being close to nature. The concept of knowing and *feeling* that you have a relationship with nature is definitely lacking today. In most capitalistic societies people tend to look at nature as a resource that they can profit from in the financial sense, whereas for us as Diné, being able to go to an undisturbed landscape is one of the most valuable experiences. These are the places we can restore ourselves and connect. It's different than going to a parking lot or backyard that's been landscaped, when you go into a natural place that is growing wildly and perfectly without human manipulation. I think people are craving that.

You look at society today and everything is so planned; "This is your schedule. You're going to go to school from 8:00 am to three o'clock in the afternoon. You come home, do homework." It's this indoctrination of values that we constantly have to deal with in this civilization. Whereas in the traditional sense you wake up in the morning, you go out, you make your offering and pray for that beautiful, long life. You pray for harmony, to be in balance with all things, with all life and nature, with all the life forms that exist on Earth. Even down to the rocks. People don't see that as a life form, but there's a lot of microorganisms and such that are all part of that life cycle.

I see people thinking that buying a smudge stick and a dream catcher will bring them closer to their truth, and perhaps it will. But spirituality is not about buying things in order to attain a spiritual connection. It's not about all the stuff that people think they need to buy in order to have a spiritual sense of oneself. It's simply in the relationship of being present.

I definitely see why people look to indigenous peoples throughout the world for some kind of wisdom. Many indigenous populations still maintain that relationship to the Earth. You watch the trees and the trees will tell you a lot about what to expect in the coming year. When you watch what nature is doing, it's a science as well. People forget this! What is science? It's observation. Indigenous peoples have that knowledge base of observing their cultural and spiritual landscapes since the beginning of their existence. For me, it's a sense spirit. Spirituality is really tied in with our traditional sciences as well. It's not magic. It's not some sort of folklore or mythology. It's just life.

CLAYSON BENALLY (Blackfire / Sihasin): Our father's generation saw that transition from where there was basically no colonization in Black Mesa (Arizona). My dad (Jones Benally) didn't see his first white person until he was a young man. Seeing the first car driving through the valley and smelling the pollution from that vehicle; he described to us those first transitional moments in our region. He learned sacred practices from his grandparents and our family were the regional practitioners. If you're sick, rather than go to a hospital our traditional medicine is our healthcare system. Many cultural practitioners use herbs, body work, prayers and ceremonies.

We continue these traditions and have apprenticed under our father, learning how to work with the body, realign bones, the skeletal system. We learned the concept that mental, physical and spiritual well-being all are interconnected. This wealth of information and knowledge is basically like a higher education system. When you're young, you might start getting your primary education all the way up to your doctorate learning how to, for example, deliver babies and understanding everything you'd need to survive without a hospital structure. This is how our ancestors survived for millennia; transmitting oral traditions and knowledge. That's a lineage we still carry with us today.

BERTA BENALLY (Blackfire manager / mother): They've always been singing together all their lives, traditional and ceremonial songs. So, when the band started it was just natural that Jones started singing along and it worked with the traditional songs and it fused perfectly. The kids rehearsed Blackfire songs out of our home so we were always around. They've been singing together all their lives and when the band started, Jones would start singing and it was perfect. My kids were born into an era of genocide, the forced relocation of 10,000 families we've been fighting ever since. The music was a way to release the genocide that's going on right now and support in fighting the government that's trying to force relocation. My children were raised traditionally and my husband Jones is a traditional medicine man, a healer, so that's where it's rooted. Using your voice is critical; singing is powerful. They write songs like "Resist" with words like, "Walk upon the screaming ground, no respect for the dead." That song is about all the massacres of indigenous people and came out of our first trip to Pine Ridge and Wounded Knee, where we learned about not only what happened in the past, but what's still happening today. We have to resist!

CLAYSON BENALLY (Blackfire / Sihasin): Being born in Black Mesa, this is the place my umbilical cord was placed on this Earth. My mom (Berta Benally) placed my umbilical cord at the base of a sacred tree up in Black Mesa, not far from Big Mountain. And a bulldozer uprooted it. They were basically laying the fencing that was going to separate the Navajo and the Hopi for the relocation of all the people. I was born in 1977, so the Navajo Hopi Relocation Act of 1974 was already enacted and people were in the midst of this struggle to remain upon the land. Our family are resisters and we fought to remain at the place of our ancestors. We recognized that, at the root of this relocation violence was that there's coal here, a resource. Our lives were not considered of the same worth as this coal below our feet. So, the removal and displacement of 14,000 families in the 1970's when you add the multiplier effect. That's had such a detrimental impact upon our communities. Our spiritual connection was ripped apart. When I went to Flagstaff later—when we were displaced and essentially refugees—punk rock became my salvation.

"NOT ALL KILLED BY JOHN WAYNE"

Kristen Martinez is a doctoral student in the Department of Musicology at the University of California, Los Angeles, and she co-coordinates the online Indigenous Punks Archive. Her 2019 thesis for a master's degree in American Indian Studies at UCLA was titled "Not All Killed by John Wayne: Indigenous Rock 'n' Roll, Metal and Punk History 1940's to the Present." In the introduction Martinez writes, "I argue that Native punk is not just a cultural movement, but a form of survivance. Bands utilize punk and their stories as a conduit to counteract issues of victimhood as well as challenge imposed mechanisms of settler colonialism, racism, misogyny, homophobia, notions of being fixed in the past, as well as bringing awareness to genocide and missing and murdered Indigenous women."

KRISTEN MARTINEZ (Observer Syndrome / Indigenous Punks Archive): The title of my thesis is *Not All Killed by John Wayne* and this was something said by Clayson Benally from Blackfire. He encapsulated everything about indigenous punk rock and how he and his sister Jeneda, and brother Klee, are *still there*; "We're still here. We're not killed off. And . . . we're playing punk rock!" The framework of my thesis is survivance. That's what Clayson is saying; indigenous people are not absent. They've survived and prospered. But pop culture and Americanism want to portray this image of *poor Native Americans*. It's a victimhood and despair without seeing that they're thriving in music, art, scholarship, sports, every aspect of life. I think that *survivance* is very much in a lot of the punk rock lyrics, attitude and fashion. Some musicians have incorporated their indigenous culture with Goth or punk attire. There's rockabilly women that incorporate beautiful Pueblo cultures into their 1950's rockabilly attire.

There's pushback now against being the victim or being erased and learning what a brutally racist pop culture figure John Wayne was! There's a ska punk band Low Cash Ninjas and their song "Still Here" pushes back against stereotypes and being a mascot and these narratives pushed upon indigenous people. A big thing that changed everything and drew us into punk in the 2000s was post-9/11 and xenophobia and distrust of the government. At the same time, bands came out that really changed everything. For me that band was AFI, A Fire Inside. They were punk, but they also had that goth side so they opened the door to The Cure and all that music. I also love metal. I'm wearing this Motorhead shirt! I listen to the darkest, craziest stuff but I have my own spirituality.

I love the ideology of punk. In high school I thought, "If you look tough, nobody will mess with you." In high school you don't want to get bullied. It was like an armor. I grew up in El Monte, California, so it's heavily Latinx and Asian and a lot of kids really loved that kind of music. In my dissertation work I'm looking also at Emo, which came out at that time, too. A lot of kids of color really loved Emo even though it's a Caucasian kind of aesthetic; straight hair and things like that. All the Emo kids I knew were Black, Mexican and Latinx. Emos in Mexico in the 2000s got beat up because of the way they looked and their emotional vulnerableness. There was candidness to sing your emotions and also an androgyny to the style. Many people just didn't like that. It even goes higher with the surveillance aspect, especially post-9/11. You know, "Why are these young people saying how they actually feel? What are they conspiring to do?" In the Southwest (USA) there's a lot of bands like Heart Museum from Albuquerque (New Mexico) that were in that 2000 Emo era. Arizona had a pretty popular scene and a lot of indigenous bands were doing Emo.

JM: You mentioned in your thesis that the Ghost Dance was banned in 1890. That reminds me that for some time in the United States, African drumming was illegal. It was a way of communicating for slaves and the oppressors said, "Now, that's illegal." Often music of rebellion receives some backlash.

KRISTEN MARTINEZ (Observer Syndrome / Indigenous Punks Archive): The first ever recordings of music are of indigenous people. Some of the first sounds that people ever recorded were indigenous music. Regarding indigenous music being banned, what comes to mind is this great documentary *Rumble*. I remember learning about Johnny Cash's music and how this white artist was talking about indigenous issues and getting banned. And I'm thinking of Alcatraz where the radio waves were banned. Indigenous punk rock is talking about issues that the government and Americans do not want to hear like giving the land back, which to Americans is like, "What?" These themes counter the imposed narratives.

Another great indigenous punk band is 1876 from Portland, Oregon. They're Blackfeet and Cheyenne. What they tell me is that in their experience, they play somewhere and it's punk rock and it's all *stick it to the man*. But once they start talking about indigenous themes or white supremacy, people don't want to hear it. Even in the punk rock community it's like, "Hey, you're going too far."

With War is a straight edge hardcore band, and they're talking about Land Back and Missing and Murdered Indigenous Women (MMIW). There's violence and murder against indigenous women and two spirit queer people in Mexico, Canada and America. When Black or Indigenous individuals go missing, it's not the big news story and it gets wiped away. When people are talking about that in their music, some people become allies. And others don't want to hear about it. They want to have a beer and have a good time. That is very unique of indigenous punk and sometimes it gets backlash if it's too radical.

Blackfire and Klee (Benally) was a really big proponent of putting out these ideas even if people in certain spaces don't want to hear it. It is very unique to indigenous punk to discuss these topics. The way indigenous folks are approaching their music and lyrics is very unique and powerful. Some spaces can't fathom them, but that's what punk is for! Punk is to advocate and educate. Indigenous punk rock is about taking care of community. Some punk bands unfortunately are misogynistic and homophobic.

KRISTEN MARTINEZ (Observer Syndrome / Indigenous Punks Archive): Observer Syndrome started in the pandemic, a period where a lot of people had time to create. And there was xenophobia; because of the pandemic you could see how lower-class people are treated and the disparities. It really prompted me and others to make this band and speak about things. One of the bands I'm really inspired by is the Clash because they had lyrics about working-class people and economic disparities. The pandemic was a really hard time, seeing how many people were passing away, left and right. And seeing some people I know going into a depression. It was a dark time. So, that's where some of the lyrics came from. We have a song "Dynamite in the Well" that's talking about empowering people. It's about not just standing by, but living life fully. That's also where the name of the band comes from. Observer Syndrome is when we're all just watching and not doing anything about anything.

KRISTEN MARTINEZ (Observer Syndrome / Indigenous Punks Archive): My family is Mexican and come from the Yaqui people in Sonora, Mexico. They were mistreated by the Mexican government and they're one of the few tribes that are still in Mexico and have sovereignty.

A lot of indigenous people are very punk rock and have dealt with a lot of government abuse. A lot of ideology from indigenous people is in UK anarcho-punk music; grassroots organizing, animal rights, environmental activism and community building. That's a lot of the indigenous ways of life. The bands are really cool and definitely take their ideology and practices from indigeneity.

I grew up Catholic and our family is primarily Catholic. I don't agree with some stuff, especially the abuse. Just look at indigenous communities and the boarding school system. There was an Indian boarding school in Riverside (California). Now it's been changed to an actual school, with indigenous people doing great things with it. But the boarding schools were there to assimilate people. These were all over the United States and Canada. I've seen some of what the Catholic Church has done but I never let go of believing in God. I have my own spirituality. I believe in a higher power and I love mythology. I gravitate toward the spirituality of the ancestral Yaqui culture but they do have a lot of Catholicism in their culture and have incorporated that into their spirituality, ceremonies and festivals. I've gone to see them in Sonora. There is also the spirituality with the Yaqui Deer Dance, which is not maybe accepted by the Catholic Church.

JM: Tell me about where the word *punk* came from originally.

KRISTEN MARTINEZ (Observer Syndrome / Indigenous Punks Archive): I don't want to speak for the Lenape people and it could have been a little ambitious of me, but there is a root word in Lenape—"punkw"—that looks like the word-"punk"—in English. It means "ashes." The word punk has had many meanings and later took on derogatory meanings like *prisoner*. But we got the word from the Lenape people.

YAOTL MAZAHUA (Iconoclast / Aztlan Underground aka Anahuak Underground): The word *punk* is actually a Delaware (Lenape) word that means "ember." When the colonists of the East Coast (United States) started populating the area they were introduced to tobacco, which is commonly medicinal and spiritual. The colonizers that consumed tobacco looked like they had embers in their hands and the Delaware word for "ember" was "punk." The settlers that looked down on the whites that were partaking in this native custom were called "punks" as in outcasts, as the Delawares referred to the whites smoking tobacco.

CLAYSON BENALLY (Blackfire / Sihasin): The punk rock mohawk goes back to the Akwesasne warrior societies that were on the East Coast. Historically, there was a subsidy from the United States government with bounties, even in California. They were subsidizing murder and paying people for the scalp of Indigenous men, women and children. So, some tribes on the Eastern Coast going up into Canada started to have the mohawk style, where they would shave the sides of their head and just keep the center lock of hair. That's part of that spirituality. It's also a way of saying, "Fuck you! You're not going to steal my hair!" It was a way of identifying, "This is resistance."

YAOTL MAZAHUA (Iconoclast / Aztlan Underground aka Anahuak Underground): I am Mazahua People of the Deer of Meso America from my father's side and Tarahumara foot runners from Chihuahua from my mother's side. Lakota spirituality has been a big part of my spirituality as well as Aztec dance practice known as Danza. In indigenous culture, prayer is everyday and I give thanks for my life and send prayers to my family, loved ones, humanity and Mother Earth in need of peace and strength.

Bands like The Stains, Crass, and Discharge inspired us toward self-discovery and, ultimately, spirituality with regards to our indigenous world view. The Stains affirmed we could be brown without shame. Crass, and artists on its label, explored the idea of Mother Earth and decentralization of power and Discharge deconstructed imperial wars. It was positive punk band Southern Death Cult that put me on the path to reconnecting with indigenous culture with songs like "Fatman" and "Moya." It was a Death Cult poster that had my dad question my interest in native symbols. After that, he informed me I was native! This nearly brought me to tears and my path to reconnecting to my roots began. Up until then I had internalized that I was a "wetback" and didn't belong here because I was not white.

Anarchist punk informed me about property is theft, mutual aid and the decentralization of power. All these ideas align with indigenous world views. In fact, anarchism was inspired by indigenous lifeways. Read Jack Weatherford's book *Indian Givers*. The common ground with punk and indigenous culture is that both are at odds with empire and the dominant culture. Both understand that another world is possible and that the dominant culture is a deathstyle disconnected from human connection and respect for all living things. To advocate and recognize all living things, and how we are all connected, is spirituality. The importance of Land Back is that the original caretakers still hold the sacred knowledge of the lands they have resided on for time immemorial and if we do not honor that and return the land to the original caretakers for guidance, then it affects everyone.

JM: I enjoyed hearing you perform on Indigenous People's Day in San Francisco. (October 14, 2024) It was great to hear John Trudell's voice on one of your songs. There's a video where Trudell says, "A religious perception of reality was used to replace a spiritual perception of reality. Because the spiritual sense of reality, you're connected to everything."

YAOTL MAZAHUA (Iconoclast / Aztlan Underground aka Anahuak Underground): Bullseye! Religion inherently indoctrinates judgment against people who do not believe in the respective religion, which was one of the factors driving colonialism. But spirituality is understanding that all living things are interrelated and have a connection to the cosmos. Therefore, God aka creator is not only in the church, mosque or temple, but everywhere. We know that the air we all breathe comes from the same life-giving force, which is tangible as long as you are mindful. But religion is based on dogma and creates tunnel-vision, preventing these understandings. Creator and spirituality is not only tangible, but ever-present and nonjudgmental, because we are creator, too.

KLEE WAS A MODERN-DAY CRAZY HORSE

JM: Any thoughts about the significance of Klee Benally's music, activism and writings?

YAOTL MAZAHUA (Iconoclast / Anahuak Underground): We were blessed to cross paths with Blackfire and Klee Benally in the 90s. I know in the spirit world Klee would not like to hear this but, for us he was a modern-day Crazy Horse or Pontiac, Tupac Amaru or Zapata. He lived his life to the fullest to disrupt the colonial reality. In individual action and collective efforts, he pushed the envelope to confront colonial power. He put his words and music into action. During Covid he practiced mutual aid in his community, critiqued nonprofit funding that perpetuates complacency and produced a decolonial board game—*Burn* *the Fort.* He joined us for an action against caged kids in Adelanto (Immigration Detention Prison in Southern California). We also shared the understanding that anarchism was inspired by native life ways and that direct democracy is part of our heritage. Klee was laser-focused on decolonizing our minds and land. His legacy lives on as his spirit continues to inspire us.

JENEDA BENALLY (Blackfire / Sihasin): My brother Klee was remarkable. Exclamation point, exclamation point, exclamation point! He was incredibly passionate and saw the injustices of the world and the beauty of the world. We can't forget that passionate lens of his life. To have grown up together into this punk rock world—traveling throughout Europe, the squats and punk clubs—was a gift. We're coming up pretty soon on the one year of his passing. (December 30, 2023) Klee knew that his life was not long, as did we. Our brother worked really passionately and fiercely to fulfill some of the dreams he had as a kid. *Burn the Fort* was something he's always wanted to do. When we were kids, we would always create our own games. My brother created *Burn the Fort* because he saw a need of educating people, but also having fun with it, because a lot of people don't know how much fun and silly Klee was! *Burn the Fort* is just as educational, passionate, fierce, silly and strong as my brother Klee. The game is so much a reflection of who he was and who he still is, because I still feel him strongly in this world.

I haven't read his book yet (*No Sacred Surrender*) but every once in a while when I'm looking for some guidance from him, or I'm missing him terribly, I open a page and read it. And it seems to land just where it should. We're still grieving and I don't know that we'll necessarily ever stop grieving the loss of our brother, but he changed the world. For him it was so important to open people's minds and eyes to injustices and then make them hopefully act upon that. It's so much a family teaching of ours that *you are part of the solution.* You're not the complete solution. You are part of the solution.

CLAYSON BENALLY (Blackfire / Sihasin): When he took his last breath his final words were, "No spiritual surrender." That was his truth. I feel that he's still continuing on that fight against injustice and continuing that warrior legacy that our grandmother, Roberta Blackgoat, and all the countless generations that have come before us, stood in defense of our Mother Earth. It's a powerful legacy and it lives on through the music that we created.

JENEDA BENALLY (Blackfire / Sihasin): Klee created tools of resistance to help guide people. He always felt that the burden should never fall on one person. We shouldn't have to have heroes that are out there alone doing the hard work. He would always have these lessons like; step-up-by-stepping-back, allowing others to take that step into leadership. This resistance is a community, a family. When we look at equality, justice and all the different rights that we're struggling for, we're all in this fight together. We can all step forward and share that responsibility. The spiritual movement is one for health, well-being and balance, not just for ourselves but for every living creature.

BERTA BENALLY (Blackfire manager / mother): We're going to fight and resist. We're in for a bumpy ride. (2024: Trump re-elected US president) Klee's life was being a warrior. Everyone should be a warrior, not a sheep. It's a very thin veil right now. Always ask for guidance from your ancestors, and hopefully the message arrives. We don't know what's going to happen next but our world's going to change.

MORNING STAR GALI (Indigenous Justice): I met the Benally family close to twenty years ago when I was living with my family in Flagstaff, Arizona and was aware of their efforts to protect the sacred San Francisco Peaks (Dookó'oslííd). The city of Flagstaff, which borders the Navajo Nation, was proposing to utilize the city's sewage wastewater for an artificial snowmaking process. My mother and stepfather, who is Diné, have lived on the Navajo Nation for over twenty years. As a small child I was very aware of the Big Mountain resistance movement and I would go visit Roberta Blackgoat and the Big Mountain resisters and it really impressed upon me that it was grandmothers that were leading this fight. Roberta held a sign saying, "The only one who's going to move me is the Creator." The history of indigenous resistance was led by the matriarchs.

Blackfire utilized punk rock and indigenous music to share indigenous resistance and history all around the world. I organized a number of shows that featured Blackfire as a headliner and Aztlan Underground, now Anahuak Underground. I became good friends of the Benally family and we did a lot of organizing and grassroots media over twenty years. The mixing of punk rock and indigenous resistance and spirituality always seemed to be a very natural occurrence for me. Especially growing up in the Bay Area, living in Berkeley and attending shows at the Gilman, I understood that the anti-authoritarianism of punk rock and indigenous resistance were very much in alignment with one another. There was always a critique of US capitalism and imperialism. There were values that were very similar in being able to use music—which is very much connected to our spirituality as indigenous peoples—as a way to effectively get our messaging out.

Punk music and culture are very much in alignment with the spirituality of indigenous peoples; it's like a spiritual orchestration. I say, "Every day as a California Indian woman is a fight against invisibility and against erasure." The values within punk culture also very much represented that sense of being outside of the norm, of fighting against being silenced, and of using your message in a way that could be loud but also attract a following of people that were also marginalized and did not fit into the societal norms of American culture.

JOEY RAMONE—TRADITIONAL MEDICINE

CLAYSON BENALLY (Blackfire / Sihasin): The Ramones were very pivotal within our journey. I knew Joey (Ramone) in his later life when the band (Ramones) had come to an end in 1996. Joey Ramone had been diagnosed with lymphoma and he was on the path where he wanted to get well and he came out to be with our family and our father (Jones Benally) did some treatments using traditional medicine that helped him. Because our family has been rooted in spiritual and cultural traditions, we have always been somewhat of a refuge.

Part of the gift that we were raised with is that healing process of being able to identify root causes of illness and using music and tools that we have. I feel blessed as a drummer, through the drum itself. I can help the youth within our community have a better understanding and connection to that beat, to that art that we all have within us. And hopefully use that as a tool to help them on their journey and give them strength and solace and a foundation they can draw upon. I think of music and healing as synonymous.

PATTI PATTEX (Cut My Skin): I was blown away by Klee's voice, the music of Blackfire and especially the lyrics. Indigenous issues were always on my mind. It's frightening how white people assume the right to wipe out indigenous people who are so close to nature, who are our only hope of surviving on this Earth. It's understandable to rebel against this oppression, to fight for survival and to protect the habitats and living spaces that leave room for spirituality and nature. That's what Blackfire and Klee did!

JEFF OTT (Fifteen): Last year (2017) I was working as a nurse practitioner for the Karuk Tribe on the Klamath River south of the Oregon border in a town called Happy Camp, which is three thousand people. They technically had an official government but anybody's grandma could go up to the chairman of the tribal council with whatever their issue was and he'd sit there for five or six hours and talk to them. It wasn't exactly no formal government at all, but the absence of that thing where some people are worth more than others and get more say than others. Small, loosely organized government forces people to participate and therefore it's way more democratic than anything we call democracy. What we call democracy is most people being completely uninvolved on a daily basis. They might be involved one day a year when they vote. These days I'm left with the impression that when you get a group of people that's more than a few thousand, you're starting to deal with too many people to have a formal organization of governance that won't corrupt.

H. PAUL MOON (*Hamac Caziím*, director): I'm drawn to the notion that punk is less of an identifiable musicology or sound, and more of a spirit that accesses timeless practices and customs like religion and ritual. I remember an epiphany moment hearing Hamac Caziím cite their influences from metal bands like Metallica, but then sitting in the edit suite marveling at how their music sounds to my ears like hardcore punk. Maybe living on protected indigenous land, just like stewarding its ecosystem, gives rise to art which authentically and independently transforms influences, within useful limits, compared to the digital jukebox and constant interconnection we feel in urban America. Even if mainstream metal made its way into their mostly isolated world, it jammed with their other primary influence; sacred folk songs. Their organic fusion of those musical styles resulted in a provocative thesis: that punk is really the sound of the sacred, manifested on modern, mostly electric instruments. The music of Hamac Caziím is like a defiant rallying cry for the rising generations of this Comca'ac tribe. Each song has the effect of a war anthem, that they're justified to win. They are not imperialists trying to expand their territory; they are defenders led to battle, armed with anthems.

JM: On *Remain in Light* is the song "Listening Wind." This still just brings chills up my spine. The lyrics bring to mind US colonialism and violence and resistance to that.

JERRY HARRISON (Talking Heads): I agree with you, it's an amazing song. Peter Gabriel does a great version. The song is about the development of thinking of someone perhaps becoming a terrorist. I think maybe we'd be investigated by some part of the government if we wrote that song today! (2024) I don't think it's particular to American colonialism or imperialism. It's the idea of someone being disenfranchised. And that can be the Chinese or the Arabs and lots of countries that have this ability and are doing this all over the world right now. The United States held that particular position in the 50s when so much of the rest of the industrialized world was damaged by World War II. And they made massive mistakes, in my mind.

JM: So many governments have displaced people. Now people all over the world are saying, "We want our land back."

JERRY HARRISON (Talking Heads): The difficult thing is how many generations of land stealing are we going back to? Sometimes there's multiple land seizures. The other thing is that *every place* has seen a clash between indigenous, nomadic people and others who arrive who establish property rights and laws. You look at something like the history of England, and see the establishment of property rights, fences and trespassing. Settlers come in saying, "I own this land" and they're running into grazing societies or societies that had a public commons they shared, and the result almost always is that the ones that have established property rights then become enforceable and dominant. And very often it's indigenous people that lived off the land, usually with less density, that lose out. This obviously happened in the United States. Suddenly, you had these rich landowners and people were forced to work for them. The landowners would say, "You're stealing the wood of the king to build a fire and you can go to jail for this, or be killed." It was ridiculous. That dynamic between nomadic populations and stationary land-owning populations; it's always the stationary land-owning populations that displace the people that were there before, living with another natural system of life. This also goes back to the invention of agriculture. It's just not very much fun to be on the other side of that.

9

"JESUS DIED FOR SOMEBODY'S SINS . . ."—JESUS AND CHRISTIANITY IN PUNK ROCK

He's the preacher on TV / the false sincerity.

—"American Jesus" by Bad Religion (1993)

I'm the son of rage and love / the Jesus of Suburbia.

—"Jesus from Suburbia" by Green Day (2003)

Jesus was a terrorist, enemy of the state / That's what the Romans labelled him / so he was put to death.

—"Jesus Was a Terrorist" by Jello Biafra and No Means No (1991)

Jesus died for somebody's sins, but not mine.

—"Horses" by Patti Smith Group (1975)

JESUS CHRIST SUPERMARKET

The world of punk rock is filled with images and lyrics referring to Jesus and Christianity and the crucifix symbol has been used widely in punk artwork. Crass named their debut album *Stations of the Crass* (1979) and another *Christ—The Album* (1982). Their album cover for *Yes Sir, I Will* (1983) has an

141

interpretive image of the crucifixion of Jesus and the band referenced "the body of Christ" when they established Corpus Christi Records in 1982. In 2010 singer Steve Ignorant performed Crass music in a tour titled *The Last Supper*.

The Dead Kennedys creatively modified the crucifix symbol for the cover of their 1981 album *In God We Trust, Inc.*, as did Killing Joke with their album *Absolute Dissent* (2010). The album cover for *Coral Fang* by The Distillers (2003) has a female body bleeding on the cross and punk artist Raymond Pettibon's cover art for Black Flag's 1984 album *Slip It In* has a nun wearing a cross, holding onto someone's bare leg. Band names like Econochrist, The Crucified, Crucifix, Crucifux and Teenage Jesus and the Jerks all refer to Christianity, obviously. The black-and-white music video for "American Jesus" by Bad Religion has singer Greg Graffin wearing protective goggles as he walks among blindfolded zombie-people chanting in unison, "One nation, under god."

The 1989 Depeche Mode song "Personal Jesus" has been covered by Johnny Cash, Iggy Pop (with Trevor Horn) and Marilyn Manson. Then there's "Big Jesus Trash Can" by The Birthday Party, "Jesus Made Me Feel Guilty" by The Buzzcocks (1979), "Jesus" by Johnette Napolitano and Holly Vincent, "Jesus Was a Communist" by Reagan Youth (1984) and the sardonic "Jesus Is Love" by Tartar Control (2011). To name a few. Have you heard "Irish Catholic Boy" by Seanchi and the Unity Squad? How about "Catholic Day" from a very early Adam and the Ants demo for Decca Records? (1978) Writer Sean Murphy combined Jesus and punk rock in a six-part comic book series titled *Punk Rock Jesus* (Vertigo Comics 2012–2013). Green Day is probably the best-known punk rock band on planet Earth and Jesus has been a subject of some of their songs including "Jesus of Suburbia." Singer Billie Joe Armstrong told Spin Magazine in an October 2005 interview that this is the Green Day song he's most proud of. He added that his biggest regret is not having named the *Insomniac* album *Jesus Christ Supermarket*.

MORE POPULAR THAN JESUS

Years before punk exploded, John Lennon expressed his frustration about the ways that Jesus' teachings had been "twisted" and even predicted the demise of Christianity. Lennon also famously described the Beatles as "more popular than Jesus." Part of a 1966 interview with his journalist friend Maureen Cleave went like this: "Christianity will go. It will vanish and shrink. I needn't argue with that; I'm right and I will be proved right. We're more popular than Jesus now. I don't know which will go first—rock 'n' roll or Christianity. Jesus was all right but his disciples were thick and ordinary. It's them twisting it that ruins it for me." (London Evening Standard, March 4, 1966)

ROBYN HITCHCOCK (The Soft Boys): John Lennon made a casual remark to a British journalist at the beginning of 1966, about how the Beatles were more popular than Jesus. He was a bit gung-ho. Surfing on three years of Beatlemania I guess will do that to you. If you've had that many people trying to get into your car or your bed or your head, you are definitely going to have quite a big idea of your own importance. Six months later, this remark suddenly turned up in the American press: "Lennon says the Beatles are bigger than Jesus! It means he's saying down with Jesus. Jesus sucks." And wham! "We're 'gonna burn their records!" People started burning Beatles records and that was the end for the Beatles as a live act. Now this kind of thing is instant on Twitter or Instagram. So, you 'gotta be careful.

REBEL FOR JESUS

Many punk bands are critical of the great damage that's been done by religious extremism and the ways "God" and "Jesus" have been co-opted by authoritarian systems. Clearly, religious institutions have been core supporters of genocides, slavery and caste systems in places like the United States, Yugoslavia, Germany and India. Indigenous punk bands in the United States like Blackfire, Heart Museum and 1876 remind us that the Catholic Mission system was not carrying forward the loving teachings of Jesus, but advancing violent systems of slavery and murder.

There have been dozens of punk and metal bands on Christian record labels like Tooth and Nail, Blood & Ink and Small Step Records who release music, "written from the Christian faith perspective with messages of hope, love, and restoration." Christian punk is often evangelical, emphasizing personal redemption and salvation through God and promises of an afterlife. The Altar Boys were one of many Christian punk bands that combined this evangelical angle with the rebellion of punk for songs like "Rebel for Jesus" from their 1987 album *Against the Grain.*

> *You're out there telling your friends the good news / All they think about is partying and being cool / You tell them who Jesus is / And they look at you like you're just so out of it.*

—"Rebel for Jesus" by the Altar Boys

Given the social-political awareness of so many punk bands, surprisingly few Christian punk bands have embraced Jesus as a radical critic of militarism (hatred) and capitalism (greed) and as a prophet who saw the potential in everyone to not only shape their personal experience, but also share responsibility in shaping the social-political structures we live within. Bands like Crashdog and Ballydowse stand out as Christian punk bands that have integrated these political and spiritual aspects into their music and lyrics. The Psalters from Philadelphia describe themselves as an "Anarcho-Christian community with homemade world-music," and they support radical activists like Christian Peacemaker Teams. Grrr Records in Chicago releases music by Christian bands like Headnoise and is connected with Jesus People Chicago, an organization established in 1972 for "living together in intentional community and serving the poor." The song "Weapons of Mass Destruction" by Ballydowse begins with an audio clip from a 1996 interview with former (and first female) US Secretary of State Madeline Albright who was asked if killing 500,000 Iraqi children had been worth the price. She answers, "I think that is a very hard choice, but we think the price is worth it."

> *In Mosul in northern Iraq's no fly zone / We saw flocks of sheep which had been blasted to eternity / With the small child shepherds who tended them / No other targets in sight.*

—"Weapons of Mass Destruction" by Ballydowse from
Out of the Fertile Crescent (2000)

> *My God doesn't call His people to judge and kill / My God doesn't need your guns to bring His will.*

—"My God" by Crashdog from *Cashists, Fascists and Other Fungus* 1995

> *From war to war, death and genocide / We've fought for money, power and lies / But the war we fight now rages deep inside / It's God against man / Spiritual suicide.*

—"War" by Headnoise from *No Compromise* (2001)

HORSES—FORTY YEARS OLD

I'm watching Patti Smith and Lenny Kaye perform with their band in Santa Cruz, California. It's January 2016 and forty years since their album *Horses* was released (December 1975) and they're performing the whole album, song by song! The audience of course chants along with Patti during the final words to the song—"Jesus died for somebody's sins, but not mine!" Lenny Kaye then told the appreciative crowd, "The *Horses* album is forty years old but the greatest band out of New York City is *fifty* years old!" The Patti Smith Group then launched into a rousing medley of Velvet Underground songs.

JM: A lot of Crass album art, lyrics and album titles refer to Jesus. Tell me about that.

PENNY RIMBAUD (Crass): It was all very well, Patti Smith saying, "Jesus died for somebody's sins, but not mine." My response was, "Jesus died for his *own* sins. Not mine." I think that's very different. Patti was being moderate or she wasn't thinking hard enough. At that time, I took a great disliking to her because she'd said the wrong thing as a philosopher. I don't judge things by faith or religion, I judge them by philosophy. Philosophy is about intent and is a form of mathematics; there are rules of reason which one tries to turn upside down but not in a surreal way. In a rational way.

Jesus was on a fairly good run until he hung around in Gethsemane. It was shocking bad theater at that time. You could say that the guy was quite cool, sort of on the level of someone like Allen Ginsberg; a prophet with a sense of humor. But Gethsemane was a big mistake. He had the choice. He could've run. He should've got away. It was bad theater. The net result is this crucified, emaciated figure that haunts everyone in the Western world, until they find a way around it. I spent a large amount of my life trying to deconstruct that as a fundamental. That's the nail through the very head of capitalism and materialism as we know it. That was the great schism. I said it in "Reality Asylum." Christ dug the pits of Auschwitz. He created the schism. Well, it's quite possible that it wasn't *he* who created the schism, it was actually Christianity created the schism, under the writings of Paul and the other people who were latter day. Mary Magdalene is completely lost from the picture and she's probably the only one talking any sense at all.

I've got no time for Christianity whatsoever because of the crimes that have been committed in the name of Christ in things like the First World War. That's bad philosophy. Let's not call it a religion, let's call it philosophy. Then it comes home a little bit more. Christianity has been deplorable, from its inception. I tried to deconstruct the whole Christ myth.

I've been writing a thing called, "And He Was Cut Down," a long poem. Which actually is more about Magdalene; why it wasn't that we listened to her rather than to Christ. So, I haven't shed that manacle entirely. It allows for other bad theaters. It almost allows for the Charles Manson conundrum. That guy had a few good things to say. He's a demon, monster, mad hatter and egotistical fool. But he certainly had some good points about society. That was in the earlier days before he was locked up too long with his own thoughts. If ever you could find another Christ figure, it was he. ("And He Was Cut Down," was later released and performed in 2019.)

Figure 9.1 Cover detail of the fifth album from UK anarcho-punk band Crass, Yes Sir, I Will (1983): "Our love of life is total, everything we do is an expression of that." Contributed: Penny Rimbaud / Gee Vaucher.

THE DEVIL'S MUSIC

In his 2009 book *Deflowered: My Life in Pansy Division*, Jon Ginoli mentions a documentary film about Christian rock music titled *Why Should the Devil Have All the Good Music?* (2004) named after the Larry Norman song from his 1972 album *Only Visiting This Planet*. In the opening scene a woman tells the story of how she'd almost committed suicide but instead made her way to a Christian rock concert on July 25, 1980. She was beckoned inside by the lead singer of one of the bands, The Redemption Band, and it's while dancing that she accepts Jesus as her savior. "Spirit is in control of the music," she says. Mark Nicks of the band Cool Hand Luke is interviewed saying, "God writes our songs for us." Dan Sinker, founder and editor of the now-defunct *Punk Planet Magazine*, speaks about the rise of Christian punk and Tom Wisniewski, guitarist with MxPx, talks about how his band started off playing in churches. When musicians and fans are interviewed in the film, they refer to music that is *not* Christian as "secular." Musician and producer Steve Albini (Nirvana, The Pixies, Godspeed You! Black Emperor) discusses the commercialization of Christian punk and offers the view that many bands have been used by the church: "That bugs people," he opines.

The organization Rock for Life is highlighted in the film. Their website says, "Rock for Life is promoting human rights for all people born and pre-born, by engaging the culture through music, education and action. We believe that each and every human being is a person from his or her biological beginning." Their website has photos of "missionaries" who traveled with the 2017 Vans Warped Tour to sell T-shirts with "Adoption Saves Lives" emblazoned on them and to give out pro-life (anti-abortion) literature. Their blog boasts of having had a presence at forty-one concerts in thirty states on the tour. The Rock for Life website lists bands who call themselves pro-life as well as bands who "advocate abortion" and, "donate money or play concerts to raise money for Planned Parenthood, Rock for Choice, Axis of Justice, America Coming Together, Punkvoter.com, Air Traffic Control Project and other pro-choice projects." Some of the bands listed include Against Me!, Alanis Morissette, Bad Religion, Circle Jerks, Dixie Chicks, Fifteen, Good Riddance, Henry Rollins, Laurie Anderson, New Found Glory and Rage Against the Machine.

Christian ideas have been mixed with many types of music: gospel, folk, classical, jazz and rock 'n' roll. There's also a rich history of Christian propaganda *against* rock 'n' roll. Rev. David Noebel wrote a series of books in the 1960s for Christian Crusade Publications that described folk and rock music as a communist plot to, "nerve-jam our children" (*Rhythm Riots and Revolution* pg. 30). Noebel also wrote that the rhythmic roots of rock 'n' roll were from Africa; " . . . where it was used to incite warriors to such a frenzy that by nightfall neighbors were cooked in carnage pots!" (pg. 78)

Terry Watkins from Dial-The-Truth Ministries is the author of *Christian Rock: Blessing or Blasphemy* (website: http://www.av1611.org/crock.html) Watkins criticizes musicians like Amy Grant, Ozzy Osbourne and Nine Inch Nails for having satanic imagery or anti-Jesus elements; "There's no mistaking the new age/satanic influence of the group Earth, Wind and Fire." Watkins, a former rock guitarist turned evangelical Christian, also offers a theory on the origins of the term "rock 'n roll"—"In the early 1950s, Cleveland disc jockey Alan Freed revolutionized the music world . . . . Borrowing a ghetto term for sexual fornication, he coined the term "ROCK N ROLL." The Encyclopedia Britannica Yearbook for 1956 described rock 'n' roll as, "insistent savagery . . . deliberately competing with the artistic ideals of the jungle."

Music is very important in the spiritual life of a child of God.
And the wrong music can spiritually destroy the child of God.

—Terry Watkins (*Christian Rock: Blessing or Blasphemy*)

Today all major record companies are flooding our teenager
with a noise that is basically sexual, unchristian, mentally
unsettling and riot-producing.

—David. A Noebel (*Rhythm, Riots and Revolution*—1966, pg. 79)

Time Magazine reported in the summer of 1956 that rock and roll shows had been banned in New Jersey and Texas after the city of Santa Cruz, California imposed a ban on June 3, 1956, after SCPD Lieutenant Richard Overton shut down a performance by Chuck Higgins and his Orchestra. ("Pachuko Hop") Lt. Overton explained that the audience was, "engaged in suggestive, stimulating and tantalizing motions induced by the provocative rhythms of an all-negro band." Expeditious protests pushed the city manager to remove the ban. ("Authorities Impose Ban on "Rock and Roll" Dances Here" Santa Cruz Sentinel News June 4, 1956)

San Francisco's Brother Karekin goes by the moniker "Punk Monk." His website includes writings described as, "Reflections of an unabashed political and social radical, Christian anarchist, activist, Gen-X poet, and Episcopal Friar" (punkmonksf.com—2018). Brother K writes, "I earned the nickname Punk Monk as the first Gen-X member of the Brotherhood in 1995. This is from my years as a street savvy, anti-autoritarian [*sic*], punk kid who came to religious life with a mohawk and an attitude and a suspicion of my parents' merely cultural Christianity. My work is about trying to live the Gospel." Similarly, Austin Williams started the Underground Church NYC in 2002—"An organization that ministers to Christian punks." It's not unlike Dharma Punx, in applying a punk attitude to an established spiritual realm. A post on the MySpace page for the Underground Church eulogized, "Underground Church NYC is dead. This occurred on September 3, 2006 . . . may God be with you all."

TOTAL PUNK ROCK MOVE

If you saw TSOL perform back in the day, you might be surprised to know that Jack Grisham is Christian. Jack and I spoke at his house in downtown Huntington Beach, just a few blocks from some of the best beaches in the

United States. He tells me that he views Jesus as something of a spiritual anarchist and Jack's emails to me include Bible quotes at the bottom: "Romans 12:2—Adapt yourselves no longer to the pattern of this present world, but let your minds be remade and your whole nature thus transformed. Then you will be able to discern the will of God, and to know what is good, acceptable, and perfect . . . "

JACK GRISHAM (TSOL): I'm Christian-based but I don't know if that's what I should be calling myself anymore. I study and see how best I can serve. That's what meditation comes down to for me. Thinking of others—"How can I apply this to make someone's day easier?" The first sin in Christian mythology was will. If you're based on that, then there will be suffering.

STEVE IGNORANT (Crass): When I was at school I decided, believe it or not, that I was going to be a priest. I wanted to be a missionary and go and help the poor savages in South America and spread the message. But that all got blown out the window because this new religious education teacher came in and said, "Okay, we're going to talk about different religions every week. This week we're talking about Buddhism." I'd been at Dial House at this time and I'd picked up a book called *Zen for the West* and it was little anecdotes and a lot of it made sense. "Leave your bed like you would an old pair of shoes." I was getting into it and I liked that there wasn't really a figurehead; you didn't have to kneel down and pray. And then the religious education teacher said, "Guatama Buddha is said to have lived on one grain of rice a day for seven years. Personally, I find that very hard to believe." I knew this man was a Christian, so I put my hand up and said, "If you find that hard to believe, don't you find it hard to believe that Jesus rose a dead man?" He said, "Sit down and shut up, lad!" I was like, "That's it. Fuck you, it's a load of bullocks!"

I realized when I started flipping through the Bible, there's a lot of incest and child procuring going on there. A lot of pretty nasty stuff. I decided this was not for me anymore, as it says in our song "No Gods No Masters." When we were in Crass, I realized the way we were living, you could actually have called us Christians except there was no Christ figurehead. Until this day, you could say I'm almost a Christian, yet I don't believe in God. It's just not for me. Throughout all of that, what came out of it for me was that I realized that what I was trying to talk about, and trying to deal with, was the loss of innocence. And where's compassion in this world? To this day that's still what I'm talking about. The little tiny bit of Zen Buddhism that I read gave me hope and helped me through a bit. But then of course, at the same time there was David Bowie, so . . . (*big laugh*) It's a pretty good mixture.

RON REYES (Black Flag / Piggy): I walked as a born-again Christian for many years and had a very deep faith in Christ and all of the great things he talked about and showed. But I have huge problems with the church in general. It's been a very long time since I've been to a church. I don't foresee myself being involved in the organized aspect of religion anytime soon. But I learned a lot about peace, compassion, grace and giving and things I probably would not have learned anywhere else. It was a fantastic, life-enriching experience. Those years played a very important part in keeping my family and marriage together. My marriage is twenty-eight years and I've got kids that still live at home and don't hate their parents. That's my crown of glory! I think that played a part.

JM: Is Jesus still important to you?

RON REYES (Black Flag / Piggy): Certainly, the principles of forgiveness, grace, tolerance and sacrificial love—those things, yeah! Of course! Who can't use a little bit more of that? Those things are important to me and I was presented those ideas through Christ. Those principles can be presented to you from other teachings as well. For me, those came through the teachings of Christ. I absolutely do not hold a fundamentalist view of scripture. I think interpretation is very important for anything you read, whether it's the teachings of Bad Religion or the teachings of Christ and the Sermon on the Mount. You need to look at that carefully and not blindly follow anything. Those things are still very dear to me.

JM: Any Christian punk music that you like?

RON REYES (Black Flag): I'm completely unaware. There may be some. To be honest, I don't have much interest in it. Whatever floats your boat. A good buddy of mine in Vancouver has recently joined an Orthodox Church and he's been in bands. He's finding a great sense of inner peace and a way to belong and be a very useful part of society. There are so many good things that can happen with religion. But there's also some stupid, awful shit that can happen.

CHRISTIAN ASPLUND (Brigham Young University—professor): My religion, although it's quite corporate now, was a DIY religion. Joseph Smith made these outrageous claims and created his own book of scripture and got some people together and started a religion. I believe in it, so of course to me it makes perfect sense! It has all these elements that are appealing to me—*do it yourself* and *direct access to the divine* without mediating through a priest or scripture in the way that Protestant or Catholic Christianity do. As a Mormon, I approach my own spirituality in a DIY way. I've been doing sacred music events in my own home— "The Avant Garage." The punk rock ethos has a very virulent dislike of hypocrisy and a love of directness and truth, even if the truth is couched in extreme sarcasm. Those ideas are part of my religion.

GREG GRAFFIN (Bad Religion): As you know, Bad Religion has sung many songs about suffering. The reason I used that spiritual song on *Cold as the Clay* (2006) is almost as an irony, really. Jesus' followers would say, "Suffering down here on Earth is a given, so let's just keep a' following the good word. Let's just have faith." I think more than anything, that song shows the limits of pure spirituality. It shows the limits of religion in that the people are hopeless when it comes to suffering. In the world of science, I don't think that we are *as* hopeless. I think it's a valid life quest to devote yourself to alleviating suffering in the world and through science there are ways we can do it. Through medicines, psychology and drugs we have already proven that we can alleviate suffering. The question is free access to drugs and medicine. To really make a difference globally, we are going to have to figure out how access can be had to technology's greatest prizes. If Jesus was alive today, he would probably be astounded at the remarkable progress of science and I'm sure he would be the first one in line to take antibiotics if his friends were suffering from fevers.

I wouldn't say that I'm opposed in any way to people who use Jesus as a model. Part of the great irony is that modern society doesn't really spend much time studying Jesus' ways or the fundamental tenets of Christian religion. If they did, how could they let starvation occur in their own communities? And that is just one example. The whole issue of retribution is another one; punishment and payback. It is so commonly heard among the born-again Christians; it seems they completely forgot to read the section in the Bible where you turn your other cheek to your enemy after he hits you with one hand.

GLENN WALLIS (Ruin): The radical, anti-military, anti-Capitalist revolutionary Jesus that you and I seem to be attuned to gets crucified anew every time a "Christian" opens his or her mouth. Wouldn't you think that Christian *punks* and *metalheads* would know better! I hear more soulful spirituality, more truthful religion, in a single measure of Black Metal, with its ass-kicking antinomian Satan or wild Dionysian paganism, than in that entire shitload of Christian punk bands. I am probably being unfair here. Musically, Christian punk can be just as driving and thrashing as any other. I am responding to the *ideological* content. I personally dislike improvers of humankind, like evangelicals and gurus. Like you, I would love to hear the radical Jesus channeled through Christian metal and punk.

PRESTON JONES (*Is Belief in God Good, Bad or Irrelevant?*): What happened to Jesus? He got nailed! It's a complicated world. Love is revolutionary but if you really want to put love into practice then you should be ready to pay the price. Gandhi, MLK, Jesus; two were assassinated and Jesus was executed. I believe in the power of love. But if you pursue it there's a high chance that you'll pay a price because there is this war going on.

MARK ANDERSEN (*Dance of Days* / Positive Force DC): I practice within the Christian tradition and my approach to that is, in the best sense of the word, Catholic, which means "universal." To some degree that has meant there is a wide universe of truth out there that we have to encounter and there are different ways to that truth. A lot of us believe in a God who is best described by the word "love." We try to follow someone who so deeply gave himself to Love—capital L—that he literally was crucified, which is an agonizingly painful, torturous death. That was the single most humiliating public abomination that the Roman Empire could devise to try to quell the extremely restive and uncooperative Jewish masses. What we're talking about is a *whole lot of love.* (*laugh*) To quote Led Zeppelin, although probably not quite what they meant.

NORMAN NAWROCKI (Rhythm Activism): We're really grateful to Propagandhi because they put out one of our last albums, *Jesus Was Gay,* on the G7 Welcoming Committee label. That album was so controversial. We were on tour in the United States and asked for extra copies of the album to sell on the road but we'd never get them. They'd be put in the mail and the box would arrive at our tour destination and we'd open it but there were no *Jesus Was Gay* CD's. Inside it were Christian fundamentalist pamphlets telling us that Jesus was going to save us. Somebody at the post office had sabotaged the shipments! This happened to us constantly on the road and we ran out of albums to sell. It's one of those Canadian-American-cross-border-Christian-fundamentalist-rock-and-roll stories.

JM: I didn't know that the post office provided that service!

NORMAN NAWROCKI: (Rhythm Activism): (*laugh*) The disciples of Jesus obviously do! We have a photo of Jesus on the cover smiling. The title song "Jesus Was Gay" went, "Jesus was gay and moved to Alberta—one of those super redneck provinces, like Alabama in the United States—opened up a bar for all his friends, bought a pickup, got a tattoo saying, "love your brother, amen." The story is about a gay man who opens up a bar in a small town. The bar gets attacked. He re-opens and gets attacked again; spray-painted and windows smashed. He continues to re-open and they physically attack him. He physically fights back and then they all become friends and they realize he's okay. That came out in '97.

EXENE CERVENKA (X): Mainstream Christianity is a watered-down version of what was really said. There's solace in that because it kind of mitigates all of that bad stuff that you've heard because you can say, "There was some value in what I learned." But it was also used to manipulate and control. You just have to read through things. It takes a lifetime of studying, meeting people, hanging out. That's the dialogue in the community that you have to seek out so that you can exchange ideas and learn the truth. I think the journey of life is to slay all of your demons and get everything in order before you leave.

I have total respect for Billy (Zoom) as a human being and whatever choices he makes I have respect for it. A lot of my family and friends are Christians, pretty hardcore Christians at that. They are not in any way stereotypical right-wing, people-hating fascists. The Christians I know give Christianity a really good name. It's not the Christianity that I believe in because my Christianity goes back a little further to the Gnostic scriptures, not to the 1600s when King James wrote the Bible. But other people respect that book and that's where they get their religion from, so I respect that. Religion and politics are personal to some extent and don't have to cause conflict among people who disagree. You've got to have respect for other people's beliefs.

JM: I know you made music for Christian films in the 70s and hoped to start a Christian record label. I think you became Christian around the time you started the band X.

BILLY ZOOM (X): I did. Right about the time I met Exene I was becoming Christian. It all happened around the same time.

JM: Being in a punk rock band and becoming Christian can seem like very different realms. Can you tell me about how those were coming into you at the same time?

BILLY ZOOM (X): Like you said, they were coming at the same time and one wasn't necessarily because of the other. I'd been on a spiritual quest of some sort for a while and had studied different philosophies and religions. I was reading a lot and at the same time I was a musician. That's what I did for a living. Christianity seemed to be the philosophy that made sense to me, or the only one that actually did make sense beyond a certain point. Punk rock just seemed to be the new direction. I actually expected it to be a lot bigger! I thought that the Ramones were going to be the next Beatles. I think they should've been, if they hadn't been banned from the radio and ignored by the media.

STEWART EBERSOLE (*Barred for Life*): In the real world, people are really proud of what church you go to. In punk you're really proud of what church you *don't* go to. Punks are good at knowing which religion you *don't* agree with. Now I'm at a point where I don't want to be a nihilist. I want to be part of a group that is doing good instead of separating. I've never been comfortable with separating. It was finally great to take all the things that made sense to me and put them in one constructive framework under the Quaker tradition. It's beautiful. I never would've become a Quaker when I was going to shows. I think I would've been embarrassed to say, "I'm a Quaker. That's my faith."

ROB FISH (108): At one point when we were looking for a drummer, someone brought up a kid who was really an awesome guy. But he was a Christian. It was interesting for me because I thought, "Anytime I talk about things, whether it be in a casual manner or joking around, I always make jokes about Christianity." So, I spent some time talking with him about it. It was weird because I could appreciate how his sense of spirituality played out in his life. I had made Christians my enemy but then realized that that's just as stupid. Here's a guy who actually I can appreciate where he's coming from in respect to his spirituality. Do I agree with it and want to practice it myself? No, not at all. But at the same time, it inspires him. It makes him feel good. He doesn't project the moralistic aspects of it in how he talks to others. That's where most conflict comes into play; where we feel like we've got something that no one else has. We've got to give it to them, whether it be handing it to them in a basket or shoving it down their throat. I've never spent a lot of time reading the Bible. For whatever reasons, Catholicism and Judeo-Christian theology have never sat with me. It's probably not all that different from most religions but they weren't meant to be a dividing point in people's lives. I don't know; some *are* meant to divide out the good and the bad. But at their root I don't think they were like that.

A PRAYER TO THE ALMIGHTY

Awakening is the most important message of punk.

—Goran "Max" Marić (Bjesovi)

It's 1998 and Goran "Max" Marić is leading my friend Cathrine and myself through downtown Belgrade, the capital metropolis of Serbia. We walk past clothing shops, bakeries and restaurants to a nightclub called *Klub Industrija*. Located at the end of a gently inclining tunnel in a natural cavern beneath a downtown café, *Klub Industrija* was opened in 1994 by the same people who four years earlier had established the counterculture radio station B92, which was repeatedly shutdown by authorities. B92 and *Klub Industrija* became home to youth looking for truth and music during wartime. It was a place of refuge. The splitting apart of Yugoslavia and subsequent war left lives turned upside down and everybody I met in the area had been affected by the violence. Max and his girlfriend Bojana were no different. Max had gone from being a singer in the punk-infused band Bjesovi to becoming a priest in the Orthodox Church.

Two years later I visited Belgrade again and when Max introduced me to people as, "my American friend," I found myself on the receiving end of; "Who the fuck is the United States, threatening to bomb us?" It was 1999 and a couple of months later US president Bill Clinton *did* drop bombs on Serbian kids, TV stations and the Chinese embassy in Belgrade. From March to June NATO dropped about 14,000 bombs on Serbian cities in retaliation for the Milosevic government's attacks in Kosovo. I phoned Max and Bojana during the bombing of Belgrade and they told me they'd realized that life was too short. "It's a good time for us to get married. It's maybe now or never," Bojana said. She described the two of them walking down a Belgrade Avenue, dressed in flowing wedding attire and feeling magically happy amidst the broken shards of glass and debris from explosions across the neighborhood.

My body is an empty shell / my eyes are dead lakes / Awake me.

—"Awake Me" by Bjesovi (1994)

GORAN "MAX" MARIĆ (Bjesovi): The song "Awake Me" is like a prayer to the Almighty, to wake us up from the delusion of life in this world. We don't have enough strength to do it by ourselves and we need the ultimate salvation. Awakening is the most important message of punk. We are all so cynical in daily life and often neglect our fellow people. Life is precious and we have to be aware of its sanctity. We should be more careful and caring with each other. Loneliness is the real inferno. If you are not capable of loving others than all your life is wasted. And if you choose the path of love, you have to be ready to pay the full price for that decision. It is much easier to sit at home and watch television than to think about the ways of making your own life, and the lives of others, better. Not one reform can succeed without love and love is the sacrifice. It's not easy, but it's your choice. Punk delivers great ideas in the most appropriate manner. We have witnessed that many times, haven't we?

JM: How did punk fans respond to Bjesovi lyrics about Jesus and compassion?

GORAN "MAX" MARIĆ (Bjesovi): At first, they didn't understand what was going on! Later they evolved and they took the message in. They understood that we, in a way, "baptized" punk. Punk was a vehicle for delivering the message.

JORDAN COOPER (Revelation Records): We made a list on an envelope of names for our record label and one I liked was "Schism." Ray (Cappo) liked the name Revelation Records. He's from a Catholic background and believed in Jesus and all that. I suspect that was one of the reasons he wanted it. Not only could it be positive but it would have religious bonus points, too. I probably *didn't* like it for the exact same reasons. But he played a little trick on me and coerced me into using the name Revelation.

JM: How did Ray coerce you?

JORDAN COOPER (Revelation Records): He was friends with a band called Bold which we ended up putting out. Ray said they'd do the record with us only if the label was called Revelation. I said, "Oh, all right." That was the first time I caved in when I shouldn't have. We even had records done with Schism Records that didn't get used.

ADAM NIGH (Craig's Brother / Thrush / Too Bad Eugene): My relationship with God is very explicitly Christian. My parents are amazing people and I definitely picked up my faith from them. I had something in me that I don't necessarily see in my parents and I don't know where I got it. I know my sister has it but nobody else has it in my family. It's dissatisfaction with the normal answers we got. And really honing in on ultimate questions like; Why are we here? What's our role in life? What's our relationship to the universe? I really pushed for answers to those kinds of things!

The summer before my freshman year of high school I went to a Christian camp outside of Fresno. A lot of Christian preachers do what's called indoctrination. The good ones say, "Here's my paradigm for understanding the world. I give you no intimidation to accept it. Why don't you try it out?" The preacher was saying, "I believe we are being parented, mysteriously so. Just like my five-year-old finds my parenting of him very mysterious. He often has no idea why I'm telling him, or not telling him, certain things. But he knows he's being parented. I believe we are being parented, too."

I HAD AN ENCOUNTER WITH GOD

ADAM NIGH (Craig's Brother / Thrush / Too Bad Eugene): I definitely believe I had an encounter with God. I teach in high school at Monte Vista Christian (Watsonville, California) and my students ask me all the time, "So, do you hear God's voice audibly? Does he write stuff down?" It's a very mysterious thing. I have pursued theology because I want to be able to articulate the things I believe, clearly. But I can't articulate this experience clearly! That's where the music comes in. The experience that you have when you enter into prayer faithfully and feel that you're being heard and spoken back to, not in terms of words but by all of creation. Even when things appear chaotic, I'm being mysteriously parented. Just as my parenting seems chaotic to my son, I know it's intentional.

I felt this echo of a line in scripture; when I pray to God it is just to *be still and know that I am God*. That's almost the key phrase of my entire spirituality. While I think it's rational to believe in God, I still can't prove God's existence. So, at the end of the day I'm still. God is God. My relationship with God is mediated through a sort of music I hear from everything around me, particularly my relationships with the people in my life; friends, enemies, students, teachers, my kids and wife especially. I find the proximate meeting there between myself and others, but I also understand the ultimate meeting where God is speaking to me through those things.

I had some experiences, that I understand as a relationship with God, from the time I was a freshman in high school. I wanted to express this in a couple of ways—one was being able to articulate it precisely, which was kind of the theological side. And wanting to express it poetically in a way that would move people, because I don't think theology tends to move the soul too much. Music was the outlet for that. It all begins from the one passion of the experience of God. There is something they call *process theology*. I always thought God was the same always and there's some theologians saying, "No. God is learning in the process of time." Just that question hurt my head!

ADAM NIGH (Craig's Brother / Thrush / Too Bad Eugene): There's this whole Christian music industry and it's tied in with the country music industry. A lot of the same owners of the records labels are running Nashville stars, both country and Christian. My parents love country music and we get into arguments all the time. I saw that a lot of that music was there to put people to sleep. To turn them off socially so they're filled with the sense, "God's in control. Everything's fine. Go to sleep. The president will make all the right decisions. Be happy." I became convinced that Nashville was killing Jesus. The root for that song ("Theological") was I was having a conversation with a guy and I said, "If Jesus was born today, who would kill him?" I asked it and it was a loaded question. It would not be Jerusalem. It's Nashville.

The anger and loud hatred of some of it (punk) was a hatred of injustice and abuse of people and of the poor. There was an alignment of a lot of 80s punk rock with a lot of Christian ideas, particularly Liberation Theology. This says that God is on the side of the oppressed, the poor. I think those guys were saying the same thing. They weren't doing it in a spiritual way; they weren't talking about God. They were saying "we" were on the side of people who are being screwed over and I think Christians are supposed to say the same thing. That's how I was able to embrace both punk and Christianity.

If some of the Old Testament prophets had lived now, they might have been in punk bands. If you read some of the stuff from Isaiah and Amos, you hear absolute screaming against the social structures of the time and all of the bullshit that was going on. They were saying, "We've got to tear this down!" When you take Jesus out of the Bible he's painted almost as a hippie; "Just love each other!" That's his message and he's absolutely furious with the religious leaders and institutions of his day, which are all about money, greed and power. He's very angry with them!

Who would Jesus be directing anger against today? Probably the same people as punk bands. I remember getting a lot of grief from pastors and Bible teachers in high school for listening to punk rock because they were bashing the church so much. I didn't know how to defend myself. But as time went on and I studied more I thought, "They're only attacking the church where they find hypocrisy." In that vein I think Christ attacks it, too.

I first got really involved in the music scene with Craig's Brother in 1997. We got signed to what was basically a Christian record label, Tooth and Nail Records. They were careful not to call themselves one but we all knew they were a Christian label. We put out our record in '98 and were touring with other bands that were mostly like us; Christian bands who didn't want to be cheesy and say, "Jesus! Jesus!" all the time. They wanted to be a little bit more artistic and spiritually insightful than that. But they were basically Christian, so we weren't getting any flack from them. We never faced anything like persecution (from punks) but I did notice that when our CD came out and it was at Streetlight Records the card behind it said, "Man, these Christians can rock!" It was a little dig in trying to specify what we were. That was probably the worst of it.

As time went on, some of the bands that we played with—notably MxPx—started to get pretty big even among secular bands. I think people were starting to get comfortable with the idea of a Christian punk band. As I was able to leave the Christian ghetto-almost of music and play some regular tours and clubs, I was never shoving it down anybody's throat backstage. I never ran into any kind of opposition. We became friends with MxPx and I heard plenty of stories of them getting a lot of crap from punk bands.

MxPx put out an EP on Fat Wreck Chords and the label had to release this defense for having put out an album by MxPx because they were getting a lot of letters saying, "Why are you putting out this Christian stuff? Are you going back on your stance?"—"No. We like their music. We don't necessarily agree with their spirituality. But who cares?" I thought that was interesting. We heard about it from other bands but we never experienced it much ourselves.

"MxPx meets the same criteria as all of our bands: they make great punk records, have an awesome live show, and are terrific people. This in no way means that we support Christianity or Christian punk. I mean everybody knows Fat Mike is a Jew, how else do you explain his success as an entertainer? Fat Wreck Chords is a label committed to giving back to the punk scene and furthering progressive causes, and we will continue to be so." Fat Mike was more lighthearted, "We got Jews, Japs, Krauts, Queers, Catholics, Capes, Canucks, Muslims, and morons on the label. Why not Christians?"

—May 22, 2001, PunkNews.org

NICK ELDRED (Dun Bin Had): There are a lot of good bands doing stuff that is pro-religion and if people are going to knock them for what they believe, that's ridiculous. You have bands like Leftöver Crack that are pro-atheism. They write a lot of songs that are anti-God. There's a lot of kids that relate to what they're saying. It's against everything that their parents go for. Like back in the 80s when heavy metal came out it's what all the parents were against and that's what became appealing to the kids! If a band is good and they're singing about what they believe in, more power to them! Whether it's anti-spirituality or pro-spirituality. Personally, I've never been real big into church. I've never gone and don't believe in anything like that but I'm not going to knock anybody about their beliefs.

JAKE ELDRED (Dun Bin Had): There's been a lot of bloodshed in the name of religion but I'm not going to be there on stage and preach to people; "Don't believe in this!" I think Christian punk rock shit is just hilarious! A little fun fact: in the Midwest in the Bible Belt, the banks they have out there, if you come out to exactly $6.66 in your transaction they'll actually kick in another quarter because they don't want you to leave with bad mojo. Shit like that is hilarious!

CLIFFORD DINSMORE (Bl'ast / Dusted Angel): The whole Christian punk and Christian metal scene is ludicrous and preposterous. I don't buy it at all. It's ridiculous. It makes my stomach turn. I don't think music should be a format for preaching of any kind. But people can do whatever they want. That's what's awesome about music; it's an individual expression and it allows people to express who they are and what they believe. Some people get more preachy about it than others. That's their deal. It's never been ours.

"JESUS IS PUNK"—CHRISTIAN PUNK IN SOUTHERN CALIFORNIA

THE ALTAR BOYS AND UNDERCOVER

If you want to live eternally / God said pick up your cross and follow me, and then he was crucified / So I can live again.

—"Life Begins at the Cross" by the Altar Boys (1986)

Jesus said he was the only way / And he stands here calling you today / And if you believe (I do) then you shall live.

—"I Am the Resurrection" by Undercover
(1983 album *God Rules*)

Living for Christ is what we do / That's the definition of our hardcore / We don't need drugs or booze / Christian punks we won't lose.

—"Jesus Christ Hardcore" by Officer Negative (1998)

One of the locations that gave rise to both hardcore punk and Christian punk was a part of Southern California called Orange County. It's south of Los Angeles and home to Disneyland, sandy beaches, a towering glass megachurch called The Crystal Cathedral and military weapons manufacturing corporations like Raytheon, Boeing and Lockheed Martin. Commonly referred to as "politically conservative" the area was home to La Casa Pacifica, the "Western White House" where US president Richard Nixon lived after resigning to avoid impeachment in 1974. In 1988 former US president Ronald Reagan gave a speech in the city of Fullerton to support George Bush for president and declared, "Orange County is where the good Republicans go before they die." Trump signs and "Make America Great Again" slogans are common sights there, in California's deep south.

As punk rock and new wave spread in the late 1970s and early 1980s, Los Angeles and Orange County became a breeding ground for new bands like The Weirdos, The Screamers, The Flesh Eaters, Black Randy and the Metrosquad, The Germs, X, Bad Religion, Black Flag, Circle Jerks, TSOL, Agent Orange, Social Distortion, China White, The Alley Cats, The Plugz, Suicidal Tendencies, Adolescents, Descendents, D.I., The Dickies, The Plimsouls, Suburban Lawns, Alice Bag Band, Wall of Voodoo, Minutemen, Fear, The Go-Go's and many more.

In Orange County, Christianity was combined with punk rock in bands like the Altar Boys, Undercover and The Crucified. The merging of punk and the teachings of Jesus later inspired bands like MxPx and Peter 118 and led to JCHC or "Jesus Christ Hard Core," which the band Officer Negative sang about in their 1998 song of that name. Numerous Christian record labels appeared across the punk rock landscape including Tooth and Nail, Blood and Ink and "faith-based" Small Step Records, which began in 2021 with the motto "Love God, Love Others—Listen to Pop Punk." In the 1970's Chuck Smith and his Calvary Chapel in Costa Mesa hosted many "Jesus People" bands from the emerging Contemporary Christian Music scene like singer Larry Norman and the band Love Song. Later they welcomed Christian punk bands like the Altar Boys and Undercover.

CARPENTER OF NAZARETH

JM: How did you come to Christianity, Jesus and punk rock and how did these realms connect for you?

MIKE STAND (The Altar Boys): I always had known about Christianity and went to churches when I was younger. I was a Mormon for a while, believe it or not. But that didn't totally connect with me. Many people that come to Christianity have had a life of drugs and total debauchery. I had my share of struggles but I was never a drug addict or drunkard. I liked girls; who doesn't, right? So, I came from a different point of view.

I came to a point in my life, in 1980, when I was in my early twenties and I realized I had to make a decision. I knew all the information about Jesus and his claims and I said, "I'm going to make a commitment to following Christianity and Christ. I want to see what it is to be a follower of Jesus, the carpenter from Nazareth." That's the way I like to coin it, because when you say you're a Christian, that brings all kinds of stuff with it. So, I wanted to be a follower of that carpenter from Nazareth and thus began that journey.

I'd always been a musician and appreciated those bands that shared the message of Christ through their music. I was a big Hendrix fan and the Beatles, Grand Funk Railroad and garage rock. Loved it all up to Emerson, Lake and Palmer. As my journey with Christ began in 1980, I said, "Where do I go from here? Well, I've got my music. Maybe I have something to say." So, I started a band with my cousins called Image. In March, 1981 I saw a band called The Lifesavors because my brother Kevin was their original drummer. (Kevin Lee Annis) The Lifesavors were Chris Wimber, Mark Krischak and Michael Knott. (Knott founded Christian punk record label Blonde Vinyl and inspired Brendon Ebel, who founded the Tooth and Nail label.)

The Lifesavors were really cool and they were Christians. My brother said, "We're playing Calvary Chapel in Costa Mesa." (Orange County, Southern California) Back in the late 1970s and early 1980s, to play Calvary Chapel Costa Mesa was something huge! If you played there, it was like you hit the big times as far as Christian music goes. I thought, "No way! They've only been together two months. I've been playing two years! We can't even get in there!" The Lifesavors were like the Nirvana or Beatles of Christian music. When I saw the Lifesavors I saw the kids connecting with the music and thought, "I can do that. That's music I understand. And we can do that in church? Wow, have I been missing it!" I thought, "I'm going to try this." There's a documentary being made right now about the Orange County Christian new wave and punk music scene called *Us Kids*. They raised $50,000 and they're done with all the filming.

WHEN YOU'RE A REBEL

MIKE STAND (The Altar Boys): We started the Altar Boys with the intent of sharing the good news of Christ through our music within punk rock. It's about being a rebel. It was a reaction to so many things; hippie music and everyday musicians not having a voice in music. There was a lot of unrest after the Vietnam War and a lot of economic uncertainty. Punk had that message of . . . What's the term I'm looking for? Anarchy! So, we thought we'd do something different than that. Instead of being destructive we'd be rebellious against the world. The Bible says, "Do not be conformed to this world, but be transformed by the renewal of your mind. That by testing, you may discern what is the will of God, that which is good, acceptable and true. Do not conform to the pattern of this world, but be transformed by the renewing of your mind." (Romans 12:2)

We had a song called "When You're a Rebel" and it talked about, "When you're a rebel, they don't understand the things you do / When you're a rebel you got to make a stand / cause we're getting close to the end." We had to say it like it was and proclaim the good news of Christ. We did that using punk rock. I wouldn't say we were *totally* punk rock. We were punk rock in the way that Hüsker Dü or The Replacements were punk rock. Same with The Lifesavors and some of the first Christian punk rock bands like The Crucified and Nobody Special.

We brought that message of Christ and it seems the message connected with kids, particularly here in Orange County (Southern California) where punk rock really took off. Orange County made punk its own thing and the Altar Boys played at a lot of different clubs and college parties. We played at Edison High School and other schools during their lunch hours. Even though we were Christians and our lyrics were very much upfront—very simplistic in a lot of ways, but very profound—we found that although some people did not agree with our message, they liked our music. There wasn't the contempt there is today if you're a Christian. It was a different time. We're talking forty-five years ago with the Altar Boys. Our message connected with a lot of youth. It was one of hope and faith. Instead of partying and drinking all night and throwing up, you could be a rebel against the world and get your life cleaned up and have hope for the future.

We found a lot of people reacted to that message in a very positive way. Many became missionaries. I'm thinking of Dan Kimball, who is a writer. That message resonated deeply with him. There's a book he put out two years ago, *How (not) to Read the Bible.* I read it as much as I read the Bible! It lays out the scripture in a very different way, with the message of Christ going all the way back to the Hebrews. These days I'm playing rockabilly in a band called The Altar Billies and Dan's come down here to see us play. He digs early rockabilly and punk rock, so we stay in touch with each other.

DAN KIMBALL (The Elephant Boys / *Adventures in Churchland: Finding Jesus in the Mess of Organized Religion / How (not) to Read the Bible*): Jesus was punk rock in a way because he was stripping away the layers of what religion had become. He said, "Look at what this has turned into! There is hypocrisy and religious elitism and forced guilt." It was like the punk rock guy coming in and saying, "We have to turn this upside down." That's why I related to Jesus and still do today. Jesus was rebelling against what religion had become. It's the punk rock attitude. It's like the Ramones saying they were tired of some of the big pop-bubble bands. They birthed out of that. Or Malcolm McLaren and The Sex Pistols coming from the New York Dolls. Punk rock was trying to push out what was shallow in surface-types of music. Jesus was punk rock by breaking the shallowness of what religion became at his time.

MIKE STAND (The Altar Boys): I didn't come to Christianity as a punk beforehand. I came as a sinner, a person who didn't have all the answers. I began a journey to find answers that I continue today. As a Christian, some fifty years down the road, I've learned a lot about myself. I know less than I thought I did. I'm still learning how important grace is in the message of Christ, and how this world truly does need hope. I found hope in Jesus and not in religion. Jesus is not religion. As a believer, we don't look at it as religion. Some people may not understand this but the difference in Christianity is that God is reaching down to mankind, whereas—and I'm not saying this to put down other religions—but the tendency of man is to try to reach up and justify himself through rituals. With Christianity and God forgiving us, we receive mercy and grace that, quite frankly, we don't deserve. That's the message we preached with the Altar Boys. We didn't realize the band would make that big of an impact to where, here I am talking with you about it today. (2024) I never would have thought in my wildest dreams that our songs and messages would continue to live on.

JM: Tell me about the connection the Altar Boys had to Calvary Chapel, and if you felt connected to the earlier cutting-edge 1960s Christian music, the "Jesus People" movement.

MIKE STAND (The Altar Boys): I did feel somewhat connected, yes. I understood what they were saying and I appreciated it. I didn't totally absorb it, but I had gone to some of the Calvary Chapel concerts where you just sat and listened. Being the nervous guy, I couldn't sit very long and I had to get up. The music they put out was mellow and they were the founders of taking the laid-back music of early Larry Norman and Love Song and making it relevant. I saw Larry Norman perform several times. At a festival in 1986 in Kentucky, Larry took our band out for lunch. He was very kind and gracious to us.

We did connect with Calvary Chapel Costa Mesa in the 80s, when I started the Altar Boys. We connected with their Ministry Resource Center that would take young artists such as myself and give them different avenues to play and build them up in the ministry. In the early '80s I connected with Bill Valenzuela at Calvary Chapel in the Ministry Resource and he said, "Your music is going to be remembered. I have this profound revelation." I laughed because it was 1981 and I hadn't started the band yet! I said, "What are you talking about?" and he goes, "They're 'gonna remember the music of the Altar Boys fifty years from now." I just laughed at him because I'm thinking, "I'm still looking for a lead singer and a guitar player!" I originally started the band but I didn't even want to sing! I didn't feel I had those gifts to be able to express myself musically. So, kudos to them for encouraging artists and for Love Song and Chuck (Smith).

It was hard for Chuck to back all those early bands. He was in his fifties when those groups came out. Chuck Smith embraced what we were all doing, but he struggled with it and eventually he let us go. I think it was because the music was so aggressive. Those early 70s Christian groups that came before punk like Larry Norman and the Love Song; it was pretty mellow, laid-back, easy and listenable. Chuck (Smith) did his best to embrace what we were doing but I think it wound up being a little bit too much for him. God bless him.

I don't know if you saw the movie about Greg Laurie, Chuck Smith and Calvary Chapel but it was a stretch for Chuck. (*Jesus Revolution*— 2023) God bless him for saying that there's other ways besides hymns to reach people and share the good news of Christ.

I've never been proselytizing as much as just sharing the truth. I may not have a perfect understanding; I don't think any of us do. But I'm convinced of the message of Christ. It's true and I've seen miracles in my life and other people's lives. The Altar Boys have been so important in my life, and still are to so many people. I'll always be forever grateful for the platform I've been given, which wasn't expected.

JM: A lot of punk rock is anti-organized religion with lyrics about changing social and political systems. In the 80s, there was really that sense that a nuclear war could happen at any time and a lot of punk rock artists were expressing that angst. What was your relationship like with other punk bands who were not Christian, who were singing more about politics? Was there tension?

MIKE STAND (The Altar Boys): We weren't there to create any tension. The message of Christ creates enough tension on its own! It's really the antithesis of what punk rock was saying. You've got punk rock with anarchy and, "The end is near and who gives a crap?" In a lot of ways punk rock was, "Live fast, die young, because tomorrow's not going to happen." We thought it was better to rebel against the world and take all that angst and put it into hope. When we interacted with other bands, we tried to be gracious, because everyone deserves that. We never argued with other bands. It was a time where, if you had a different message and you were doing something different, in punk music that was okay. Maybe our message wasn't the same as theirs, but there never was angst or contempt against us. "We don't agree with you. But we like you guys and your music." That's the way it worked for us.

JM: How is it that so much violence occurs in the name of Jesus, Islam and Judaism? We see this now (2024) again in one of the religious centers on the planet, the Middle East. I wonder if you have any ideas about how this religious violence happens?

MIKE STAND (The Altar Boys): The fall of man is awful. The fall of man created literally hell on Earth. And this goes for the Christian religion, the Jews and the Hebrews back to Adam and Eve when they chose to say, "We don't need you, God. We can do this on our own." That separated us from God. Dan Kimball uses an atom bomb as a metaphor for this; that a huge bomb exploded on mankind. When an atom bomb explodes, what do you have? You have radioactive pollution and that radioactivity has stayed with mankind. God had a plan to deal with that, and the only way that plan could happen is through Jesus, God himself. Because that's what Jesus claimed to be. We've got to remember that's what makes Christianity different. Christianity says God Himself had to come down and he paid the ultimate price. Whether you believe that or not, it's another thing.

Islam and all major religions believe Jesus lived. And they all have their different take. But according to the word he said, "I'm God and the only way we can get out of this mess is that I have to die for mankind." But still, that radioactivity continues with us today. Man's imperfect. That's what's difficult. I find myself still struggling, doing things that I should know better, being a Christian for so long. So, if I struggle . . . I can't imagine how another person gets through this life.

Jesus did address people doing (violent) things in his name and somehow justifying it. He said, "They're going to come on the last day and they're going to say, "Lord, here we are." And he said, "I didn't know you. I know there's people that are of my sheep and if you're of my sheep, you're going to bear good fruit." He did address that there will be false prophets and people that come in His Name who will do horrible things. I'm not justifying all the horrendous things that mankind has done, but it was addressed. The Bible says even those that know the truth barely make it into heaven.

I'm not a Bible scholar but I do know what Jesus said. There will be many that do miracles and different things in his name. He said, "Depart from me if I never knew you because you didn't bear the fruit." There are many things going on in our lives that aren't good, yet Christians build churches and hospitals. Some of the first colleges were built by Christians, like Harvard and these huge colleges in the East that the Quakers built. We forget the great Christians like Isaac Newton and Johann Sebastian Bach. We're believers. I don't think anybody can explain why certain things are done in God's name. It's horrible, and

I just have to shake my head sometimes. I'm just thankful about what my life is, and that's where I am right now.

> *Look at what they're teaching in our schools today / Evolution's*
> *a fact / Creation's a dream /Well, I question it!*

—"I Question It" by the Altar Boys (*Gut Level Music* 1986)

JM: A lot of punk bands in the '80's sang about sociopolitical issues like war, poverty, racism and pollution. Did you address some of these issues in Altar Boys lyrics?

MIKE STAND (The Altar Boys): Yes. I did a song called "I Question It" on the GLM record (*Gut Level Music*—1986) where I talked about injustice. But if you go too far outside, then you're missing the point on the message of Christianity. So, you have to be prudent about it. At the time Jesus came, Rome had conquered Israel and they believed that when the Messiah came, he was going to overthrow the government by political means. That's what many of the apostles were hoping for. And it didn't happen the way they hoped. Many of the apostles were hoping he was going to establish heaven on Earth. "Alright! This is the Messiah!" But he raised Lazarus from the dead and he was healing people and that wasn't the way it's supposed to be. Jesus said, "No, I have to die."

I equally look around this world and wonder, "Why do we have so many homeless people? Why are things so expensive?" I've been a music teacher in a school in Santa Ana (Southern California) for thirty years. I see about seven hundred kids a week and I'm wondering if these kids will ever be able to afford a home or place to live.

There's so much injustice that it's hard to reconcile it in our minds. As Christians we have to stay focused on the fact that social injustice and loneliness are horrible, but that Christ is the answer. Even Jesus said, "The poor, you'll always have among you." Not meaning, "Too bad." But meaning, "I won't be here all the time and you need to address that." In fact, it talks about our fruits of giving to the poor in his name, but doing that not because we're justified by some good works, but because that's the fruit of being a Christian. So, when we call for these things it's not for social justice in and of itself, as much as this is injustice biblically. There is injustice that we have to address as followers. But if we go too far in that direction, then the message of Christ gets hijacked where social justice, in and of itself, is great. It's enough if you adhere to the message and teachings of Jesus. You may disagree, but I'm just telling you where I am. And Dan (Kimball) would back me on that!

DAN KIMBALL (The Elephant Boys / *Adventures in Churchland: Finding Jesus in the Mess of Organized Religion*): A lot of criticisms about the church are valid. But generally, the criticisms aren't about the kind of churches that I believe Jesus meant to exist. I had to get passed some of my surface impressions about the weird stuff about church. That's why the Bible is so important. Not what *might be said* in some churches or in the news, but what does it say in the Bible? Christianity gets a bad rap for teaching the Bible as the *only* way but if you explore most other faiths, they'd say the same about themselves. If I said, "He's the one way to salvation," you'd have to know what *salvation* means. If something has changed your life so much and you put your faith in Jesus and believe that there's one God, you can't help but want to share that with others. It's because you care about others.

That's a whole different vibe than going outside the HP Pavilion (San Jose, California) in an impersonal way with loudspeakers just blasting people. We went to see Barry Manilow. I have two ten-year-old daughters, and it was really fascinating. Outside, there were Christians yelling at people and I said, "We're going to see Barry Manilow! Leave us alone!" I think they're doing more damage than helping. Everyone in line is thinking, "There's those crazy Christians again!" But it's about love. If you care about something then you can't help but let other people know.

> *I can say with confidence that we can intelligently, and with faith, believe that the Scriptures are from God.*
>
> —*How (not) to Read the Bible: Making Sense of the Anti-women, Anti-science, Pro-violence, Pro-slavery and other Crazy-Sounding Parts of Scripture* by Dan Kimball (Zondervan, 2020—page 9)

DAN KIMBALL (The Elephant Boys / *How (not) to Read the Bible*): My entry into the church and spirituality came when I was at Colorado State University. I didn't have a bottom-out experience. I wasn't addicted to some drug and needed God. It was more of an intellectual quest. This was while I was in the band (The Elephant Boys) and studying different religions. When I moved to England, I met an eighty-three-year-old pastor and began understanding the Christian faith. When I moved back to the States, I attended an evangelical church.

JM: You wrote in your book *Adventures in Churchland*: "Every time the band played somewhere, I took a gym bag containing my drum sticks, a towel, my hair gel, a couple of cans of beer and my little brown Bible."

DAN KIMBALL (The Elephant Boys / *How (not) to Read the Bible*): Being in the band made me not defensive but offensive, and think more about Christianity. It caused me to not just take things at a surface level about the Christian faith. Actually, some of my friends were concerned about me; "Why are you reading this Christian stuff? Christians are homogeneous, lose their creativity and are brainwashed." I'm very thankful for that because it reminded me that I never want to fall into that. It reminds me to think, "Is this true?" They were doing it out of care and not out of confrontation. The Sex Pistols were important to me because they were so fresh. I loved their style and their visuals. It was a little disillusioning learning that it was all planned! But their music spoke to me—"Don't be satisfied with normality! Always be thinking, is this truth?" That's why I think that Jesus was a punk rocker way back then; he also asked these questions.

PUNKS IN CHURCHES—ORANGE COUNTY TO EAST BERLIN

JM: It's so interesting to me that during the '80s when you and the Altar Boys were playing in churches in Southern California, halfway around the world in East Berlin, behind the Berlin Wall, there were also punk rock bands playing in churches. In that authoritarian society, churches retained some autonomy and some, like Zionskirche, became sanctuaries for youth and punks to discuss political issues, have concerts and print opposition literature.

MIKE STAND (The Altar Boys): Wow! I didn't know that about those bands in East Berlin. The churches were giving them a place to play; I think that's wonderful. That's the way it should be. You're always going to have some conflict with certain churches. They did with us, but we were pretty much embraced by most of the churches because we tried to be transparent with the message and we had accountability with some elders. We could get a lot of pushback, just like some other bands did. But if we did, we were oblivious to it because we were so busy. We were playing ten to twelve times a month and recording albums in between. It was crazy. I don't know where I got the energy, because I don't have it today! (2024) The East Berlin punk and church story is worth a book in itself!

Here we are in America where we have freedom, where in Russia and some places you're executed for your beliefs. Christianity is now the most oppressed religion in the world. I don't know if you're aware of that. In China you're put away forever and they have these underground churches and people are literally putting their lives on the line. Here in America, the discourse has changed, but it's certainly not like other parts of the world.

JM: My family moved to Orange County when I was seventeen, in 1979, when punk rock was *the* vibrant music happening. We all loved KROQ. And then punk rock concerts started to become violent, like gang fights. There were kids wearing swastikas and often people were hurt. How did you maneuver within that Orange County punk violence?

MIKE STAND (The Altar Boys): At first, when I saw the violence at shows I was like, "Wow, what's going on out there?" At the shows at churches that didn't happen as much. We played church one weekend, a club the next, and a college party and high school the next. But during a show I'd just say, "Stop doing that." I would call them out. After a while, I got upset: "We're not here to kill each other. We want you to have a good time, but we don't want to see kids getting hurt." There's a line there, and usually they would stop. I didn't let things get out of control.

At first, I wasn't quite sure what to do about it, but we talked and decided, "We can't let this happen. They want to bounce around a bit, that's okay. But as soon as it gets out of hand . . . " We didn't specifically point people out but just, "Let's be cool here. We're not here for violence." And that took care of it, or there were people in the crowd that would pull these people to the side. I have no big regrets about someone getting bashed over the head with a beer bottle or slashed. I'm grateful for that. I know some kids got hurt, but not too much. We addressed that early on saying, "This is not our message. It's not what this is about. Yes, it's fast, loud and furious and it's in your face. But you 'gotta maintain here!"

KEITH MORRIS (Black Flag / Off!): Because of the energy of the music we played, and where we came from, we were the ones accused of bringing that into punk. I'm speaking of Black Flag, which was a bunch of hairy-Hodad-surfer-wannabe-skateboard-riding-goofballs from the beach. We were surrounded by athleticism with a certain mentality that was, "Go for it!"

UNDERCOVER—GENUINE YOUTH REVOLUTION

JOSEPH OJO TAYLOR (Undercover): We did get a lot of support from Calvary Chapel as long as you didn't get too far out doctrinally or you didn't get too crazy. There was a legitimate huge revolution among Christian teenagers. They could finally lay claim to styles of music, whether it was Undercover or anyone else. In a lot of ways, we happened to meet the right people at the right time. It was a genuine youth revolution: "I don't have to dress conservatively or listen to Amy Grant!"

As much as I love Amy, that was about as wild as Christian music was allowed to get until that punk scene broke out.

Another angle would've said, "Is this punk rock?"—"No, it's not." Even if you want to look at some of the groups that could mimic punk music—the drums, guitar and speed and look on stage—in the final analysis, Undercover was very conservative and establishment. It didn't come from punk rock organically. I'm not sure how to make sense of all of that. It's a world of contradictions and dichotomies and I'm not sure I still can make a hundred percent sense of it.

We bought into it hook, line and sinker. It was the whole Calvary Chapel thing. Even from the very beginning there were parts of it that didn't make sense. My faith died by a thousand paper cuts; little by little it eroded. But at first, we believed all that stuff. If you look at our first three records, they're pretty evangelical and fundamentalist. During the making of our third, I'd already started moving away from that, though it doesn't show up in the music. For a long time, I thought we had a partner in Calvary Chapel and then I realized that we really didn't.

JM: Back in the '80s, Chuck Smith and Calvary Chapel were teaching that the rapture was going to happen no later than 1988. What needs were met for you by believing that?

JOSEPH OJO TAYLOR (Undercover): That's a good one. You could look at Jesus and say he was punk rock, going into a temple and overturning money changers tables! You're talking about getting into the Pharisees and going face-to-face with the high priests and the governor of Judaea, Pontius Pilate. There's a lot in that story that's pretty consistent with that anti-authoritarian, anti-establishment mindset. I admit, and I do this with my head down a little bit, that to some degree we were utilized by the church. We were utilized. Some of what we did artistically was utilitarian. It wasn't until our third album that I decided that it was enough of that and took a whole different direction.

JOSEPH OJO TAYLOR (Undercover): I was born and raised a Roman Catholic. My mother was Italian so I was an altar boy and we had to learn our parts in Latin. I was too young to think about some of the basic issues that the church struggles with today—women's rights, sexuality, reproductive rights, much less the later scandals. (sexual abuse by priests) At the time it was a really rich sensual experience. By sensual I'm talking about the music and incense; the smell of walking into a cathedral that is one hundred years old. When I finally went to Europe, I was inside churches that were thousands of years old. It's almost a bombardment of the senses. You couple that together with the redemptive story of Christianity; it's a very powerful mythology. I don't mean that in a pejorative way. I responded to the artistic representations of that powerful story as a kid.

The older I got, toward the end of high school, I started thinking about some of the issues and it didn't make much sense. I ended up ditching the Catholic Church altogether. For a while I probably ditched Christian doctrine, too. I came back to it through Calvary Chapel. My mother's brother told me they were having concerts down there and I was a musician and I might like to check it out. So, I went and I responded culturally. There were people my age and they were excited about their beliefs and it was a much looser religious experience than I was used to in a traditional Catholic Church.

JM: Do you think there is an intelligent being or force that oversees the universe? What's your thinking about this now compared to 1980?

JOSEPH OJO TAYLOR (Undercover): There might be something out there but I don't know and no one else does either. As imperfect as it might be, the best way we have to know the world is through science and rational discourse. I have no problem labeling myself a free thinker and I define that like the *Freedom from Religion Foundation* does, where I'm really interested in the truth claims of religion more than anything else. Not whether God is real, but you can back into that by looking at the truth claims that religion makes. A lot of those claims can either be rejected outright or held onto. I defer to science in terms of what we know about the universe. It's even stranger than we can possibly imagine! Is there something behind it? My vote on that would be so meaningless and such a small voice.

I'm reading Walter Isaacson's biography on Einstein, again. (*Einstein: His Life and Universe*—2007) The universe is a fascinating place and I'm looking at what he said about it and his own metaphysics and what has been discovered since. I do defer to Thomas Huxley and the quote I love from him is, "Trust a witness in all matters in which neither his self-interest, passion, prejudices nor the love of the marvelous is strongly concerned." The next sentence carries the day, "Where they are involved, require corroborative evidence in exact proportion to the contravention of probability by the thing testified." When he says, "testified" those are the truth claims I'm talking about which religions make all the time.

I'm often accused of arrogance. People put words in my mouth. They say, "You don't believe in God. You hate God." It all boils down to this: all the religions of the world make an awful lot of truth claims that I'm requiring, "corroborative evidence in exact proportion to the contravention of probability." And until anyone's got that, I do the best I can with what I know. I don't think anyone can rule out the existence of God but as Victor Stenger said (*God: The*

Failed Hypothesis—2008, Promotheus Books), you absolutely can rule out certain versions of God simply based on their truth claims. I ruled out the evangelical God a long time ago. It was a painful and long journey.

JM: Was it painful because you lost community?

JOSEPH OJO TAYLOR (Undercover): Not so much. From the time of our last album in '94 up until the time I resurfaced on social media on Facebook and Twitter around 2007, I wasn't getting a whole lot of phone calls from fans wondering how my journey was going. All of a sudden, everyone is now *wildly* interested. I think the only reason they're wildly interested is because I'm in a different place than I was then, and I've got something to say about it.

JM: Are there Christian punk bands that you appreciate now?

JOSEPH OJO TAYLOR (Undercover): Yes. A lot of my Christian musician friends are excellent musicians. I appreciate them on that level. I don't listen to punk rock anymore to tell you the truth, because I've been there and done that. My Christian musician friends fall into one of two camps: either they're still trying to do a Christian music thing, to sell things to a Christian audience. And then there's a group of Christian friends that are trying to free themselves from any kind of Christian marketplace. It's interesting to me that a lot of the ones that are still having to market to a Christian marketplace have almost completely lost any sense of prophetic or angry voice at all because they can't afford to. Nothing is further from punk rock than that! They've got to pay the rent and put food on the table; "I really can't speak my mind. I can't take a stand on the social issues of the day."

Here we are in the midst (2015) of this wild thing in Kentucky and the Supreme Court ruling on same-sex marriage and the only voices that I hear are from people that have nothing to lose by saying so. That's disillusioning. A lot of them are saying, "I don't want to get involved. That's not what my music is about. I just want to write good songs. I don't want to be controversial and rock the boat." When you talk specifically about Christian punk musicians, they've gone totally the other way. They are completely toothless, other than to dig into their fundamentalism.

JM: Have you ever heard of Christian punk bands singing about Jesus as a political person, with anti-war messages, challenging authoritarianism and advocating social change?

JOSEPH OJO TAYLOR (Undercover): No. It would be unfair to interpret the lyrics of early groups like ours as such, in light of where Christian music has gone since then. It was hard for the Catholic Church to allow even acoustic guitars in their church! And then the Protestant Church would have bands dressed the way they were and playing guitars and drums. One sacrifice we chose to make; if we were going to work alongside the church then we knew that the lyrics and songs had to have some kind of purity. A lot of pastors said to us, "I can't get behind the way you guys look and sound. But I can't argue with your lyrics." We heard that a lot. I don't think a Christian band playing aggressive music that was talking more about social justice than religious issues could find a place inside the church. There were bands like that, like U2 and the Alarm.

I never really considered us a punk band. I can't even say that I came from that sociology. I never considered myself a punk activist except in the sense that we were overturning young Christian experience. We had to be staged because, to get the church's imprimatur, we had to be safe. But there were bands after us that took it much further. Look up Mark Salomon from The Crucified. They were the real deal when punk came into its own within Christian music.

NEW TESTAMENT

C. J. RAMONE (The Ramones): I grew up very Catholic. I went to Catholic schools and mass every Sunday when I was a kid. The thing that really helped me see the world in the way that I do is that I read the New Testament when I was a kid. Without prompting from anybody, I just became interested. I got a message from it that resonated really deep within me. I got an understanding of the world and what it means to be alive. It's a message I've carried with me my whole life. I don't profess to be a good person or even a good Catholic! (*laugh*) I try my best. But that has been my guide.

Along the way I've studied all different religions and I look for the common message. Every religion does seem to have the same message but people use the message to get power and money. They bend things and twist it and make it into something different and they get people to follow them and it turns into something bad. Then people end up hating that religion because of what it's become.

All I can say is that I'm the person I am, because I got the message. And I didn't worry about all the stuff that men invented—I just listened for the message in the words. Anyone can say, "But all the words were created by man." My response is, "If what is in the Bible was not handed down from anywhere else, and it's completely the creation of men, it was created by men who were intensely knowledgeable about existence, and they tried to pass a message to us to help us survive." So, whether you want to believe it came from God or that a bunch of old guys got together and made it up . . .

C. J. RAMONE (The Ramones): People say, "Religion was created to control people." I look at it way more like a survival handbook. The control that people think that it's trying to exercise did not come through the message that I got at all. And I've done some really crappy things that I regret. I hurt people and I hurt myself—everything that everybody else does, I have definitely done. But the cool thing about having got the message when I was young is that you have to be able to forgive yourself and find your way back to walking on that good path again. I always come back to it and work hard to get myself straightened up. I've been a good dad to my kids and good to my friends and family.

I've tried to share some of what I know with the fans, people who come to my shows and buy my records. I try to help people understand that regardless of who you are or where you live—you're important. You have an opportunity to do something with your life if you can shake off all the stuff that the world tries to put on you and if you follow your own path. Unfortunately, that doesn't come from many places anymore. Everybody wants you to think you're just another cog, "We're under somebody's thumb." If you live under the illusion that someone else is controlling you and you don't have the freedom to think or do what you want, then you're resigning yourself to a life of exactly what they're talking about and that's *slavery*. You're just a slave to everything around you! You're letting your environment control you and that's one thing I've fought hard to not let that happen to me.

Right now (2018) being Catholic or Christian in punk rock, or music in general, is not popular. Once you label something there is an expectation and you're limiting who you're going to play to. I'm a message guy and it doesn't matter where the message comes from—Jewish, Catholic, Muslim, Buddhist—every religion has the same message. It really does! But people get so caught up in the ceremonies and books—all the manmade stuff—that they completely miss the message. It's super frustrating as I travel the world and see that everybody wants the same basic things in their lives. Everybody wants to live somewhat free. They want to be able to express themselves, feed their kids, live with a modicum of comfort. Everyone's needs are so simple and similar. But it seems we're so distracted with all this other garbage that it gets in the way of moving past where we've been for a couple of centuries. So, I'm not really big in labeling music Christian this or Catholic that.

11

CHURCH FROM BELOW
KIRCHE VON UNTEN (KVU)
EAST GERMAN PUNKS/ZIONSKIRCHE

*Our big concern was; there's an enemy against youth in the
GDR, so we have to change the society.*

—Dirk Moldt (*Kleine Prenzlauer Berg Geschichte* / Fatale)

*When the better-known bands started to play, the church
exploded as the punks, packed into the sanctuary, started to
hurl themselves around and pogo up and down in a writhing
mass of black.*

—*Burning Down the Haus* by Tim Mohr (page 115)
describing the first concert by East German
punk band Namenlos on April 30, 1983
at Christus Church, Halle

*Berlin, Church of the Saviour, The Blues Masses; word got
around that we punks could play there, too.*

—Mita Schamal speaking about June 24, 1983
Namenlos concert at Erlöserkirche, East Berlin
(2006 documentary *OstPunk! Too Much Future* directed
by Carsten Fiebeler and Michael Boehlke)

*It might seem strange that the Ramones Museum is in Berlin
and not New York, but upon closer inspection, it makes sense.
Nowhere has punk burrowed deeper into the socio-cultural
woodwork than in Germany.*

—*Culture from the Slums: Punk Rock in East and
West Germany* by Jeff Hayton

In the 1980s Christian punk was taking shape in evangelical churches in Southern California with bands like the Altar Boys and Undercover, while halfway around the world behind the Berlin Wall in East Germany (DDR / GDR) some Protestant churches were offering critical support to punks and activists agitating against the authoritarian culture and struggling for liberation. East German punk bands like Namenlos, Planlos, Feeling B, Die Firma, Schleim-Keim and Antitrott sang out against the police state and West German bands like Die Toten Hosen snuck into East Berlin for clandestine concerts with help from people like Mark Reeder. One opposition group that coordinated meetings and punk concerts in the DDR was Kirche von Unten (KvU), translated into English as either Church from Below or Church from Under. In recent years this history has garnered more attention in articles, academic writings and books by historian Dirk Moldt and others. Paul Hockenos writes in his 2017 book *Berlin Calling: A Story of Anarchy, Music, the Wall and the Birth of the New Berlin* that the relationship between East German punks and churches played a major role in overthrowing communism there and bringing down the Berlin Wall.

*"Punks are not normally associated with Christian churches.
In fact, the image many people have of punks seems antithetical
to Christian religious beliefs. Although it may sound strange
at first, there was an important relationship that developed
between the punk subculture and the Protestant churches in
East Germany. This relationship was complicated, and there
were tensions between the groups at times."*—*"Punks in the
Church: The Relationship Between the Punk Subculture and
Church in East Germany" by Ruth A. Aardsma Benton (Master's Thesis 2018—Western Michigan University)*

In 2022 Andrew Hanna wrote a Master of Arts thesis in Security Studies at the Naval Postgraduate School in Monterey, California titled "Punk Rock's Impact on the Fall of Communism in East Germany" that concluded: "Understanding the impacts that music cultures have on social movements is relevant in today's global security environment." He compared the 1980s punk movement in East Germany to Black Lives Matter activism in the United States: "Much like the GDR punks in the late 1980s, this movement continues to protest and fight for political change across the United States." (page 72) Hanna also wrote:

> *"The (East German punk) movement needed to find sanctu-ary in response to the party-state's harsh attacks. Thus, punks retreated to the protestant church. Not for religion, but for protection . . . The church became the new center of gravity for the punk movement." (page 62)*

ISLANDS INSIDE COMMUNISM: CHURCHES

DIRK MOLDT (*Kleine Prenzlauer Berg Geschichte* / Fatale): There's a pre-history to the relationship between churches and punks in the DDR, starting in the 1970s. The big churches were empty and people came only at Christmas or Easter. In the middle of the communist system, it was a question of survival. This is why the church started slowly to be a bit experimental. People who went to church for prayer were also citizens of the DDR, with fears and hopes. Many people were searching for freedom. Even long-haired fans of Blues and rock music asked to make an education, or for a job, in the church. It was like an island in the middle of the communist society and people were looking for friends.

Often, young people came to the church and asked for a free room to have discussions because they were not allowed into the state youth clubs or pubs. When you wanted to refuse the army, such questions were not allowed officially because the army was required for all men in the DDR. People also had ques-tions about the environment and human rights and you couldn't speak freely in government youth clubs. Other young people wanted a room for hanging out in their free time. For punks and young people, it's necessary to hang around and talk bloody shit! Others asked the church for rooms to use as a small theater.

There were a lot of reasons for young East German people to contact the churches. It was *not* normal that the church then said, "Okay, come in." The churches were *not* politically radical. Only a very small part of the church was interested in youth and people on the street; maybe five or ten percent. We had a lot of experiences when the churches said to youth, "No, you don't believe in God. You're not part of the church. Stay outside." That was the majority. So, it's absolutely false to say that the Evangelic Church was friendly to the oppositional groups. But the churches in the DDR were the only institution with a democratic structure. When church decisions were made, the state security tried to influence them but the decisions were really made in a democratic process.

HARALD HAUSWALD (GDR photographer): You have to explain to people from the West that it was normal for concerts to take place in churches in East Berlin. Church halls were the only possibility for punk bands to perform because everything was controlled by the state. In the Zionskirche there was an Umweltbibliothek (Environmental Library) where literature was collected which was banned in the GDR. Posters were also produced to draw attention to environmental pollution or other grievances in the GDR.

DIRK MOLDT (Fatale): In about 1980 came the first punks to ask the churches, "Do you have a free room?" The punks were young, wild and relatively destructive because their orientation was *planless*. They were absolutely frustrated and knew only their own way and their own music and the state defeated them absolutely hard. Pfingstkirche in Friedrichshain, East Berlin became a point to meet and Bernd Schröder and his successor Lorenz Postler became real friends to the punks for years. In 1983, the state helped this church to close out the punks because of the noise and rubbish. The punks have their own world and the church could not understand this world! Then the punks searched to find a new place, and they found one in March, 1983 in the Erlöserkirche (Alösa) in the Pro-Fi-Keller, a cellar.

SILKE AHRENS (Kirche von Unten): Erlöserkirche (Savior Church) was written by the punk community as "Alösa." The "er" sounds similar to a German "a" so the first "A" was then capitalized and put in a circle, the sign for anarchism or antifa. The punks from the Erlöserkirche (Savior Church) thus were called "Alösa-punks." The "Alösa" fanzine was produced by punks in East Berlin in the so-called "Pro-Fi-Keller" (Professor-Fischer-Keller) rooms offered to the punk community by the evangelist church and the deacon Lorenz Postler!

MITA SCHAMAL (Namenlos): In the DDR it was not legal for punk concerts to happen in the official rooms because the government was fighting against the punks. The churches were the only places where the government couldn't go. The churches were something like an embassy of God! (*laugh*) The pastors had such a big heart to help the young people and bring them to God. They said, "Come to us here! You can eat, drink, smoke and you can play music." They hadn't any idea what kind of young people would come to the churches!

CHAPTER 11

BLUES MASSES TO PUNK CONCERTS

DIRK MOLDT (Fatale): The punks were not the first music in the church. The church had her own music and classical music. The first big experience the church had with popular music was in the 70s when a lot of Blues bands arose in East Germany. You can't march to Blues music! It's absolutely impossible. In 1979 there was a big event in the church, the so-called Blues-Messen (Blues Masses) in Friedrichshain. It was a trial, but not an error!

Bernd Schröder was involved as well as Rainer Eppelmann, the priest at Friedrichshain Samaritan Church who later became the post-revolution minister for disarmament in the GDR. The Blues musician Günter "Holly" Holwas came to Rainer Eppelmann and offered to play a concert. Holly said, "I promise the church will be filled!" Eppelmann was skeptical but deacon Bernd Schröder told Eppelmann, "We have a lot of classical concerts and now we'll try Blues concerts." And the church was filled! Two-hundred-fifty long-haired hippies!

When people came to the next Blues-Messen, Bernd Schröder said, "Welcome! Some of you have come all the way from Leipzig." The people shouted, "Yeah!" It was like a party! Then he began a discussion that is a tradition for many hundreds of years, of talking about problems. He said, "Welcome into our church. Now, imagine you're not here. Imagine you're in America, in a southern state, and you have to work the whole day in the fucking cotton fields."

For the young people, this was an association they could relate to because it was forbidden *not* to work in East Germany. Whoever did not work came in prison sometimes. The young punks understood, "This story is also *my story*." He continued, "You work in these cotton fields and you see on the horizon a train going to the northern states. Next, imagine you want to go to the freedom in the free states." All of the people then understood, "We are part of a universal freedom movement." Bernd Schröder explained that in this horrible slavery situation, the workers created a very fine music and, "We in this church want to hear it and see how it makes us feel." That is how Blues music came into the church in the GDR. The youth loved the Blues and they understood, "We are a part of a worldwide freedom movement." No one spoke directly about the GDR and communism and yet the young people understood this was about freedom. This approach was a big new invention, I would say.

The Blues Masses at churches in the GDR paved the way for the punks. A great field of experiences, including agreements and conflicts, brought young hippies and punks into peace, environmental and human rights activism and they became members of the resistance against the Communists. The state tried to defeat the church and freedom groups under the roof of the church. The punk movement in the GDR would've had a different character without the Blues Masses that came before in the church.

On June 24, 1983 there was a Blues-Messen and the organizers decided to let a punk band also play in the open-air courtyard nearby the Erlöser Church in East Berlin. The name of the band was Namenlos. There were a lot of conservative Blues lovers who said, "No! This is a Blues Mass. It's not a punk mass!" The younger people said, "We want to see this!" For a lot of people, it was the first opportunity to hear a punk band. The conservative Blues lovers thought, "I'm not in the right place." Later the members of Namenlos were arrested because of the lyrics in this concert and they were punished with prison.

MITA SCHAMAL (Namenlos): The churches first had Blues-Messen (Blues Masses) that were something like the ghost of poor Black people from America singing about freedom and fighting against oppression. Here the poor, young East Germans with long hair were fighting for their freedom in the church with these Blues-Messen. One girl was singing like Janis Joplin and later they said that young punk boys and girls can play in the church, too. Then my band Namenlos played at Erlöser Church. The concert was so crazy! Nobody knew what we were doing! There were twenty or thirty punk friends pogo dancing and fighting and we played and the drunken Blues guys and girls were shocked! When they heard our music they threw stones. My drums were making this sound; boom, boom boom! I was playing the drums but the loudest sound came because bottles and stones were hitting the drums! Oh, my God! I was loving it! It was the best concert in all of my life! And then on August 11, 1983, the Stasi caught us and took us to the prison.

It was not surprising at all that we were arrested. From the winter to the summer of 1983 there was a war between the government and the punks and we knew clearly that we are going into prison soon. The day we were caught by the government we had planned to move all this stuff out of our flats so the state would not find any texts, placards or cassettes; things that would help them put us in the prison. But at eight o'clock, they caught us. I was not thinking about how long I will stay in prison. I was too young to think about that. I was just thinking, "I have to play in this group Namenlos with these political texts." It was something I couldn't stop. Namenlos played our first concert in Christus Church, Halle, East Germany on April 30, 1983. Our second was at St. Michaelis Church in Karl-Marx-Stadt on June 11, 1983, and our final show was on June 24, 1983, at Erlöser Church in East Berlin.

I knew I would go into prison and I didn't care how long I'd be there. The first three days in prison I was alone in one room and it felt relaxing. You know why it felt relaxing? Because to be a punk was very stressful in East Berlin and in prison it was like a holiday! I didn't have to go to work or fight against any bullshit bull (police). I didn't have to fight against anything. I could just wait and relax. It's strange, but I remember it like this. I was there just seven weeks and I was seventeen years old.

Six weeks later I went to the psychological hospital in the north of Berlin. The doctor made psychological tests with me and after three hours he called into the prison station to say, "I need more time with Schamal." After one week, I was released from the prison hospital and it was a shock. It was not a shock to go in but it was a shock to go out.

I had depression because I wanted to be together with my friend Jana (Schlosser), the singer from Namenlos. We were like twins. I heard what Jana went through in the worst women's prison in East Germany and saw that she was depressed. She'd been with twelve women in one small room without any privacy, with people who killed people and fascistic people. The women had to work and the food was bullshit and Jana was alone in an isolation cellar for three weeks. My trauma from prison was not so big as hers. My first and biggest trauma was when I was really young, a trauma of isolation. My mother couldn't be with me and gave me to a home where you bring children. Doctors take you and you're together with other small babies. There was no warmth and love. I don't remember it exactly because I was so young, but when I meditate, I can go into this feeling. I also feel it in my problems with relationships; I need a long time to feel trust and safety.

JM: Did you know Mita Schamal and Namenlos who were arrested for playing punk music?

PAUL LANDERS (Feeling B / First Arsch / Die Firma / Rammstein): Yes, we all know each other and we say hello if we meet. You could get arrested very easily but you could also get away with it easily. It depended on many factors. I was arrested two times, never imprisoned. We were one of the bands who got permission to perform and we changed some lyrics in English. After you got permission from the state you could play in every club and do pretty much what you wanted. A bit like after passing your driving test; you can drive a lot more reckless but you have to look out for the police. We were more of the fun punk side and tried to avoid head on collisions with the authorities, because you lost most of the times. We saw ourselves more as partisans, like the jester who can say things while others can't.

DIRK MOLDT (Fatale): The band Namenlos came under pressure and they were arrested in 1983. But the church leaders felt a guilt because they knew the church should be a shelter. The church was the only place for bands to play and for a lot of young people to gather because the youth clubs were closed for us. For a lot of bands, it was forbidden to play in a normal club because you have to have permission and many people were saying, "Whoever gets permission is no longer a punk." In the 80s, a lot of bands played punk music but they weren't punks. These were "Die Underren" the so-called "Other Bands." It was a great time for young people interested in music and politics; it was like an explosion.

WENKE ROTTSTOCK (Kirche von Unten): It was extremely dangerous to be a punk in the DDR. I personally experienced many repressions like being put into custody arbitrarily many times, having the police camp outside my home. Sometimes, I was put into custody on a daily basis. My father was also put into prison in the early 1980s for "trying to escape the republic" (Republikflucht). Stasi infiltrators mostly came from colleagues at work, teachers, directors of the school, and sometimes even friends. Even after I was let out of prison, the Stasi was still following me and even tried to recruit me, which I always opposed.

I was not active in a punk band in the GDR. In the 1980's I was involved politically in the punk scene in Dessau. I was taken into custody by the Volkspolizei in 1983 and was imprisoned in the Halle-Goldberg home for political "re-education." From there I was sent to Zeitz into the children's home for political re-education until the end of August, 1986. After my release I was involved in many underground punk concerts and joined the Blues-Masses. End of 1989, I joined the political movement and citizens' initiative "Neues Forum" in Dessau, where the local church supported us to print flyers at night—which was illegal and persecuted as a criminal offense—and offered meeting rooms and space for events. I also went to the mass demonstrations in nearby cities at the time, mainly in Leipzig. I started organizing punk concerts around 1987. When I was in prison or in "re-education homes" I used to listen to, or sing, punk songs to keep myself sane. Many others who have experiences being persecuted by the regime speak of the same thing; the punk music not only kept our spirits up but also kept us sane. The sense of belonging, of not being alone, of fighting for what is right, fighting for freedom. And by just humming or singing a punk song in prison, I felt free.

JÖRG "JOLLY" ZICKLER (KvU): In the Environmental Library in Zionskirche there was a printing press on which various samizdat magazines were printed. The newspapers *Kopfsprung* and *mOAning star* were published as part of the KvU. The KtvU (Kirchentag von Unten) held two events with anarchist themes: "Jesus is an anarchist?" and "You can't build a state with Jesus—Jesus from below." Silke (Ahrens) learned the first layout program Pagemaker in the basement. Myself, and other punks, took part in the layout parties. The printing presses and accessories came from West Berlin via friends and diplomatic channels.

WENKE ROTTSTOCK (Kirche von Unten): For me, punk rock was a form of liberation in the GDR. The song lyrics spoke about what we really felt about the regime. Punk rock bands expressed our desires for revolution and liberation. They gave us a space to be free and the courage to resist. Like the song "DDR Terrorstaat" (Gleichlaufschwankung) which came out many years later and was suppressed by the regime, where they sing: "DDR Terrorstaat, wir haben deine Scheiße satt!" ("East German terror regime, we are sick of your shit!"). Joining the illegal punk concerts in the DDR meant a freedom of the spirit. I felt I wasn't alone in my opposition. In East Berlin, the Umweltbibliothek (Environmental Library) had printing presses at Zionskirche which the punks used secretly at night. Hans Simon, the pastor of the Zionskirche, allowed the punks to use these rooms.

SPEICHE (Gesellschaftliches Fehlverhalten / KvU): There were two printing presses. One in Friedrichsfelde to realize the *Friedrichsfelder Feuermelder*. The other was possessed by the Umweltbibliothek (Environmental Library) at Zionskirche where they printed the *Umweltblätter*, *mOAning star* and *Grenzfalldruck*. The first *Grenzfall* was numbered as "number three" to confuse the Staatssicherheit (state security). One of the printing machines is in an exhibition right now at Zionskirche. (2024) Sometimes we also outsourced our printing of fanzines to Poland.

WENKE ROTTSTOCK (Kirche von Unten): KvU was like a second home to me. It offered a room for open political discussion, events and organizing concerts. KvU helped keep alive the spirit of the revolution and continue the heritage of the punk scene. There were some churches that didn't allow punks into their premises, but most pastors did allow the punk community to operate under their protection. That was crucial for the survival of the punk community and the spirit of revolution, because the police and Stasi weren't allowed on church premises or were kicked out so the punks were safe there. The religious community was just as oppressed as any other part of society. The only difference was that the churches in the DDR had relative autonomy on their own premises. The ideology of the DDR called for the eradication of religion, which was difficult because a majority of the people were Christian/Protestant. It was probably because the religious community was just as repressed and persecuted as any other opposing group of society, that the churches embraced the punk community.

Christians weren't allowed to openly express their religion in public spaces, like wearing a cross around your neck in school, just as punks weren't allowed to show their identity and ideology. Both groups—religious people and punks—were oppressed by the GDR regime. And in that, they probably felt a sense of sympathy toward each other despite the differences in beliefs. Although the punk scene was anti-authoritarian the Protestant churches embraced the punk community in the spirit of resistance against the regime.

All the pastors of the Zionskirche were extremely open and friendly toward the punk community. They embraced the punks with enthusiasm and supported our movement. The collaboration between Zionskirche and the punk community is an enrichment for the religious community, the punk community and the local community. Until today, we organize exhibitions in collaboration with Zionskirche, like the thirty-year memorial concert held in 2017 for the neo-Nazi attack on the October 17, 1987, Zionskirche concert. Or the thirty-five-year memorial concert of the "peaceful revolution" held at the Zionskirche in 2024. In recent years, over ninety percent of the local community was gentrified so the clientele is different now. We continuously organize events together to keep the joint history of the KvU and the punk scene alive. Unfortunately, the KvU will discontinue next year (2025) as we received the termination of the lease this year. Additionally, the old KvU members split into a separate, autonomous group called the "KvU Förderverein" as there were disagreements among the members of the KvU.

PATTI PATTEX (Cut My Skin): We were amazed because it didn't match our cliché ideas of church. It was more like a normal performance venue. The impressive stories that were told to us there showed that it is important and possible to change a society through solidarity and courage. It's the church as it should actually be with compassion, "love your neighbor" ethics and respect for outcasts, regime critics and free spirits. Even to protect them from the merciless destruction of the rulers who want an obedient mass.

KEN CHITWOOD (Dept. for the Study of Religion at Universität Bayreuth): I don't think East Berlin punks moved the church in a particular direction. Most people were in the middle; not wanting to be a vehicle for the authoritarian regime *and* not wanting to be a Trojan horse for the revolution. But many people of the Kirche von Unten and members of the clergy were influenced by the punk scene and got deeper into the resistance because of the punk music and conversations. Elements from within the church became key parts of the peaceful revolution.

JM: Do you remember any punks or activists in the DDR who viewed Jesus as a model for nonviolent revolution? Anti-war, anti-capitalist?

SPEICHE (Gesellschaftliches Fehlverhalten / KvU): Forget it, there was nobody! Maybe some punk people kept it as a secret. We had Jewish people in our groups and also Muslims. Many of us found some deeper meaning of what religion should be. Religion goes back eight thousand years, not two thousand years like the Jesus history.

SILKE AHRENS AND JÖRG "JOLLY" ZICKLER (KvU): We used the opportunities offered by the churches to organize events there, but neither of us were Christians. In the Open Work and later in the KvU there were people with a Christian background, which they lived to varying degrees. The church is a hierarchical organization and we—like most punk bands—are opponents of organized religions. We have met people who, out of a religious/spiritual attitude engage in humanistic, emancipatory actions, which we treat with respect. We have experienced that it's always individual people in the church who derive a domination-free coexistence from the "message of Jesus."

CHURCH FROM BELOW—"OPEN WORK"

DIRK MOLDT (*Kleine Prenzlauer Berg Geschichte* / Fatale): The Blues-Messen went until 1986 when it was closed by church leaders as a concession to the state because the leadership wanted to celebrate a big church congress in East Berlin in 1987 called Kirchentag von Unten (Church Day from Below). Later the Kirche von Unten (Church from Below) was started as a protest against this official connection between the state and church leadership. Our big concern was; there's an enemy against youth in the DDR, so we have to change the society. But we were not the best fit for the leaders of the church and we were not given a room for discussions. In 1987 the Offene Arbeit (Open Work) and other groups founded together the Kirchentag von Unten. The leader of the official church gave us the Pfingstkirche for three days and this was the start of Kirche von Unten, the Church from Below (KvU). The punks said, "Enough is enough. We want also to make a meeting, but our meeting is not the official church, it's the Kirche von Unten, the *Church from Below*. We want this to be a center to talk, make music and theater. The official Evangelic Church has to give us this! If not, we will squat!" And a big fear was in the official church.

WENKE ROTTSTOCK (Kirche von Unten): To stop squatting of the churches, the church leadership decided to allow the "Church Day from Below" from June 24-26, 1987, and was originally organized in the rooms of the Pentecostal Church at Kotikowplatz (Pfingstkirche) and exceeded all expectations with over six thousand participants. The Galilää Church (Galiläakirche) at nearby Rigaer Straße offered additional space.

SILKE AHRENS AND JÖRG "JOLLY" ZICKLER (Kirche von Unten): The KvU was an amalgamation of opposition groups in the GDR; Open Work, Environmental Library, Solidary Church, Initiative for Peace and Human Rights and subcultural groups like hippies, punks and goths. The basis of our work in the KvU was Open Work (Offene Arbeit) which had existed since the 1960s with young people who tried to practice partnership-based, non-hierarchical interactions, non-prejudiced acceptance, consensus, DIY, shared living, fun and spontaneity. This remained a major part of the KvU and there was a feeling of togetherness under the motto: "Live simply, live together, live nonviolently." For us, and certainly for the punks, the joy of life was more important than political work. In *Berlin Calling* Hockenos, to our surprise, translates "Kirche von Unten" as "Church from Below." In the GDR era we liked to say "Church from Down Under" in the sense of "Church from the very bottom." Actually the "below" comes from South American grassroots activist communities.

WENKE ROTTSTOCK (Kirche von Unten): At the 1987 "Church Day from Below" many important topics were discussed like nuclear power, criminal persecution in the GDR and the relationship among oppositional groups in Eastern Europe. The KvU then organized the concert at Zionskirche on October 17, 1987, with Die Firma and Element of Crime.

ZIONSKIRCHE CONCERT OCTOBER 17, 1987

DIRK MOLDT (Fatale): By 1987, normal society and church members in East Berlin were more open and interested in new perspectives because of Gorbachev and the human rights movement. That's why in 1987 the Zionskirche said, "Let's make a punk concert." Silvio Meier said, "We'll make a punk concert, but we want to have Element of Crime, a band from West Berlin." They were not known as a punk band, but New Wave. We organized the gig and asked the East Berlin band Die Firma to lend us their PA. We didn't want them to play, but it was their condition for lending the PA. Pastor Simon was not at the concert on October 17, 1987.

KEY PANKONIN (Die Firma / Ichfunktion): I was a founding member of East German punk band Die Firma but I left the band in 1987 because of internal disagreements and joined another band, Ichfunktion. I wasn't at the October 17, 1987, concert at Zionskirche with Die Firma and Element of Crime. Unfortunately, the punks were attacked by neo-Nazis there.

SPEICHE (Gesellschaftliches Fehlverhalten / KvU): The 1987 Zionskirche concert was organized by KvU people like Silvio Meier and myself. Most of the punk audience left after Die Firma finished and Element of Crime were about to play; about four hundred of six hundred fifty people. In the end, fifty-six people were injured by the fascists. Five hours earlier at a soccer game in Berlin-Köpenick people decided to form a mob and look for trouble. The same day there was also a punk concert in Rummelsburg at Erlöserkirche with No Means No and Mike Gödes with his band Reasors Exzesz. The fascist mob had sent some people as spies to check out what kind of defense they might expect. They realized there were too many punks; no perfect target at all. The fascists knew that punks are more likely to fight back, so they decided to change their target to Zionskirche.

I also helped organize punk concerts with Die Toten Hosen with support band Die Vision, whose lead singer Geier was a Stasi spy. All opposition groups had been infiltrated by the Stasi on different levels. The "Initiative für Frieden und Menschenrechte" (Initiative for Peace and Human Rights) was observed pretty heavy. Compared to other groups in Berlin, the KvU group wasn't infected that much. In one church in Weimar the priest was a Stasi spy.

SILKE AHRENS (Kirche von Unten): I was at the concert in the Zion Church. Silvio Meier, one of my best friends, helped organize the concert. Silvio was murdered by fascists in Berlin in 1992. When the concert was almost over and attacked by the fascists, I was standing at the other exit with a donation basket and suddenly people were rushing out in panic. I tried to get inside to find out what was going on but the church was almost empty. At the other exit there were loud, violent clashes. It was a frightening atmosphere.

HARALD HAUSWALD (GDR photographer): I left the concert before they attacked. In my opinion, they weren't neo-Nazis. I got to know some of them because I was taking photos at soccer matches. Most of them were right-wing, but not extremist. But they were drunk and said, "Let's go and clap left-wingers."

WENKE ROTTSTOCK (Kirche von Unten): I did not attend the October 17, 1987 Zionskirche concert but in 2017 I organized the memorial concert "Remember 1987!" to give the legendary concert the ending it deserved; a peaceful concert to remember. Because in 1987 the concert was attacked by neo-Nazis and ended violently. For us at the contemporary KvU it's more important than ever to set an example against right-wing propaganda, Nazis and hate in our country.

JM: What was your experience playing at the October 17, 1987, Zionskirche concert? What happened when neo-Nazis attacked the audience?

PAUL LANDERS (Feeling B / First Arsch / Die Firma / Rammstein): There was a very euphoric atmosphere in the air and the evening was peaceful. It became ugly in the moment we realized that the event was being attacked. You could not really see what was going on because of the dark lighting. I think it was a very small group of skins who made the assault and it was over in a couple minutes. But because it was a first, people did not really understand exactly what was going on. We just felt violated and cold.

I was summoned in to the Keibelstraße police headquarter and they showed me pictures of skinheads and asked if I recognized someone. After the second session at the police station, I realized that it was not the police and my interrogation was not even about the event at Zionskirche! It was the Stasi and they were trying to recruit me! Immediately I walked around and told all of my friends that they tried to recruit me! And it worked; the Stasi never contacted me after. (Author's note: Rammstein drummer Christoph "Doom" Schneider was also in the 1980s East German band Die Firma and in a 2020 interview he revealed for the first time that their new wave / punk band had two members who were spies for the government; the singer and keyboardist. ("Rammstein Drummer's Early East German Band Had Two Government Spies In Its Lineup" by Jon Hadusek, consequence.net, June 29, 2020))

Figure 11.1 André Greiner-Pol from East German band Tacheles plays guitar on the chancel balcony in Zionskirche in October 1987. Rafael Insunza (vocals) with Alex Kriening (Feeling B) on drums and Frank Tröger (Die Firma) on keyboards. At another illegal Zionskirche punk concert the same month, the audience was attacked by neo-Nazi skinheads. Photo by Harald Hauswald / OSTKREUZ.

HARALD HAUSWALD (GDR photographer): Everyone had dealings with the Stasi when they were trying to recruit people. I don't know anyone to whom that hasn't happened. They tried to recruit me too, but the Stasi file says that I wasn't suitable for recruitment. Now I have my file; they followed me for twelve years.

SILKE AHRENS AND JÖRG "JOLLY" ZICKLER (Kirche von Unten): We always expected Stasi people to infiltrate the group, but we tried to live relatively freely in keeping with our name Open Work. When we later read our Stasi files, we found that hierarchically-minded government employees were less able to deal with our style than groups with a fixed group of people on a specific topic. There were significantly fewer Stasi infiltrators in the KvU than in the conspiratorial groups.

KEY PANKONIN (Die Firma / Ichfunktion): Our October 2024 performance is called "Wir Kriegen Euch Alle!" ("We'll Get All of You") with dialogue about the 1987 Zionskirche concert when Nazi fascists attacked the concert. "We are going to get you all," is what the neo-Nazis shouted at the punks. Two of our actors—Hans Narva and Torsten Füchsel—are punk musicians from the bands Herbst in Peking and Rosengarten and they share their memories about this horror story. The attack at Zionskirche was exactly a way to do intervention by state authorities. Simply, they had found a tool to change the Schutzraum Kirche (Shelter Church) into something very unsafe. When you think about the personal history of the church attackers you will find that most of them were punks before they turned into fascist skinheads. Finally, it was "Punks gegen Punks" (punks against punks) which is good for the government, isn't it?

PLAYING ON THE CHANCEL / PULPIT

DIRK MOLDT (*Kleine Prenzlauer Berg Geschichte* / Fatale): At another Zionskirche concert the guitarist André Greiner-Pol with the band Tacheles acted like a diva, "I am the greatest!" But we knew the chancel balcony is a very special place in the church. The priest from Zionskirche, Pfarrer Simon, told me that this photo of André on the chancel helped state security to make arguments against us having more concerts in the church. It was a wonder that Silvio Meier was successful with the next concert.

WENKE ROTTSTOCK (Kirche von Unten): The photo was taken by Harald Hauswald, a very prominent photographer in East Berlin. The punk musician in the photo is André Greiner-Pol. I asked Delia, the wife of André, to confirm this. André died in 2008. Many members of the punk scene from back then don't identify with the photo of André with Tacheles at the Zionskirche in 1987. Their music could be considered Krautrock or improvisational music and therefore wasn't strictly punk music.

HARALD HAUSWALD (GDR photographer): I was surprised he dared to play on the pulpit but nobody said anything against it. I didn't think it was so great he climbed up there. Zionskirche didn't often do concerts and events; most were at Ritterkirche and Erlöserkirche and it's funny that at these church events they always had big banners: "Please don't smoke." I never heard there were problems from the photo of André. Nobody told me anything!

KEY PANKONIN (Die Firma / Ichfunktion): I played punk rock at Zionskirche on the chancel!

KEN CHITWOOD (Dept. for the Study of Religion at Universität Bayreuth): I love that image from the 1987 concert at Zionskirche with the guitar player (André Greiner-Pol) with his leg up on the top of the pulpit, hitting a riff. It's iconic in so many ways. It's undermining of the pulpit and what's being proclaimed there, but also the image embodies the liberating anti-regime message of Jesus across time. It was also an opportunity for bands like Die Toten Hosen to come from the West and perform at East Berlin churches, who saw something in the liberation and power of being anti-establishment.

JM: How important was punk rock in the DDR, in terms of self-expression and challenging the authoritarian government?

PAUL LANDERS (Feeling B / Die Firma / Rammstein): Punk rock was a tool to express an alternative opinion to the official line. So was Blues, hard rock and metal. Punk was a way for creating liberation and freedom in the DDR, but it was not the only way. The DDR was not the tight-knit Stasi State most people now think. It was full of holes and gaps, where an easy-peasy life was possible. The churches could host parties and punk concerts on their own ground, unobstructed by the state. The Stasi could only loiter around the premises and take pictures of the arriving people. Churches and weddings were the only places for alternative bands to play without getting permission to play. Therefore, there was an unusually tight relation between the churches and punk rock. It was not always entirely peaceful. But a lot of "Langhaarige" (people with long hair as a sign of opposition) worked at the churches and the common enemy of the state bonded us all together. Religion had nothing to do with it.

JM: Do you feel that some of your original punk sensibilities are still alive in you and the music you make with Rammstein?

PAUL LANDERS (Feeling B / First Arsch / Die Firma / Rammstein): What's alive is still the idea of playing with the boundaries of good taste. What can you do, or say? And what not? Where are the ends of patience from our society? What kind of art are we able to tolerate?

JM: The DDR was a very controlled society but they allowed churches to have some autonomy. I still wonder why.

KEN CHITWOOD (Dept. for the Study of Religion at Universität Bayreuth): There's a long history of liberal Christianity and church activists. They were some of the main homes of the abolition and civil rights movements in the US. So, why not resistance to the GDR regime? It makes a lot of sense within that tradition. The GDR did not see the church as an institution that could undermine it and so gave it a certain degree of autonomy. The government viewed it as a dying institution; "Secular socialism will be the wave of the future, so we don't have to worry about the churches." So, the churches were kind of left to their own. There were pastors and people who started to become part of the pushback against the DDR regime and some churches began allowing East German punk bands to perform at churches because there were no places for them to do so. This provided a platform.

SILKE AHRENS AND JÖRG "JOLLY" ZICKLER (Kirche von Unten): In contrast to other "socialist" countries, the GDR had a special relationship between the state and the church. Due to its proximity to West Germany, the GDR was unable to completely suppress the influence of the church. From 1978 onwards, the language used was "not to endanger the good relationship between the state and the church" and the church defined itself as the "church *in* socialism." Not for or against. This meant a certain amount of freedom for the congregations and their activities, but at the same time the fear of losing freedom. The GDR was a control society that included all areas of life: work, leisure, religious, parties, clubs, schools, etc. It was fundamentally dangerous to express or live one's own opinion or deviations from the norm in public. It was particularly difficult for associations that were clearly acting as groups. "Rioting together" was a criminal offense. This naturally affected the punks and the KvU, as well as all other subcultural groups.

The GDR was unbelievably bourgeois and had not really dealt with fascism. Due to their conspicuous appearance and extroverted behavior, punks in particular were exposed to harassment by the police, state security and "good citizens" and the withdrawal of identity cards, youth work camps, conscription into the army and prison. The first punk generation was hit particularly hard until around 1984, but even up until the end of the GDR (1989) individuals were repeatedly punished.

CARSTEN FIEBELER (*OstPunk! Too Much Future*): The church in the GDR wasn't "radical." Before the fall of the Wall there was a connection to the punk scene with the Protestant church, but the Catholic side didn't play along. The church was enormously important during the time of the first punk generation and an important point of contact for the punks, who actually had nothing to do with the church. The deacons in particular gave the punks a place to retreat to, to make performances in church spaces. And when punks were arrested, they took care of legal advice, among other things.

KEY PANKONIN (Die Firma / Ichfunktion): "Schutzraum Kirche" (Shelter Church) refers to the fact that the DDR government and police were not allowed to enter church space. I remember walking around Alexanderplatz (East Berlin) in the early 80s. We carried two guitars and tried to play some songs right in front of the television tower. Soon two policemen came along and ordered us to leave, so we made our way. One minute later a guy told us we can just walk a few meters to the Marienkirche which is also near the television tower. There we could simply sit on the lawn next to the church and play music. It was a safe place to make some early punk songs on acoustic guitar.

I remember a close friend of mine invited me to a Junge Gemeinde (Church Youth Community Group) near Ostbahnhof train station next to the Berlin Wall. There were rooms where you could have a discussion about almost anything; no need to chat about god and religious matters. They also had a space for a church band and all of the members were young people like me. It was a great experience, to have a free place like this outside the space of authority. One month later Pfarrer Schneider asked us to join some real church events. It was no problem that not one of us wanted to do that. We weren't there for religion. Only a few members of this Junge Gemeinde didn't like us because of our no-religion-at-all attitude.

SILKE AHRENS AND JÖRG "JOLLY" ZICKLER (KvU): It was always only individual church employees who opened their rooms to punks, for example at the Galilee Church (Galiläakirche) and the Redeemer Church (Erlöserkirche). There were also so-called "disposable churches" that you could get in for one concert, but never again afterwards. The churches in the GDR were just as bourgeois as the society around them. The punks were kicked out of the Pentecostal congregation in 1983. At Galiläa there was a committed pastor, Gerhard Cyrus, who worked openly with punks. Later, the Redeemer congregation had the Pro-Fi-Keller—a former morgue—which the punks could use almost autonomously. This is where we first saw No Means No in the autumn of 1988, who had secretly come over from West Berlin. There were two employees who arranged contact between the church congregation and the Alösa punks. There was of course a circle around the first A! In the Zionskirche there was Pastor Simon, who had a very open nature, especially through his cooperation with the Environmental Library, who made concerts possible from time to time.

However, there were always discussions and arguments in the congregations about things like order and cleanliness, noise levels, political orientation, the missionary orientation of the church and fear for the "good relationship between church and state" and thus fear of losing the church's own freedom. At the upper church level, these things were always viewed with suspicion, not least by many church employees recruited by the Stasi. Two-thirds of the Thuringian regional church leadership were Stasi employees.

ANTI-NAZI CONFESSING CHURCH

DIRK MOLDT (Fatale): In the 1930's the Galiläa Church was part of the Bekennende Kirche (The Confessing Church) that opposed the Nazis. In March, 1983 Gerhard Cyrus was the priest at Galiläa Church and decided, "I want to help the people." Cyrus was always interested in young people until the end of his life and he always offered questions; "What do you think? What do you feel?" I visited him in his last month of life and I think he was asking these questions even more! Father Cyrus had two daughters. One daughter died and the living daughter was part of the movement of youth in the church, and was interested in Blues-Messen (Blues Masses) and punk rock. Cyrus decided, "I'll take a little bit of my daughter's interest for myself." He was alone in the church in this regard. The church community was against the punks not only because the church was conservative, but because during the Nazi times the church aligned with Hitler. The Deutsche Christen were a group that loved Hitler and brought Nazi flags into the church.

The Bekennende Kirche was a church movement that started in the 1930's against the Nazi dictatorship. A lot of Christians believed that Adolph Hitler was the new messiah and the new Christ. Really, you can't imagine! But another part of the church said, "No. Our leader in the church is Jesus Christ. Nobody else." Dietrich Bonhoeffer was one of those in the Bekennende Kirche and they tried to assassinate Hitler. The church communities were divided, with some supporting Adolf Hitler as the new messiah and others opposed to the Nazis.

One Sunday in 1986 Father Cyrus held a Lord Service and invited the young punks into the church; "Let's listen to the silence and talk about our problems." He said; "I also have problems. I fear the police." So, the young punks understood, "This person is not strange. He's old, but you can deal with him." In 1985 or 1986 a band called Zerfall played at Galiläa Church and this year (2024) they had a forty-year anniversary at the church. Cyrus told his community in 1986, "When I have sorrows and don't know what I can do, I sit in the church in the silence, face-to-face to God." But these young punks became loud! So, he wanted to build a bridge to understand. Then Zerfall played songs and a small part of the old community went outside. It was a sign, "We don't like this situation." But a lot of people stayed in the church and listened more.

SILKE AHRENS AND JÖRG "JOLLY" ZICKLER (KvU): We knew the "Confessing Church" with Dietrich Bonhoeffer as Christians who opposed Nazi fascism. Walter Schilling, a pastor we greatly respected, based his theology on the "Confessing Church." But we were not aware of Dietrich Bonhoeffer's work in Zionskirche at the time. Christian theology was only relevant to a few of us. We also knew about Ernesto Cardenal and the Christian movement of grassroots communities from Latin America. Books from the West on these and other topics were read and exchanged. Our name Kirche von Unten "Church from Below" is based on this idea.

KEN CHITWOOD (Dept. for the Study of Religion at Universität Bayreuth): Dietrich Bonhoeffer and the history of resistance at Zionskirche reminds us that Berlin is a place of constant change and resistance. At each historical juncture, religion has been a persistently ubiquitous force. This is not what you'd assume, given Berlin's reputation as a free-thinking, secular, cosmopolitan metropolis. But religion and Berlin are inextricably linked. You can go all the way back to the founding of Berlin to find this kind of resistance movement. Imperial forces were dominating that area in the Prussian world and Berlin and those pre-medieval villages were some of the last people to convert to Christianity. They held on to what we now call "pagan" beliefs and practices longer than anybody else in the area. This was already very punk! To be anti-establishment and say, "You will not tell us what to do!"

DIRK MOLDT (Fatale): Punk was really the best. It was dynamic and funny and it was absolutely cool. No other music was so dynamic and so simple to play. I played for a year in a punk band (Fatale) and then we split. Two bandmembers went to the West and our time was over. It's really necessary for every young person to be a part of theater, music and fun. And stress, also! It was really the best music and the best time.

SPEICHE (Gesellschaftliches Fehlverhalten / KvU): The KvU started in 1984 and later there were bigger events in 1987. Kirche von Unten was a place of freedom. We were the lost children, trying to renew the church from its base. By doing this we had unknown possibilities and free spaces. Sometimes our activities ended in complete chaos! In general, we felt we were part of the GDR population who had the right to treat the church like a kind of possession. We didn't destroy anything. It happened that we ruined the floor right in front of the altar by pogo dancing but two of us came back to do some repairs. (Hoffungskirche) Different groups had access to church keys and sometimes there was tension because there were so many people who wanted to use those free spaces inside the church. It was about making changings in the society and, "How can we do it?" There were people around like Bärbel Bohley who later co-founded *Neues Forum* (New Forum political movement) and Carlo Jordan (Green Party activist).

WENKE ROTTSTOCK (Kirche von Unten): Those who opposed the regime in the 1989 demonstrations all over East Germany, especially those in Berlin, played a significant role in bringing about the "peaceful revolution." It was the desire of all the people for freedom. Squatting played a central role in the KvU. In the early 1990s, I squatted an empty house in Dessau with friends which until today is an "alternative youth center" which we bought from the original owner later for 1DM. Many spaces that are used by alternative subcultures were originally squatted and today remain autonomously organized like Tuntenhaus, Schokoladen, Linie 206, Schöne Christine, Fehre 6 and Freudenhaus.

SILKE AHRENS (KvU): I occupied an apartment in Berlin with my boyfriend (Thomas Kremer, singer/guitarist with Antitrott) in 1985/86 and later again alone, as many people did at the time in Berlin, especially in Friedrichshain and Prenzlauer Berg. Most of the apartments were in very poor condition and were no longer rented out. Many apartments were used as meeting places for readings, vernissages and concerts, not always to the amusement of the neighbors! In the special situation in Berlin, the open apartments were the replacement for the Open Work's rooms until the KvU finally fought for their own rooms in January 1989. Jolly (Jörg Zickler) and friends occupied an entire house in Jena in 1983, the "Autonomous Republic of Zwätzengasse" which was the creative center for various subcultures in Jena.

MY PARENTS WERE COMMUNIST

JM: Mark Reeder helped sneak Die Toten Hosen and other bands from West Berlin into East Germany for clandestine concerts in the late 80s. Did you go to any of these concerts?

DIRK MOLDT (Fatale): It was so secret that almost nobody knew about it! Die Toten Hosen played not in the church, but in the courtyard. They played later again in Pankow. My parents were communists and I was also in this direction in my youth, but I changed to an anarchist direction. There was so much despotism in normal life that we tried to live without this. We were filled with hope for less violence, but in a dictatorship it's difficult to live this dream. My question has always been, why is it so split? The words from the church versus what they do in the world. I think it's not the structure of the church. In every case it's the leadership. Some were liars, some were not liars. Some were helping people in need and some did not. This is all.

WENKE ROTTSTOCK (Kirche von Unten): I was never religious and I'm an atheist until today. I did not attend the church in East Berlin or my hometown. I only went to the church for political events and punk concerts during the DDR. A lot of punk rock bands oppose the concept of churches and religion. I think of Schleim-Keim's "Antichrist" song. I'm against organized religion and the power of the churches, especially the corruption of power.

JM: In *Berlin Calling: A Story of Anarchy, Music, the Wall and the Birth of the New Berlin* (2017) Paul Hockenos writes, "In Autumn 1989, Prenzlauer Berg and its Protestant Churches, including the Church of Zion, would be the focus of the "peaceful revolution" that overthrew communism and ended the Cold War." What role did Kirche von Unten (KvU) and the punk movement have in bringing down the Berlin Wall and communism?

JÖRG "JOLLY" ZICKLER (Kirche von Unten): The KvU (Church from Below) was one of the few places that offered space for free discussions about changing society and trying out non-hierarchical interactions. Our focus was mainly on changes in our own country. Young people from the KvU, the environmental library and other groups took action on the streets in 1989 including demonstrations, vote counts, protest drums, vigils and autonomous Antifa actions. Unfortunately, the peaceful revolution in the country we hoped for could not be completed, as all positive emancipatory processes were nipped in the bud by the collapse of the GDR and colonization by West Germany.

HARALD HAUSWALD (GDR photographer): The punks helped bring down the wall, that's true. But they were just one cog in the machine that was on its way to bringing down the wall. There were also other musicians, writers and theater people who helped bring down the Eastern Bloc and showed solidarity in Poland. Punk rock contributed to the fall of the Berlin Wall, but as a small part of many.

SILKE AHRENS (KvU): I was busy sewing lots of black and red flags for the big demonstration on November 4, 1989, which for many of us was the beginning of the end of the hoped-for changes in the GDR. Representatives of the old system suddenly started posing as reformers. Many of us had ideas for concrete change within the GDR in the direction of council communism/anarchism. This idea failed at the founding congress of the "United Left" in November, 1989 and all further attempts became impossible with the capitalist takeover of the GDR.

MITA SCHAMAL (Namenlos): When the Berlin Wall came down (November 9, 1989) some changes were very good and some were very bad. But I think the revolution is part of a social evolution, and this evolution is something we don't have in our control. It's in the order of Mother Earth. We are living on this beautiful Earth and in this evolution there have been created "isms" like communism and capitalism. It's bullshit because life is full of everything we need and we don't need any isms!

JM: Zionskirche is organizing a celebration on October 12, 2024, to honor thirty-five years since the "peaceful revolution" and fall of the Berlin Wall. Will you and KvU participate?

WENKE ROTTSTOCK (Kirche von Unten): Of course! Horst Edler is organizing the event and asked me to recruit some punk bands for the concert! (Planlos, Rosa Beton and author Henryk Gericke) Although it's thirty-five years ago, I still feel like just back in the 1980s and the fight isn't over. There is too much neo-nazi propaganda in our country, too many right-wing bands. Sometimes, it feels like it's just getting worse. Today the KvU is a youth center. In the last few years, the original members have either left the KvU or died. As a result, the "KvU Förderverein" (the KvU Sponsorship Association) was founded in 2022, where I am a board member. This KvU association is now organizing concerts outside the KvU, like in the Zionskirche, Schokoladen, Freilichtbühne Weißensee and Supamolly. The KvU will most likely be closed next year (2025) but the "KvU Förderverein" will continue.

CALM FOR THE REVOLUTION
MEDITATION/AWARE AND PRESENT/LIVING FREE

*I am not a spiritual person, but I always like looking at monks:
there's a floating strength about them that I admire very much.*

Occupants: Photos and Writings by Henry Rollins
(Chicago Review Press, 2011, pg.153)

*I want to challenge the idea that there's necessarily an opposition
between trying to calm one's mind and trying to produce more
justice in the world.*

—Sara Marcus (*Girls to The Front: The True Story of the Riot
Grrrl Revolution*)

*I don't even want to speculate how my life might have been
without meditation.*

—Glenn Wallis (Ruin)

SARA MARCUS (*Girls to The Front: The True Story of the Riot Grrrl Revolution*):
You hear a lot about self-care these days because it's a long haul. I want to challenge the idea that there's necessarily an opposition between trying to calm one's mind and trying to produce more justice in the world. At points throughout *Girls to the Front* I did a lot of thinking about feminist consciousness-raising as a quasi-spiritual conversion, these kinds of rituals that were part of life in Riot Grrrl that gave containers and repeatability to the ways that we were acting on

the feminist commitment. Riot Grrrl helped us find language to be able to inhabit our identities in a way that felt less constricted than the female identities that were being pushed upon us by sexist culture. I wrote about feminism as almost a spiritual commitment in the way of, "What's a collective worldview with an articulated almost-eschatology?" We talked about the revolution! This idea that there's a more perfected version of reality than the one we're muddling through right now. That feels quite spiritual.

DAN MCKEE (*Anarchist, Atheist, Punk Rock Teacher*): I think calmness is essential for any meaningful revolution. A sustainable alternative can't be based on anger in a world where we have been trained to be retributive against those who make us angry. I'm angry most of the time when I look around the world, but if it was anger that guided me toward revolution it would not be revolutionary, it would be some glorified version of dumb street justice. Any supposedly revolutionary movement which advocates punishment for those who currently oppress has already failed. We can't change the world through the paradigms of the present. We need better alternatives. Calmness sounds passive, but to borrow from Buddhism, I think calmness simply means acceptance of the chaos and anger of the world.

TRANSCENDENT COLLECTIVE MOSHPIT

EDDIE STERN (Chop Shop / Lou Reed's Yoga teacher): As you know from your own meditation, there's a difference between being relaxed and calm and being aware and fully present. The purposes of meditation and yoga practices are not so much to find a state of calm as they are to find a state of total presence in the moment. Can you think of anything which makes you more in the moment than a mosh pit? You know you're in tune if you're doing it right with everyone around you because it's not a fight, it's a collective ecstatic dance. It's transcendent.

You see echoes of that in Osho's dynamic meditations where you jump and dance, breathe fast and scream. What's more punk rock than that? And it's not a violent anger, it's a primal expression. There are strains of hardcore punk that are violent and aggressive, but largely the kind of anger that you hear expressed in punk music is anger toward the oppressive structures that confine people to certain modes of being and keep the world in a state of oppression, chaos and violence.

I likened myself to be a peace punk. In the village down on St. Mark's Place (New York City) we had the skinheads who were super violent if they wanted to be. And then the punk rockers who were not so much, and the peace punks who had huge mohawks but were reading Gandhi. Very aware and very conscious.

JM: Do you practice meditation?

DAVE WAKELING (The Beat): Yeah. I was doing it quite heavily a year or two ago. I had a teacher and we were messing with jhanas. I'm kind of a bit scattered now. I sit in the van a lot and mainly I do Metta prayers of compassion, visualizing everybody in the van or to myself. Really what it's done is I've learned to be a little more compassionate and have given the great value of it to other people. The backside of it was that I found I was being more compassionate to myself and didn't know it. That's nice. Over the past three years I've fallen in love with myself again. I don't have to keep running away. It's nice because it doesn't matter what comes up—you can just sit with it and it goes. You keep running away from it and it chases you forever. They say you feel the sharp point of the spear—fear—on your chest. If you move away, it follows you. You walk backward the whole of your life. The first time you move straight onto the spear, the spear disappears! There's no fear!

There's been a few things in the last year or so that shook me a touch, but it hasn't taken long for me to get my equilibrium back. And I don't have to get loaded to get out of it. I'm pleased with that. Makes me more able to communicate about the true plight of things. A bit more clarity and a bit more insistence. If you've got no painkillers going, the pain does feel greater. No doubt about it. It's a workable pain. I turn on the news and start crying some mornings. Fucking piles of little brown babies. It should make you cry. I'm amazed that not everybody is crying. I think the whole world ought to be crying. There is awful, painful stuff going on. You'd like to *forgive them that they know not what they do.* But c'mon, some of 'em do! (*laugh*)

There's a lot of Buddhism cropping up in the songs now. Tons of it. I started doing modern translations of my favorite prayers. I'd like to make them a bit more accessible: "May all sentient beings be free from danger, may you be safe, may you be happy, may you be whole and may you have peace." That's the Metta prayer in rhyming English. We sing that at the end of "Save It for Later." It's not easy fitting an English translation of the *prajnaparamita* into a song with a reggae beat! There's a lot more of it cropping up. I've got to that post-motorbike stage of my life now. I made it!

JM: Meditation is noticing what is presently occurring within ourselves and learning to relax our beliefs about, and response to, that experience.

GABRIEL KUHN (*Sober for The Revolution*): If you call that meditation, then I partake in some meditation practices. Otherwise, there is nothing that I do that would be referred to as meditation or spiritual practice. I think the closest I get to it is sports, in the sense of certain focus and awareness and releasing certain emotions and getting in a state that is a peculiar sort of perception and consciousness. I get that through sports. I ended up playing soccer in Austria because it was the easiest sport to earn some money, which was very good for me as a student. But in terms of enjoying sports, I really enjoy downhill skiing. Now in Sweden, I do more cross-country skiing. It has that meditative effect.

PENNY RIMBAUD (Crass): I thought, "We've been promoting peace and we don't even know what peace is." We'd never experienced it, so I needed to experience peace to talk about peace. I'd been playing around with Zen all my life but I'd never taken it seriously. I'd never really been prepared to look at it in the deep sense. The Zen joker! Alan Watts wrote about himself about this. *Dharma Bums* by (Jack) Kerouac is one of the most beautiful Taoist expressions. Then you end up as a drunken, nationalist, slightly right-wing wanker. That's bad philosophy and that's why I go back to the Christ story. If you've seen light, if you've seen heaven, you never can leave her. You can't end up a corpse on the bloody cross or a drunk sitting in a chair blabbering on about nonsense. That means you haven't actually touched light.

CAMILLE ROSE GARCIA (The Real Minx): In high school I tried the kind where you stare at the candle. Now I meditate while I'm riding my bike or on a hike. I also do yoga and that's very meditative. It's important to quiet the mind and get to a space where you remember what the world *used* to be like. "What was it like before you had to be so busy all the time?" There are theories that the Mayan calendar is counting down and the world is actually spinning faster and that's why it seems like everything is going faster and you can't catch up.

I was just reading this great book on Vedic, which is the root of Hinduism and Buddhism. It closely mirrors what I've always thought but I never gave any formal name: that the creator and the presence of life is in everything. Everything you do makes a difference. How you treat animals, nature and other human beings; it's all a part of the same thing.

MOANA STROM (Stalin's War): Liberation Prison Project is a Buddhist non-profit organization based in San Francisco, directed by Venerable Robina Courtin, an amazing, articulate Australian nun. It supplies spiritual support to Buddhist practitioners in prison. If a prisoner is interested in Buddhism or if they want to continue with their practice, we'll send them books and set them up with a corresponding teacher. We also have about twenty visiting teachers who go into prisons and teach group meditation and dharma classes to prisoners.

JOHNETTE NAPOLITANO (Concrete Blonde): I have to really work at keeping my mind where I need it to be, when I need it. The thing is to give each and every little thing you do your absolute full focus, not to be distracted by the hustle around you.

DARIUS KOSKI (Swingin' Utters): I appreciate things about meditation; I don't do it. I should. When I was a kid, my uncle used to meditate and I'd go to his house and I did it off and on for a couple of years. It's something I should be getting into now at this point in my life because I'm completely filled with stress.

JON KING (Gang of Four): You mentioned meditation. I've done that sort of thing over the years and it's interesting. At a certain point you can get a sense of emptiness. Karl Marx said the point is not to *describe* the world but to *change* it. That was a fantastically acute thing to say. It's almost banal to say, "What you think changes how you act," but it is quite hard to change what you think. In moments of meditation, somehow or other you're freed from the way you used to think.

EXENE CERVENKA (X): What's so great about art is not just what you're giving to other people that are listening to your music or looking at your art, which is so valuable. To give something back is an important component. But while you're making the art, you're not thinking about the people who are going to see or hear it; you're only thinking about the process of creating. And if you get lost in that, it can be like anything else. Like a craftsperson or a gardener, parent or teacher. When you're really focused on something it is the best thing in the world because you're lost in that moment and nothing else exists. That's why people gamble, because it's similar to creating art. It makes you lose sight of everything else except that moment you're in, what you're focusing on. Art is healthier than gambling, I think. I love doing art because you get lost in it. It's the same thing with making music. If you're playing guitar, you don't even know how many hours have passed. That's the most valuable thing about being an artist: the creative process.

JM: I'd be curious to hear more about how you cultivate being present in the moment.

JOHN DOE (X): Well, children are certainly a great way to do it. They won't tolerate you being *anywhere else* than paying attention to what is going on in front of you! Maybe that's one of the reasons people like sports so much, because sports are certainly in the moment. The way I've tried to cultivate it is just to enjoy things as they're happening rather than thinking about what did happen or what will happen. There's no trick. I think it's just experiencing what it's like when you're in the moment and then understand and regain that.

JM: Some people would describe meditation the way you're talking about cultivating being present. Have you experimented with meditation?

JOHN DOE (X): No, I haven't. But I do think about the past a lot. I think about the future a lot. I use that for creative purposes and writing songs and poetry. It's difficult to do that in the present. You're trying to figure out what happened, how you felt about it, the impact it had, how you wished it could've been different. No, never meditated. But that's OK. I didn't feel the need. I think everybody envies people who have that sort of discipline. I've known a few people who do it pretty regularly and they seem incredibly centered, satisfied and happy in a deep way. Seems like a good idea.

JM: How important has meditation been to you? Do you continue to have a practice?

GLENN WALLIS (Ruin): Meditation has been extremely important to me. I don't even want to speculate how my life might have been without meditation. From my very first session to my last, meditation means being in a weird paradoxical space where seemingly contradictory modes of being were in play; stability with fluidity, acute concentration with vivid openness, self-awareness with self-negation. Very strange and also very rich in results! I carry with me into everyday life what happens on the zafu. (meditation cushion) In that sense, I understand Dogen's remark that true meditation is non-meditation. *Life* is the zafu. This understanding is also the reason I no longer formally meditate.

JM: How important do you think it is to be calm and compassionate for the revolution?

GLENN WALLIS (Ruin): I believe in the wisdom of prefiguration in the anarchist sense. What we get in the end will be infused by how we act, speak and relate to one another at the beginning and in the middle. If we value calm and compassion as necessary dispositions for the kind of world we want, then we had better start cultivating those capacities *now*. But the question of what we want those values to *mean* has to be addressed as well. I have seen "calm and compassion" used in ways that I would describe as passive-aggressive. The same goes for "right speech." It's sometimes just a means for censorship and control. *Calm and compassion* can too easily become cudgels in a power dynamic. But yes, any revolution worthy of the name must give serious thought to the nature, and place, of calmness and compassion in its formation.

JM: How does meditation and calming the mind relate to the chaotic cacophony of punk?

GLENN WALLIS (Ruin): Haha! The *chaotic cacophony of punk* is a good way of describing *the mind*, isn't it? Maybe that throbbing, thrashing, punk beat *is* the mind at work. I don't think the point of meditation is to calm the mind. That's boring! I think the point of meditation is just to sit *with* the mind and the body, emotions and the world. Really, all of this is one reality. Because of certain linguistic and historical contingencies, we say *mind* and *body* as if these are distinct phenomenon but when regarded from the inside, so to speak, it is obvious that it is one whole. Punk can be calming. It can also be achingly beautiful.

JM: Can you describe some ways you have transformed or changed through music, regarding anger or expressing yourself?

LENNY KAYE (Patti Smith Group): I've been able to channel a lot of my own personal idiosyncrasies to my music. By playing these, I can give them a release. Especially playing rock and roll. Sometimes when we play hard, I'm able to indulge all of my tendencies, from my most romantic and caring to some of my *let it all out*. You are what you play. I've realized that no matter where you are on the spectrum of, "How many people are in the audience?" Or how your career is doing, really what I get most pleasure out of is the simple act of playing music. Even if it's in my basement for an hour. *That* is one's meditation and the closer you're connected with your inner self, the more you can see it come out of you when you're playing.

I know exactly how I'm feeling when I play that night because if I'm feeling uneasy with myself, I will see it in my playing. If I'm feeling like I know who I am that day, I can make that microtone of a bend and get it right exactly where I want. It's like *The Zen of Motorcycle Maintenance*. When your machine is running great, whatever it is, you're in tune. A few years ago, I really got into riding a motorcycle, and I found a lot of parallels between how you are on a bike and how you are with a guitar. Being conscious of your place in the universe, but not stepping outside yourself so that you are too aware; it's that space. When you're in the zone playing a guitar solo or going around a curve at eighty miles an hour, these things show you just how in tune you are with yourself. That's why they call it "in tune."

JONATHAN RICHMAN (Modern Lovers): Sometimes I'll play music in the morning to know how I feel, to know if I'm angry. To me, a sound can tell me how I feel. Do I have a spiritual practice? Is there something that I do? Yes! *I love life*. That is my spiritual practice. And anything else I might do—if I meditate, pray or anything else—it's all because of that.

JACK GRISHAM (TSOL): I do a lot of meditation in the morning. It's more contemplation than meditation, really. I sit quietly and do a reading. It could be something that happened and I just go over it. What does it bring up in me? How can I apply this to serving someone?

ROB FISH (108 / Resurrection): When I do different types of meditation or spiritual practices, it's really nice because I don't think if it's truth or fiction or if it's right or wrong. It's this thing I find really touching, endearing and beautiful. I want to experience it. And that's where it ends. When I'm done and I get up and unlock my door and walk out, I don't judge other people in the context of what I just experienced. If they do experience it in some respect, it's probably going to look a little different than how I experienced it.

There's one guy I'm really close with and from a spiritual standpoint I really appreciate him, but when it comes to practical aspects of life, we couldn't disagree more. He's of the feeling, "I know things I should do to better facilitate what I receive, so I'm going to pull out the stops and start doing all those things today." I think, "Maybe I'll get there one day." I enjoy what I have *now*. Do I hope for more? Yeah. But I want to let it come up organically. I'd never look at someone and say, "You're doing it the wrong way."

MATT CLEAVER (Stalin's War): There are different types of meditation. For someone who's got a very out-of-control mind, one good technique is to not focus on anything. You also don't try to block thoughts from happening. You're just acknowledging that thoughts are happening. One reason our minds go so crazy and go off on tangents is that we attach ourselves to a thought. We'll acknowledge that the thought has essence and think that it's real, and our minds might continue with the thought and we start thinking of scenarios and our mind will go crazy. I'm not that great of a meditator; I have to use this meditation technique a lot. Just work on not attaching yourself to a particular thought. If you don't follow weird fantasies that come into your head then they will eventually fade. It may take a while, but eventually you'll get to the state where you just concentrate on nothing at all.

I Must Not Think Bad Thoughts

—song by X (1983)

EXENE CERVENKA (X): It's a mantra of some sort—*I must not think bad thoughts*. It's a meditation and it doesn't necessarily mean putting your head in the sand. It means keeping your head above it and keeping your head clear. You can think about the negative and think about what needs to be fixed, but you cannot let your head get stuck in the negative. You can't get your spirit stuck in the negative because then you're completely ineffectual. It's an interesting song because it refers to all these things that are happening and then says, "But I must not think bad thoughts." It's like that inner quandary of fighting to stay abreast of things and wanting to fix things but also not wanting to get dragged down by them.

I find that allowing negative experiences and negative people—negative theories—into your life is extremely physically, emotionally and spiritually self-destructive. If I see somebody who is angry and cuts in line in front of me, I immediately just let it go. I don't think that negative things other people do impacts me at all. When you let go of that tendency for negative people to impact you, you become more positive, functional and clear about everything. I've let go of fear, as much as you can. And definitely let go of anger and resentment as much as possible. The best thing about twelve-step programs is letting go of resentment. Resentment is what leads to a lot of the problems that people have with substance abuse and interpersonal relationships going wrong. Other people's behavior is no business of mine. I try to be for what I think is the good, righteous path to be on. I just stay on my own path and don't let anybody pull me off. I know what my agenda is for the day.

JM: In my experience it sometimes takes a lot of courage to stay on a path. There's a lot of people who are very ready to offer other paths that they think are *better*.

EXENE CERVENKA (X): Well, that's nice. But part of getting older is knowing more about yourself and about the world and other people's agendas and learning what's true. There are certain things that I just know to be true. There are a lot of things that I just don't have answers for. But the ones that I do, I just can't be persuaded to change my mind because I know from experience what works and what doesn't. (Author's note: A few years later Exene posted online theories describing some mass shootings in the United States as being staged with actors as part of a left-wing plot to support gun control. ("X's Exene Cervenka Calls Santa Barbara Shootings a Hoax" by Chris Payne, Billboard Magazine, May 29, 2014)

REVOLUTION IS A PROCESS

JM: You write that, "There is no way to revolution, revolution is the way." This reminds me of Gandhi who said, "Be the change you want to see" and of Thich

Nhat Hanh, "There is no path to peace, peace is the path." I spoke with Greg Graffin and Ian MacKaye about meditation and they hold the common view that people who practice meditation are having a peaceful experience yet when they themselves try to meditate, their minds are too busy.

MARK ANDERSEN (*Dance of Days* / Positive Force DC): Thich Nhat Hanh has said that devotion is not what matters, practice is what matters. I'm paraphrasing. Part of what is deeply meaningful about what Thich Nhat Hanh has to say is that actually the cultivation of this awareness—mindfulness—is the practice. You have to concentrate on that. It's not simply being still and letting peace rush in. It's honestly engaging whatever is there. Accepting it and through that process of acknowledging, embracing it and letting it go; it's in that sometimes challenging or brutal encounter that we're able to grow.

The practice of slowing down to be present is very much tied into the concentration that I know within punk. The truth-telling or the truth-*hearing* in this case! I understand the terminology may be foreign to Greg or to Ian, but I fully believe that the most powerful art that they create has come out of, in some sense, a meditative state. And it's deeply connected to the spirit. I'm sure Ian would acknowledge that to an extent.

Part of what I'm talking about in this thing called revolution is you've got to be out there. Part of it might be up on barricades in the streets. On the other hand, one of the great paradoxical things about spiritual practice is when you see an injustice in the world and the reaction is, "Don't just sit there, do something." I have come to understand that equally reasonable, and increasingly important is, "Don't just do something, *sit there!*" We may be driven by our desire to see things change but we're not engaging on a deeper level. We've got to have both things. If you see an injustice and you do something, you could make the whole situation worse. Doing something is not necessarily part of the solution.

GREG GRAFFIN (Bad Religion): I am not a good meditator. I don't know how to do it. In writing music, I can hear something the way it's supposed to sound before it's actually played. I can definitely get into a mode where I'm seeing the result before I actually put it down on paper or hear it. But I don't know how to relax and, from what I hear, that is a really important part of meditation! (*laugh*) I'm just not good at it. It's probably because I'm hyperactive or something!

JM: It's very common that when people try to meditate, they think they don't meditate well. We have this idea that meditation means that you become instantly peaceful. But mostly what people are doing when they meditate is returning their attention, over and over, to a chosen object each time they notice their attention has gone away.

GREG GRAFFIN (Bad Religion): In that sense, I'm probably a very strong meditator because every time I write songs, I end up going back to the same thing. You go to comfortable places when you are writing and then you have to step back and listen to it a day later and realize that you've already been down that road.

JM: People sometimes notice when they meditate that sensory experiences happen *before* thinking. Albert Einstein wrote about how some theories came to him in a sort of "pre-thinking" way. They came in the sort of way you've described music coming to you.

GREG GRAFFIN (Bad Religion): If that's meditation, then I retract what I said!

JM: You're a great meditator after all!

GREG GRAFFIN (Bad Religion): Yeah! (*laugh*)

JM: There's a Bad Religion song "Tiny Voices" from *Stranger Than Fiction*. There's a line that says, "If we don't confront them, they will never go away." In a lot of ways, meditation is about noticing the voices in our head. Tell me about that realm of changing how we think and how that can create difference in the world.

GREG GRAFFIN (Bad Religion): Those little voices are your conscience. I don't think they just happen spontaneously. They happen because of past experience. Hopefully they are good experiences, but as the song implies, they could be trauma that you need to confront in order to get on with your life. As Dick Lewontin said in my dissertation, an organism is the nexus of a highly complicated set of experiences and events that preceded it.

DEEP BREATHING WONDERLAND PROCESS NUMBER ELEVEN

CRIS KIRKWOOD (Meat Puppets): It (meditation) would interest me if I had the brains for it. It would be nice to have the ability to participate actively in a healthy lifestyle. But it became apparent to me at a young age that I was bereft of that particular trait. Ultimately what you have are a lot of individuals that have their own way of going about life and yet there's also the delight of tradition. We're all ultimately the same kind of creature. There's certain things people have found that are calming or centering. There's meditation, but I've never gotten into that particular type of practice. I'm a big fan of discipline and crafty little humans.

I think they're really neat little critters in a lot of ways and some things they manage to come up with I find very impressive. I'm a big fan of systems. Something like the airline industry is mind-boggling to me, the level of cooperation and attention to detail. I find it interesting.

JM: Do you apply this to music as well?

CRIS KIRKWOOD (Meat Puppets): We've been doing this close to thirty years and one of the things that was there from the inception was allowing ourselves to grow old doing this; have the basic tenets of the project be so broad-based that we'd be able to continue to push back our own boundaries indefinitely. But in terms of applying systems to music; no more than my imagination will allow me to. Which is somewhat systematic in that I sit and think, "All right, how do I get beyond the confines of my mind? How do you allow inspiration to happen?" But I'm not that specific in terms of, "Now I'm going to do my Tantric exercises." I don't have intimate sessions where we are now going to explore *deep breathing wonderland process number eleven.*

IAN MACKAYE (Minor Threat / Fugazi): I do like to take inventory of this life. I look at all the things I have and figure out which of these things I actually need. Which of them bring me joy and which should be gotten rid of? I'm talking about not just material things, but ideas or ways of thinking. There is so much input coming in constantly that it's important to take some moments to just go through it and try to make sure that what is in there isn't toxic. If it is, then everything becomes toxified. You then get yourself into trouble.

JM: A lot of people identify so much with their thinking and we often may not be aware of what we're thinking about. One method of becoming aware of thoughts, beliefs and ideas is what some people call meditation.

IAN MACKAYE (Minor Threat / Fugazi): It's funny. I have often thought about meditation but I don't think I have ever done it. If I have, I didn't know it. My thinking usually comes in the form of conversation with people. Quite often it is with people who are struggling with something and I sort of stand back and think about their dilemma. Here is an image I often use—if you and I are sitting at a table and you have your hands under the table and you have two pieces of a puzzle that you are trying to fit together and you're having a difficult time with it—*that* is a dilemma. I think that just talking about that dilemma and bringing it into the air is, in essence, bringing your hands above the table. When you bring your hands above the table it's much easier to figure out the answer to the dilemma. And the answer is either how those things easily fit together. Or that those things will never fit together. But at least you have arrived at the answer and the dilemma is gone. It is in that process I arrive at my own thinking. It's that business about how much easier it is to help someone clean their room than your own. I talk to people and I give them ideas or advice, but then I recognize that I have to take my own medicine, too. It is hard but it's really productive. I'm not saying that this is the way everyone has to do it. I'm just saying that this is the way that I mostly get into this way of thinking. Now, there are times I do like to get up early in the morning. I will look out a window and do some thinking. I will stop and look at something that nobody else would see. But not because I'm constantly in a sort of dream state, but rather that I think it's important to be idle from time to time; to let your mind kind of wheel away. And then you can jump into it with the rest of you.

DARIUS KOSKI (Swingin' Utters): I wanted to be a writer when I was in high school and realized I was a really shitty writer. I don't understand how to come up with an interesting plot so I abandoned that altogether. But lyrics came pretty easily. Maybe I'm thinking something and a phrase just pops up and I go from there. I always have a little notebook and pen with me. I never sit down to write something—it just happens. If I try to sit down and write a song, I may get one or two lines I can use later. It's always the stuff that pops into my mind that's the best. I don't know where it comes from. It's just something that happens. Melodies are the same and sometimes come at the same time.

JM: It sounds like you just trust the process.

DARIUS KOSKI (Swingin' Utters): Yeah, that's the only way it works for me. There's months where I don't write a song but I never get writer's block. It's not like I'm going to write a brilliant song but I could always come up with something. It's the one thing in my life I feel I can do really well. I have no doubts about what I can do when it comes to music. I feel comfortable with myself. And it's frustrating because I don't make a living playing music. That sucks! It would kill me if I had to stop playing music.

IAN MACKAYE (Minor Threat / Fugazi): I have nothing to sell and I'm not advocating any particular group or organization, no books, nothing like that. All I'm interested in is encouraging people to think about things. To maybe find arrival. And see that maybe not everybody in the world is trying to sell you something. It's a nice thing to think about.

JM: It is a nice thing to think about. I like the way you put it as *arrival*. We always seem to be on our way somewhere. So, when is the part where we get there?

IAN MACKAYE (Minor Threat): When do we get there? We are always on our way. Always! (*laugh*) And therefore we are always there. Works out pretty good!

JM: Have you experimented with meditation or contemplation to deal with intense emotions and to expand your awareness?

KLAUS FLOURIDE (Dead Kennedys): I have meditated, but not enough. I'm sort of a lazy meditation and yoga person. Now I'm sort of forcing myself back into doing that just because there's a lot of very anxious things going on in my life right now. In order to control the anxiety and keep it from turning into say, an illness. Because too much anxiety can make you ill basically, you have to do things to be able to find that quiet place and not necessarily wipe out what you're anxious about, but deal with it so it doesn't rule you. Anxiety can really be crippling.

I believe totally in psychiatric medications for when they're needed because chemically you could just have the wrong chemicals pumping through your brain. People who have things like schizophrenic conditions; it must be like having a bad acid trip every day. I can't imagine that! If you need chemicals to help out in an anxiety situation, but they don't become an addiction in themselves, that's helpful too. It should be coupled with helping yourself figure out what causes the anxiety and that can be done in therapy and with meditation.

When I was eighteen, I took about six months of yoga. No, I must have lasted about three months. The main thing it taught me—and it's a great trick that I pass onto people at parties—is how to get rid of hiccups! (*laugh*) I know it sounds absurd but yoga has to do with controlling your body. I learned how to control my diaphragm, which was spazzing and causing me to have hiccups. If someone says, "I never get over my hiccups once they've started," I've said, "Sit down and do this." In three minutes, they're gone and the person is saying, "Oh my God!"

It reminds me of how Kurt Vonnegut's brother, a scientist, responded when someone commented on how cluttered and messy his house was. He said, "If you think this is messy, you ought to see it up here," and he'd point to his head. That's how I feel about how my life runs. The outside clutter is a reflection of the inside clutter. If I ever want to get the outside more organized, I'm going to have to work on the inside a little more. It's an ongoing process, as is life in general. You don't stop learning at any point.

JM: About your song, "True to This" you've said, "It's just being free from accumulated garbage, whether it's emotional or physical." Tell me about the journey of freeing yourself from what is not essential.

JOHNETTE NAPOLITANO (Concrete Blonde): It's something you don't realize until you have all this crap you haven't seen in years. It just becomes karmic baggage after awhile. But for a nation of people that are supposed to be so free, we sure burden ourselves with a lot of obligations and pressures we really don't need. Of course, typically the things we own start owning us. We're less mobile, not discovering the world around us, caught in a cycle of working to maintain the things we have. We have more than most people on the planet and it's never enough.

THE WAY TO LIVE

IAN MACKAYE (Minor Threat / Fugazi): As a kid I used to play touch football in the street. I grew up on Beecher Street in Washington DC. We had a regular game of touch football, me and these other little boys, about ten to twelve years old. It was not tackle, it was touch. But when you got touched you really got slapped. You really hit the person and there was an aggression. And there was one guy who played, whose name I have forgotten now, but I remember that he was so gentle with his touches that it surprised me. I thought it was weird because it didn't seem like he was keeping up. He wasn't doing it right! I couldn't understand where he was coming from. It was so strange. It was supposed to be this, "Gotcha!—you're out!" Whereas he used these really gentle touches. What was notable was that he always got you. He didn't need to make a show of it. He was agile and quick and when you ran with the ball, he would just gently touch you. He didn't need to hit you hard because he got you. He was relaxed. Every once in a while, I think about him; "That is the way to live."

Instead of being in a constant state of frustration and reflexive anger, to feel more relaxed. If you are working for goodness and happiness then be good and be happy. That just seems so clear to me. Or maybe I'm an idealist. But I feel there is no strategy for being happy. That's the problem; people believe that there is a strategy, something they must do to be happy. If they believe that, then they can be sold ideas and products they're told will bring happiness! The only way to be happy is to be happy! It's just too easy, but they keep going to the wrong shop.

HUDSON RIVER WIND MEDITATIONS—LOU REED

Lou Reed's twentieth and last solo album was released in 2007. In the liner notes for *Hudson River Wind Meditations* Reed explains, "I first composed this music for myself as an adjunct to meditation, Tai Chi, and bodywork, and as music to play in the background of life, to replace the everyday cacophony with new and ordered sounds of an unpredictable nature." When the album was re-released in 2024 an article in Yoga Journal noted how few people knew this album. ("Lou Reed Has Recorded . . . a Meditation Album?" by Sierra Vandervort January 20, 2024—Yoga Journal) Lou Reed passed away in 2013.

EDDIE STERN (Chop Shop / Lou Reed's Yoga teacher): I met Lou Reed in 2006. He was a very good friend of an artist named Julian Schnabel, who was a student and friend of mine. Julian invited me to his sixtieth birthday and Lou and Laurie (Anderson) were at that party. Lou was seated next to my wife, who is French and not a part of American music culture. She didn't know who Lou Reed was. Lou picked up her French accent and he could tell she had no idea he was a musician, so he spoke very freely with her all evening about France and cheese. That was funny.

When Julian put on the Berlin concerts at St Ann's Warehouse (2006) he invited us and Julian brought us backstage and introduced me to Lou again and said, "Lou, you really should do yoga with this guy." Lou said, "I don't like yoga. It makes my knees hurt." Julian said, "No, this guy is different. You should try him." I went over to his house to teach him, and that became the start of a friendship until he passed away in 2013.

Every Tuesday was his day off from Tai Chi and we would do yoga, meditate, chant and we would talk. He would ask questions. As I mentioned in the liner notes (*Hudson River Wind Meditations*) when we got to the part of doing yoga poses, Lou would always put on this record he'd made. It wasn't available at that time because it had a limited release and didn't do well commercially. Lou was always ahead of his time. He had *Metal Machine Music* (1975) which now is revered but back then, people were like, "What is this?" So, Lou would put on the *Wind Meditations* when we'd do the yoga practices. Once in a while he'd say to me, "I don't even know how I made this music. I couldn't play this again if I wanted to. I can't even remember the instruments I used." There was this feeling that here was this one-off piece of music that could never be recreated because he didn't know how he made it! It existed as this music of hypnotism, drones and odd beauty. It was the soundtrack to our weekly yoga classes but I never thought once to say, "Where can I get a copy?" It was Lou's music for meditation and Tai Chi and it was before he decided he even liked yoga!

JM: The meditation album actually reminds me of *Metal Machine Music* in some ways.

EDDIE STERN (Chop Shop / Lou Reed's Yoga teacher): Yes, it reminds me of that album, too. I was with Lou once a week, an hour each time, over a span of about seven years from 2006 to 2013. I was really intimidated to teach him because he was Lou Reed! I grew up in the 1970s and 80s in Greenwich Village and we all knew who Lou Reed was! When I started learning how to play guitar one of the first songs I learned was "Sweet Jane" by the Velvet Underground. So, it was definitely intimidating to meet Lou. I was scared of him! I did my best to go over and teach him and always be like, "Okay, stay on point." Because if you weren't present, Lou would know it really quickly. He could sense very acutely what was going on around him, if people were responding to him in that moment. It's kind of like, if you imagine an old-school Zen master and as soon as your attention wavers, they throw a brick at your head! In his own way, Lou was like that with knowing who was tuned in and who wasn't at that moment. So, you had to be present.

JM: How does making music relate to any spiritual sensibility?

JAMES WILLIAMSON (Iggy & The Stooges): Honestly, when I was that age, I wasn't thinking about things like that. We were very much in the present. Our band was all about our band and we didn't much care what anybody else thought about us. All we cared about was what we thought about *us*. So, I'm not sure that there was a spiritual consciousness that entered into it too much, although everybody took all the usual psychedelics. It was the late 60s and 70s.

CONTROL THE MIND—JACK GRISHAM

I'm in downtown Huntington Beach, California at Jack Grisham's house just a few blocks from the ocean. The mail carrier stops by and Jack greets her warmly, "Hi Becky!" and then returns to telling me about his joy of exploring religions: "I've got books all over the house. I'm comparing a lot of religions. I'm reading a book by this Jewish Rabbi Lewis Browne, *This Believing World*. He ended up killing himself. I recently read some Viktor Frankl. I read the Koran, the Bible. I'm always reading something."

JM: I've been thinking about Viktor Frankl. He presented the idea that, "Between a stimulus and the response, there is a space. And in that space is where freedom is possible." Frankl was saying that we can choose our responses, independent from the experience. Do you think that's true?

JACK GRISHAM (TSOL): Yeah. If you call my house the phone machine says, *"Have a great day cause it's your choice."* So, that's it. But it takes a lot of work and a lot of training to basically control the mind instead of having your mind control you. I used to sing songs saying "Wake up, wake up, wake up!" And I didn't realize that *I* was asleep! (*laugh*) It's actually pretty funny if I think back about it. "Wake up!" But *you're* asleep, sir! Real strange; a man that's asleep telling other people to wake up.

JM: Your new album *Wilder Shores* (2017) is based on Kundalini Yoga mantras. Tell me about your yoga practice.

BELINDA CARLISLE (The Go-Go's / The Germs): I started practicing Kundalini Yoga twenty-six years ago when I was pregnant with my son. My first teacher was Gurmukh Kaur Khalsa. At that time Gurmukh used to come to people's houses to do prenatal yoga and I was really sick with my pregnancy. She would come to my house and that was my introduction to yoga. During that time, I was also battling my own addiction demons, which is well-documented. But when I got sober, almost thirteen years ago, I started a consistent practice and so I know its power. The past thirteen years it's been pretty much a daily practice.

One of the things I loved when I was introduced to Kundalini Yoga was the music and chanting. Even way back then, before I got sober, I was chanting a lot and I was part of Soka Gakkai, an organization of Buddhists all over the world. At that time, I was thirsting for something. I was chanting a lot and even being in the throws of addiction, chanting would still alter my perception in a good way. So, when I decided I was ready to make this serious change, I was chanting two to three hours a day. Not Kundalini chants but, "Nam-Myōhō-Renge-Kyō." My life was a complete mess, but I was flying high! So, that was proof to me. And through the years I've had a few experiences with my yoga practice and chanting, where things would happen, which is a whole other story.

About one and a half years ago I thought, "Okay, I'm just going to experiment with it." To be honest, almost everybody didn't want to know about it. They didn't really understand what I was trying to do. In the spiritual community, they didn't understand it and my record company and the straightforward pop and rock people also didn't get it. So, I just thought, "Well, whatever. If nobody hears it or responds to it, then at least *I* liked it!" That's been my attitude anyway with my last albums like *Voila* which was all in French, and the album before that (*A Woman and a Man*—1996). I just thought I'd experiment. I listen to mantra, The Bee Gees, and then I'll put on Wall of Voodoo. But mantra is ninety percent of what I listen to. I know its power. It transforms things energetically. Chanting is not just airy-fairy; it's a science. I love it. Whatever I do next it won't be for a couple of years. I'm taking six months off now. I like doing nothing. Doing nothing is under-rated!

JM: I agree! I really put effort into doing nothing. That's funny to say! But it can take effort to create spaciousness.

BELINDA CARLISLE (The Go-Go's / The Germs): I totally get it. It would take me months. My last show was in Singapore about a month ago and before that I was in India and it took me a good while. I ended my tour in the UK at the beginning of October, so today is December 1st (2017) here in Bangkok and it's taken me two months to really be able to be happy with doing nothing. It takes an effort sometimes to be okay with that. Because all of us in this world, especially now with social media and so much stimuli—more so in the States than here—but you always feel that if you're doing nothing then something is wrong. And doing nothing is—just—the—best. It's just the best.

JM: I think people don't know how to do it. We were raised to believe that if you watch TV then you're doing nothing.

BELINDA CARLISLE (The Go-Go's / The Germs): It's funny that you say that. I'm going on a silent retreat for ten days where it's no reading, no speaking. It's full-on silence. It's supposed to be a completely incredible experience. I've always liked the idea of it but I don't think I've been ready until now, but it kind of scares me. Everybody I know that's done it has said that it is just the most psychedelic thing that you can do.

RAY CAPPO (Youth of Today / Shelter): The mantra holds the mind, but it also scrubs the mind. The mind is very busy and can go all over the place. Even if I say, "I want to sit for fifteen minutes and chant mantras," as soon as I start "Hari Krishna" the mind will go somewhere else immediately. So, the mantra is a practice of holding the mind. When you say a mantra with the appropriate, not just attention, but *intention*—which is calling divinity into your life—then the mantra becomes even more powerful.

EDDIE STERN (Chop Shop / Lou Reed's Yoga teacher): I started doing yoga in 1986. I was working in an iconic record store in Greenwich Village called Bleecker Bob's. I was in the back selling T-shirts. There was a guy named Ted Byoric working at Bleecker Bob's and he started talking to me about yoga, enlightenment and transcendental states of consciousness. He was my first introduction to yoga as a spiritual practice. I ended up going to India when I turned twenty-one after going to some yoga classes in New York City. Ted and I ended up starting a business together and we sold a lot of bootleg punk rock T-shirts. I realized I'd found something purposeful and I wanted to commit myself to it. It was in a very different form than the yoga and spirituality world is today. It was much more fringe culture and it had the spirit of freedom and creativity. This was the spirit of punk rock, but it had the clothing of hippies. Yoga was a very strange crossroads between absolute freedom and discipline. I had no idea that India was going to become a lifelong habit for me, where yoga was going to be the only thing I ever did again. All these years later, that's still the same state of mind I'm in. I still listen to punk rock and post-punk, all the music I listened to during my formative spiritual years, but my life is fully dedicated to religion and spirituality. For me, music is transcendence and I'm pretty sure I'll always love punk rock.

P.1   Hudson River Wind Meditations *by Lou Reed (2006). From the liner notes:*
"I first composed this music for myself as an adjunct to meditation, t'ai chi, and
bodywork, and as music to play in the background of life, to replace everyday
cacophony with new and ordered sounds of an unpredictable nature." Contributed:
Sister Ray Enterprises / Canal Street Communications.

P.2   Punk Rock Jesus (2012) by Sean Murphy. The story of a reality TV show in the future titled "J2" that stars a human clone of Jesus created from DNA lifted off the Shroud of Turin and implanted in the womb of a virgin teenage mom. Contributed: DC Comics / Vertigo.

P.3 Bad Religion concert with singer/scientist Greg Graffin in Santa Cruz, California, on June 3, 2016. Photo by John Malkin.

P.4 *"Punk made me aware of political injustice and Buddhism has taught me how to respond to it skillfully."* Dharma Punx: A Memoir by Noah Levine. Copyright (c) 2003 by Noah Levine. Used by permission of HarperCollins Publishers.

P.5   Kyaw Thu Win, singer/activist with Myanmar punk band Rebel Riot, at screening of My Buddha is Punk in Berlin on July 28, 2023. Photo by John Malkin.

P.6   Poster for October 12, 2024, concert at Zionskirche in Berlin celebrating thirty-five years since the 1989 peaceful revolution and fall of the Berlin Wall with former East German punk bands Planlos, Rosa Beton, and author Henryk Gericke. Poster contributed: Wenke Rottstock (KvU). Photo of Planlos by Wenke Rottstock.

P.7   Drummer Mita Schamal plays with Namenlos during an illegal concert on June 11, 1983, at St. Michaelis Church in Karl-Marx-Stadt, East Germany. The band was arrested on August 11, 1983. Photo by Machulla / Heldenstadt Anders e.V.

P.8 Billy Zoom playing guitar with X on January 25, 2009, in Santa Cruz, California. "Playing music is a spiritual experience." Photo by Matt Fitt.

P.9 Joe Clements performing with Buddhist punk band the Deathless on July 20, 2018, in Santa Cruz, California. Photo by John Malkin.

"DON'T DRINK DON'T SMOKE"
STRAIGHT EDGE/POSITIVE MENTAL ATTITUDE/ MINOR THREAT AND BAD BRAINS

I'm a person just like you / But I've got better things to do than sit around and smoke dope.

— "Straight Edge" by Minor Threat (1981)

I've lost so many friends to drugs. I've seen so many punks go down the tubes with intravenous drugs, with alcoholism, right down to being a glutton. I don't mean to use that in a biblical way. I mean having no discrimination about what they put in their mouth. That's a big thing.

— Ray Cappo (Youth of Today / Shelter)

Within our hearts and minds we know everyone has a soul, and in that soul there is what we would call the inner spirit. And there is a heart that beats. We're dealing with the wisdom time now.

— H.R. (Bad Brains)

Heifer whines could be human cries / Closer comes the screaming knife / This beautiful creature must die.

— "Meat is Murder" by The Smiths (1985)

an MacKaye was the singer and guitarist with Washington DC punk band Minor Threat and coined the phrase "Straight Edge" in 1981. MacKaye had no way of knowing that this song about his own experience refraining from consuming alcohol and drugs would become an international counterculture within a counterculture; a safe place for punks who chose to live without drinking, smoking and casual sex. Punk bands and fans later combined straight edge with a variety of ethical, spiritual, and religious traditions like veganism, Christianity and Krishna Consciousness. Many physically identified themselves as straight edge by drawing, or permanently tattooing, an "X" on the back of one hand, a reference to the "X" that was traditionally penned onto the hands of minors attending concerts, signifying they were too young to buy alcohol.

Many straight edge bands became advocates for vegetarian or vegan diets, with animal rights being widely embraced by punk musicians including singer Chrissie Hynde. The website for People for the Ethical Treatment of Animals (PETA) says: "Over the years, PETA and animals have always been able to count on Chrissie Hynde. In fact, there is absolutely nothing that the gutsy, outspoken Pretenders frontwoman and founder wouldn't do to further the cause of animal rights." Hynde operated The VegiTerranean Restaurant in Akron, Ohio, for years and led a 2004 protest against Kentucky Fried Chicken in France where, "she and other activists smeared "blood" on the windows and were arrested."

Multi-instrumentalist singer Moby owned a vegan restaurant in Los Angeles called Little Pine from 2015 to 2022 and donated all profits to animal welfare organizations. In 2019, Moby had the words ANIMAL RIGHTS tattooed across his arms in bold black lettering and on his neck is the phrase "Vegan for Life." In 2023 Moby directed the playful and insightful documentary *The Punk Rock Vegan Movie* which illuminates his path to veganism via punk rock and includes interviews with dozens of vegan punk musicians including Ian MacKaye (Minor Threat), Davey Havok (AFI), Captain Sensible (The Damned), Steve Ignorant (Crass) and H.R. (Bad Brains). Moby's 1996 album was titled *Animal Rights*. Moby was originally a member of hardcore punk band Vatican Commandos and in 1983 played guitar on their debut EP *Hit Squad for God*.

The film *10,000 Saints* (2015) is set in the late 1980s about kids who move from Vermont to New York City after the drug-related death of a friend. There they encounter the straight edge Krishna punk scene and a fictitious band called Army of One. *10,000 Saints* portrays punk as a radical drug-free breakaway from the world of dazed and confused hippies. The parents of the main character, Jude, are stoned hippies who forgot to inform him that he was adopted until he's a teenager. Eleanor Henderson wrote the story and in an online video explains: "The book is about how we interpret and invent new ways of rebelling . . . straight edge was the richest material I came across to write about." The movie uses humor to raise questions about spirituality and punk rock as exemplified by the dialogue in this scene where Jude's step-sister Eliza meets the lead singer from Army of One:

ELIZA: "Want a cigarette?"

JOHNNY: "No. I'm straight edge and Krishna."

ELIZA: "Quite a double bill."

JOHNNY: "They complement each other perfectly: clean living and transformation and transcendence."

"IT IS WHO I AM"

IAN MACKAYE (Minor Threat / Fugazi / Positive Force DC): It wasn't that being straight edge brought me so much joy. It's just that it is who I was. I didn't at some point say, "I'm not enjoying any of this stuff." I just never did it. There wasn't a point in time where I hit a wall and needed to pull out. I'm not saying that I did it right. I'm just telling you the way I lived. I don't ever think about it as this incredible shift in my life or as a realization. It is who I am.

I wrote the song "Straight Edge" because I was being ridiculed by friends in high school for not drinking or getting high. In the early days of the punk scene in Washington (DC) some of the older punks were really tickled by what they saw as a sort of *temperance* movement. If you didn't drink at a party people said, "Why are you making *us* feel bad for drinking?" I wasn't! It's a social activity. If you didn't do it with them, then people got self-conscious about it. That becomes amplified depending on the setting.

I don't think of it as a lifestyle. People have said, "That is an interesting lifestyle." But that suggests somehow that it is an affectation. It's not an affectation—it is life! It is the *basis* of life. People are born naked and they are not born drinking alcohol. I do understand that in theory there are babies born with drug addictions because of their mother's addictions, but by and large, I think we can agree that babies are born sober. That is the idea! They are born without all of the accoutrement of this society. Everything that we do beyond that is an additive.

JM: Monastics who refrain from drugs, alcohol and sex describe it as renunciation. Does that resonate for you?

IAN MACKAYE (Minor Threat / Fugazi / Positive Force DC): I would never think of it as renunciation, whatsoever. If I think about renunciation, it suggests that I'm carving away that which is part of me. I don't see it that way at all. If anything, I'm engaging in life with fewer filters and less distractions. I'm just trying to be alive *now*! Entirely alive. I want to feel things and I want to remember things. I don't actually think that intoxicants make things better. What I think they do is they allow people to *feel like* things are better. It's an enabler. It helps people get to a certain point. But that point can be gotten to without the elixir. The idea of getting high or getting drunk; so much of that is tied into such a creepy economy that is clearly preying on people's lack of self-confidence and insecurities.

GABRIEL KUHN (*Sober for the Revolution: Hardcore Punk, Straight Edge and Radical Politics*): My connection to straight edge in the beginning was very personal. I basically never drank as a teenager and I wasn't interested in doing drugs. In the circles I was hanging out—first the heavy metal and then the punk scenes—this was very odd. I then discovered that within this very exciting movement called punk there was a faction of people who didn't drink or do drugs! It was very exciting for me because it meant I wasn't the odd one out. I discovered that there was a global network of people who had a similar lifestyle. That was very uplifting for me and I identified with that group when I was seventeen years old.

When you look at straight edge politically and socially there are inspiring aspects, as well as very problematic aspects, that became pronounced in the late 1990s. At that time, it became more difficult for me to embrace that term. But since I never changed my lifestyle or consumption habits, I always felt a close connection to that scene. Within punk rock, straight edge has always been a marginal or minority movement but it has shown quite impressive persistence since the term was first coined over thirty years ago. It's a movement that's still going and I have the impression that it has grown even more in the past few years. Straight edge is known in punk circles; it's a clear reference point. People know what straight edge means, whether they have a positive or negative impression of it.

FRANCIS STEWART (*Punk is My Religion*): I have claimed a sXe identity for over twenty years. I don't think it's quite the centralized part of my identity it once was, rather it has just become a core part of me. I no longer have the desire to wear X's on my hands as much as I used to although I feel no need to hide my sXe tattoos either. Research into aging punks, especially aging punk women, indicates that this is a normal part of aging within a subculture. The overt markers fade in significance and aspects like the ethics, activism or core values take on greater importance. For many sXe punks that I've interviewed, living free was a form of resistance against capitalism, against family history of drug and/or alcohol addiction—and in some cases the abuse that can come with addiction—and a means to push back against social norms they found troubling. That could be understood as a form of striving for liberation.

THURSTON MOORE (Sonic Youth): Some of the strongest statements for youth politics were made by people like Ian MacKaye. It was really important as a seventeen-year-old kid hearing these lyrics saying: "This is my alternative to living in a way that's expected from teenagers who are into rock 'n' roll. I'm going to cut these things out of my life because I'm going to be smarter than that. You can make your own choice." Those lyrics were incredible! I wish I'd been seventeen at that time; I was already too old! I would've loved to see Minor Threat talk to an audience like that. They created a camaraderie. The first two or three years of Minor Threat were incredible.

JON GINOLI (Pansy Division): If the straight edge thing had been around when I was in high school, I probably would've embraced it, but I got out of high school a couple of years before Minor Threat were around. My parents drank. They were social drinkers and had a lot of parties. My parents are pretty fun actually. But I knew people who drank and did drugs and they seemed pathetic to me. I remember thinking, "These people are drinking so they can do things and the next day say, "I didn't know what I was doing!" They can pretend that they forgot what they'd done. I didn't want to live like that. I was idealistic. I drink now, but I didn't start drinking until I was almost forty. At a certain point I said, "I had these ideas about drinking that were valid at a certain point and now I don't agree anymore." But that was my thinking at the time.

JAMES SPOONER (*Afro-Punk* / *Black Punk Now*): I was thirteen when I first heard Minor Threat. When someone told me there was such a thing as straight edge it was instantly attractive to me because I was scared of drugs. And the idea that I could *not* do drugs and still be punk rock was awesome! Then I heard Minor Threat and I was sold. "I'm totally straight edge." When I think of Ian MacKaye and his ideals I don't think about straight edge. I think about the fact that Minor Threat is as well-known as any underground band and can sell out Hammerstein Ballroom, five thousand people. Their shows are $5, all ages. They've never played a show that is not all ages! Ian refuses to be in magazines that have cigarette or alcohol ads. He completely plays by his rules. He told me Dischord Records doesn't have a lawyer and he's never signed a contract. To me that's punk rock. The fact that he's been able to do Dischord for over thirty years, doesn't have a lot of business enemies, tells me that punk rock *can* work if you believe in it. I drink. That's not really my issue. It was cool when I met him

(MacKaye) and he said he still doesn't drink. I thought, "Wow, you're really the same dude from the record." That's exciting in a certain kind of way. This says to me that it's possible! The stuff that we believed in as fifteen-year-old idealistic kids can work as adults. You have to believe in it.

CAMILLE ROSE GARCIA (The Real Minx): I worked at Revelation Records briefly in Huntington Beach (California) and they had a lot of straight edge bands on their label. By the time I was seventeen I was sober and only recently started drinking wine. I'm not into extremes. I'm also not into extremely denying yourself anything. The straight edge scene never really appealed to me but it worked for some people. I'm just not that disciplined.

JORDAN COOPER (Revelation Records): For most people that were into punk it goes to just rising above the rat race and the herd. That's the majority view and there were factions that got into Krishna, Buddhism. Some got away from punk rock entirely because it slowed them down for opening their eyes. Then there's people like me that just built their own treadmill and didn't think too much about it.

AMY RAY (Indigo Girls): There are so many different kinds of punk music and there have been so many different movements, just from the late 60s on. Some have been more patriarchal and macho, fisticuffs and really anti-authority in a way that wasn't politicized. Then there's the strong riot grrrl thing and the straight edge movement, which is *so* disciplined and so thoughtful about everything. It's almost impossible to live that. It's a great way to live, if you can.

TIM MCKEE (North Atlantic Books editor): I remember hearing Minor Threat and 7 Seconds and *not* identifying with it. "I *do* take drugs and drink alcohol!" It revealed to me that there were a lot of differences within punk rock. Because all the bands I liked ended up being straight edge, I accepted their lecturing. But I didn't like it. I thought, "Hey that's cool for *you*, but why are you telling *me* what to do?" It felt a little un-punk rock to me. When I read interviews with Ian (MacKaye) or Kevin Seconds and they'd talk about that, I would feel a little talked down to. I wasn't *against* the idea of straight edge but it felt too doctrinaire. I didn't feel that with other ideas presented in punk lyrics like "Nazi Punks Fuck Off" and the anti-racist movement. I ended up respecting songs and interviews from punk rockers I looked up to immensely. They'd spell out anti-racist ideology. The anti-drug ideology; not so much. Drugs, alcohol and racism were all a problem within punk rock.

CHRISTIAN ASPLUND (Brigham Young University professor): Minor Threat came here when I was a freshman at BYU. It was a very exciting concert in Salt Lake in this basement venue. Ian's (MacKaye) microphone broke after the first song and he kept singing. His voice is so loud that you could still hear him above the band! He hung out with BYU punks after the show and he was very positive about

Mormonism. I think because of the Word of Wisdom and our clean lifestyle, he was sort of promoting that. That wasn't the main thing for me. It's more opposition to the hypocrisy and the decadence of the 70s and opening up a place for a person to be cool but not partake in things that he or she doesn't like or agree with.

ADAM NIGH (Too Bad Eugene): Within that same punk scene there was a lot of stuff that was on the opposite side. A lot of bands were embracing drunken, self-destruction.

YISHAI ROMANOFF (Moshiach Oi!): When I was heavily into punk rock, I was doing a lot of drugs. Minor Threat was one of my favorite bands, which is ironic. I appreciated the straight edge ideas even though I wasn't straight edge. By the time I cleaned up from drugs in 2007 I wasn't into punk rock as much. Since then I've been, for the most part, totally clean and straight edge.

JM: There's a punk subculture called straight edge where people refrain from alcohol, drugs, meat and casual sex. Were you ever interested in this?

JOHNETTE NAPOLITANO (Concrete Blonde): Definitely nothing I'm interested in, but to each his own. I see the value in the approach but whenever people feel the need to create too much discipline in their lives—too many rules—life just isn't about that to me. I do like a framework but within that framework is some built-in flexibility. I have goals, year to year. If I basically accomplish what I set out for myself in terms of my own sense of personal progress, I have no problem with blowing off to Vegas for a couple of wild days or some good, long wine-fueled dinners with friends.

JAMES WILLIAMSON (Iggy & The Stooges): A couple things happened around the same time. I realized this band wasn't working out and secondly that drugs weren't working out. So, I just stopped. It was very closely tied together. If you're in the music business, it's pretty hard to avoid. Getting out of the music business was very helpful in that regard. I removed myself from that scene. But I wasn't totally out of it because there was an interim period where I was working at a recording studio. I thought that's what I wanted to do until I transitioned into digital electronics. It was an intermediate phase. I think that the drug thing is a dead-end street. I don't advocate it for anybody.

ADDICTION UNTREATED IS SPIRITUAL DEATH

MARK ANDERSEN (*Dance of Days* / Positive Force DC): Addiction is something that impacts many of us directly through ourselves or the ones we love. Addiction untreated is a spiritual death. I'm acquainted with addiction and I always want to be honest how much this is still a process for me. It comes back to—*revolution is a process*. It's a state of becoming. So is the spiritual life. When it stops, then you're in trouble. For those of us who want a revolution that is personally significant and spiritually powerful, we're trying to figure out how in the hell we got here, what in the world we're supposed to do while we're here and what it all means. We want to do something that is real.

RAY CAPPO (Youth of Today / Shelter): I've lost so many friends to drugs. I've seen so many punks go down the tubes with intravenous drugs, alcoholism, right down to being a glutton. I don't mean to use that in a biblical way. I mean having no discrimination about what they put in their mouth. When you're twenty you might say, "Fuck you, Ray Cappo! If I want to eat a bag of Cheetos, I'm going to eat a bag of Cheetos!" You know what? I'm talking to these people now who are forty-five and it makes a huge difference!

JM: Did you ever hear about straight edge?

PENELOPE SPHEERIS (*The Decline of Western Civilization*): Hell yeah! The first straight edge person I met was Henry Rollins and I think it made him crazy! (*laugh*) He's from D.C. and there was a whole straight edge thing there.

JOHN DOE (X): The Musicians Assistance Program is a charity I've championed for many years. Buddy Allen was one of the founders. He was a jazz sax player and addicted to heroin for a long time and finally pulled himself out. MAP is a very rigid assistance program to help musicians who traditionally don't have any medical insurance, to get off drugs. But they have to really want it. They're given a place to live, money. Four years ago, they had a couple of big concerts with Keith Richards, Norah Jones and Lucinda Williams playing Graham Parsons' songs. It's not tied to religion, like twelve-step AA programs.

JM: It brings to mind the straight edge movement. Minor Threat and other bands sang about abstaining from drugs and alcohol, not eating meat and for some, not having casual sex. Was any of that interesting to you when it was happening?

JOHN DOE (X): We came from a different side of that track. More like William Blake where the road to enlightenment is through excess. But I see straight edge as valid. Whichever way you find your path, whatever way you find your power is good.

JONNY WICKERSHAM (Social Distortion): I was the exact antithesis of straight edge. I knew about Minor Threat and there was a band from Orange County called Uniform Choice that was a straight edge band. I was playing drums in a band in 1984 and we played a party with Uniform Choice and I got so hammered that I couldn't even play the set. It was just ridiculous. I remember the guy from Uniform Choice giving me a lecture about drinking! I always liked Minor Threat but I wasn't interested in being part of the straight edge movement because I was interested in getting fucked up! (*laugh*)

DAVE WAKELING (The English Beat): I did it the other way. I overdid all of them—drugs, alcohol and sex—until I saw how redundant it was and then worked backward from there. I had to check it out myself. Like the Buddha said, "Don't believe anything that anybody says, including what I just said. Go and check it for yourself—if it's your truth, then it's the truth." Now it's not a matter of renunciation for me. I prefer being sober at the minute. I struggled with pot over the years. I used pot to get off alcohol; it is a gateway drug and the gateway swings both ways. I was a dreadful alcoholic and started smoking pot again to get off the drink and now I don't care for either.

"I'm naturally high, dude!" Actually, I'm so busy that I haven't got time. Now I'm doing fourteen-hour days on the computer, so I'm jazzed doing that. Not quite as scared of myself, so I don't need as much anesthetic. Life's no better but I'm used to the suffering now. I've accepted it and it doesn't hurt so much. You get to a nice little point where being alone doesn't necessarily mean being lonely. I don't need to grasp for anything else to stop me feeling lonely. I've had to get to some really despondent places to really see it. Jean Genet says that you see the stars the brightest when you're lying in the gutter. The Buddha said that the biggest lotuses grow out of the dirtiest swamps.

JOE CLEMENTS (Fury 66 / The Deathless / HotLung): I got sober when I was twenty-three and started playing music and eventually started hanging out with Noah (Levine). The straight edge scene was getting pretty big in the late 80s and I caught the tail end with more metalish hardcore stuff. When I really think about it, straight edge itself became a platform. It was another way of saying, "I'm better than you."

JM: In your documentary *Cleveland's Screaming* Vince Rancid of Slam Magazine mentions the "dogma of straight edge." It seems that any idea can become dogma, no matter how beneficial it began.

BRAD WARNER (ODFX / *Hardcore Zen*): Other people have said the same thing about straight edge. Some of it became very dogmatic. There were people going around trying to beat you up if you drank a beer! Anything can become dogmatic. For me, straight edge was something I was very interested in because, like probably every kid growing up in the late 70's, I had done drugs in high school. There was still this lingering idea that that was the cool thing to do and that you were going to find some kind of answer there, which was my reason for doing it. Then I found straight edge that said, "No, just get rid of all of that stuff; the answer is to just be who you are." I thought that was pretty amazing. I was very attracted to it. But when it became about everybody tattooing X's on their hands it becomes too much of a dogma. There is an idea within Zen that when anything becomes too dogmatic, even if it is a good thing, it needs to be thrown away.

> *Wake up you little boys and girls / And go and tell it to the whole wide world . . . / Take out all unnecessary things bringing you down.*
>
> —"Morning Song" by Too Bad Eugene

ADAM NIGH (Too Bad Eugene): When I was in high school and discovering punk rock, what really got me going was 7 Seconds and their message of, "Let's have a positive youth and not be like what our parents are telling us we're like," which is a bunch of alcoholics addicted to drugs. Let's pick ourselves up! Minor Threat, Youth Brigade and this whole, "We're not going to be what the stereotypes say we are." It started with a love of self. I love the idea of trying to oppose things that are self-destructive.

The line in "Morning Song"—I wasn't straight edge when I wrote it. It's this idea of getting to a place where you can live life in a meaningful, joyful way while still being socially conscious. You want to eliminate things that keep you from that like drugs and alcohol. But more what I had in mind was my own life and being too busy. Simplify. Don't say "yes" to everybody that asks you for your time because that will rob you of your own life. I look at it now and it sounds like birds chirping, smelling the roses—kind of naive. But it was *stop and smell the roses every once in awhile.*

DRUGS AND ALCOHOL

JENEDA BENALLY (Blackfire / Sihasin): Drugs and alcohol have always been used as a weapon against indigenous peoples as a way for the government to take our land, our culture and to take our youth and future away from us! I never considered myself to be straight edge but I do remember some people having X's on their hands. Some people were against anything that was considered to be an intoxicant, even caffeine.

CLAYSON BENALLY (Blackfire / Sihasin): Growing up on the Navajo reservation, as a youth band, we were all under eighteen and trying to play in a venue was next to impossible because at that time music was synonymous with bars. If you wanted to be a band you had to play in a bar. We said, "Fuck that! We're creating our own scene." Even our own community here in Northern Arizona—Flagstaff— we'd have amazing festivals and it was about community and diversity. Whether you're straight edge or whatever, it didn't matter. It was just about expressing yourself and we had such a diverse range that it became a hub. Touring bands used to love to stop here, like Naked Aggression and The Offspring.

To be straight edge, there was a lot of respect in that. We never considered ourselves straight-edgers because we were just indigenous people that said, "No! Fuck you! We're not giving into this system that has been used to crimi-nalize, demonize and destroy our people. We're doing something completely different than that. Whatever you say is the norm—especially as youth—we're going to do the complete opposite!" Any discrimination that was thrown at us, we would turn it around and use that to empower ourselves. We wrote music. If somebody said to my sister, "You're a girl. You can't play bass," that was empowering! It was a compliment. "Okay—Thank you! That gives me more ground to stand on!" Anytime something was used to harm us, or was put in our way as an obstacle, it was like, "Great! We're going to rise."

JENEDA BENALLY (Blackfire / Sihasin): One of the songs we wrote as Blackfire is "Painkiller" about substance abuse and it was really important to inspire our peers because at that point we were just teenagers going into high schools to play and talk to kids about the importance of making healthy decisions. It was really important to give the message of being clear-headed so that you could make good decisions. Indigenous people in small communities have been impacted by drugs and alcohol in horrific ways. That's not just because we're on a reser-vation—that happens all over. But when we were growing up, we were asking, "Why are our youth completely disregarding our cultural ways and values in order to escape with some substance?" We saw that as a death to our culture and our future. We really tried to nurture an environment free from drugs and alcohol and discrimination. As Blackfire we only *ever* played all-ages shows because we didn't want anybody to ever feel discriminated against because that's how we grew up. We grew up being clearly discriminated against. We wanted to foster our audience's understanding that they were in a safe place where they were valued and respected.

CHRISTIAN ASPLUND (*Sacred Music & The Punk Ethic*): As a Mormon I feel that punk rock is in some ways a negative movement, but not in a bad way. It was a reaction to the excesses of the 70s and hypocrisy of that era. This worship of materialism came so quickly on the heels of the hippies-sixties thing. It just felt so hypocritical and ostentatious; rock stars destroying hotel rooms and having concerts at big arenas. I found that distasteful. It had nothing to do with music. And there was this phony spirituality of New Age vibes and horoscopes. It felt like a really nice cleansing of the palette.

The straight edge impulse goes way back because the 70s rock scene was all about bragging about cocaine, marijuana, booze and lots of sex. Punk rock talked about love and dating in a more innocent, teenager kind of way and seemed more authentic and fun. Of course, punk rock ended up going a different direction in terms of lyrics. But that was similarly interesting to the young person—or at least the young male—about politics and conspiracy, anti-Reagan and alienation. It was exciting to have songs about, and made by, losers. Because the losers never had their own platform and then it suddenly became cool to be a loser or an outsider.

BRAD WARNER (*Hardcore Zen*): Whatever clouds your mind, you have to get rid of it. For me it really wasn't about renunciation. Even though I had done drugs, I found that I didn't really like them. So, it was never hard to give up something I didn't like. But there are other ways that you can intoxicate yourself. You can be completely intoxicated without using any drugs at all. So, getting rid of those other intoxicants—certain television, gossip, fantasies—can be difficult. A lot of times these are hard to identify because society is telling you that that this is the way you're supposed to live and you don't have any reference point to say otherwise. We're told that there is not a different way to live, other than to keep reinforcing this identity that you have and to try to make it as big as possible. We learn to strive to be number one and be on top. Especially Americans have this drive.

VEGETARIAN BUT NEVER MILITANT

JM: You've written about your own drug and alcohol addiction in your 2011 memoir *Lips Unsealed*. Were you interested in the straight edge sub-genre of punk?

BELINDA CARLISLE (The Go-Go's / The Germs): To be honest I didn't even know what straight edge was. Of course, I wouldn't have been interested in that back then because I wasn't a vegan and I wasn't militant in that way. I would do stuff for PETA and yell at people on the street for wearing fur. (*laugh*) I was vegetarian but I was never militant. I didn't even know that there was such thing as a straight edge. I never heard of it!

DAVE DICTOR (Millions of Dead Cops): We were upset about this culture that we came from that wants you to mindlessly consume a "Corporate Death Burger," which is the title of one of our songs. They don't want us to even consider what goes on in the meat industry and the stealing of resources. If everyone in America is eating burgers, how does that affect the economy of the rest of the world? From clearing out rainforests in Central and South America to soybeans not being fed to people but to fatten up cows. I've given up meat now for over thirty years.

If you don't find yourself fitting in, or you're not liking what you're seeing, there is very much the temptation to over-party. And then you get to see that reality. Then you make a conscious decision to not over-party. In fact, let's *under-party*. With that comes a clarity. For myself it has, anyway. Then you start trying to find other things to fill up your life besides alcohol and drugs. A spirit-full nature is a nice thing to fill up your self with. To fill a void that we all have; the hunger that we have to get through and survive and imagine something greater than what we're seeing.

JM: When you were in the band in Israel, were you interested in straight edge bands?

ETAY LEVY (Nekhei Naatza): Absolutely. I appreciated the ideas behind it but I wasn't straight edge. I became vegetarian shortly after meeting Federico (Gomez) and Santiago (Gomez) and have remained vegetarian since.

FEDERICO GOMEZ (Nekhei Naatza / Dir Yassin): We were straight edge pretty much all the time since we started the band.

RUSS RANKIN (Good Riddance): Veganism happened because, while I was growing up eating meat, I never really felt good about it. I was always told, "You have to." I was getting into a lot of straight edge bands in the late 1980s and going to see all these shows. Bands were starting to sing about vegetarianism; Youth of Today and Cro-Mags. I'd think, "I like this band and if they're singing about it, I'll check it out."

I read this book *Diet for a New America* by John Robbins and it absolutely floored me! After I got over being really pissed about how I'd been lied to for so long, I decided to pursue the lifestyle outlined in the book. It was 1993 when I went vegan and it was pretty easy, living in Santa Cruz (California). But even a few years after that when Good Riddance got signed and we were touring a lot, I found it not that big of a deal. It meant enough to me where I was willing to eat fries at Denny's on tour.

What's cool is that since 1993 I've been able to see the awareness grow and see much more available to people who are vegan or vegetarian. It's much more part of our cultural lexicon now. It used to be a freakish thing. Now everybody knows somebody who's vegan! The punk and hardcore scenes can take a lot of the credit for that, as far as espousing that lifestyle and getting people involved. A lot of people latched onto it as a trend. I'm not qualified to talk about what straight edge is now. I'm part of a generation where straight edge was pretty much just a positive thing. For me it's still a valid lifestyle.

ABDULLAH EL-KHATIB (Inqirad): I've never been into straight edge. I've been a vegetarian for over a decade and it's changed my life drastically. I was underweight and managed to get healthier as I refrained from eating meat.

ROB FISH (108): We played a show a few months ago and there was this band Gather who is pretty cool; young vegan straight edge kids. And another band Seven Generations Again; different ages but also vegetarian straight edge. I was talking to the singer from Gather and they were just back from their first time in Europe. She was talking about how she was having problems with her throat, singing, and we were talking about different ways to deal with throat issues. She was talking about how in Europe everyone smokes and drinks and it's really annoying. She liked playing the show that night because everybody was straight edge and vegetarian. I said to her, "To me the strangest thing was coming to the show tonight and there were probably one hundred fifty kids here and they're all vegetarian and straight edge, yet there's five frickin' PETA tables here showing me videos of animals getting killed!" I said, "What's the point? What do you find exhilarating about that?" I would rather play a show where I didn't agree with anybody! As least then there's some form of communication.

That was one of the things I really appreciated about the first era of 108—you'd have a bill with 108, Rorshach, Ass Suck and all these bands that really ran the gamut, socially or politically. I remember we played a show one time in Colorado Springs—Shelter, 108 and Not For the Lack of Trying. They had three guys from Downcaste and this girl who used to write for *HeartattaCk* and *No Answers*. Before the show we pulled up and I saw the guys from Not For Lack of Trying and we were hanging out. We went out to dinner together and a few punk kids at the place we went for dinner were looking at us like we were insane! They could not figure out how the singer from 108 could hang out with the kids from Downcaste and NFLOT. People said, "It was weird that you were all hanging out." I thought, "How thick are these people that they think we have these lines drawn?" We don't agree on some things but we probably agree on more things than you think. The few things we don't agree about are not a source of anger. We talk about it and we might make fun of each other a little bit. Maybe we'll debate a bit back and forth. Ultimately, I don't think any of us think we've got some corner on the market of truth.

You might shock someone into being a vegetarian because you made them see fifty videos of cows being hung upside down and killed. But when I got into straight edge in 1986, how many kids were into that scene that are still straight edge today? Probably a dozen. For a lot of them it never got any deeper than, "Drinking sucks. Smoking sucks." It's the same with vegetarianism. How many kids were vegan or vegetarian fifteen years ago that still are today? Not a lot. When I confront the idea of vegetarianism, I can think of PETA videos but really what it comes down to was that when I was in fifth grade my dog died. It broke my heart and I realized that this dog meant more to me than the people around me. That's why I'm still vegetarian.

FRANCIS STEWART (*Punk is My Religion*): Your sense that many sXe punks have viewed these choices as a moral, religious, spiritual precept very much aligns with the data I got on fieldwork over sixteen years of qualitative ethnographic work. Most interviewees talked very earnestly of those choices as a moral code, often describing them as akin to a wedding vow—a code that once broken, cannot be remade. What was really interesting was two-fold; First, the differences between those who took personal offense when other people—especially icons— "broke edge" and those who were more accepting of people whose decisions changed over time. Second, a large percentage of sXe people I interviewed have supplemented that precept by adding veganism and many of them consider it on a par with refraining from alcohol and drugs.

COMMUNITY OF DEVIANTS

IAN MACKAYE (Minor Threat / Fugazi): In the punk scene there was such a *fashionable nihilism* that when me or my friends engaged in that scene and *didn't* behave like that, it made some people uncomfortable. This started a kind of dialogue between us and them. I discussed it through lyrics. In the beginning I was writing songs like, "I Drink Milk" which was sort of making fun of this idea. All my friends wanted to go drink beer and I said, "I drink milk."

"Straight Edge" was a song I wrote in 1980 about my decision in my life to not get high and not drink and not be involved with manipulative or exploitive sex; conquest sex. What happened was that it resonated with people. I was thinking about it like it was a deviant position, especially in the 70s. It was a time where everybody I knew was always getting high. It seemed pretty crazy to take that position and sing about it. It seemed radical and really true to punk. I felt that punk rock was a community of deviants. I felt like a deviant because I did not share what the rest of society thought about partying and having fun.

At some point I wrote the song "Straight Edge." The lyric was basically that I am a person just like you but I've got better things to do. And then I list all things I am not going to do. Like, I'm not going to get high. I sang, "I've got the straight edge."

The idea was if I am fully present then I would have an edge on people. I did not think that I was attempting to create a movement. I certainly was not trying to organize something where people are going to go on a crusade against other people. That was just never my idea! I was thinking about my right to live my life the way I want to. If those words sound at all familiar it might be because they come almost directly from a Jimi Hendrix song. The song is "Six for Nine." At the end of the song there was a little spoken word bit where he says, "I am the one who has to die when it is time for me to die. So, let me live my life the way that I want to." Even though what I imagined what Hendrix was singing about was about being a kind of freak, those words really connected with me. I felt the same way about how I lived! This is my life; let me live the way I want to.

IAN MACKAYE (Minor Threat / Fugazi): People who have issues of violence, aggression or power are generally looking for devices that will serve as triggers for their violence. That's because they are trying to get the violence out of themselves. So, they look for things that will easily trigger the violence so that it will spring out of them.

One way of looking at straight edge is that it has a series of basic rules and if those rules are not followed, then you can fight. Then your violence can come out. In most organized religions there are similar tenets. These are principles, practices or beliefs that—if you think of them as triggers—then they provide a perfect format for violence because suddenly someone has broken a rule and they either have to be educated or punished. This applies to things like nationalism. Violence preys so intensely on things like nations because nations have borders. They are imaginary lines by and large.

Straight Edge resonated with kids around the country, and eventually around the world. By the mid-80's there was a fairly recognized and militant straight edge movement. Before long there was a kind of fundamentalist straight edge movement. There were people who actually were using this basic idea of straight edge as a position of education and saying that if you didn't accept the education, then you waived your rights to your own well-being. The media loved it! How much more sensational can you get then, "Here are these crazy punk rock kids who don't drink and don't eat meat but they are totally violent! Blowing up McDonald's!" The whole thing got so completely surreal.

Again, even though I coined the phrase *straight edge* I never intended it to be a movement. In fact, I am literally on record saying that! Minor Threat released a song called "Out of Step" and we redid the song on another record and during the instrumental bit I say, "This is not a set of rules. We are just talking about life. It's just something to think about." What developed out of it was something that was so far out of my or anybody else's control. It is a true phenomenon. That is what straight edge is.

ADAM NIGH (Too Bad Eugene): I listened to Minor Threat. My brother is seven years older than me so he saw 7 Seconds, who became my favorite straight edge band. Gorilla Biscuits and Youth of Today—I loved it! I saw them saying the same thing I was saying which was stay away from all this stuff that clouds the mind and wastes your humanity. I really embraced that for a period. But then I became aware of how prideful that was making me.

If you listen to Ian MacKaye through the Minor Threat discography there's "Out of Step" and then they do "Out of Step" again later on and he gives a mini-explanation like, "This is not a set of rules . . . " He was trying to distance himself from sounding like he's giving us a new Ten Commandments. But I couldn't help thinking, "That's not going to work. As long as you say, "I don't drink, I don't smoke, I don't fuck . . . " you can't help but call that a creed. That is the creed of a religion! I've heard him say that he didn't intend to start a movement, but he did. And that movement was very prideful. As much as you would want it to be rooted in a positive sense of self, I think it became largely a negative view of others. That's what happened with me.

There was a Christian straight edge movement because it saw that we have a shared value. But what was missing was compassion! I didn't see any. What I saw was a looking down upon smokers and drinkers. The song "Filler" that Minor Threat did was not sung with a sense of, "Hey man, let me pull you up. Let me give you wisdom that might help you in life." It was a total put down, "You're an idiot. You've just filled your life. You're crap." I had to face that at a certain point. It was not just something that had to do with my musical life, but my spiritual life. I had to find that authentic side of Christianity that was more about loving good than hating evil.

I love the idea of trying to oppose things that are self-destructive. But I do feel, in my experience of the straight edge movement, that it was a bit too prideful to really accomplish much positive. Since my younger days of putting the X's on my hands when I went to the punk shows, I do enjoy alcohol every now and then and I have a wife and think sex is an awesome thing. I don't think there is anything damaging about those things. One of the things that was short-sighted in my own straight edge was seeing those things as inherently damaging. It's more the *addiction*. Addiction to anything is what is going to keep you from living a fulfilled life. Total renunciation of alcohol is necessary if you are addicted to it. If you are not, I don't see the need to eliminate that from your life.

RON REYES (Black Flag / Piggy): Through history there are sheeple. There's a human tendency to want to be led and have a leader and some of that is good. It helps focus your energy and thoughts. But when it becomes mindless and thoughtless and you're not putting critical thinking into it, it becomes dangerous. You have to be careful.

REID CHANCELLOR (*Hardcore Anxiety: A Graphic Guide to Punk Rock and Mental Health*): I love that punk has a place for straight edge vegan kids and also a place for *we just wanna have fun and drink beer* people. The problem is when you start to view your own camp as better or more important than others. We're all outside the box. The whole idea of punk is a rejection of the "box." I've always identified with the straight edge movement. I used to drink and smoke but I quit a while ago. Straight edge is a perfect example of a camp in punk culture that can get out of hand. The first time I heard someone say they made the choice to "claim edge" I thought it was a joke. My decisions that I made for my health don't require any explanation or label, and neither does anyone else's for that matter.

VEGAN REICH

In one of its manifestations, straight edge hardcore punk drifted into hardline, a smaller movement with bands like Vegan Reich, who's singer Sean Muttaqi established the Uprising record label and a zine called *Vanguard* to support like-minded punks. Hardliners embraced a set of ideas and beliefs that emphasized animal liberation, veganism and refraining from drugs and alcohol. Vegan Reich lyrics also embraced war and a reverence for Islam and Taoism.

> *The war outside / manifests from the war within / Eternal jihad / Born on this battlefield / After all these years, I'm fighting still?*
>
> —"Eternal Jihad" by Vegan Reich

> *I'm not a vegan and I have had sex / So some hardline kids tried to kick my ass / If you're not like them they want to clean your clock / They're nothing but a bunch of jocks.*
>
> —"Indie Sux, Hardline Sux, Emo Sux, You Suck!" by Anti-Flag

SEAN MUTTAQI (Vegan Reich): I never felt much of an affinity for the straight edge movement in my earlier years. I knew about Minor Threat and liked them as a band, but I wasn't drug-free. My anti-drug stance arose within the anarchist scene, unrelated to straight edge. Years later our band Vegan Reich probably drew it's biggest following from the straight edge movement. Overall, I'm not sure that the general direction straight edge later took was a healthy one in terms of spiritual development. Overall, I find it really went down the path of a sort of Nietzschean *Will to Power* type mentality. Purifying one's self to become a sort of superman, as opposed to seeking some clarity for self-development. Once it devolved into crews beating people up for harming themselves—ostensibly by smoking or drinking—it missed the point. It certainly didn't have anything to do with Ian's original intentions.

FRANCIS STEWART (*Punk is My Religion: Straight Edge Punk and 'Religious' Identity*): In some scenes, sXe did become very rigid. The most extreme versions of these were hardliners but, in some ways, the most concerning were those who identified as posi-edge. They were very much invested in that identity to the point of being unable to see how rigid it was in some regards.

MATT CLEAVER (Stalin's War): I don't usually find myself in a position where I explain why I'm vegan or why I don't do drugs; why I'm straight edge. A lot of people that know me only find out after months. I don't like to be preachy. The best way to go about getting that message across is to lead by example rather than by dictum and telling people what they're doing is wrong.

JM: Was straight edge interesting to you in terms of clearing one's head, not consuming stuff that clouds the mind?

JACK GRISHAM (TSOL): I wasn't a big fan of it, man. Hey, that's great if you want to do it. Well, you do it and shut the fuck up about it! You know what I mean? Don't start telling me what I need to be doing! I've got a real problem with that. One of the things I have trouble with is *preachers*. I've got a big problem with people preaching. Tell me your view—don't tell me that this needs to be my view, because it doesn't need to be my view! The last thing someone drinking and getting high wants to hear is someone telling them not to do it!

I would've been all for it if they had done it and then shut the fuck up. I give talks all of the time and never say one thing about playing in a punk rock band. They're clueless. I've had guys come up to me and say, "Are you fucking kidding me? You're in *that* band?" They had no idea. You want to start a movement? Start a quiet movement! Keep your mouth shut about it. Don't start forcing it down our throats and separating people. That's immediately what they did, "This is the mark of the straight edge, you're not one of us." Shit! I think that it had a lot to do with destroying punk rock, at least the scene.

JAMES SPOONER (*Afro-Punk / Black Punk Now*): Ian (MacKaye) was nineteen saying, "I don't do drugs and I don't drink. I've got my head on straight. This is what works for me. I'm straight edge." He coined this phrase and people took it to mean this whole other thing. They took it on as their identity and warped it into all kinds of stuff. On the extreme level you had skins in Salt Lake City beating up people who smoked cigarettes and carving X's in their foreheads! That doesn't have anything to do with what Ian MacKaye was talking about! That's how things evolved.

I can relate to that because when my movie *Afro-Punk* came out in 2003, it really tripped me out when I started hearing people identify themselves as "Afro-Punk" or using it as an adjective, "That kid's all Afro-punked out." What the hell does that mean? It's one of the reasons I stepped away from it. To me *Afro-Punk* was this film I made. The media gets hold of things and all of a sudden it has to have a definition and a sound. I just saw an article that NBC did on the (Afro-Punk) festival this year and it has Afro-Punk on mainstream and it's like, "What are you talking about?" It's crazy to me. It wouldn't surprise me if in twenty years I'm talking to somebody about something ridiculous someone did in the name of "Afro-Punk" and I have to defend it. I think the combination of people desperately needing an identity and the media desperately needing to put things in a box is dangerous.

STEWART EBERSOLE (*Barred for Life*): In the United States there were bands that were dividing; "I'm straight edge!" That's great dude, you're straight edge. But nothing politically motivated. The Dead Kennedys really appealed to me. I was hard pressed to find bands that spoke to me politically in that era. I thought, "Okay, I'll take the skateboarding songs and the anthems." I got into Minor Threat and Uniform Choice and straight edge in the late 80s. That was all fantastic, but these were anthems for division and not anthems for unity. While they were singing songs about unity, they were really saying, "I want all the people that think like me to be on my team. I want the rest of you fuckers to clear out. Anyone with mohawks or dreadlocks is out and you have to have a shaved head and wear basketball jerseys." I thought, "I graduated from high school already and now I have to go through this again? Fuck this!" I always had a love/hate thing with straight edge.

I knew straight edge was supercharged in a political direction. I loved loud, fast music. There were political bands like Crass and Discharge but at times I thought, "This sounds more like Flipper singing songs about politics." It didn't make me feel empowered. I thought, "I don't want these guys doing my anthem." But if you wanted heavy fast stuff like Suicidal Tendencies, there wasn't shit about politics. They mentioned Ronald Reagan once or twice and the rest was about skateboarding, Satan, getting hit by a car, wanting a Pepsi; nothing touching on the political.

Getting introduced to Minor Threat's first record and learning about straight edge I realized, "There's other people who don't drink who have gone through the exact same scenario." That to me was revolutionary! Someone introduced me to a way of living that I'd already been living and this gave it a bit of validity. It was like saying, "You're not alone, man." And then straight edge became a little fanatical. By 1987 it became, "I'm vegan and straight edge and if you don't like these seven things that define my crazy life, then fuck you!" I thought, "Not again—this can't be happening again!"

When I first got into punk my mom said to me, "Why are you doing this to me?" I said, "Because I know there's more out there to discover and you aren't letting me do it and a lot of other people aren't either." I wanted to discover my own path and *that* is revolutionary. Punk rock isn't a collective revolution. We're always going to get into those Fugazi moments of, "I want everybody to be as free as possible within the confines of what I define is okay." I thought, "C'mon Ian—Don't do this to me! I'll agree with three of those, and four of them I won't. Don't penalize me for that." I'll never be able to agree with a collective idea of freedom because I don't think we as a species really get collective ideas of freedom. As soon as one person decides to be really free, you impinge on someone else's freedom.

MODERN-DAY MONASTIC MOVEMENT

SEAN MUTTAQI (Vegan Reich): The whole hardline thing was absolutely a modern-day monastic movement of sorts. A sort of synthesis for me between very American counterculture and revolutionary influences such as Nation of Islam, MOVE, and Rastafarianism, alongside anarchist thought with a heavy Buddhist/Taoist overlay from my immersion in Chinese martial arts. I think many in punk rock misconstrue what hardline was due to their inability to see it outside of straight edge, or as not conforming to their own dualist worldview of atheist or agnostic punk rock, fighting against a conservative religious right. It was more nuanced than most give it credit for. It certainly had no commonality with right-wing political thought, or any sort of evangelical Christianity.

JM: When I spoke with Ian MacKaye about being Straight Edge, I equated this with renunciation but this didn't resonate with Ian at all. What about you?

DAVE DICTOR (Millions of Dead Christians): I never thought of using the word *renunciate*. But I sure resonate with *foregoing it*. I'm just saying, "I've had my fill and I'm not going to tell you how to live." When you *renounce* something, it's almost like you're making a judgment about it. I'm someone who drank and drugged for many years of his adult life and then I gave it up ten years ago. When I was younger, I always looked skeptically at people who were older than me telling me that I shouldn't do something.

Even when I'm up on stage I'm conscious of communication. I have a song about drugs called "Going Nowhere Faster Than You." It's about being on speed; "For awhile in my life I was going nowhere faster." I knew that I was going nowhere, but I was doing it *fast*. I make a joke about it on stage and the crowd will laugh. And then I'll say, "I'm clean now for eight years and I feel good that I can share that with you tonight." Generally, I get a lot of positive attention for that.

On this other level I don't want to make judgments. I don't want to be standing in front of people saying, "I renounce!" I might even be playing in a bar where they're selling alcohol, so I'm not going to verbally announce that I'm renouncing anything. But I will certainly share that at this point in my life, I'm not using it and I find it to be a good way for me to be going. I'll generally preface it by saying, "Don't let your good times become your addiction," because that's where it went for me. On the other hand, if someone comes up on stage and they're very drunk I will say, "Wow, friend, you're very drunk. You should sit down and think about it. Make some better choices. You might put yourself or someone else in danger." But that's just where I'm at.

POSITIVE MENTAL ATTITUDE—"WE ADVOCATE NONVIOLENCE"

H.R. (Bad Brains): We advocate nonviolence and through these years there's been a few other groups that did not understand those advocations and because of their lack of discipline, they did suffer the consequences. But thank you for reminding me. It is a priority to be able to reach out to the masses and express ourselves in a peaceful manner. I do want to say that the good news is that the war is over. I would be available to share ideas and not allow our differences to make us indifferent to each other.

STEVEN BLUSH (*American Hardcore*): One thing in hardcore was that you had the Bad Brains in Washington DC. They were a very interesting band; they played jazz fusion, had good chops and got turned onto punk rock and Bob Marley. They were into PMA—positive mental attitude—self-help books and were really charged by that. They combined this positive attitude with new Rastafarianism, suburban punk rock and vegetarianism. It was incredibly strong. When Bad Brains came to New York, they kind of changed New York City. In the *American Hardcore* film Ian MacKaye talks about how the Bad Brains didn't have a practice space, so they'd come to their house and use their equipment. As they'd trade off the equipment, Ian realized how poorly they played compared to the Bad Brains. Also, punk rock had been very negative but here was this very positive energy!

JM: Where did your focus on positive mental attitude and love come from?

H.R. (Bad Brains): Those songs from the early days of groups like Cream, The Beatles and the ever so popular Bob Marley and the Wailers were about how you should never give up. One day my father asked me to read a book written by Andrew Carnegie. In my learning of the teachings of PMA—the laws of success—I discovered a new way to communicate through positive mental attitude. Those ideas improved many children's desire to learn to improve. (*Success Through a Positive Mental Attitude* (1952) by Napoleon Hill, based on interviews including with Andrew Carnegie. Hill was an advisor to President Roosevelt from 1933–1936. "What the mind of man can conceive and believe, it can achieve," is one of Hill's famous expressions.)

JM: I'd guess that you view making music as a spiritual practice and I wonder if you enjoy meditation or prayer or other spiritual practices?

H.R. (Bad Brains): It's a big part of being an earnest musician. One does have to pray and meditate. I do understand from learning from the angels that when one doesn't pray there can sometimes be a transmission breakdown that happens. One's inner spirit becomes affected or infected with a disease. That disease can cause patterns that would lead to psychological malfunctions. (pause) Yes, sir. Good point.

RAY CAPPO (Youth of Today / Shelter): HR's music touched my heart. Bad Brains were such a great seminal band in that music genre. They definitely had a lot of influence on me. So did Norman Vincent Peale and *The Power of Positive Thinking*. It's important to be positive and that principle is important if it's blended with spirituality. If you're just positive about the material world it's not great. When people haven't dealt with hate, greed, envy and anger and they're constantly killing just to survive, this is exactly what's happening in the animal

Figure 13.1 H.R. of Bad Brains. (Human Rights is the stage name of Paul Hudson):
"I discovered a new way to communicate through positive mental attitude."
Photo by Matt Fitt.

kingdom. There has to be a spiritual caveat to add onto positive mental attitude. If you don't see the bigger picture that your soul is eternal—that we are eternal beings—then positive mental attitude is like sticking your head in the sand.

YISHAI ROMANOFF (Moshiach Oi!) I was very into Bad Brains. While some punks had a much more negative and nihilistic attitude, Bad Brains sang about PMA. That was huge for me, and it was a very positive influence on me at the time. When I began becoming religious, I also appreciated the fact that Bad Brains was one of the only punk bands who had religious beliefs. They read the Bible and sang about God in their songs, despite the fact that almost no other punk bands did. That's punk.

JM: You quote Ian MacKaye in your book *Dance of Days*, "You are not as capable of changing politics as you are capable of changing yourself. If you're able to change yourself, that's for the better. When you get that out of the way, then maybe the other things will shape up." Then there's H.R. from the Bad Brains who sang about destroying Babylon from within each of our own hearts. You've said that you learned more from Ian than anyone else except your parents.

MARK ANDERSEN (*Dance for Days* / Positive Force DC): Anyone who knows the history of Bad Brains knows that H.R. is a different person than Ian MacKaye. (H.R. stands for Human Rights and is the stage name of Paul Hudson.) They are two of the crucial figures in the D.C. punk community. In certain ways the Ian MacKaye that we know is, maybe not impossible but, unlikely without the inspiration that H.R. gave. When H.R. made that comment to me about, "Destroy Babylon in your own heart," that was the truest thing I probably heard him say in a decade or two. This is a person who is in a deep struggle. I say this as someone who admires him profoundly as an artist. There is tragedy in that story, partly because his gift is so immense. I'm a person of brokenness as well, so I'm saying this with great love for H.R. whom I know as Joseph.

MUSIC FROM THE SOUL

H.R. (Bad Brains): Love, Jah, Rastafari, Prince of Peace. We are honored and privileged to do this interview with you. Brother John, approaching the spirituality of the transfiguration of the most high. And, in the midst thereof, there is music to teach the children, the masses, different transpositions so we go to these different transpositions. We're playing soul-reggae-hip-hop-rubadub-love-groove-on music. And it's good music, from the soul. It's good for the mind and the body. It helps us in our improvement to understand what are the spiritual teachings of the beautiful family of God and also our loved ones. We want to be able to have fun with the people, with those transpositions and the music.

JIM LINDBERG (Pennywise): When we started playing music as a band, Jason (Thirsk) was our chief lyricist and was very much into the PMA thing, Positive Mental Attitude. He was listening to bands like 7 Seconds and Minor Threat. They were a response to the nihilistic late 70s and early 80s bands. Reaganomics was killing everything and there was nuclear proliferation. We had a decade of punk rock songs attacking society. But there was a real movement with bands like Dag Nasty saying, "We've written hundreds of songs about how messed up the world is." There were bands that started saying, "What can we do to change things? Let's try to provide some answers or at least try to inspire people to affect change in their own lives." Bands like Minor Threat and other straight edge bands were trying to say, "Look at our scene and what's going on around us."

There was a lot of drug abuse and alcoholism, violence and vandalism. The whole destructive nature started to wear on certain bands and they started to say, "Let's make something positive." It's never a popular choice, to put that in your music. Most people want to have their rock and roll down and dirty and sinful. Our first four or five albums were very much about a positive message and the whole idea of making the most out of your life and "seize the day." It was straight out of Thoreau and Emerson's guidebooks of self-reliance. That's been something that's helped us along. We've also written songs later in our career that are critical of government officials and the president. But at our core, our band has always been about a positive message and putting that out there as much as possible.

MOANA STROM (Stalin's War): Music is so powerful, especially to young people. When you're young you're listening to music all day, everyday. You hear every single word and you're holding on to all of it. If you can be a positive role model and be singing about things that matter and are positive, then you can help form people's lives and ideas. If you're talking about *spirituality* and *social change* rather than booze and drugs it can be incredibly beneficial.

MEDITATE AND DESTROY
DHARMA PUNX AND NOAH LEVINE/THE DEATHLESS

Punk made me aware of political injustice and Buddhism has taught me how to respond to it skillfully.

—Noah Levine (*Dharma Punx*)

Buddha was an anarchist.

—Joe Clements (The Deathless / Fury 66)

More important than truth and justice is compassion! We don't want to create a new form of oppression. It's important to understand that sometimes people are hurting inside and that's why they hurt others.

—China Martens (*Future Generation: The Zine-Book for Subculture Parents, Kids, Friends and Others*)

Punk and Buddhism go well together.

—Sarah Fisher (*Meditate & Destroy* director)

My first interview with Noah Levine was conducted in the forest in Santa Cruz, California. We sat in the sunshine on a wooden deck overlooking Branciforte Creek, outside the house where I was living at the time. At the top of the dirt road, Levine had parked his decked-out car with "dharmapunx" inscribed on the license plate. His groundbreaking book *Dharma Punx* had

Figure 14.1 Poster for 2007 documentary Meditate and Destroy directed by Sarah Fisher. Contributed: Sarah Fisher.

recently been published (2003) and our interview was broadcast on Free Radio Santa Cruz, a commercial-free, unlicensed radio station with roots in anarchist self-organization and nonviolent direct action. I told Levine I usually interviewed people about social change and spiritual growth, from Vietnamese Buddhist monk Thich Nhat Hanh to Bad Religion singer Greg Graffin. Levine laughed and said, "Well, now you have both in one!" *Dharma Punx* tells the personal story of Levine's own transformation from serving time in jail to help-ing others who are incarcerated and/or struggling with addiction.

Levine later wrote additional books: *Against the Stream: A Buddhist Manual for Spiritual Revolutionaries* (2007), *Heart of the Revolution: The Buddha's Radical Teachings of Forgiveness, Compassion and Kindness* (2011) and *Refuge Recovery: A Buddhist Path to Recovering from Addiction* (2014). Levine founded the Against the Stream Meditation Society and a meditation center in Venice, California, and continues to offer consultations and lead meditation retreats. In June 2024, a conference in Santa Cruz, California celebrated the tenth anniver-sary of Refuge Recovery, a program established by Levine to heal addiction.

More recently Noah was accused of sexual misconduct and was subjected to a series of investigations by Buddhist organizations he's been affiliated with. His website includes this statement: "In 2018 Noah was falsely accused of sexual misconduct. This caused great harm to the communities he had spent thirty years creating and supporting. He is now in the process of rebuilding and recreating structures and organizations to continue sharing Buddhism with all who seek his guidance." (noahlevine.com—2024)

Buddhist punk band the Deathless was conceived in 2014 and included Noah Levine providing lyrics with singer/guitarist/producer Joe Clements (Fury 66 / HotLung) and Dharma Punx co-founder Vinny Ferraro. Levine is the subject of the 2007 documentary film *Meditate and Destroy* by director Sarah Fisher.

DHARMA PUNX

NOAH LEVINE (*Dharma Punx | Against the Stream*): My search for happiness, acceptance and freedom led me to punk rock. Punk had the energy, the infor-mation and the politics that I resonated with. But I took it to the extreme nihil-istic, self-destructive, drug-addicted, crime side of things. There definitely was an intense drive to escape from my own mind, from my emotions and my body. Drugs and alcohol offered that escape for a long time, to the point where I was so numb I wasn't even aware of the pain I was causing myself and others. I just didn't care because I had really lost hope and wasn't able to take responsibility for my actions. There came a point where I was strung out and locked up and I had even lost my punk ethic in the pursuit of oblivion.

But that same energy of dissatisfaction and suffering eventually led me to start meditating while I was in prison. At the time, I thought that doing spiritual prac-tice would be like completely fucking selling out. That was for hippies and my parents and brain-dead religious followers. That was the masses to me. But I had lost all other hope. I felt like I had nowhere else to turn. Meditation was a profound experience for me. I was able to just be present for that moment in my jail cell, rather than in the terror of prison and shame and regret for the crimes I'd committed. I had been looking for that experience of freedom in punk, drugs, sex and crime, but I hadn't found real freedom.

JM: You wrote in *Dharma Punx* that the spiritual path described by the Buddha is one of being against the stream, against selfish desires and ignorance. You wrote, "This fits perfectly with the punk rock ethic."

NOAH LEVINE (*Dharma Punx / Against the Stream*): Yeah. As I began to meditate and it really worked, I thought, "Actually, most people *aren't* doing this. This *isn't* mainstream! This isn't selling out. This is the punkest thing I've ever done." To learn to tell the truth after living a life of lies, to learn how to be kind to myself and other people was the most rebellious and difficult action I've ever taken. This isn't buying in. This is waking up from this delusion I've been in. I found a teaching where the Buddha said that practice is "against the stream" or an act of rebellion. Most people are suffering and don't even know it. They're so attached to seeking pleasure all of the time that they'll never wake up. I understood that teaching, because my whole life has been against the stream! I began integrating the punk ethic—that anti-establishment acknowledgment of suffering in the world—with the Buddhist philosophy that awakening, happiness and freedom are possible by acknowledging suffering and its causes. And cultivating awareness, morality and wisdom.

JM: You were in jail and got a phone call from your father Stephen Levine, who was a prominent Buddhist teacher in America. (Stephen passed away in 2016) He offered meditation instructions over the phone and that was the first time you practiced meditation, in jail.

NOAH LEVINE (*Dharma Punx*): Yeah. In a gentle and supportive way he said, "Look, what you're doing is just not working. Why don't you try something else?" It was the first time I ever meditated. I had been around it since I was a kid, but I'd never tried it. That was the turning point for me, of having the direct experience. I'm a pessimist. I'm skeptical about everything, so until I experience something for myself, I think it's bullshit. And that was the first time I experienced it for myself. I was in enough pain that I was willing to even check out meditation. I thought, "Wow, this actually works to relax me a little bit, to calm me down." For a half a breath at a time. Not for hours, not for days. But just for that moment of awareness. I feel incredibly fortunate that I had my father on that level. There is a way in which it did save my life.

JASON MURPHY (Rebel Dharma meditation instructor): Noah and I were locked up together when we were fifteen. We'd met each other on the street, downtown, in the mid-80s punk and metal scene. We hung out in two different groups, but we were half a block from each other. We were often in the same institutions at the same time.

JM: In *Dharma Punx* Noah writes about breaking into people's houses to steal stuff to pay for drugs. He also mentions he sometimes used his own name in his graffiti—noahcore.

JASON MURPHY: I was a little smarter than that! My idea was to be dead or in prison by the time I was twenty-one. When I was ten years old I got arrested for breaking and entering. I stole some guns and pot from a neighbor's house. When the police came, I was hiding behind my mom's leg saying, "Please don't take me!" The cop said, "I don't see anything in your son's future but state prison." It was an imprint in my head at ten years old. There was also a time when I was in seventh grade that a teacher called me "stupid" in front of the whole class. That was an assault! I threw a desk at the teacher and punched the principal and got thrown out of the school. I rebelled against school. I was off and running. I was burning out and didn't have anywhere else to go.

JASON MURPHY (Rebel Dharma meditation instructor): We're moving a little away from the Dharma Punx brand even though it's been extremely helpful. After five years of having this group I'm thinking about whether we are limiting ourselves by calling it Dharma Punx which gives the impression that you have to like punk rock music. People say, "I can tell you're a Dharma Punk because one, you're ringing a meditation bell, and two, you're covered in tattoos." We're breaking out of that mold and talking more about the inner rebellion. We're thinking about Rebel Dharma.

I wrote a paper in an Anthropology of Religion class called, "The Buddha was Punk Rock" about how the Buddha ran away from home and hit the streets. He was a gutter punk. The Buddha rebelled against class and the social structure and changed the face of India. He did so not with anger but with the energy of revolutionary action. Instead of destroying the system by blowing up buildings—with the anarchist mentality that was made into a stamp of punk rock in the 1980s—his rebellion is still felt in the dharma. Noah (Levine) has a phrase I like—*meditate and destroy*. It's about destroying greed, hatred and delusion. The punk rock ethic is also deeply rooted in destroying the greed by not wanting or needing anything, except maybe some more beer. They didn't do so well on hatred.

SEARCH AND DESTROY

The phrase "Search and Destroy" has been reconfigured within the punk rock realm since its apparent origin as a military strategy during the devastating US war on Vietnam from 1968 to '75. Similar to the phrase "carpet bombing" it's worse than it sounds. Noah Levine repurposed "Search and Destroy" to reflect a commitment to ending the causes of suffering with "Meditate and Destroy" which also established a powerful trademark for his Dharma Punx meditation franchise. Later Levine and his Buddhism-infused punk band the Deathless included a song called "Adapt and Destroy" on their 2015 EP *The Gates to the Deathless Are Open*.

Much earlier Iggy Pop and James Williamson titled a song "Search & Destroy" on the 1973 Stooges album *Raw Power*. And then there's the infamous *Search and Destroy* punk magazine from San Francisco that was published from 1977 to '79. Bl'ast had a song called "Surf & Destroy" on their debut album *The Power of Expression* (1986). Artist Shepard Fairey included two phrases on his posters for OBEY Propaganda Printing Services—"Think and Create" and "Print and Destroy."

JM: Iggy & The Stooges had the song "Search & Destroy." Henry Rollins, who was in the band Black Flag . . .

JAMES WILLIAMSON (Iggy & The Stooges): Yeah, I know who he is.

JM: Henry has "Search and Destroy" as a tattoo. I don't know if that's where he got it.

JAMES WILLIAMSON: It probably is.

BUDDHISM AND PUNK ROCK

It's August 2007 and I'm in San Francisco at a nicely furnished upstairs yoga studio, sitting on a smooth wooden floor watching people socializing in small groups, sipping slim glasses of wine. An event has been organized to raise funds to complete a film by New York artist Sarah Fisher called *Meditate and Destroy* that tells the story of Noah Levine and the connections between Buddhism and punk rock. The event is MC'd by Wes Nisker, a prominent Buddhist meditation teacher and humorist. He sings a clever song about, "getting off the wheel" which reminds me that John Lennon sang of the same wheel and no longer being snagged by it; "Just sitting here watching the wheels go round and round . . . " A year after the fundraising event I spoke with Levine when *Meditate and Destroy* debuted at the 2008 Santa Cruz International Film Festival. Featured in the film is footage of Levine hanging out with his buddy Russ Rankin, singer with Good Riddance.

RUSS RANKIN (Good Riddance / Only Crime): Over the years I've been able to find spirituality in unlikely places. I consider myself to be a pretty spiritual person today. That wasn't me fifteen or twenty years ago, but that is me today. I think if I didn't have that side of me, where I can meditate and get in touch with something that's greater than me, I think I would probably be locked up or in a straight jacket by now.

JM: The lyrics from the Good Riddance song, "All the Joy You've Ever Known" go; "I've waited for freedom from bondage of self." Lots of suffering is due to wrong perceptions and self-created suffering. And some is created by cultural systems and political structures.

RUSS RANKIN (Good Riddance): Through trial and error, and thinking these things through and having so many conversations with people who know more than I do, I agree with you that there are a lot of problems in the world that I didn't create. At the same time, I can control how I react to them. Or what kind of action—if any—I'm going to take. It reminds me of when you get on an airplane and they say, "Put the mask on yourself *first* and then put the mask on your kid." I can't really be any good to anybody unless I can get straight with myself first. Only then can I become useful to somebody. If I'm sick, depressed and suicidal and hating everybody, I'm not going to be much help to anybody. Over the last ten years I've adopted this philosophy to do what I can to get straight with myself first so that I can be in the best position to be helpful to other people.

I remember a line in a Dead Kennedys song where Jello says, "What can just one of us do against so much greed and power, trying to crush us into roaches?" I remember when I'd read political books and listen to hours of Dead Kennedys music; I felt overwhelmed. I'd think, "There's nothing I can do. I'm so small." I've wanted to put into action my vision of a compassionate and just world. Even though it may not exist outside my front door, I can carry it with me wherever I go. I don't think that's naive or idealistic. It's practical. At the end of the day, I'll settle for that rather than just throwing up my hands and saying, "I can't do anything, so screw it!" Or even worse, saying, "What do you mean? There's nothing wrong!" I don't want to be that guy either!

SARAH FISHER (*Meditate & Destroy* film director): Punk and Buddhism go well together. That's why Noah has received so much attention. There is this stereotype about punk rock as being very rebellious, but it's a question of how you define *rebellion*. The Buddha was someone who went against the stream. He went against the norm of society and didn't follow the Hindu religion. He discovered a form of spiritual practice that he thought was *more true* and in accord with the way the world works. As a punk rocker, I think that's the same attitude and approach to life; not going with the norm of society and finding out what's true for yourself. That's the way Noah lives in the world and how he's chosen to integrate punk rock with Buddhism and spirituality. They are parallel paths and they integrate very well together.

In the punk scene it doesn't seem naturally acceptable to come out as a spiritual practitioner. And within the spiritual scene it doesn't seem natural to come out as a punk rocker! But if you're on the spiritual path, you have to find a way to be *in the world but not of it* and be true to yourself. It's liberating to be yourself and really find a way that you can live in the world and not feel stigmatized by any group you belong to. It's closing the circle of these opposing worlds. Making the film has been a coming out of the closet experience for me. If I'm talking about the film, people ask how I got interested in Buddhism and what my practices are and how I got interested in *Dharma Punx*. It's been a way to introduce people to meditation and the dharma.

NOAH LEVINE (*Dharma Punx* / The Deathless): I grew up in the punk scene and had been very wary of religion. I found out that the Buddha talked about his teachings and practice as a form of rebellion and called it *against the stream*. When he was defining Buddhism as being the middle path he was questioned: "The middle path of what?" He said, "Well, it's the middle between two dead ends." One dead end is seeking happiness from blindly following a religious tradition by just accepting what the religion is teaching, and not critically analyzing it or using discernment. "Likewise," he said, "Looking for happiness in material things as a source of your well-being is also a setup for disappointment and bound to end in suffering." This practice and path that he is laying out, that I'm practicing and teaching now, leads between that of worldliness and that of blindly following religion. I wrote *Dharma Punx* seven years ago and that put me into a bigger, national arena. In Santa Cruz I've trained Jason Murphy who runs a weekly class he calls Rebel Dharma. Up in San Francisco, Vinny Ferraro runs a weekly group called Urban Dharma. Josh Corga teaches up in Vancouver. We now have over twenty affiliated meditation groups around the country, Canada and Europe.

> *The idea of being calm and peaceful was appealing to me, but I*
> *couldn't get with the bell-bottoms and the hippie beads.*

—Jason Murphy (Rebel Dharma)

JASON MURPHY (Rebel Dharma instructor): I wasn't into being spiritual—the idea appalled me. The idea of being calm and peaceful was appealing to me, but I couldn't get with the bell-bottoms and the hippie beads. I preferred the idea that instead of letting go of who you are, let yourself *be* who you are. If you're angry then *know* that you're angry. Also know that anger is an emotion and it's not *who you are*.

We get into identity—*selfing*—and creating personas. Punk rock is a persona. Even though I wear a leather jacket, ride a motorcycle, have tattoos and go to punk shows I understand the concept of *that which arises passes away*. The feeling of anger arises and I don't attach to it. When I was younger all I knew was anger, so it was my identity. That's what Pema Chodron is talking about with self-righteous anger. Activists have a bit of that, which gets in the way of mindfulness and being with what is arising and seeing impermanence.

The way to deal with anger is not by stopping the anger but by practicing being loving and kind. That's the transformation that many of us dharma punks had to make in the Buddhist perspective. Buddhism is about being a spiritual warrior. Jesus and Buddha were rebels against what was being done in the name of religion. Religion in some ways can be considered the *opiate of the masses*, to get people to do what we want them to do—we can kill and steal land in the name of religion.

JM: How did you come across meditation?

JASON MURPHY (Rebel Dharma): I had anger management issues. I got kicked out of schools. I was referred to a local psychologist in town. After a few sessions he suggested a self-hypnosis technique. I'm grateful he didn't call it meditation because I probably would've said, "That's for the fucking hippies and I don't want anything to do with it!" In Santa Cruz there was a definite division between young and old, hippies and punks. We felt like we had to fight back. I learned some basic mindfulness meditation. I had an experience of changing. I really began to meditate when I started studying karate with zazen. There was no instruction. Meditation helped me calm down and clarify.

NOAH LEVINE (*Refuge Recovery / Dharma Punx /* The Deathless): Engaged action in the world is the total integral part of any spiritual practice. We have this vision of the Buddha as a renunciate. He was a renunciate but he renounced greed, hatred and delusion. He renounced his possessions. But he stayed incredibly engaged in the societal issues of his times. He spoke out against racism and sexism, war, hatred and violence. The Buddha pointed out that there is suffering. This is the credo of punk rock. There is suffering and we don't like it—it sucks! The Buddha took it a step further and said, "Yes. And there is a cause of that suffering and there is a solution, an end to it, in the individual." Punk made me aware of political injustice and Buddhism has taught me how to respond to it skillfully.

Our generation has lived through the Cold War and Reaganomics and the birth, death and maybe rebirth of punk rock. To actually have a whole crew of punk rockers, or Generation Xers or Ys or whatever it is now! There is something incredibly special about having a community of spiritual rebels, spiritual revolutionaries. Being a punk rock Buddhist is really fucking lonely! I did it for ten years on my own. I was the only young, tattooed punker at the meditation retreats! I love the fact that I now have a community. That's why I wrote the book: to take the hippie peace-loving stigma off of spiritual practice. To say that punks can do this. Punks maybe even have a head start because they understand suffering so well. Buddhist practice is simple, but it takes the courage of a warrior.

I've been putting more effort into creating a Buddhist approach to treating drug addiction and alcoholism. The twelve-step program is a very theistic and Judeo-Christian approach to addiction. A lot has been done around Buddhism and twelve steps and not much has been done in bringing a purely Buddhist approach to addiction. I'll probably do a book. (*Refuge Recovery* was published in 2014) We've been having meetings in Los Angeles. The next few years of my life feel clearly dedicated to creating more alternatives to the twelve steps and more Buddhist approaches to recovery for people.

DO YOU RELY ON A PRAYER?

In the introduction to his book *Dharma Punx* (2003) Noah Levine writes of the influence that Bl'ast and other punk bands had on him: "I raise a fist to all of the punk rock and hardcore bands who have inspired and motivated me over the years. Since there are way too many to name them all, I will name only the important ones: The Ramones, The Clash, The Sex Pistols, Minor Threat, Black Flag, Bad Brains, Bl'ast, GBH, Agnostic Front, Judge, Shelter, 108, and a big fucking middle finger to my friends in Good Riddance and Rancid." Bl'ast's second album, *It's in My Blood* (1987), has an album cover that features a pair of hands brought together in prayer, an iconic Christian/Buddhist/Hindu image that years later Noah Levine would relocate to brand his Dharma Punx school of mindfulness.

CLIFFORD DINSMORE (Bl'ast / Dusted Angel): That was a really weird album cover, how it came about. (*It's in My Blood*) It really didn't have any significance for what we stood for. It was something that someone at SST (Records) drew and it looked pretty cool. The praying hands. There's a contradiction of what that cover represented and what we stood for in terms of, "Do you rely on a prayer to get you through life? Or do you take the initiative and survive on your own and make a world on your own?" I still think about it to this day; how that was such a trippy cover for that dark, heavy record. It's kind of funny.

JM: Did you hear of fans getting the wrong idea about the band because of that cover?

CLIFFORD DINSMORE (Bl'ast): I think they saw it as the anti-religious thing that it was.

THE DEATHLESS

Buddhist punk band the Deathless was conceived during a Buddhist meditation retreat in Big Sur, California in 2014 and features Joe Clements, Vinny Ferraro and Noah Levine, who provides lyrics and spoken word sections. The band formed in Santa Cruz amidst the seventeenth anniversary of the publication of Levine's book *Dharma Punx*. The Deathless create energized punk rock with clear Buddhist themes. Their song "Three Gems" opens with a spoken word excerpt from a dharma talk by Vinny Ferraro followed by Clements singing a traditional Pali chant; "Buddham Saranam Gacchami . . . "

The first time I heard about the Deathless was at a Vipassana meditation retreat where one of the instructors was Jason Murphy, a local Santa Cruz colleague of Noah Levine in the Dharma Punx tradition of mindfulness mixed with punk attitude. As Murphy gave a dharma talk on impermanence one evening, I noticed his black T-shirt with the image of a skeleton arm raising a sharp blade above a sea of skulls with the words "The Deathless."

NOAH LEVINE (*Dharma Punx* / The Deathless): The Deathless is the culmination of my life's passions of punk rock and Buddhism. It's an organic offspring of Joe's (Clements) meditation practice and Joe moving from a punk rocker being interested in Buddhism to really practicing Buddhism and saying, "Hey, let's do a Shelter type of spiritual hardcore band." And me *not* being a musician and saying, "Let's collaborate on the lyrics and the writing. Let's do a split seven-inch where I could do teachings." It was natural. Everything in my life has been very organic—*Dharma Punx* leading to *Against the Stream* leading to *Refuge Recovery*. And that leading to the Deathless.

AJAHN AMARO BHIKKU (Buddhist monk, author and meditation teacher): The Deathless. Coincidentally "Amaro" means deathless. I don't know if there's a connection between Noah's choice of punk band name but that's my name, too. I met Noah when I was co-leading the second meditation retreat he was on. Mary Orr was the teacher on the first retreat he joined there in Santa Cruz. That was 1993 and he was about twenty-two or twenty-three years old. So, he was fairly fresh into the meditation world. He had rebelled against his dad, Stephen Levine. He came on that retreat, so I knew him from that time. And when I moved to the States in 96, I ran into him at Spirit Rock. (Meditation Center in Woodacre, California) I'd just been at the Nicholas Roerich Museum in New York City and I noticed he had a Roerich tattoo on his arm. Noah said, "Not many people recognize that." I've known Noah more than thirty years and he still comes along to retreats that I lead in Thailand quite often these days. We still have a fairly close association.

AJAHN AMARO BHIKKU: I was around at the very beginning of the punk era and Noah takes it as sort of a badge of great value in the punk ethos that I went to see The Damned in 1977 at the Marquee. Oftentimes, when I've been chatting with Noah and he would introduce me to some of his punk friends, he'd say, "He saw The Damned in 1977!" I also saw Bob Marley. I went to see David Bowie in '73, Led Zeppelin, The Pink Floyd and a whole array of rock bands and hippie festivals as well. To me the heart of the punk and hippie ethos is the same.

The guy I shared an apartment with my last six months at University in England was a fellow student at the University, but he was very strongly enamored of the whole punk movement, and particularly the first album of the Clash. He played it seven or eight times a day! So, when I entered the monastery, I could still recite lyrics from that album. That went on most of the first couple of years in the monastery, because I spent so much of my teens with my head filled with music off the radio or playing records. And going to gigs. Everything was a cue for a song, the mind is so hungry. The Clash are deeply embedded on account of that friend, Patrick Field, playing that album over and over. That was January of 1977 and the whole punk thing was kicking off. In the *New Musical Express* the previous year, they had that famous review of the first Sex Pistols gig, "This isn't music, this is chaos." And then other bands rose up very fast.

TOTAL LIBERATION IS POSSIBLE

AJAHN AMARO BHIKKU: Growing up in my teens, the issue that was at the center of my struggles trying to understand life was; how can we be free in a world of limitation? You haven't got enough money. People make rules for you in school, society, in the family. This is right, that's wrong. From early childhood I wondered, "Who says so? Prove it! Why is the line here and not there?" I wondered, "How can we be free?" Also noticing the limitations of the human body, not just the social situations, but the laws of gravity and nature. In terms of spirituality, there is a strong intuition that we can be free. That's a possibility that we have as human beings, that a total liberation is possible. But how can that work in a world of limitation?

I was born in 1956. I was a sort of late flower child but I was around lots of hippies and the anarchist movement that was going on in Britain at that time. People like Ubi Dwyer and Sid Rawle and the Free Festival Movement. I was along at a number of those. I was at the Windsor Festival that got broken up by the police, though I left the day before the police arrived, fortunately. It was all revolving around: How can we be free in a world of limitation? And where is freedom to be found? The instinct was to go against any kind of rule or boundary. I managed to get through high school without being expelled, but largely because a couple of the teachers vouched for me, and they wouldn't sanction me being kicked out. I was continually just pushing the limits as much as I could. But then there's always another boundary.

AJAHN AMARO BHIKKU: The punk movement was a kind of pulling down the lovey-dovey values of the hippie world and honoring the feelings of anger, rage and frustration and "I want to tear it all down." There was "London's Burning" and "I'm So Bored With the USA." *No Future* and those kinds of anthems were being touted or "Anarchy in the UK." You're trying to rebel against limitations and you're being honest with your feelings. But still, there isn't an actual quality of freedom other than in that endorphin flash of being in the mosh pit, being completely carried away by the drug or the dance or the sort of beauty of the moment. And there is a moment, like the luminous sunset moment. Yes, it's all perfect colors and they're radiant and beautiful. And then it can't be kept or owned. So, there was that sense of release and freedom, but it's incredibly fleeting. And then there's the damage done in order to get to that place where everything is good. I could see, "If I carry on like this, I'm not going to live past twenty-five." I didn't really "figure it out" until I came in contact with meditation and Buddhism when I wandered into the Wat Pah Nanachat Monastery in Thailand, January of 78.

TYRANT IN THE MIND

I'm sitting in the control room at Compound Recording Studios and Joe Clements lights a thick stick of Palo Santo, the light smoke wafting upwards. As the fresh scent permeates the room Clements tells me of his days playing in Fury 66 and how the Deathless came together. We also discuss empathy, the nature of suffering and overcoming addiction. He's preparing to leave for Germany later that day to meet up with Noah Levine in Munich for Wanderlust 108, a world tour "mindfulness triathlon" sponsored by Adidas that includes meditation, yoga, a 5K run/walk and concerts. (2016) Clements mentions that he and Levine want to hook up with Ray Cappo (Shelter) to make some music; "Have you heard what he's doing lately? Music with tablas!"

JM: How do Buddhism and punk go together for you?

JOE CLEMENTS (The Deathless / Fury 66 / HotLung): In doing this band I wasn't thinking how Buddhism goes with punk rock. It wasn't like, "We're anarchists." I'm very personal with my music, so what I'm going through and what I'm feeling—that's what my lyrics are. I got into Buddhism and really started practicing at a time where I was coming out of some heavy addiction. I was sober but still pretty miserable. I was still searching outside of myself for the answer, for freedom from suffering. Until I really let go a little bit and said "yes" to go to one of Noah's retreats.

Meditation can appear to be this hippie-bullshit, blissed-out thing. I thought, "There's no way I can shut up my mind! You fucking haven't heard *my* mind!" In doing the practice I found some freedom. For me it's this personal thing. Noah and I were on retreat in 2014 (Big Sur, California) and I said, "Wouldn't it be cool to do a Buddhist punk band like Shelter, 108 and Cro-Mags did with Krishna? And Bad Brains did in a different sense with Rastafari?" That's where that inspiration came from.

Have you heard my fucking mind? If you've heard my mind, you'd know I couldn't meditate. With my bands, what's in the mind is coming out here, loud! This is giving me some freedom. I just want to share it—not shove it down your throat. It's an inspirational thing to me. It's a message of positivity. I know that people might think of Buddhism as Zenned-out blissful, spiritual bypass. That's not my experience. It's fucking *sit down and check out what's going on inside*. And it's fucking brutal in there! There's a tyrant in the mind. Wow! But I can meet it with some tenderness, some love, kindness and compassion.

JM: One of the first insights in Buddhism is to notice what's happening in the mind and body. And the practice of concentration and mindfulness does lead to blissful states.

JOE CLEMENTS: I've found the bliss when I've changed the relationship I have to the thoughts. Not taking the thoughts so personal and then dropping into the body. When my mind and my heart meet it's like, "There you are, old friend." The body is here and it has a message.

MY BUDDHA IS PUNK
KYAW THU WIN AND REBEL RIOT IN MYANMAR

The day our consciousness becomes awake / There will be no prejudice in the world.

—"One Day" by Rebel Riot from 2021 album *One Day*, recorded just months before another military coup in their home country, Myanmar.

Buddha is like my teacher and not a superhero. I'm not a Buddhist. I don't want to be a part of any religious organization.

—Kyaw Thu Win (Rebel Riot)

Buddhism is similar with the punks because punk is a DIY lifestyle. Do It Yourself.

—Kyaw Thu Win (Rebel Riot)

Rebel Riot is a punk band that was founded in 2007 in Yangon, Myanmar, (formerly Rangoon, Burma) after the onset of the Saffron Revolution, a series of pro-democracy nonviolent mass protests that challenged fifty years of military dictatorship. Kyaw Thu Win, Zarni, and Oakar formed the band and also established a local chapter of Food Not Bombs to provide free vegan food to hungry and unhoused people in Myanmar. Rebel Riot's recordings include *No Place to Live* EP (2016), *One Day* (2021) and *The Rebel Riot* (2021).

My Buddha is Punk (2015) is a documentary by German director Andreas Hartmann that highlights Rebel Riot singer Kyaw Thu Win and his community of street punks who have embraced a unique blend of Buddhism and punk rock. *No Spicy No Fun—The Rebel Riot in the UK* (2021) is a documentary directed by Robert Bononi and Kim Ford and produced by Punk Ethics that follows Rebel Riot on their 2017 tour of England.

Since the 2021 military coup in Myanmar, the country has been dominated by an unelected dictator, and thousands of civilians have been killed with tens of thousands now imprisoned. One former member of Rebel Riot is now living in exile in Thailand, while another joined the rebel forces fighting the military regime.

Rebel Riot singer/lyricist Kyaw Thu Win continues to be an outspoken critic of the military regime in Myanmar. Kyaw Kyaw (pronounced Cho-Cho, as he's called affectionately by friends) has blended teachings and practices from his

Figure 15.1 My Buddha is Punk (2015) documentary by German director Andreas Hartmann presents Myanmar punk band Rebel Riot and singer/activist Kyaw Kyaw Thu Win. "It's great to be a rebel with love and kindness." Contributed: Andreas Hartmann.

country's traditional religion of Buddhism with high-energy, political punk rock. He practices meditation to enhance clear thinking and actions, engages in direct action to relieve the suffering of people living in poverty while also advocating for social change in songs like "Freedom," "Abolish Military Slave Education," and "Fuck Religious Rules/Wars." Their song "One Day" imagines a time without racism, sexism, war, and poverty. Kyaw Kyaw and Rebel Riot offer yet another dynamic, living experiment in blending personal liberation with social revolution.

BUDDHISM AND PUNK

KYAW THU WIN (Rebel Riot): For me, Buddhism is not a religion. It's a way of living and thinking. Punk is not only a fashion statement but also an ideology and way of life. I've found that punk and Buddhism can connect with each other. Buddhism teaches me about love, compassion and generosity and punk teaches me about rebellion. It's great to be a rebel with love and kindness. The common ground between Buddhism and punk is the desire to make a better world! That's why I believe these two things can go together.

JM: Do you think of Rebel Riot as a Buddhist punk band?

KYAW THU WIN: I don't think RR is a Buddhist punk band. We just like some of Buddha's ideas. We are not Buddhist and we do not promote any religious organizations.

JM: I appreciate how much you talk and sing about compassion and I like the quote on your Facebook page, "Revolution can't exist without love."

KYAW THU WIN: Yeah, bro. I really feel that the whole world needs love. Love is very important. Love has no boundaries; no nation, no religion, no race. I learned from Buddha that love, compassion, joy and equanimity are the very nature of humanity. Buddha is like my teacher and not a superhero. I'm not a Buddhist. I don't want to be a part of any religious organization.

May all beings be free of suffering. May all beings be at peace.

—"My Buddha is Punk" by Rebel Riot

JM: How were you and other punks in Myanmar influenced by the Saffron Revolution? (2007 pro-democracy mass protests against government corruption in Myanmar/Burma.)

KYAW THU WIN (Rebel Riot): This revolution gives me a lot of energy to be part of changing the system. We've been so long under a military system so when we saw this Saffron Revolution a lot of people came and joined on the street for solidarity. This revolution is our hope to change the system and create a better situation.

JM: Do you see Buddhist monks and nuns as allies of social revolution and punk rock in Myanmar?

KYAW THU WIN: No. But if we have to fight against common enemies, like the military, yeah, of course we can be allies.

JM: What about Aung San Suu Kyi? Many of us have held her as a great hero and she was under house arrest by the government for so long. Now she's in the government (2018) and some accuse her of not helping enough to stop the harming of Muslims. What do you think?

KYAW THU WIN: Myanmar politics is very complicated. I just don't understand her situation well enough and her position now and what she is doing and thinking. I can't exactly say anything about it right now, bro. Also, in Myanmar there are not only problems with how Rohingya Muslims are treated, but also Kachin, Shane, Kayin have problems, too. They are all fighting and killing each other. But the Muslim situation is a big headline for the media. So, being in her position the situation is not so easy to solve with all of the problems happening at the same time.

JM: Tell me about the photo where three of you from the band are dressed as a Christian, Buddhist and Muslim. I like the idea of people getting along and not forcing their ideas on each other. Tell me about the trouble that came from that photo.

KYAW THU WIN (Rebel Riot): Yeah, bro. This photo was shot by a photographer in Thailand in March, 2017 when we were touring in Bangkok. After we came back, I posted it on our Facebook page. The message of the photo is to create peace between religions. But one guy from MaBaTha (The Patriotic Association of Myanmar) shared our photo on his (Facebook) wall and wrote an untrue message that we are a destroyer of Buddhism and that some Islamic organization was behind us and the photo was hate speech. People were so angry at us! Many people wanted to fight me and kill me. Some wanted to put us in jail.

In Myanmar there is a religious law that could've made us spend two years in jail for that. Everyday a lot of people called my phone and were giving me shit and were rude to me. I put off my sim card from my phone. So, I didn't know how I could solve this problem. It got bigger and bigger every day during that time. Finally, I got the idea to call the guy who posted our photo with the false message. I explained to him what the photo meant to us and I asked him to delete it from his Facebook wall. He apologized to me and deleted it. Then I used him like the media to make his apology public to people who had misunderstood us. Now everything is finished and okay. No problem at all.

BERLIN SYNCHRONICITY—*MY BUDDHA IS PUNK*

JM: The screening of *My Buddha is Punk* in Berlin last year (July 28, 2023) was high-energy and packed with Berlin punks. There was a Food Not Bombs table and people were very excited. It was quite hot in the theater! I happened to be in Berlin and the screening was sold out but luckily you had an extra ticket!

ANDREAS HARTMANN (*My Buddha is Punk* director): That was a great synchronicity that you could see the film! It was great to see Kyaw Kyaw again. It was good to see that the film still draws a lot of people to the cinema. It was also wonderful to experience the solidarity of people because he raised a lot of funding that evening for Food Not Bombs in Myanmar. The first screening we did together was in Thailand at the Bangkok Underground Film Festival. (2017) I invited Kyaw Kyaw and his band members and some other friends to Bangkok. The film went viral in Thailand. Three or four hundred people were at this open-air screening and afterward, the hanging screen was pulled up and there was a stage with instruments and the band gave a live concert and the whole audience was super amazed!

KYAW THU WIN (Rebel Riot): This movie was very important in my life. In Berlin I was able to convey a few of my thoughts to the public. I want to bring about positive change with the energy that comes from punk. That's why such exhibitions are very beneficial for me and I value such experiences because I can share a good message among people.

PUNK SCENE IN MYANMAR

JM: What drew you to make this documentary?

ANDREAS HARTMANN (*My Buddha is Punk* director): I made a film in Vietnam (*Days of Rain*—2010) and was traveling in Asia. In 2011, I was back in Berlin and read an article in a German newspaper about the punk scene in Myanmar. I was immediately intrigued by this story of a young community living in this former military dictatorship.

I was interested in how they found a way of living and expression to deal with everything that happens around them. I found Kyaw Kyaw (pronounced Cho-Cho) on Facebook and I told him I'm interested in making a film about the punk scene in Myanmar. I didn't know yet that I wanted to make a film about Kyaw Kyaw because I didn't know him yet! I traveled to Myanmar and very quickly after meeting him for the first time and experiencing his presence, personality and character, I decided to make a film focused on him and this community, shown through their actions and activism.

JM: In your film, Kyaw Kyaw is so compassionate. In my view, he gives little Dharma talks to people he encounters on the train or to other street punks. He offers teachings on cause and effect and on not viewing people as higher or lower than yourself; that we're all the same. Then the film cuts to Rebel Riot in the studio and they're recording a song screaming, "Fuck the military!" Punk rock often is viewed as angry and chaotic. Buddhism is seen as peaceful and meditative—your film shows both of these aspects. What do you think of this combination of punk and Buddhism?

ANDREAS HARTMANN (*My Buddha is Punk* director): What you describe is exactly the thing which drew my attention. I'm not particularly interested in punk music. I wanted to observe how Kyaw Kyaw was traveling around and trying to combine these two ways of living—his philosophy of punk and also this deep spiritual background of his country, where he grew up.

In this scene with the train journey to Zigon (Northern Myanmar), he suddenly started talking to all these people and everything got really silent. The whole train was listening to his story. This happened multiple times during the film shooting. I was really fascinated by his magnetic presence and how he could reach people. I also thought of these as small Dharma talks.

But when I first arrived in Myanmar, I didn't know this! In the German newspaper article, the spiritual part was not mentioned. When I went to Myanmar, I saw this punk community and political background of the military dictatorship and this was the story which was fascinating me. But after I arrived Kyaw Kyaw told me, "Tomorrow I'm going to the Shwedagon Pagoda in Yangon." This is the biggest and most holy site in Yangon and he asked me if I want to join him. We went together and he showed me how he meditates there at least two or three times a week. He told me it was his time to prepare for his tasks and actions of the day. He wanted to use his time to meditate and find inner peace in himself. From that moment I was really intrigued by this combination of punk and Buddhism. Very soon after I came up with this idea for the film title: *My Buddha is Punk*.

JM: Rebel Riot has a song with that same title, "My Buddha is Punk." On the train, Kyaw Kyaw tells a young man, "It's not good to be a soldier or a police officer." Later, he adds, "The Buddha said, 'Don't believe your parents, don't believe teachers, don't even believe what the Buddha says. Think for yourself.'" *Think for yourself* is a big idea in punk rock and anarchism.

ANDREAS HARTMANN: This quote you're talking about was, "Don't believe what your mother or what your father says. Don't believe what a teacher says." Kyaw Kyaw told me this quote early after I met him, when we talked casually between filming. This was the quote which really struck me and then gave me the idea of the kind of film I could do with him. This quote also gave me the inspiration for the title. Because actually the film title is not inspired by the song title. It's the other way around. The film title inspired Rebel Riot to make a song with the same title. There is another song title, "Punk is My Religion" so it's maybe a bit inspired from that. It was just an instinct, like a quick inspiration. I felt with this quote, he found this connection between Buddhism and punk. He found some belief or philosophy which goes both ways. He's a very reflective person.

JM: Andreas told me that you named the song "My Buddha is Punk" after the film title.

KYAW THU WIN (Rebel Riot): Yes, it was Andreas's idea. I liked it, too. *My Buddha is Punk.* This title reflects my life because I also practice Buddha's meditation methods. From there, we started making music for the next few years. But there are a few problems—the lyrics. I like Buddhist philosophy, but I am not a Buddhist. I'm not a religious fanatic. So, writing lyrics is like announcing Buddhism. I don't want any kind of propaganda. I do not believe in any religious organization, but I believe in truth. This song is such an idea. Humans face physical and mental suffering in their daily lives; greed, anger, ignorance, and torture. Humans can also free themselves from that suffering. It was created with imagination.

WITHOUT JUDGMENT

JM: One scene in the film shows Kyaw Kyaw sitting in a room with his local street punks and they've realized someone is stealing from their collective money. This situation is handled very differently than how it's usually handled, where punishment is the goal. Would you describe this scene?

ANDREAS HARTMANN (*My Buddha is Punk* director): Kyaw Kyaw looks at things as they really are; somebody stole money and they're discussing this. But they're not judging each other. But Kyaw Kyaw contradicts himself a little bit in this scene when he says, "In punk, there's no rules and no regulations. Everybody can do what they do. But. . . if you have a different opinion, then you cannot be part of this group."

During the shooting, I experienced this challenge to be true to one's own ideas. This also became a narrative of the film. Later he goes to Zigon (Northern

Myanmar) and meets all these young punks and they're sitting under the tree. He realized that none of these young punks are actually interested in the punk philosophy. They're more interested in the fashion and these jackets and you can see his disappointment.

How you described this scene reminded me also of my filming process of observing the group in this nonverbal situation. During many weeks of filming, I didn't understand what they were talking about. When I returned to Berlin I worked with Burmese translators. I was telling people about this experience and somebody made the analogy that this is a kind of meditative work, because I'm also observing people without judgment. Of course, I was trying to understand what they're saying with different senses, or trying to read the energy in the room, but because I don't really understand the exact facts of what they say I'm looking at them without judgment. In meditation and Buddhism you're looking at how things really are. Maybe this kind of method of filmmaking is similar, or has some connection.

JM: In the film we see images of Adolf Hitler and swastikas. These are on posters and T-shirts for sale alongside images of revolutionary heroes like Che Guevara and Aung San Suu Kyi. Kyaw Kyaw directly asks some young Myanmar punks, "It seems like you're promoting Nazism. Do you you know that Nazism means the murder of six million Jews?" What was your understanding of why Adolf Hitler and Nazism are supported in Myanmar?

ANDREAS HARTMANN (*My Buddha is Punk* director): When I saw this, I was also very surprised. I learned that Myanmar (Burma) was occupied by England (before and during the Second World War) and because Germany was fighting against England, they have this very positive view of Germany and Hitler as a nationalist leader. For many young people (in Myanmar) Hitler is an idol, but also a fashion. Many young people don't understand what it means and they use a swastika as fashion. Kyaw Kyaw told me in school the history is tweaked. They don't learn about the Holocaust and Hitler is described as a very powerful and great leader.

JM: Myanmar has had a lot of suffering for decades, with military dictatorship and revolutions and now, once again, an authoritarian government. Aung San Suu Kyi helped lead a democratic revolution in 1988 and was under house arrest for fifteen years from 1989 to 2010. The Saffron Revolution of 2007 involved mass protests that included Buddhist monastics and in 2015 and 2020 Aung San Suu Kyi's NLD Party (National League for Democracy) was voted into government. She literally shared political power with the very military leaders who had imprisoned and tortured thousands of pro-democracy activists in Burma. She was later criticized for not supporting Myanmar's Muslim Rohingya population, who were attacked and forced to flee to Bangladesh. In 2021 there was yet another military coup and now (2024) Aung San Suu Kyi is once again under house arrest. All of this is the background of Burma/Myanmar, where Kyaw Kyaw has brought together the compassion of Buddhism with the political attitude of punk.

ANDREAS HARTMANN (*My Buddha is Punk* director): It was shocking when the last coup happened, again. When I was there in 2012 it was this moment of hope and the country was in a place of positive change. Next to T-shirts of the swastika there were Aung San Suu Kyi and NLD (National League for Democracy) T-shirts. People had hope for change, democracy and a better future. This was a very interesting moment to witness in Myanmar. I have other friends in Myanmar and what they wrote me during this coup was very hopeless. (2021) They were very traumatized. They couldn't believe that their country is falling back again to fifty years ago. Many people left the country.

One of the Rebel Riot band members—Oakar—is now living in Thailand. And Zarni, the one who was drawing the cartoons for the zine—has now joined the rebel groups and is trying to fight against the military. A lot of things have changed and Rebel Riot also had to split. But now Kyaw Kyaw has other band members.

JM: After the film screening in Berlin, Kyaw told the audience, "I may have problems when I go back to Myanmar if they know what I'm talking about here." I heard later he didn't have any problems returning home.

ANDREAS HARTMANN: I also think he had no problem.

KYAW THU WIN (Rebel Riot): I had no problems going home. Everything is OK. I am working on a new album with new band members (Rebel Riot). But unfortunately, two months ago one of the new members, the guitarist, passed away. The new album is finished and will be released on the 23rd of this month (To... Dear Comrade - May, 2024). It was produced by friends in Japan. The band had also to stop performing for a year. Then we will find a new guitarist and continue the activities. In Yangon, we still cook and share food for three hundred people on the street every Saturday. Sometimes if there is a budget problem, we stop for a while. Otherwise, we are cooking every week. Keith McHenry is who I admire and emulate. (co-founder of Food Not Bombs in 1980.)

After the July 28, 2023 screening of *My Buddha is Punk* at the Kino Moviemento cinema in the Kreuzberg district of Berlin, Kyaw Kyaw Thu Win and director Andreas Hartmann answered questions from the audience. Here's an excerpt from Kyaw Kyaw's comments:

DO IT YOURSELF

KYAW THU WIN (Rebel Riot): I'm not a religious person. Of course, my parents are Buddhist and I carry the tradition of Buddhism. We usually believe what our parents believe. But I also learned a lot about Buddhism. What does Buddhism mean? I found one thing: Buddhism is similar with the punks because punk is a DIY lifestyle. *Do It Yourself*. In Buddhism we also don't believe in God, we don't believe in the creator; we believe in ourselves.

I was very confused in this time because I am the center in two ways. I'm a punk and the other side is religious. I think I need to choose one. What do I choose? (*laugh*) I was confused! Finally I realized, "Oh no. Fuck! Buddhism is not a religion for me. It's a way of life, a way of living, of thinking." So, I don't need to go to a religious organization where they're talking about bullshit. I don't believe that. I believe that if you want to free yourself, you have to do it yourself. Punk means to make yourself free in your life. No racism, no sexism, no homophobia. Everyone can be punk; it doesn't matter if you have a tattoo or not.

Punk is very meaningful in my life. Punk saved my life and helped me think about so many things. People can be free by dancing, making music, writing. Everybody can be happy in their life and they don't need to be punk. Then I created the band Rebel Riot and I'm thinking "Fuck the system, fuck the government, fuck everything!" After that I think about myself and I see I've already complained about the system and the government; "What about me? What am I doing?" Wow! I think a lot about this. We *should* complain about systems and governments, all the time. Sure. But don't forget we also have to complain about ourselves. This is very important.

It's very easy to read the newspaper and complain about that. It's easy! But you have to think about what *you* are doing. It doesn't matter big or small, I should do a little bit to change the world or change the universe. But you need to change yourself first. So, I think, "I'll try to change a little bit." Normally we get drunk—spiky hair drunk punk—and we shout! But in this time, Myanmar is one of poorest countries in the world and we've seen war since 1962, so we should do something. We cook food for the homeless and street kids. We started this in 2013 and now Food Not Bombs movement is not just in my city but all over Myanmar. So many people are inspired and they create something.

After the military coup (2021) the money was so crazy. One of the poorest countries is getting more poor! If you buy rice, onions, garlic and basic food for your kitchen, everything is three times more expensive. There are more poor and more homeless. We see this and ask, "What can we do?" We should cook something, even one meal for lunch or dinner." This is not charity. We have to show them, "Hey guys, we are together." Homeless people have no hope—no future—nobody cares about him. When we give the food to him or her they think, "We are not alone, we are together." Not only do we give food, but we give compassion.

Everyone likes kindness. You need kindness from your girlfriend, your boyfriend, your parents, from your friends. They are all human, like us. They need kindness from us. Right? So, we should show them, we are together! We are all human. You are poor, homeless because of this fucking system. This is our project. Food Not Bombs is not charity, it is solidarity to show that we are together. We say, "Don't be hopeless." For me, I want to be a little bit useful in this life.

HARDCORE ZEN

BRAD WARNER/ODFX/PUNK ROCK AND THE TRUTH ABOUT REALITY

Zen is more punk than punk could ever be.

—Brad Warner

Everything that you hear about enlightenment or about some other transcendent existence is just an idea in your brain. It might be really, really beautiful. But if you got there, if you got to heaven, you'd be complaining about having to hear harp music all the time. Or your wings itch.

—Brad Warner (*Zero Defex*)

The past is a kind of memory, and the future is a kind of hope. Being alive in this world is just action in the present.

—Gudo Wafu Nishijima
(Japanese Zen teacher of Brad Warner)

It's entirely wrong to say that Buddhism is a religion without a God. In fact, it's quite the opposite. To me Buddhism is a way to approach and understand God without dealing with a religion.

—From introduction to *There is No God and He is Always With You* by Brad Warner (2013)

"**B**ohemian Rhapsody" by Queen is playing on the jukebox at the Saturn Café in downtown Santa Cruz, California. The music is no longer background music; the volume is definitely louder than the last two songs that played by Tom Petty and Joan Jett. Clearly, one of the wait staff has pumped up the volume and the operatic song grabs everyone's attention and all of us—mid-meal or still hankering for a salad or cup of tomato soup—joins in singing the lyrics together, out loud. We all seem to know the words from this beloved rock-opera of a song; "Thunderbolt and lightning / Very, very frightening to me / Galileo, Galileo . . . " A food server waves his arms like a conductor encouraging us to sing along with Freddie Mercury. Meanwhile, Brad Warner and I are sitting at a table enjoying dinner and conversation after his local book event for *Hardcore Zen* and he's just all smiles. "This is great! Everyone's singing 'Bohemian Rhapsody.' I've got to write about this," he declares. When the chorus comes up, the place is loud and energized, singing back and forth with joy.

Figure 16.1 Cover of 2019 edition of Hardcore Zen: Punk Rock, Monster Movies, and the Truth about Reality *(2003) by Brad Warner, Zen monk and bassist with 1980s punk band ODFX in Akron, Ohio. "Zen is more punk than punk could ever be." Reprinted by arrangement with Wisdom Publications.*

Back in 1982 Brad Warner was playing loud and fast bass in a hardcore band in Ohio called Zero Defex (ODFX). Warner filmed a lot of the 1980s hardcore scene in Akron and Cleveland and produced a DIY documentary called *Cleveland's Screaming* (2007). He also released five albums of psychedelic rock under the name Dimentia 13. Warner's first book on punk rock and Buddhism was published by Wisdom, a Buddhist publisher based in Massachusetts. He wrote *Hardcore Zen* (2003) while living in Japan working on Godzilla-type movies and becoming a Zen priest under the mentorship of Buddhist teacher Wafu Gado Nishijima. Warner has written a dozen more books including *Sit Down and Shut Up: Punk Rock Commentaries on Buddha, God, Truth, Sex, Death and Dogen's Treasury of the Right Dharma Eye* (2007), *There Is No God and He Is Always With You: A Search for God in Odd Places* (2013) and other books on Zen, sex and karma. Warner is the subject of the 2013 documentary by Pirooz Kalayah, *Brad Warner's Hardcore Zen*.

ZEN IS MORE PUNK THAN PUNK

JM: In *Hardcore Zen* you write, "In its early days punk rock had a lot in common with Zen Buddhism." And you've said, "Zen is more punk than punk could ever be."

BRAD WARNER (*Hardcore Zen*): I guess I did say that! (*laugh*)

JM: What the heck did you mean by that?

BRAD WARNER: What *did* I mean by that? Punk was all about anarchy or no rules or being completely true to yourself. In the days I was into it, everybody shaved their heads which is also a neat connection to Zen. They believed in this philosophy, or they *said* they believed in this philosophy. But I think it fell apart rather quickly and became kind of a trend where *everybody had to think differently in exactly the same way*. In that way, it had a lot of connection to Zen Buddhism, which is about being absolutely true to yourself and discovering what you really are.

JM: On the surface people might say that punk rock is based in anger. It can be pretty loud. And that Buddhism and meditation are peaceful and quiet. How do you reconcile this?

BRAD WARNER (*Hardcore Zen*): I don't think that meditation—at least Zazen—is quiet necessarily. If you're truly doing Zazen practice you become aware of all of these levels going on within your own mind that can be extremely loud, disorienting and disconcerting. You need to find a way to deal with that. You're sitting there not moving as all of these things are coming up in your brain. After you've done it for awhile, you'll notice that almost *shocking* things will come up. In that way, a lot of meditation—which they say is devoted to quieting the mind or still-ness—to a certain degree, is not true. You're just adding whatever you imagine as stillness or quietness and trying to use that concept to drown out whatever is actually going on! Zazen practice is allowing that stuff to come up and actually confronting it. But confronting it by not really doing anything particular about it other than just letting it happen. This is a really important process because if you can learn to let your brain cough up whatever the hell it wants to cough up and not react to it, you find a strength that you can't find any other way.

JM: I sense there's also common ground between punk rock and Buddhism in the idea that liberation comes from creating social systems that are free and not rigid, but that people are a bit afraid of living without structure. In Buddhist terminology this might be described as a fear of realizing that self is an illusion. Maybe in anarchist or political terms we can say that the rules and laws that we think hold things together are confining reality in a way that ends up causing suffering. I wonder if you see that connection?

BRAD WARNER (*Hardcore Zen*): There is a certain amount of connection. The rules that we have are the causes of our suffering. They're rather arbitrary and we just believe in them. If you go to a Zen monastery, there are a lot of rules! There are rules about how to get up and how to bow. In the very strict ones, there are rules about how to use the toilet. But there is also an understanding that these rules are arbitrary, more or less. They're just to make everything run smoothly but we don't *believe* in them.

The mistake that we make in this society is that we have rules and we *believe* deeply in these rules as if they're some kind of a profound truth that we can't possibly violate lest the whole world fall apart. There's a difference between just following rules and *believing* in them. Believing in them may be where we get in to trouble. We believe in our set of rules and then we come across a society that has a different set of rules and we are damn well going to teach them *our* set of rules! This can cause a lot of trouble. Belief is sort of the foundation of a lot of the problems.

BRAD WARNER (Zero Defex / *Hardcore Zen*): When I first came across punk rock it was at a time when I was interested in what was *true*. I was always interested in music and rock music in particular. At the time when I was a teenager the rock music sucked! The music being played on the radio was awful! I was in this state of despair because I knew that there was truthful rock music because I had this collection of rock music from the 60s that I knew was good. And then it all disappeared. I thought that there had been this great force for truth that had gone away by the time I got old enough to experience it.

Zero Defex existed before I joined. They were around for about six months with a different bass player and when I went to see them it was amazing. Here was some true rock music! I found out they were looking for a bass player. Their guy disappeared. Nobody ever saw him again; he just vanished one day. When I found out that I could join this force of truth, I thought this was a great thing!

I came across Buddhism at about the same time (as punk). It was also a situation where I was looking for something truthful. I was a freshman in college and looking for some way to study Eastern religions and there happened to be a class called "Zen Buddhism." I thought, "Zen Buddhism isn't really my style. It's kind of silly, with people trying to will themselves to float on fluffy white clouds of enlightenment all day." But it was the only Eastern religion class on offer that semester, so I took it. My teacher, the guy who became my first Buddhist teacher who was masquerading as a mild-mannered college lecturer, read *The Heart Sutra* to us. A sutra is a Buddhist scripture. It was profound. I wrote a whole chapter about *The Heart Sutra* in the book. It floored me. I had no idea what it meant. It was just a bunch of words that I couldn't understand but I was astounded by the truthfulness of this set of words.

Form is no other than emptiness / Emptiness is no other than form.

—from Buddhist Heart Sutra

BE A LIGHT UNTO YOURSELF

BRAD WARNER (*Hardcore Zen*): Only when you doubt something can you find the truth of it. There is a famous passage in one of the accounts of Buddha's life where Buddha says, "It is proper to doubt. Don't believe in anything just because some authority has said it or because it's written in scripture." He's saying that you should doubt everything and find the truth for yourself. That was just incredible to hear because no other religious authority was saying that. Religious authority is always saying, "I'm telling you the truth and you've got to believe me. Forget about finding it yourself because I've already found it and here it is!" I couldn't accept that. I don't know how anybody can accept that.

JM: You wrote in *Hardcore Zen*, "Buddhism is about letting people know they do not need to follow any authority." I also appreciate another section where you explain that an authentic teacher will hand authority and responsibility back to you if you try to give it to them.

BRAD WARNER (*Hardcore Zen*): Buddha's dying words were, "Be a light unto yourself," or "Be a lamp unto yourself." Meaning: don't follow any authority. The idea of a teacher throwing authority back at you was something I'd experienced with my two teachers. You'd go to them saying, "Oh master, please show me the way," and they'd be like, "I'm not going to show you the way. *You* have to find the way." That was extremely refreshing but extremely challenging to have somebody tell you, "If you try to follow my way exactly, you're just going to end up an imitation of me and there is no point in that."

I can understand it because of the position I'm in now as a so-called "teacher" of Buddhism. People come up and ask me, "Brad, tell me the way." I feel stupid when people ask me that. I think, "Who are you talking to?" You're talking to a guy who's on his website dressed in a rubber bug costume and you're asking him to show you the way! Do you know what you're getting into here?

BRAD WARNER (*Hardcore Zen*): After the book came out (*Hardcore Zen*—2003) people wanted me to be their authority figure or master. When you accept an authority figure what you're really doing is deferring responsibility for your own actions or your own life. This is the way cults work because nobody wants to be responsible for anything. If your guru tells you to go put poison gas on the Tokyo subway system . . .

Everybody has buried within their psyche these destructive urges and if you can find an authority figure who says, "Go and gas the Tokyo subways or crash into the World Trade Center and I give you permission to do that by taking on the responsibility for that action." Or by saying, "This is God's will" or whatever, you have lost something very important in yourself. That's tragic even when it happens on a lesser level than terrorist attacks—which I'm using as a kind of shocking example—it happens in all kinds of ways in everyday life.

JM: You write about Buddhist teacher Pema Chodron and her idea of the *wisdom of no escape*. In your own words you say, "You can't escape yourself." Do you think the notion of enlightenment points to giving up trying to escape ourselves?

BRAD WARNER (*Hardcore Zen*): That's part of it because we're always trying to escape from wherever we are. There is also always the idea of mundane reality. If you look in most books about spiritual matters, especially Eastern spirituality, they're always speaking of transcending mundane reality and trying to get to the truth. There was a band years ago in Akron called The Mundanes. I always think of them when I come across this idea.

Reality—whatever you are living through—is something you really understand. You really understand talking on the phone or you really understand sitting at home listening to Free Radio Santa Cruz. You understand that and it's just mundane or normal. But we think there is maybe something that transcends that and you want to get to the extraordinary, enlightened reality. But the life you're living isn't mundane at all! It's incredible! Just the very fact that you're here at all—existing and breathing air and farting and whatever you're doing—it's just an amazing thing. It's the most amazing thing because it's really real.

Everything that you hear about enlightenment or about some other transcendent existence is just an idea in your brain. It might be really beautiful. But if you got there, if you got to heaven, you'd be complaining about having to hear harp music all the time. Or your wings itch. Or whatever. Wherever you are, you think of as mundane and you want to get somewhere else. The fact is, if you're always in that kind of a frame of mind, even if you have some super-mystical experience you'll be thinking, "Oh my God—isn't this great! Too bad I'm going to have to go home in an hour, away from the angels!"

CAUSE AND EFFECT ARE SIMULTANEOUS

JM: What struck me strongly in *Hardcore Zen* was the view that cause and effect happen *simultaneously*.

BRAD WARNER (*Hardcore Zen*): That is one of Nishijima's pet lines; that cause and effect are always simultaneous. He used to always say that to me and I would think, "Yeah, yeah. Cause and effect are always simultaneous." But it didn't make much sense to me. But the cause *is* the effect and we somehow miss that. This may be something that is so difficult to explain or to put into words that it might be a matter of just having faith in it, which is a dangerous thing to say.

One of the things that the practice of Zazen does in its own slightly magical way is allow you to see this more and more clearly as your practice continues. When you start to notice this, you realize that you have to be very, very careful about what you do and what you say because it has this tremendous ripple effect. Like dropping a stone into a lake; the ripples will go on forever. At some point the ripples will be so far away from the stone that the stone can't possibly know what it's done by its action, but the effects are always there. And they are always going to be felt.

JM: Brad Warner was your Zen student here in Japan for ten years. Have you read his book *Hardcore Zen*?

GUDO WAFU NISHIJIMA (Japanese Zen teacher of Brad Warner): Yes. When it was drafted, Brad sent it to me and I read it. Brad is a very a sincere thinker. To play music comes from his sincerity. And to study Buddhism comes from his sincerity. I think he's a very nice Buddhist because he's so sincere in how to live. So, I think he's a very nice personality.

JM: Tell me about the Buddhist view of cause and effect in the present moment.

GUDO WAFU NISHIJIMA: According to Buddhist theory, we can never live in the past and we can never live in the future. The time when we can live is only the present moment. Actions in the present moment are not sense perceptions; they are a simple fact. Action is always in the present moment. The past is a kind of memory, and the future is a kind of hope. So, those are not real. Being alive in this world is just action in the present.

Buddhism also accepts the principle of the *instantaneousness of this world*. Because action exists just at the present moment, the world *also* exists just at the present moment. Relying upon such a theory, Buddhism solves the very difficult philosophical problem that is the contradiction between determinism and human freedom. If we believe in determinism of human beings, we can never be free. And if we accept human freedom, there is no cause and effect. So, this contradictory problem in philosophy has never been solved throughout more than thousands of years. It is very strange, but in ancient India Gautama Buddha solved this problem and he relied upon the instantaneousness of this world.

The reverence of cause and effect is a reverence of modern science. Therefore, Buddhism can never be contradictory to scientific knowledge. Even though we are caught by the rule of cause and effect at the present moment, the present moment is such a short time, like the edge of a razor. So, if we put a piece of paper on the edge of a razor, a part sometimes falls down to the right side, sometimes to the left side. And true freedom occurs like that. That is the human freedom situation. Gautama Buddha utilized the instantaneousness of this world and solved the human contradictory situation of human freedom and determinism.

Buddhism believes that the value of action at the present moment decides everything, even the universe. To be true in our actions is the most important matter in the Buddhist philosophical system. Buddhism believes that to live morally is human life itself. Our life is just the act at the present moment. We can notice that there is only action at every moment and that is a scenery of our life. I think that such age of realism has begun already, since the beginning of the twentieth century. That is my idea.

SIT DOWN AND SHUT UP

JM: In your book *Sit Down and Shut Up* (2007) you mention that in the punk world, "It became uncool not to be pessimistic."

BRAD WARNER (*Sit Down and Shut Up*): That was definitely one of the things I had a problem with! I just wasn't so pessimistic. I was generally happy. Well, I would vacillate between generally happy and really dour. But I couldn't take the idea of just being completely pessimistic as being realistic. Especially now, it doesn't seem like a realistic attitude because being pessimistic just means you don't try as hard because you think, "Everything is going to be awful anyway."

JM: Do you have a sense that punk rock or Buddhism embodies elements of cooperation and mutual aid rather than competition?

BRAD WARNER (*Sit Down and Shut Up*): Buddhism is about that always. It's about trying to cooperate rather than compete. There is no real sense in competing. Of course, there is no real sense in giving in to something that you don't agree with just because you don't want to compete. Sometimes you just have to leave the playing field, if you want to pursue the metaphor further. As far as punk and competition, one of the people in my movie *Cleveland's Screaming* says that punk was always this matter of being very reciprocal. One of the lessons he learned from being in punk rock was that if somebody gets you a gig in Cleveland, then you would get their band a gig in Akron. It's just something you did to help each other out with the understanding that the scene as a whole was bigger than you are. We also knew that being on top doesn't really satisfy. You can notice people who are on top of this or that and you look at their lives and see how miserable it is to be in that position.

JM: Most religions and philosophies seem to include an idea that no matter which path you choose it's beneficial to respect different paths chosen by others. But that seems to get lost when people become enthusiastic about the path they've found.

BRAD WARNER (*Sit Down and Shut Up*): You can't force anybody to take your path. I wouldn't want to go out and knock on doors and say, "Would you like to hear about Zen?" It's just ridiculous! That stuff doesn't really work—even when it works, it doesn't work! You just get people paying lip service to something and not really getting it. Or they get into it just because it offers some sort of social environment they find comforting, but it's not really any kind of deep understanding. On the other hand, I'm accused all the time of being dogmatic or insisting on my own way. I learned this from my own teacher, who was very insistent on his own way. But when you examined it, he was saying, "This is my way and this is what works and I don't deviate from what works." But that's not the same as trying to force everybody else into doing what works for you. There is a big difference, although sometimes it's difficult to see that clearly.

NOT ABLE TO MEDITATE

JM: Often when I talk to people about meditation, they may have seen images of meditation that appear peaceful. Or they compare themselves to others and think that when other people are meditating, they're experiencing peace but when they try it, they find that maybe it's not so peaceful.

BRAD WARNER (*Sit Down and Shut Up*): They think, "All of these other people can meditate, but not me!" Yes, I hear that. The truth is that it's hard for everybody! That's the kind of fantasy I work hard to break down. It is difficult for everybody—it was difficult for Buddha. By the same token, it gets easier after you do it for a while. It has gotten to the point where if I don't do it everyday, I feel like crap. I get up in the morning and I want to practice Zazen because I know that it's a beneficial thing to do.

When I first started, my teacher said, "You should do Zazen everyday, even if it's just five lousy minutes." I was a struggling indie-musician putting out records. Even after Zero Defex I put out all of these albums as Dimentia 13 in the 1980s and tried to make this music thing work. I was coming home from out-of-town gigs because I couldn't afford a hotel. I was driving all night and getting home at four in the morning, which seems insane. But I didn't feel right without Zazen. When I didn't do it, my whole perspective—my body and mind—everything was all screwie. I would give it up from time to time because I was thinking, "Well, I'm not getting enlightened and this is just stupid." When I would give it up the sort of buzzing horribleness that you get in your brain would just get so loud and awful that I'd think, "Well, I gotta do that Zazen thing. I can't avoid it."

IDEALISM, MATERIALSM, REALISM, BUDDHISM

GUDO WAFU NISHIJIMA (Zen teacher of *Hardcore Zen* author Brad Warner): Buddhism insists that to know reality, we have to leave the intellectual area—idealism and materialism—and enter into the area of action. We need to act. And the practice of Zazen is the fundamental basis of action. Even though it does not have any movement, keeping the spine straight is a kind of act, and such acts are the basis of Buddhist philosophy. Therefore, we practice Zazen and we experience what action is and such experience teaches us what reality is. That is the structure of Buddhist philosophy.

Usually, scientists think that the material world and reality are the same, but according to Buddhist philosophy materialism and realism are different. In the case of materialism, the source of their ideas is sense perception and sense perception is just excitement of our sense organs. So, it is not matter itself. According to Buddhist philosophy, there is a clear difference between a materialism and realism. Zen says that both the materialistic and the spiritual view are incomplete and mistaken, that we are neither body nor mind, that our actual reality cannot be defined in such narrow terms. Even the word God is too limiting. Or as Dogen says, "Even the whole universe in ten directions is just a small part of the supreme truth." The supreme truth is, to me, another name for God.

—From introduction to *There is No God and He is Always With You* by Brad Warner (2013)

JM: It seems the wisdom and compassion teachings of Buddhism have come to the United States after massive amounts of violence, including the US wars on Japan and Vietnam.

BRAD WARNER (Hardcore Zen): I hadn't really thought about it that way, but that's true. We bombed Japan and then got their Buddhism. We bombed Vietnam and got Thich Nhat Hanh.

JM: It's almost like compassion travels like water; it seems to flow where it is not yet.

BRAD WARNER: It does seem to move in its own fashion without so much conscious intervention. You're right. I was thinking about India. The British had tried to conquer India and take it over and what happened as a result was that Indian culture became extremely influential in Britain. It's not what you would expect. It's the same thing with Japan or Vietnam. The US government tried to suppress and control their cultures, but then aspects of their cultures end up becoming a part of us. It is a sort of assimilation process.

"NOT A BUDDHIST PUNK BAND!"
RUIN/SENSE FIELD/DEATHLESS/BUDDHADATTA

Take away the structures and the boundlessness remains.

—"Freedom Has No Bounds" by Ruin (1984)

The late 1960s and early 70s was an explosive period worldwide for social, political and spiritual revolutions and many styles of music became conduits for liberation and living free. Eastern spiritual philosophies and practices had migrated to Europe and North America and by the 60s meditation and yoga were widely practiced. In 1968 the Beatles famously went to Rishikesh, India, to practice Transcendental Meditation with Maharishi Mahesh Yogi. The band reportedly wrote forty-eight songs during that period, which became the White Album. John, Paul, George and Ringo extolled the benefits of meditation but ended up leaving Maharishi when the guru was accused of sexual misconduct.

("The Beatles in India: 16 Things You Didn't Know"—
by David Chiu, Rolling Stone, February 14, 2021)

Buddhism gained wider attention when teachers like the Dalai Lama, Thich Nhat Hanh and Chögyam Trungpa Rinpoche visited Europe and North America and established meditation centers. By the late 1970s Buddhism was directly combined with punk rock and this vital pairing led to the formation of bands and organizations that focused on overcoming the suffering of addiction, anxiety and depression.

In 1979, Glenn Wallis founded the hardcore punk band Ruin in Philadelphia. He later became a translator of Buddha's teachings and associate professor of Buddhism, Hinduism and Indian Religions at the University of Georgia. A 2013 interview with Wallis in the Buddhist magazine Lion's Roar refers to Ruin as, "the first Buddhist punk band."

Then there's the Clash song "Ghetto Defendant" (1982) with Beat poet Allen Ginsberg chanting the Buddhist Prajnaparamita sutra; "Gate, gate, paragate, parasam gate, bodhi svaha." This mantra sets an intention to transcend suffering: "Over, over, completely over, not to return." A 1986 concert video features Shriekback singer Barry Andrews introducing the song "Gunning for The Buddha" as, "Perhaps the world's first Zen pop song" and the first demo album from Blink 182 was titled *Buddha*. (1992) Punk and Buddhism would later be merged by Dharma Punx meditation teacher Noah Levine, punk musician and Zen priest Brad Warner, Myanmar punk singer/activist Kyaw Thu Win and others.

JM: Ruin has been described as a Buddhist punk band. Your thoughts on this?

GLENN WALLIS (Ruin): Four of us were serious Buddhist practitioners. The practice gave us a discipline that was otherwise lacking from our lives. It also gave us a way to process the intensity of life. It was calming, even peaceful. It produced insight into situations and issues you were dealing with. It was really good for me. But I would *not* say we were a Buddhist punk band. We did not write Buddhist-oriented lyrics the way that Krishnacore or Christian metal bands injected their beliefs into their lyrics. We were not even explicitly ideological in the way straight edge, political or vegan bands were. I guess you could say that Buddhism was not our message. So, does that disqualify us as a Buddhist punk band? Having said that, Buddhist philosophy certainly played a role in informing our worldview and our attitude toward life. So, it couldn't help but seep into our music. I can think of several songs with Buddhist-inspired themes, though the Buddhism remains implicit. But I can think of more songs infused with ideas from Dada, surrealism, the Situationists, Jungian psychology, Nietzsche, and anarchism. Maybe this is the point; a *punk spirituality* will be eclectic, minimally ideological, open and expressive.

JM: Was Ruin understood and respected by other punk musicians of the 80s?

GLENN WALLIS (Ruin): I think we were respected by other punk musicians of our time. We were definitely respected by other Philadelphia bands, bar owners, scenesters. There was very little of the competition that I knew from other scenes. Were we understood? Probably not. I vividly recall reactions from certain well-known bands that suggest we took them a bit by surprise! When we opened for Public Image, John Lydon watched our soundcheck. Afterwards he told me that what we did was pretty strange, but he liked it. I heard similar reactions from members of The Dickies, Red Kross, The Dicks and Discharge when we opened for those bands. My point is that we had something going on in our music that struck them in unexpected ways. Why? I think because they had an image of what a punk band was supposed to sound and look like, and we didn't fit the image.

NOT A BUDDHIST PUNK BAND!

JOHN STOCKBERGER (Sense Field): We were definitely not a Buddhist punk band! I don't know if I'd ever want to be put in the position of representing Buddha dharma or trying to get people interested in Buddhism. That's not how my punk rock works. In 2005 we did a tour in Japan with a band and they were more or less a Buddhist band (Running from Dharma). But there weren't any Buddhist bands.

I put together the artwork for those first Sense Field singles that much later got transitioned onto the Sense Field albums for Revelation (Records). The name of the band does come from an experience I had; I was living in Venice Beach (California) in the late 80s and had a copy of *The Dhammapada* with Tibetan on one page and English on the other. One afternoon I had consumed about twenty-seven hits of acid (*robust laugh*) and I was reading this book and all the words slid off the page except for two: "sense field." That's the story of our name that doesn't get told much, for obvious reasons.

I don't consider myself a Buddhist. I'm resistant to hierarchical structures and to spirituality being carved into a tablet and becoming a static form. In most of the Buddhist practices I have experience with, it's always a living tradition and having an experience and finding a new way to share that with others. There's something in Buddhist tradition against becoming codified and it's revolutionary in a way. My understanding of Jesus and his actions; he seemed to take this same revolutionary approach of breaking people out of mental prison with a spiritual shock therapy. What happened since then is clearly different.

JOE CLEMENTS (Fury 66 / The Deathless): I don't know any Buddhist punk bands. But there are people online who will tell you that we're not the first! The article came out in the Santa Cruz Good Times saying that we were the first Buddhist punk rock band and I thought, "You don't want to *ever* fucking say that!" ("Mosh Path: How Santa Cruz's the Deathless Became the World's First Buddhist Punk Band" by Mat Weir—June 22, 2016)

NOAH LEVINE (*Dharma Punx* / The Deathless): I don't think it's correct to call the Deathless the first Buddhist punk band. There are other bands that have been heavily inspired by Buddhism and I know when that article came out in the Good Times some people wrote in and said, "Hey wait! What about this other band?" They were talking about some 70s and 80s bands that were a little obscure but were Buddhist punk.

GLENN WALLIS (Ruin): Punk sees itself as a path free from certain suffering. I saw it that way, too. In many ways the punk path—the Tao of Punk, perhaps—took you there. I developed many attitudes from my engagement with punk that even now, forty years later, made my life better and made me more confident in my questioning of the status quo. It encouraged me to stand up and express my opinion. It infused me with the DIY spirit which has completely informed all of my life projects. It gave me an ear for discordant views, and to consider the value of what I would otherwise have dismissed. It opened me to taking risks, and to see possibilities in radically alternative pathways. It reduced suffering in very real ways. It saved me from the pain that comes from living a safe, predictable humdrum existence.

What I value is the *hidden influence*. I believe that when the *real* of the thing—anarchism, Buddhism, punk spirituality—is truly embodied and genuinely lived, then all of the outward signs can be dispensed with. The *outward sign* saps the vitality of the real of the thing. Imagine meeting a person who yammers on about "punk spirituality" but who strikes you as self-righteous. Now, imagine meeting a person who says nothing about "punk spirituality" yet exudes it. I tend to get suspicious around the improvers of humankind, for whom punk spirituality or Buddhism or whatever is the answer. It's easy to get stuck in the ruts of borrowed thought. How absurd that would be for someone who embraces punk values!

BECOME WHOLE WITH MYSELF

DAVE DICTOR (Millions of Dead Christians): I find Buddhism a great place to become whole with myself. A lot of times in this world I'm pulled in a lot of different directions. My day might look like I'm practicing music, going to a demonstration, organizing a tour and then I've got a child in my life. I'm sometimes being pulled apart. It's important to take time on a daily basis for breathing and relaxing. When the Dalai Lama came to New York City a few years ago (September 22, 2003) it was wonderful to spend that weekend in a safe spiritual place and to become whole. I was moved by his compassion and not arousing anger about the world.

JM: How important is compassion and meditation in the punk world? The mainstream portrayal of punk is chaos, violence and anger.

DAVE DICTOR (Millions of Dead Cops): Media likes to hone in and make simple out of complex situations. I'm not going to tell you that there is a whole lot of spirituality actively being displayed in the punk rock community, but there is some. And it's rather ignored. I was mentioning to you about Gary Floyd and his band Sister Double Happiness. People do make conscious efforts in that direction that have come from the punk community.

At the same time "Punk" is one of these catch-all terms. It's almost like saying "Rock." Punk and rock are almost the same thing, but rock is a term from the 60s and 70s and punk might be a term from the 80s up to the present. It's a very gigantic catch-all. There's all kinds of different people involved. Bands like the Bad Brains who will be Rastafarian, have that going on with their spirituality. I'd say eighty to ninety percent of punk doesn't try to capture that at all. It's mostly people between seventeen and twenty-five, it's alcohol driven and just trying to capture the angst of this society we live in. It's a society that is de-individualized, where people aren't fitting in or aren't *wanting* to fit in. There's rebellion going on. But there is a healthy amount that's rather ignored. People aren't conscious on many different levels. They are aware of Buddhism and spirituality and they try to practice it in their private lives. Sometimes it bleeds over into their community that they're working within.

I'm now booking myself a sixty-five-city tour. (2006) It's going to be about two and a half months and I named it *The Davey Lama Incense Tour*. I'm trying to get people in our music community to think about the Dalai Lama. Everyone sees the Dalai Lama as this older Tibetan man who's praying and they don't necessarily take it any further. I'm just hoping to get people to explore a little bit more. I'm not actively telling people to like the Dalai Lama. I will tell people to enjoy life and be at peace with yourself. Usually, I do tours with titles like, *Kill A Cop and Yourself and Hope the Rest Will Follow*. Or *Destroy Amerikkka*. Something that's got visceral teeth in it! This one is more of a personal evolution type thing. I'm hoping that the audience gets it and reflects.

I hope they don't carry on "*Destroy Amerikkka!*" at the show and aren't thinking that as they watch me on stage. But thinking about self-healing, evolution, growth and spiritual-ness. On a certain level we'll still be singing songs that don't necessarily reflect everything that's so Dalai Lama-ish. There will still be songs like, "John Wayne Was a Nazi," which is probably our most famous song. It talks about how a movie star icon got put in this place to make it to look good for people to die in wars, to make it look good that white man conquered the Indians. But along with that, I want people to see that I'm trying to grow through my own anger. Here I am fifty-one years old. I don't want to be like, "John Wayne!" The person's been dead for twenty-eight years!

DRUMMING WITH BUDDHISTS

D. J. BONEBRAKE (X): I learned to play drums from Buddhists. It was kind of a pop Buddhism of Soka Gakkai established by Nichiren. We chanted, "Nam Myōhō Renge Kyō." I was twelve years old and my older brother became a member. I wanted to do everything he did so I said, "Let me go to the meetings!" I became a member at twelve. Then they said, "We've got a marching band. We're looking for guys to be in the band." I said, "Well, I don't play anything," and they said, "That's okay, we'll teach you." (*laugh*) I went down to one of the rehearsals and they said, "We need drummers or saxophone players." I said, "Well, how about drums?" That's where I got my early lessons, for two or three years. A couple of really good drummers taught me how to play and then I went off from there. So, it was Buddhists! Over the years I've learned a little bit about certain kinds of Buddhism. I find it fascinating, but I don't really study much. I was a Buddhist slacker.

JM: Have you been influenced by Zen or Eastern philosophy?

DAVID J (Bauhaus / Love & Rockets): Very much, especially Zen. I like the idea of direct action and also the idea of simplifying, which is the essence of Zen. That to me really is truthful. To answer your question now, I should probably not say anything and just have silence!

GUDO WAFU NISHIJIMA (Zen teacher of *Hardcore Zen* author Brad Warner): From the Buddhist viewpoint, we should revere both the spiritual and the material. It sounds a little contradictory, but it is the true situation of this world. Reality is not only spiritual and not only material. Looking at the real situation of this world, keeping the midway between spirit and matter is necessary to help us understand this world clearly. Buddhism believes in the rightness of the middle way; the belief in reality. Human beings should consider everything on the basis of real facts. Therefore, Buddhism has criticism of spiritual religions and also criticism of Marxist materialism. And this point is very important: if we do not overcome the contradictory situation—idealism and materialism—we can never solve any problems in the world today. Since the beginning of the twentieth century human history has entered into the age of realism. People do not notice such a fact, but gradually such a tendency will be increased. In the future people in the world will notice such facts, I guess.

Buddhism is just realism. Buddhism insists that one single philosophy can never explain this world or explain reality. If we want to explain reality, we should leave from the area of intellectual consideration and enter into the area of fact. Gautama Buddha recommended to practice Zazen to explain action, therefore we practice Zazen everyday, in the morning and at night. In this way, we can keep the autonomic nervous system balanced.

BUDDHADATTA

JM: Do you think of your band Buddhadatta as a Buddhist punk band?

VOGLIBONZE (Buddhadatta): No. I sing about Buddhism but I don't even know if Seiko (bass) and Takami (drums) are Buddhists! I happened to be born into a typical Japanese household, so I became a Buddhist. Many people in Japan don't follow any religion. Buddhism, as it was transmitted from India through China to Japan over centuries, has evolved and adapted to various interpretations by different monks. Many people in Japan consider themselves Buddhists, yet they also identify with Shintoism. Except for those with strict adherence to Shinto, most Japanese people consider themselves both Shinto and Buddhist. This means that, unlike people in some other countries, Japanese people don't place a significant emphasis on religious affiliation. They accept all religions and respect others' beliefs, which means that religious conflicts do not arise here. I personally believe that any religion that brings people happiness is fine.

JM: Would you share the story about the Buddhist monk who visited your father when he died and how you were inspired, listening to the monk chanting mantras?

VOGLIBONZE (Buddhadatta): In Buddhism, when someone dies a monk chants sutras and then we go to the crematorium. After that, it's said the soul undergoes a trial for forty-nine days to determine if they can reach paradise. During this time, the monk would visit our home weekly to chant sutras. Hearing these chants every week, I eventually thought of chanting the sutras in a punk rock style. I've never been a monk. But when I'm singing, I do practice meditation and chanting.

Figure 17.1 Japanese punk band Buddhadatta with Seiko (bass), singer Voglibonze, and Takami (drums): "The common thread between punk rock and Buddhism is that happiness or suffering can depend on one's mindset, even under the same circumstances." Photo by Ichiro Takami.

JM: What is the connection for you between punk rock and Buddhism?

VOGLIBONZE (Buddhadatta): Everyone has a different interpretation of what punk rock means, so it's difficult to answer simply. To me, the common thread between punk rock and Buddhism is that happiness or suffering can depend on one's mindset, even under the same circumstances.

JM: Some say that punk rock and Buddhism are both about ending suffering and experiencing liberation. Do you think that's true?

VOGLIBONZE (Buddhadatta): I can't say if it's true, but I like that way of thinking.

JM: Why is it important for you to convey the Buddha's teachings through music?

VOGLIBONZE (Buddhadatta): Conveying Buddhist teachings isn't that important to me; making music is more important. I'm not interested in spreading Buddhism. However, I believe the Buddhist perspective of wishing happiness for everyone, regardless of their religion or lack of one, is something valuable and worth sharing. Destruction and killing bring nothing but loss. I think the most important teaching can be found in the journey of the Buddha from his birth to enlightenment. Born as a prince of the Shakya clan, he lived a life that, in many ways, was contrary to what he would later teach. Despite his incredible abilities, he indulged in a life of decadence with five hundred women and alcohol as provided by the king. This led me to realize that enlightenment is achieved through experiencing desires and making mistakes. However, please understand that this view is my own!

JM: In America, sometimes it's common for Buddhist people to say that they are not Buddhist. I do this sometimes. Some people wish not to be attached to any particular form or belief, including Buddhism itself. What are your thoughts on this?

VOGLIBONZE (Buddhadatta): That's completely true, and most Japanese people see it that way. Japanese Buddhism is essentially a way of thinking for humans to live peacefully and happily. It's normal for us to not cling to any particular form or idea, including Buddhism.

JM: Which punk rock bands or musicians have influenced you the most?

VOGLIBONZE (Buddhadatta): Einstürzende Neubauten; I was influenced by their musical style. It felt as if they were chanting sutras, though I don't understand the lyrics. The Genbaku Onanies. Their rhythm (Nagoya Beat) inspired me. Turtle Island and Seppuku Pistols; these two bands taught me the fusion of Japanese culture and punk. I once thought combining Japanese and punk rock would be difficult, but they proved me wrong! This led to the birth of my "punk monk" style. Japanese band Vion and their leader Hiroshi Obiki influenced me by their incorporation of Tuvan throat singing (hoomei) and Asian musicality. Their song ideas are brilliant. Most Japanese people respect all religions, so no one talks or worries about another's religion. Most Japanese are Buddhist, but we don't place much importance on it. So, whether it's a Buddhist band, a secular band, or a band of another faith, we all get along well.

JM: Some Christian punk bands have performed in churches. Have you ever performed in a Buddhist temple?

VOGLIBONZE (Buddhadatta): Of course! Japanese Buddhist temples are places where people gather, talk, and celebrate together.

JM: Are you familiar with any of the following people or bands? Noah Levine and *Dharma Punx*, Brad Warner and *Hardcore Zen*, the Buddhist punk band Ruin, the California-based Buddhist punk band the Deathless, Kyaw Thu Win of Myanmar band Rebel Riot, or Hidé of Japanese punk band Ultra Bidé?

VOGLIBONZE (Buddhadatta): I know Ultra Bidé; they're friends. I don't know the others.

JM: Do you think intense singing and music can release emotions like anger and relieve tension, or does it amplify anger?

VOGLIBONZE (Buddhadatta): That's a hard question to answer. It depends on the character of the person singing and the intensity of the song. I believe it's good to release emotions through punk rock, but I oppose hurting others or mocking them. In Buddhism, it's thought that everything you say, think, or do eventually comes back to you. Japanese Buddhism is essentially a way of thinking about how to live a happy life and is completely different from Christianity, Judaism, or Islam. I believe it is a method of liberation from suffering created by humans for humans.

"MESSAGE OF THE BHAGAVAT"
KRISHNACORE/RAGHUNATH RAY CAPPO—YOUTH OF TODAY AND SHELTER/ROB FISH—108

Spirituality and punk rock; they're one and the same in the sense that both are striving to understand things more deeply than they seem on the surface.

—Ray Cappo (Youth of Today / Shelter)

The whole idea of literalism or fundamentalism in religion or spirituality is just something I never felt comfortable with.

—Rob Fish (108)

JM: You were a celibate monk and in a hardcore punk band. How do those go together?

RAY CAPPO (Youth of Today / Shelter / *From Punk to Monk*): It was unprecedented in the history of punk as well as the history of the very orthodox lineage I was studying under. People know Hare Krishnas as this kooky Western cult but it's actually a very orthodox tradition of Vishnu worship called Vaishnavism. It's a very strict and respected school in India. I came from a punk background. In punk, who is celibate? Who's celibate when they're twenty-two? I got turned on to yoga and my yoga teacher turned me on to the Bhagavad Gita. When I met the Krishnas, even I thought they were a bunch of kooks! Then I started to meet some sincere practitioners. When you meet somebody sincere it inspires you. It was at a time in my life when I was searching. I was a teenager and I was famous. I wasn't famous like Kurt Cobain, but I had fans all over that really looked up to

Figure 18.1 Raghunath Ray Cappo does a handstand while performing with Shelter in Berkeley, California, on June 19, 2018. John Porcelly (Porcell) is on guitar. Cappo and Porcell were in the hardcore band Violent Children (with sixteen-year-old Cappo on drums) and later founded Youth of Today in 1985. Photos by John Malkin.

me. I realized that whatever illusion they're under, I'm the same putz I always was! They might think I'm cooler but I feel I'm still as confused as they are! They just like the way I sing or scream. Or they think I'm some prophet, in the case of Youth of Today, because we had a lot of ideas, ethics and ideals.

I realized I was living in a type of illusion and I wanted to get out of it. I was fed up with the level of fame I had. I wanted to find more in life and I was ready to give up everything I had worked for and take a more humble position as a student. I really got into yoga, Indian culture, studied the Vedas and tried to absorb myself in that. Coming from a punk background it was two crazy paradigms colliding but somehow it blended together nicely. It worked in a weird way. The essence of the Bhagavad Gita was that you shouldn't abandon what you do to become a renunciate or a monk, but engage in what you do in the spirit of devotion and love toward God.

JM: You ended up leaving the punk rock world for a while, right?

RAY CAPPO (Youth of Today / Shelter): When I first got into Krishna Consciousness I thought, "I'm going to give up all this nonsense. I'm in a band—this is crazy!" I'd go into a typical bar or club and there was the smell of beer and piss and there were fights. You're dealing with this punk scene that's filled with left-wing extremists and right-wing gangs. It's enough to make you say, "This is nuts! I'm getting out of here! I'm going to India! I want to hang out with sadhus, holy men and saints." And that's what I did. At the height of a Youth of Today tour I left. I went and studied in India. Then I went back to America and decided, "I'm just going to live a simple life on a farm." I moved to an ashram and lived on a farm along with the Youth of Today roadie, Steve Ready, who is now the owner of Equal Vision Records. Studying during that time made me realize, "Actually, this isn't true renunciation. True renunciation isn't renouncing what you naturally do, but it's to engage what you naturally do in a positive way." So, I brought together the spiritual and material with the band Shelter.

RAY CAPPO (Youth of Today / Shelter): I didn't even know Poly Styrene was into bhakti! (Hindu devotion). I was always a big fan of X-Ray Spex and had all their posters and singles in my record collection. On my way to India the first time I'm sitting in the temple room (London airport) chanting to myself and I saw her walk in. Like a fanboy, I almost choked. As she was leaving, I thought, "I have to say something! I've never left the US before and now I'm in England, the hub of punk rock music with the Clash, Sex Pistols, Cockney Rejects, X-Ray Spex and the Buzzcocks. Home to all these bands I grew up listening to and I'm here with one of my teen idols!" I ran up and said, "You're Poly Styrene! I'm one of your biggest fans. I didn't know you were into bhakti!" She said, "Yeah, my spiritual name is Maharani." I said, "I also was the singer of a band, but I quit." She said, "Why did you quit? Were you into drugs and alcohol?" I go, "No, we didn't drink or smoke. We're all vegetarians!" She's like, "Did anybody listen to you?" I go, "Yeah, we had tens of thousands of fans. I just wanted something more." And she's like, "Yeah, I can understand. But you have to understand you're also doing good in this world." I go, "I know, but enough was enough." So, we became friends and I met her the next day. I mentioned in my book (*From Punk to Monk*) that after I got back from India, we ended up doing my final tour in Europe, which never turned out to be my final tour. But we ended up staying with Poly

Styrene and her husband and got to know her much better. It was very nice to come full circle. And then it was very sad when she passed away (2011). Now I'm connected with her daughters.

TAKE A KNIFE

RAY CAPPO (Youth of Today / Shelter): The analogy which is often used is a knife. Is a knife good or bad? Well, it really depends on how that knife is utilized. If I slit somebody's throat, it's bad. But if you're a surgeon you can use it to delicately extract a bullet or to repair someone's heart. Utility is the principle. So, I thought, "How can my music be a positive thing?" You have to be able to be in something without getting contaminated by it. That is where a spiritual practice—sadhana—helps. We (Shelter) would wake up early, chant, meditate and sing in Bhakti schools. The connection to God is through loving devotion.

I'm really into cleansing the body and eating primarily raw foods. Raw foods are fresh and carry the energy of Earth, which is very close to God. Once food is cooked it takes on the energy of whoever prepared it. Part of the reason we get diseased is that we eat processed food that is not cooked with love. If you go into health food stores you may find things that say, "Prepared with love."

ROB FISH (108 / Resurrection / Judas Factor): I don't think you can separate spirituality and the material world. You can have a strong positive impact through material things. There's an analogy I've always used; you can take a knife and use it for good or for bad. It's the same whether you're talking about politics or spirituality. Neither are innately positive or negative. It's what you do with them.

JM: How have your ideas around spirituality been received in the punk world and how has that changed over the years?

ROB FISH (108): There's a whole segment of the punk scene that's involved in spirituality or religion. There are hundreds of bands on Tooth and Nail (Christian punk record label) and to be honest I'm not familiar with most of them. But what's always made me different from some of the Shelter guys is that some people need things to be defined for them. I had a lot of experience with them traveling and we even lived together for a short period. Spirituality is very much what they read in a book and how they assimilate that into their personal life. I never really towed that line. I always felt that there were these books that offered some great insights but, ultimately as an individual, it's all about how you process those prophets' ideas. I've never felt the need to say, "It says it in a book, so it's got to be true."

The whole idea of literalism or fundamentalism in religion or spirituality is something I never felt comfortable with. I was friends with Vic (DiCara) for a few years before we started 108. He was in Shelter and his departure from Shelter had to do with that dynamic. He was inspired by a lot of things I was inspired by, that even some of the guys in Shelter might have been inspired by. But how it played out in our lives was very different. Shelter was there to teach you something. They wanted to present theology and almost give a sermon in a live musical setting. With 108 it was never like that.

RAY CAPPO (Youth of Today / Shelter): We almost became evangelical about the principles of spiritual life. But in my heart of hearts, I was never a fundamentalist. My own experience is that a person who truly worships Krishna understands there's one God, no matter what name you give God: Christ, God, Allah or Jehovah. There is one God. A lot of people who were big fans of Shelter became Krishna monks. And some became more disciplined in their own spiritual practice. I remember one boy who was a big fan of Shelter and he became a Franciscan Monk. Another guy became a monk in a whole other thing. I didn't think, "I lost someone—they didn't join the Krishna club!" It wasn't about that. It was about deepening your spiritual life as opposed to your material life.

ROB FISH (108): I remember when we went on our first tour to Europe, the people who were involved with ISKON, the Hare Krishna church (International Society for Krishna Consciousness), were really excited because Shelter had come through. They would set up book tables at every show and there was this whole presentation: "Let's give a class and bring lots of kids back to the temple." When we arrived at our first show, we pull up outside and there's fifty people and they've got banners and they're chanting and they have tables set up. We got out of the van and walked up and said, "Get out of here! What are you doing here?" It was hard for them to understand why we were so vehement about, "We don't want you at our show. We're not going to have a program at your temple!" The common thread in 108 was this inspiration in the theology of Gaudiya Vaishnavism but it wasn't about preaching to people. It was about processing what we were experiencing as individuals, positive and negative.

That is the defining difference between us and a lot of bands that use spirituality or religion as a context for their music. We're not trying to present a specific line of thought or a specific teaching or book. It's really us trying to express ourselves. It's a pretty contrasting difference between how I processed spirituality versus how Ray Cappo or the guys in Shelter did. Or even the guys in Cro-Mags.

YOUTH OF TODAY

RUSS RANKIN (Good Riddance / Only Crime): I never really cared much for religion or spirituality. The singer in Shelter was previously in the band Youth of Today, who I saw many times. He influenced me a lot. I wanted to see what he was up to with this new band Shelter. Because of that I read The Bhagavad Gita. There were a few things about Krishna I appreciated. If someone had a gun to my head and said you had to adopt a religion, maybe I would pick that one because of the vegetarian angle. But I've always felt a knee-jerk reaction to religion because it seems so subjective, like someone is going to ask me to follow all these tenets without question. I don't know if I'd ever be willing to do that all the way. It's important to have an open mind and not suffer from contempt prior to investigation, where I'm going to write something off without checking it out.

CHRIS HANNAH (Propagandhi): Where we are from (Winnipeg, Canada) there's been a connection between a sort of conservative Christian element and hardcore punk rock. But I haven't really heard of any other couplings since the mid 80s in the New York hardcore scene. There was a Hare Krishna movement that fizzled out and died in the early 90s. Looking back there were some decent ideas in those records by bands that were otherwise considered thugs. It was interesting.

JM: Bands like Shelter?

CHRIS HANNAH (Propagandhi): I was thinking of Cro-Mags, but Shelter as well. Cro-Mags especially. Those boys were singing about street justice but they had some ideas about nonviolence and vegetarianism on their records. It's interesting to give that to a crowd of skinheads!

JM: You're doing that in a way, too, in terms of offering ideas about animal rights, activism and veganism.

CHRIS HANNAH: (Propagandhi): Yeah, I suppose so. Those ideas came because we were transformed at certain times in our lives and you feel compelled to share that transformation with others. Especially when you're younger, you suspect that what compelled you to make a change will *immediately* compel the rest of the world, once they hear your logic. Of course, it never pans out that way! But that is how issue-oriented songs came about, especially concerning animal rights. I'm still bewildered and horrified by how people, especially in Western-industrialized societies, treat animals en masse.

CLIFFORD DINSMORE (Bl'ast / Dusted Angel): Cro-Mags really initiated that. Cro-Mags were really intense people and were friends of ours. We met them when we went on our first tour and played with them in Berkeley. Then we were running into them all over the country. They're really awesome people and grew up on the streets of New York. The Krishna thing was a way for them to balance out the whole intensity of their environment.

JM: What do you do to balance out intensity?

CLIFFORD DINSMORE (Bl'ast): I'm interested in more of a personal spirituality, to be in touch with the natural elements and not really clinging to any kind of organized religion. Basically, my own trip. I would probably take more of an occult approach to spirituality which is basically not being pigeon-holed into any organized religion mold.

EDDIE STERN (Chop Shop / Lou Reed's Yoga teacher): Before I started doing yoga I was in the punk rock and hardcore scene and going to Sunday matinee shows at CBGBs and seeing the Cro-Mags and learning that Harley (Flanagan) was a Hare Krishna. I really only knew of the Hare Krishnas as a parody that you'd see in the *Airplane* movies and Saturday Night Live. I didn't know anything about the cosmologies but I was hearing Youth of Today and Raghunath (Ray Cappo) and all these guys who were at the fringes of being experimental with different religions such as Hinduism and being vegetarian or straight edge, like Minor Threat.

SOUNDTRACK FOR PEOPLE WHO DON'T FIT IN

Harley Flanagan was originally the drummer for New York punk band the Stimulators, at the age of eleven. He later became bassist and vocalist in Cro-Mags. John Joseph, former singer for Cro-Mags, recently collaborated with popular Hindu chant musician Krishna Das on a project that, "provides housing and healing techniques to inmates who have been incarcerated and are now paroled after doing very long prison sentences." (krishnadas.com—August 17, 2018) Harley Flanagan continues to record and perform as Cro-Mags today.

Robert Fish had his first contact with ISKON (International Society for Krishna Consciousness) when he was fifteen and at seventeen joined the Philadelphia ashram. His spiritual name is Rasaraja Das and he's vocalist with 108, which started in 1997. He's also been in other bands including Resurrection and Judas Factor. The first flyer for a 108 concert read: "Direct expression. Bypass mind. Bypass intellect. Self to sound. Against the dead trend. The robot me. The modern social entity stripped of color and vibrancy. Not philosophy. Not religion. True self expressed in sound." Rob Fish is featured in the documentary film *N.Y.H.C.* (1999).

ROB FISH (108 / Resurrection / Judas Factor): Punk has always been the soundtrack for people who just don't fit in. Whether that is due to social circumstance, race, sexual orientation or whatever the case might be, it's rooted in the feeling that you don't fit in. In some respects, spirituality is pretty much the same thing. It's this idea that the things you see around you aren't as simple as they might seem, and they tend to run deeper than what you can visualize. That's a link to punk rock and the same ideology that things you see around you run a lot deeper than the surface ways we encounter it, in terms of social or political circumstances.

ANIMAL LIBERATION

ROB FISH (108): Gaudiya Vaishnavism—the most esoteric and ultimate aspirations that it's supposed to draw one toward—somehow, it's found a home in my heart. I don't know why and I don't really care. I might stress something like vegetarianism because I think, "Throw out spirituality and the idea that there's any ultimate truth or karma. If it's something that brings suffering to other living beings and if I don't need to do it, then I won't." At the same time, I don't think I have the truth at my beck and call.

We submitted a song for this kid—Peter Young—who was put in jail for doing animal rights activities. A lot of people have been asking me, "You're really into animal liberation and you support what he did?" The interesting thing is that I don't really support what he did. I support that he felt something strongly and it's something I can relate to. It's something I wouldn't do and advocate, but I thought the guy was trying to do something noble. He was trying to save lives.

We did a show two months ago. There were all these kids who were really into animal liberation and they were saying, "You've got to go to these laboratories and burn them down." They told me how they got this woman's phone number and were harassing her to quit her job because she was involved with animal testing. I said, "Are you pro-life or pro-choice? What's your deal when it comes to that side of things?" He said, "I'm pro-choice." I said, "What do you think about these people who stand outside of abortion clinics and throw things and yell at doctors?" He said, "That's fucked up." I said, "What's the difference between what you're doing to these people who are involved in animal testing and someone doing that?" To me, these come from the same type of thought, "This is my morality. You're either going to agree with me or I'm going to make your life a living hell."

RAY CAPPO (Youth of Today / Shelter): The guru of the Krishna movement made hundreds of thousands of people vegetarians. Before I was even a devotee of

Krishna, they wrote books on animal rights and vegetarianism. It made me give up meat. I think it was Socrates who said, "There's different ways of persuasion." One way is through force. If I hold a gun to your head, you'll do it. But there's other ways to persuade people through intelligence. The highest way to persuade is through your actual living habits, through example. St. Thomas Aquinas said something like, "Live and sometimes preach." If you live an appropriate way, people want to be like you. Do we have to go in like animal rights activists and put glue in the locks of the animal labs and spray paint on someone's fur coat? I personally wouldn't. I think there's other ways to get the same message out that don't damage your consciousness. If the goal is to save those animals' lives and it makes me a hateful person or I get put in prison and become a martyr, what good is it? I've seen people go down that path. I remember the vegan and animal rights community was really like that. I saw so much hate. We were Hare Krishnas. We didn't like to wear leather. The only thing was that we liked to drink milk. For that one difference so many vegans hated our guts! Isn't that weird? We were probably more in league with vegans than anybody! But they were Born Again Vegans! We have to be careful about what we become fanatics about.

> *Who propagated this bullshit that meat makes you macho? My guess is it's the same big business assholes who told you the Marlboro Man was a stud.*

> —from the book *Meat is For Pussies* by John Joseph of
> Cro-Mags (Harper, 2014)

TRUTH: IT'S A BUNCH OF BULLSHIT!

ROB FISH (108): This whole idea of truth is a bunch of bullshit! There is truth, but we're not going to understand it. Most world religions have been in existence for two thousand plus years. If you're going to take their texts or theology literally, then the world is flat. There's a lot of crazy, wild theories that I've never been able to accept. Even from Gaudiya Vaishnavism books. Whether it be the Bhagavatam that talks about the creation of the universe. From a literal standpoint I cannot accept it. Same is true with science. We've encountered kids who would pound their chests, "Science is better than religion!" But the simple question is, "Was that the *same* scientific conclusion fifty or a hundred years ago?" I have this strong reaction to anybody who says they have a market corner on truth.

Some bands are there to tell you what's right and wrong and they'll wrestle over these little things that no one has an answer for. That's why 108 never had that strong backlash like Shelter or a lot of Christian bands did. We're approaching it from a very different standpoint. If you were to sit down with the three members of 108 that have been in the band the longest—Vic (DiCara), myself and Triv (Trivikrama Dasa)—and talk to us about what does and doesn't inspire us in Gaudiya Vaishnavism, you'd find that we're pretty different. We do have common inspirations and aspirations but how we feel the theology inspires us is very different. If you were to sit down ten years ago and have a conversation with Vic and a separate conversation with me, we weren't using the same lines. We would contradict each other. We didn't have this one universal message that needed to be spread.

FAITHFUL DEVOTEE

It's June 19, 2018 and I'm in Berkeley, California at a brewery/club called Cornerstone. Shelter is playing and Raghunath Ray Cappo is on stage singing for the first time in seven years. Buddhist punk band the Deathless open the show and band members Noah Levine and Joe Clements stand near the stage as Shelter sets up and tunes their guitars. As Hindu chanting wafts from giant speakers, Cappo lights some incense and says, "What kind of club is this? They don't have an incense holder!"

> *If people can sing about left-wing topics and right-wing topics why couldn't I sing about spiritual topics?*
>
> —Ray Cappo (Youth of Today / Shelter)

RAY CAPPO (Youth of Today / Shelter): Punk has always been a rebellious thing. It's very opinionated, but what good are all those opinions or rebellions if they get you to a more degraded state of life? I found ultra-left-wing liberals really bitter about everything. And I found ultra-right-wing conservative people a little crazy, too. And then I found a spiritual solution as an answer to most of the material problems. If people can sing about left-wing topics or right-wing topics, why couldn't I sing about spiritual topics? Even though I was a Krishna monk, in all my lyrics I tried to present a very ecumenical way; "What are we doing in life? Why are we here?" I tried not to be judgmental.

As much as some people got down on me and said I was a fundamentalist-Bhagavad Gita-thumping Hare Krishna I tried my best to be very broadminded. I think that's why I've lasted 'til this day and I'm still a faithful devotee of Krishna. It doesn't come from criticizing Christians. It comes from having faith that there are other worlds and higher powers. One of my goals in life is to transcend mind and body and not just be absorbed in sensual pleasure. It's been quite a journey and within that is a rebellion. That to me is the essence of punk.

Sometimes people criticized me and said, "You're always on a pulpit. Who do you think you are? You're twenty-three years old." But the fact is we were almost advanced in age because we heard some really realized people who had some wisdom. We actually put wisdom into practice. It gave us strong realizations and convictions and we could speak strongly about those things and it was infectious. Believe me it wasn't, "We're on an ego trip and our group is better than your group." It wasn't like a fundamentalist would get some joy out of saying, "You'd better accept Jesus because Jesus loves you." We weren't out to convert anybody into being a shaven-headed, robed Hare Krishna.

Some people did become shaven-head, robed Hare Krishnas and some people became Franciscan monks. It changed them! That was the beauty of that time. It was music that affected you on a deeper level. I'm not saying that just to toot my horn. I watched it like a phenomenon happening. Part of it was in God's hands and out of my hands. I look back and say, "How could I ever orchestrate a plan such as that?" To be in a rock and roll band and to be celibate is a huge thing! People *never* get it! Every type of meditation and focus—Zen, Native American, Hindu—takes intense concentration. That is a first principle in succeeding in meditation. When you develop that intense concentration, you become empowered. This attention is a key factor and the first thing that we're teaching. It can change our whole existence.

RAY CAPPO (Youth of Today / Shelter): You have to be incredibly focused to be celibate in this world that's trying to sell us lawn mowers and pizzas with sex! Drive by any billboard and they're trying to sell us out of fear or sex. Like Pavlovian dogs we're eating it up—"Yeah, we'll purchase that! There's a girl in a bikini selling me work boots!" I just passed that sign on the road. She's in a bikini but she's got on work boots. She's selling me work boots! And I'll buy 'em! So, to be celibate is to say "no" to mainstream everything. It was a great time in my life when we actually checked out of the material world!

It's funny but I missed the whole grunge scene in the early 90s. I was a celibate monk. I didn't watch TV and I didn't listen to music. I wrote all those early Shelter records never listening to any other music. People say, "Well, that sounds a little extreme." I made the choice of isolation because I wanted to very carefully decide what goes in my ears. Our ears create our consciousness, as do all of our other senses. It's like when we say, "You are what you eat." You also are what you hear and smell and see. If you expose a child to violent movies, it will really affect their consciousness as they grow. Loud sounds can affect animals and a person. If you grow up in wartime where bombs are always going off it'll affect your whole nervous system. If you live near a busy street as opposed to living in the forest; everything we take in our senses creates our new body and mind. I was focused and it was a very powerful time in my life. It was what I always wanted out of punk rock; a real focus and rebellion. I wanted a real chance to make a difference.

JM: On the surface I think we might say spiritual music needs to be calm and quiet. But punk rock is high-energy with a focused, concentrated energy.

RAY CAPPO (Youth of Today / Shelter): We created spiritual music in the form of Shelter like the *Mantra* album, which is heavy and intense. To me *spiritual* means whatever inspires you to think or change. As you develop a more meditative personality, you may be less attracted to that type of intensity. And it may still inspire you when you're an old man! Now I'm a yoga teacher in Beverly Hills (2012). My message is the same as when I was in Shelter and Youth of Today. It's just in a different format for a different audience, but the message stays the same. You can go to my yoga class and get a spiritual feeling. You could when you went to a Shelter show, too.

Now I don't believe music is an appropriate vehicle for me but I still believe in the message and I think it's more refined now. As we get older, part of our growth is to refine our spiritual ideals. I'm married now and I'm about to have my fourth child. So, "Okay, you were a celibate monk; how do you fly that here, smart ass?" How can you learn to love and be completely detached? How can I love my wife but accept that I don't possess her? How do I love my children and accept that some day they might eat meat or not believe anything that I believe? All I'm really responsible for is to love them.

JM: In spirituality there tends to be ideas about surrender and letting go and being with reality as it is. Then there's another idea that we can affect change in the world.

RAY CAPPO (Youth of Today / Shelter): One of the first things to recognize is that a lack of spirituality is the root of all the problems. Yoga teaches that we are part and parcel of a higher power. Our entire world is connected. We're part of a family. The Earth is a personality. Plants are personalities. Dogs, cats, giraffes, alligators, zebras—they're all divine personalities struggling for existence in life.

It's not me as the dominant species versus the world. We are completely in this together. In the Bible it says, "We have dominion over the animals." If we have dominion over this Earth, how are we treating Mother Earth? We build our artificial, shitty houses that will leave an ecological footprint for the next ten thousand years, with the dumpsters of waste that each project leaves behind. God knows how many thousands of years went by when nothing was left behind. We've even come to the conclusion that this planet was never inhabited or visited by other cultures, which is up for discussion.

When you develop a culture that thinks, "Me first! Whoever has the power is in charge, and everybody else has to suffer under our reign," that is a really low point. This is a crux of a Godless civilization. I'm convinced that when we have a true understanding of God, we respect other religions and we become more sensitive to our environment. One sad thing Christianity did was deify Christ and make nature a mere backdrop. They were down on Pagans who respected connection with the Earth. But Pagans were just herbalists; people who had some connection with nature and herbs and respected the divine qualities in trees, plants and animals. When the deification of Christ came about, you worshiped Christ and everything else was secondary. That can't be true religion or real spirituality because everything is connected.

JM: In the Bhagavad Gita, Krishna talks to Arjuna a lot about not being attached to outcome. What's been your experience with not being attached to outcome?

RAY CAPPO (Youth of Today / Shelter): The Bhagavad Gita was our specialty. Whenever you try to develop a career in the entertainment business you have to try your best to be detached. You have to love what you do. It was very relevant especially when I stopped being a monk. At one point, Shelter got really big and I had to be detached. I had to try my best to understand that everything's in God's hands. It's the same principle as a twelve-step program where ultimately, everything is happening exactly the way it's supposed to and if I have some issue with it then I have some issue with God's perfect plan. Everything is perfect, even the incredible amount of suffering that I might have to go through. That's a hard thing to accept.

I had a client the other day that came to me and said, "I want you to help me with my yoga and diet because I have cancer. I'm super depressed." I said, "This is going to sound heartless to you, but I'm not being insensitive. You'll get over so many problems if you can ask yourself, "How is this cancer the best thing that ever happened to me? You'll find so many incredible answers." He was a little shocked but I said, "It's documented in scientific journals that diet and mind can create cancer. You're fifty-one years old and you have a ten-year-old son. What would your son say if you got off your standard American diet and found out about foods and thoughts that heal the body and radically put that into practice and your son witnessed you change your life and heal yourself? How would that affect him? Or your wife? You would inspire everybody! This cancer could change your entire life and consciousness in a wonderful way. You could be healthier than you ever were!"

JM: It certainly seems there's no way to escape painful things in our lives.

RAY CAPPO (Youth of Today / Shelter): You only have two ways to deal with them anyway, even if there's no God or reality. If you don't escape it, the thing overtakes you and you become very bitter, resentful and a victim. A victim is not an attractive place to be. People heal themselves of all types of things; parental abuse and drug abuse. They heal themselves by accepting that *I am not the victim* and by accepting some responsibility. And then, "I'm going to use all the suffering I went through to make myself a better person." I knew a guy who was an inspiration. When he was growing up his grandfather, a minister respected in the whole town, molested him during his childhood. He became a therapist for people who dealt with similar things. That's how he forgave.

JM: All spiritual traditions teach compassion and this idea of loving people, especially those who have chosen a different path than you. Yet this compassion tends to be one of the first things that drop away when people become inspired by a particular religious tradition.

RAY CAPPO (Youth of Today / Shelter): The first time I hung out with my best friend, a born-again Christian, he told me, "Even good religious Jews will burn in hell. All Buddhists will go to hell. Anyone who existed before John the Baptist arrives will end up in hell." I was like, "Everybody? How is that a compassionate God?" It's such a paltry understanding of spirituality. I want nothing to do with it. The fact is that there's fundamentalist Muslims and fundamentalist Hindus. We have to be careful about the exclusivists because they rob from our connection with God. You've never met a culture that had more hate in the name of loving God than these fanatic Muslims? But there's been fanatic Hindus and Christians who've put swords to people's throats! What we don't like is fanaticism. It's enough to make you hate God. But we can't hate God because of a few idiots. That would be a sad waste. Do I know fanatic Hare Krishnas? Yeah! I know lots of them. I know fanatic straight edge kids and vegans. I'm not interested in hanging out with them! I don't think they even have the picture. People like that are far from God.

END SUFFERING (KARMA)

ROB FISH (108): My initial attraction to Gaudiya Vaishnavism was very much rooted in the dynamic of suffering in my life and how to bring some end to it. Initially the ideas of *karma* really helped me. Emotionally, it helped me deal with some of the things I encountered while growing up. Whether they be terrible incidents or terrible thoughts and feelings I had about myself. The idea of karma—the idea that it didn't just *happen* to me, but there is something deeper to it—helped me process it emotionally, in a way that was probably healthier than the route I was going down, in terms of being destructive physically in a lot of different ways. Ultimately that will probably work for a couple of years. I guess there are millions of people that will prove me wrong and could allow that aspect of their lives to dictate their religious or spiritual being for the rest of their life. But for me, it became evident that just having this *idea* of karma was not enough to help me process the things I'd been through.

By the time I was in 108 I was already outside of the religious context of Gaudiya Vaishnavism. I didn't fit in. I was a pro-choice kind of leftist, non-religious person. Yet, I found a lot of inspiration in some of the more esoteric aspects of Godi theology. I started to look at myself and what I went through in 108, and the way people understood 108, and I was not very happy with the place I was. I realized that the theology of karma maybe helped me deal with the suffering when I was sixteen but as I kept getting older, I was becoming more and more unhappy, to the point that on a few different occasions I almost took my own life. I realized, "I have to wipe the slate clean."

I distanced myself completely from people that were into Gaudiya Vaishnavism and dropped out of the music scene. I was still writing music but I didn't go to shows because I needed to find myself. After awhile it became clear that spirituality is a way to process. Suffering is a pretty common thing, but for me it was a negative thing. As I stepped away from everything, I realized that with the terrible things I went through as a child, or some of the terrible things I was struggling with at that point, that spirituality could be a way to deal with it, but ultimately it was up to me to make my spirituality a way to reach what I aspired to be. Versus some way for it to answer all my problems.

"MUHAMMAD WAS A PUNK ROCKER"
TAQWACORE AND MICHAEL MUHAMMAD KNIGHT

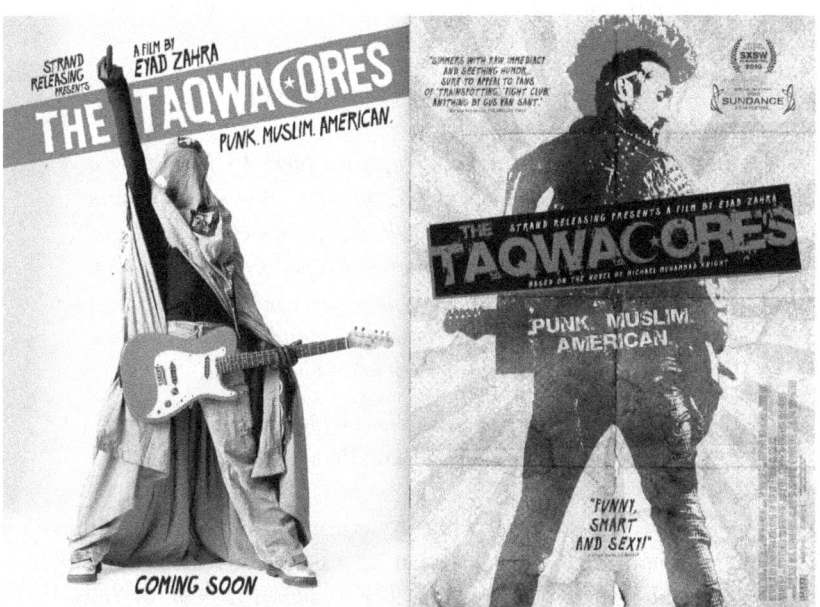

Figure 19.1 Two posters for The Taqwacores (2010) based on the novel by Michael Muhammad Knight. Contributed: Eyad Zahra (director) and Nick Riley (producer).

I am an Islamist! I am the anti-christ! Most squares can't make Most Wanted lists.

—"Sharia Law in the USA" by *The Kominas* from
Wild Nights in Guantanamo Bay (2010)

I have a particular idea or image of punk that has appealed to me, but that is not necessarily punk for everybody. Same with Islam.

—Michael Muhammad Knight (*The Taqwacores*)

When God is defined as some sort of pure consciousness—the source of energy/light that is forever self expanding, unfolding and manifesting itself, thereby giving rise to all that we know in the physical realm—I find myself entirely in awe of such a force and wanting to explore its mystery.

—Sean Muttaqi (Vegan Reich)

In 2003, blessed with easy access to photocopiers, I self-published a novel, The Taqwacores, about a community of punk-rock Muslim kids. The story overflowed with the signatures of punk culture: crass language, offensive humor, rebellion and provocation, a proud embrace of blasphemy, and a refusal to apologize or negotiate with the dominant culture's demands and sensitivities. It was, in many ways, rude for the sake of being rude.

—*Muhammad: Forty Introductions* by Michael Muhammad
Knight (2019—Soft Skull Press—page 12)

The *Taqwacores* is a novel by white American author Michael Muhammad Knight who converted to Islam when he was fifteen years old, inspired by listening to Public Enemy and reading *The Autobiography of Malcolm X*. *The Taqwacores* tells the fictitious story of a group of punk rockers living together in Buffalo, New York grappling with religious orthodoxy, racism, feminism, and other realms. Knight originally self-published the novel as a free photocopied zine and it was later published by Autonomedia in 2004.

After reading *The Taqwacores*, some punk musicians were inspired to create Islamic punk bands. The Kominas were formed in 2005 by two Pakistani-Americans in Worcester, Massachusetts and self-identified as a "Taqwacore" band. Amazingly, in a case of life imitating art, The Kominas later toured the United States and Pakistan with author Michael Muhammad Knight and other Islamic punk bands: Al-Thawra, Diacritical, Vote Hezbollah, and Secret Trial Five, an all-female Canadian band. The tour was documented from 2007 to 2009 by filmmaker Omar Majeed and released in 2009 as *Taqwacore: The Birth of Punk Islam*. In 2021, the thoughtful and creative British television series "We Are Lady Parts," directed by Nida Manzoor, referenced a 2011 Kominas song title, "Ain't No One Gonna Honor Kill My Sister But Me."

The Taqwacores was adapted into a feature-length dramatic film by Syrian-American director Eyad Zahra and filmed in Cleveland, Ohio (2010). The movie features music by some of the real-life musicians who were inspired by Knight's novel *The Taqwacores*, including The Kominas, Sagg Syndicate and Al-Thawra.

Michael Muhammad Knight has written numerous books, including the novel *Osama Van Halen* (2009—Soft Skull Press), which features Knight himself as a character, *The Five Percenters: Islam, Hip-hop and the Gods of New York* (2007—Oneworld Publications), *Blue-Eyed Devil: An American Muslim Road Odyssey* (2006—Soft Skull Press), *Tripping with Allah: Islam, Drugs and Writing* (2013—Soft Skull Press) and *Muhammad: Forty Introductions* (2019—Soft Skull Press).

Knight obtained a Master's of Theological Studies degree from Harvard University in 2011 and received his PhD in Islamic Studies from the University of North Carolina at Chapel Hill in 2016. His dissertation explores "what Islam says about the body" and was titled, "Muhammad's Body: Prophetic Assemblages and the Baraka Network," which was later published by the University of North Carolina Press (2020). Knight is currently assistant professor in the Department of Philosophy at the University of Central Florida.

JM: Two paragraphs in the beginning of *The Taqwacores* (2009) sum up your direction for the novel and the questions you'll be grappling with: "I stopped trying to define punk around the same time I stopped trying to define Islam. They aren't so far removed as you'd think. Both began in tremendous bursts of truth and vitality but seem to have lost something along the way—the energy, perhaps, that comes with knowing the world has never seen such positive force and fury and never would again. Both have suffered from sell-outs and hypocrites, but also from true believers whose devotion crippled their creative drive. Both are viewed by outsiders as unified, cohesive communities when nothing could be further from the truth. I could go on but the most important similarity is that like punk, Islam is itself a flag; an open symbol representing not things, but ideas. You cannot hold punk or Islam in your hands. So what could they mean besides what you want them to?"

You also write that, "Punk is like a flag; an open symbol, it only means what people believe it means. There was a time in China when red traffic lights meant 'go.' How would you begin to argue?" Tell me about the relationship between punk and Islam.

MICHAEL MUHAMMAD KNIGHT (*The Taqwacores*): How do punk and Islam go together? If they interact in the same body, then they're related. I don't have this essentialized idea of what punk is. Or what Islam is. There's such internal diversity in both that I'm not someone who can say, "Here is the core of punk. Here is the core of Islam. And here is how they resonate with each other." I just can't do that.

For me, I was Muslim first. For some reason, maybe it's because I'm a convert, a lot of people assume that I was punk first and reconciled Islam to it. It's the opposite. I became Muslim officially at sixteen after at least a year of heavy reading and I really went hard with it. This is kind of the narrative of the documentary (*Taqwacore: The Birth of Punk Islam* directed by Omar Majeed, 2009). I went really hard and had my breaking because Islam wasn't satisfying me anymore. I felt a lot of shame. I was just embarrassed. I felt there was something of Islam in me but I wasn't meeting anyone else's standards of what that required. So, I thought I couldn't show my face in a mosque anymore.

In my college years when I found punk, I was at the height of my convert zeal. I knew this punk kid who was staunchly individualistic and that was the personal mythology that he lived by. Now I have the tools to critique that individualism and I know maybe punk is not as individual as he said it was, but I was really drawn to that spirit of standing up and not conforming to anything and resisting and rebelling and being who you are.

Initially that's what Islam was for me. I was the only Muslim kid in my Catholic high school. Islam, for me, was standing up against the majority and the institutions. Islam came with a certain kind of racial resistance too, because I was basically in an all-white high school. But that changed and the Muslim community started to put their own demands on me. After my disillusionment period I fell in with punk kids again and really appropriated that punk ethic. I wanted that for myself. I was quiet and didn't have the guts to stand up and be who I was. It was the punk kids who were doing that. If that's being proud of being Muslim in this ocean of white people that we're in, then do that. Or if it's being a fucked-up Muslim in a Muslim community, then be OK with that, too. I found it easier to be who I was with that punk narrative.

JM: You said you'd prefer not saying what the essence is of punk or Islam. Why is that?

MICHAEL MUHAMMAD KNIGHT: These words don't signify concrete realities outside of what people say they are. If people disagree about the meanings of these things, there is no empirical science that will solve that problem. There are popular ideas about what punk and Islam mean but is Islam measured by people's relationship to the state? To gender? To theology? There are all kinds of punks, too. There are queer punks and homophobic punks. There are very social reactionary conservative punks. There's sober punks and drunk punks. I have a particular idea or image of punk that has appealed to me, but that is not necessarily punk for everybody. Same with Islam.

> *Non-Muslims (and Muslims responding to them) often mold their image of Muhammad in relation to images of Islam that they encounter in contemporary media—that is, they define Mohammed in terms of violence, religious intolerance, radical politics and reactionary patriarchy.*
>
> —*Muhammad: Forty Introductions* by Michael Muhammad Knight (2019—Soft Skull Press—page 8)

"MUHAMMAD WAS A PUNK ROCKER"

JM: The lyrics to a song—"Muhammad Was a Punk Rocker"—opens your novel *The Taqwacores*. It's a fictional story you wrote and then people who read it were inspired to start Islamic punk bands. In Buddhism there is this idea, "If you meet the Buddha on the road, kill him." This points to something you write; "Punk and Islam cannot be confined and held, and that, 'Fuck Islam' could only be said within a true Islam."

MICHAEL MUHAMMAD KNIGHT (*The Taqwacores*): This is the paradox of really trying to be God-centered. And saying that *there is no God but God* and *nothing gets* *worshiped but God.* But then you don't have access to that power. To regulate your life, you have to rely on human constructions and ideas that God wants; human interpretations and imaginations. There's this paradox that you're supposed to put that above all kinds of human imagination, but human imagination is all we have. That's the kind of thing I was speaking to there. I'm trying to submit to something that's transcendent—above human institutions—but the human institutions tell me I need *them* to get it! (*laugh*) That doesn't actually make sense to me all of the time. The institution of idol smashing becomes its own idol.

JM: Tell me about writing *The Taqwacores* and how people started contacting you and you eventually toured with Muslim punk bands inspired by your book. All of that must've been surprising.

MICHAEL MUHAMMAD KNIGHT (*The Taqwacores*): It was pretty awesome. It really reflected the incoherence of Taqwacore. The incoherence was both the play and the problem, in that you're trying to create an absolutely open space that produces a kind of incoherence that makes it hard for a thing to crystallize together. It makes it hard for anyone to speak with any authority about it. Again, that's a beautiful thing. But we weren't authoritarian with each other and the price of that is perhaps a lack of organization.

> *Historically, there's no such thing as a singular 'Islamic theology' any more than there's a singular Christian theology.*
>
> —*Muhammad: Forty Introductions* by Michael Muhammad Knight (2019—Soft Skull Press—page 60)

NO INTERMEDIARY

MICAH ANDERSON (*Ta'leef Collective*): I know Michael (Knight) well. He's a rabble-rouser in the Muslim community here. He likes to stir things up. Islam has a legal tradition he likes to flaunt and dance around, which has made him controversial. The *Taqwacores* thing seemed contrived to me. It didn't feel like an organic manifestation like Krishnacore and Shelter. I'm still waiting for that. *Taqwacores* was *not* the thing we were waiting for.

I moved to California in 92 and met Noah (Levine) and we started Dharma Punx with Vinnie Ferraro. Noah and I were pretty seriously into Krishnacore and we were also sitting Vipassana at that point. Noah introduced that to me, which he learned from his father. (Stephen Levine) I also got involved with

Sufism—a mystical, spiritual practice of Islam. That was my doorway to becoming, within a few years, a Muslim convert. I'm still one.

No intermediary is often a way that Sufism is described, especially compared to Christianity with its hierarchy. Islamic practice is almost Socialist in nature. In theory it's supposed to support the community. It's this communal aspect of Islam that I embrace. It's direct contact with the spirit, God.

We were listening to Krishnacore because there was nothing else speaking to us in the way that Shelter and 108 were. They were nailing this Eastern spirituality and using Sanskrit and it was really academic; we were all over that stuff! It gave us a framework that we didn't even realize we were looking for yet! My own framework was within Islam and Noah's was more Theravada Buddhism. The closest thing we both had was Krishnacore. I work at a Muslim non-profit called *Ta'leef Collective*. It's kind of like the Muslim *Against the Stream*. I'm a therapist there. Islam has a bad rap for not being inclusive of people's religious or political liberties. But that's mostly only been post-9/11 through Western media.

I LOVE THE HUMAN EXPERIENCE

SEAN MUTTAQI (Vegan Reich): I love the human experience. Specifically, what I think are innate qualities—to strive for self-awareness; look for meaning in the universe; to fight for justice; to create things of beauty. The labels of Punk Rock or Islam are sort of inconsequential to that; they just happen to be names given to certain tendencies that have always existed among people. For instance, there are old groups of wandering mystics within Islam called Qalandars, who exhibited punk rock behavior centuries ago. And throughout human history, in many languages, there have been equivalent words to "Islam" signifying an attempt by mankind to submit to a force greater than their own ego. To live in some sort of equilibrium with a cosmic order.

JM: Punk rock has traditionally leaned more toward an atheist or agnostic mentality. Do you feel conflicted being a religious or spiritual person and also a part of the punk scene?

SEAN MUTTAQI (Vegan Reich): No. To me there's no conflict. When someone says, "There's no God or Gods," and they're referring to a notion of some "being" or "entity" in the sky who has a physical form and watches over the world as if it's some sort of chessboard, then I'm apt to agree with my atheist friends. When God is defined as some sort of pure consciousness—the source of energy/light that is forever self-expanding, unfolding and manifesting itself, thereby giving rise to all that we know in the physical realm—I find myself entirely in awe of such a force and wanting to explore its mystery.

SEAN MUTTAQI (Vegan Reich): I tend to not like the word *religion* because it's so easily misconstrued. At their worst, religions become systems of control used by men to uphold their power and dominance over society. But this problem is actually removed from the question of theism as even "nonbelievers" can practice religion. Any idea, no matter how good, can be put to bad usage in the hands of man. One of the definitions of religion is, "a cause, principle, or system of beliefs held to with ardor and faith." In that regard, atheism was essentially the state religion in many a Communist country during times past, and likewise, was used as a system of control over their populations.

On the other hand, religion can also just mean the worship of God or the supernatural, whether in a personal setting or institutionalized system of beliefs and practices. In that regard you could say I'm "religious" because I'm on a defined path of mystical practice, for the purposes of developing self-awareness, exploring the hidden and unseen and trying to put my ego in check by submitting to something higher than my own whims. Whether or not that "something" is real is actually not that important in terms of the process of engaging in that journey. Even if it's just a focal point from a philosophical point of view that helps some of us map out the journey, it's truth in the experience of the believer.

Human beings can take any belief—even if that belief is defined as "unbelief"—and make it a basis for dogmatic, rigid, judgmental attitudes and behavior. When religion is a source of comfort, joy, solace, love, art, science, philosophy, justice and the many great things that can be attributed to it in the positive, I'm entirely in support. When it's used by the elite to keep people down and push society into darkness, then I totally understand why my atheist friends say, "No Gods, No Masters." People's behavior is what gives them their true commonality. I judge people from their actions; if their beliefs engender good behavior, that's all that matters to me.

SEAN MUTTAQI (Vegan Reich): I always had a strong connection with Jamaican culture, whether listening to reggae as a kid, knowing Jamaicans and Rastas when I was growing up, to my later associations with ska and skinhead scenes. It was always a strong presence in my life. I think there's no denying the huge influence Rastafarianism had on the emergence of Hardline. When Vegan Reich broke up, I started a reggae-influenced hardcore band, Captive Nation Rising, that very quickly dropped its hardcore element and became a reggae band opening for touring Jamaican acts. During that time, I grew my dreads out, spent time in

Jamaica and really considered Rastafarianism. Culturally, it was a natural fit. But I ultimately couldn't wrap my head around the notion of (Haile) Selassie's divinity. Even though not all Rastas take that in a literal way, it was not something I felt comfortable with theologically speaking. Same reason Nation of Islam's deification of a human being sat wrong with me as well.

Around the same time, I had been spending a lot of time in Oakland (California). One of my good friends there had left NOI (Nation of Islam) and became, for lack of a better word, "Orthodox" Muslim. It all just coalesced for me. I had spent years reading the Quran, and I was finally in a place where everything seemed right for me to convert.

Honestly, the only issue that delayed it at all was my firm belief in veganism. I didn't want to come into something with my own interpretation if there wasn't historical precedence for it. After a lot of research, I discovered many historical occurrences of key Muslim scholars and saints being vegetarian, as well as old Islamic spiritual movements that lasted for centuries in both Kashmir as well as Sri Lanka, that were explicitly vegetarian. But the final practical aspect of finding a modern community to be a part of became the last obstacle. I decided that only if I found other modern vegetarian Muslims would I take the Shahadah (declaration of faith) and convert. I had been reading Gnosis Magazine, which was edited by Jay Kinney whose *Anarchy* comics I had read as a kid, and it had an article on Bawa Muhaiyaddeen, a Sri Lankan Vegetarian Sufi Sheikh that founded a community in Philadelphia. I called up Jay and I got in touch with one of Bawa's students in Philly who I've been friends with for over two decades now and I ended up converting a short time later in Oakland.

SEAN MUTTAQI (Vegan Reich): I've never actually seen the movie. When *The Taqwacores* book came out I wasn't happy about it. As a Muslim I found a lot of its content offensive. That said, I had some mutual acquaintances with Michael Muhammad Knight who encouraged us to talk and I later became friends with the author and remain so today. To some degree, I think that book was like an albatross hung around his neck, cursing him to be defined by both fans and detractors alike for something that was simply a creative work and not an intended polemic or diatribe meant as his raison d'être.

As far as the whole Taqwacore thing; unfortunately for those who 'wanna believe it's real, it's not. It's a fiction built on a fiction. It has no organic origin within the punk scene. Michael Muhammad Knight's primary background was in hip-hop. *Taqwacore* was a fictional piece based on his fantasy about punk. It's a place setting for his otherwise creative narrative detailing the lives of disaffected Muslim youths, which was based on his experiences and interactions as a Muslim convert. But it didn't arise from a Muslim punk scene. Taqwacore as a phenomenon—and I don't label it a "scene" since it's never had the numbers to exist as such—is more akin to something like Cosplay, where life imitates art. It's a dress-up game.

JM: Have you heard of the Muslim punk scene—Taqwacore? This was originally made up in a novel *The Taqwacores* and punks emulated the book and started Islamic punk bands.

DON REDONDO (JFA): That's like *Star Trek* where they leave a book on a planet and they follow the book . . .

HARAM PUNK

ABDULLAH EL-KHATIB (Inqirad): Taqwacore has nothing to do with modern-day Arabic punk and none of the current bands are into it and we all hate being called Taqwacore bands! The word *taqwa* in Arabic means belief in God or religion. I take inspiration from other Arabic bands, just not Taqwacore. It doesn't define us as a genre. Many of the current bands have named Arabic punk, "Haram" punk.

SEAN MUTTAQI (Vegan Reich): I certainly don't want to be the arbiter about what is compatible or not with punk rock since I think the essence of punk is a spirit of rebellion and freedom. Each individual should define for themselves what punk means to them. That said, I personally think the general ethos of punk makes it more inherently compatible with spiritual traditions and political movements that run counter to the status quo of one's dominant culture. I'm more than a little wary, for instance, of the evangelical co-opting of punk aesthetics as a way to promote patriotic conservative understandings of religion, behind a veneer of hip, counterculture imagery.

That's not to say I think Christianity has no place in punk rock. Just give me John Macias and Circle One any day over Christian hardcore, or any band that's ever been on Tooth & Nail by way of example. Things like Liberation Theology or the Catholic Worker Movement seem entirely compatible with the spirit of punk rock to me. Likewise, it completely makes sense that at the onset of American punk, and then hardcore, we had bands like Bad Brains or Cro-Mags respectively embracing Rastafarianism and Krishna Consciousness and integrating those topics back into punk. It's not so much whether or not the religion itself holds liberal or conservative views or whether it has an affinity to punk or vice versa. I think it has more to do with the nature of those things within a particular society, and their relationship to the state, and the status quo of society at large.

JM: The lyrics and images from your band Vegan Reich include the word "jihad" and images of guns. I wonder if you've been confronted by authorities or other bands about this?

SEAN MUTTAQI (Vegan Reich): Well, yes, on almost all fronts. Vegan Reich did have violent lyrics, imagery and behavior. And yes, there were a couple periods in my life where there was quite a lot of harassment by the Feds. I should clarify though that Vegan Reich's violent tendencies had nothing to do with Islam. In fact, it was my journey to Islam that has ultimately made me, although not quite a pacifist, the closest to such a thing I've ever been.

We came up in a time and place where violence was a pretty normal part of our existence. So, if someone wants to understand Vegan Reich's violence, I think they need to approach it understanding the era we came up in. If they need something from the punk scene as a reference point think about Circle One and Suicidal Tendencies more than trying to situate it in later straight edge crews. We were sort of an anachronism in the scene we became known in. Straight edge may have been known for fighting in its day but Vegan Reich's penchant for guns made people in that scene think we were crazy!

JIHAD—HUGELY TRANSFORMATIVE

SEAN MUTTAQI (Vegan Reich): In Islam, jihad simply means struggle. It primarily means an inner struggle toward the purification of the soul. The outer jihad against oppression exists but it is not something taken lightly within the traditional Islamic world; it's not something waged against civilians and certainly is not an appropriate definition for wars between Muslim countries or civil wars. Neither should the term be used for popular uprisings and revolutions against unjust rulers or regimes, which would be more accurately classed as a revolution or al-Thawrah.

On the opposite end of the spectrum, it wouldn't tend to be associated with just any inner struggle either. To quit smoking for instance would not commonly be referred to as a jihad. The word implies a struggle that is hugely transformative. For instance, during the struggle against the occupation of India by Britain, that jihad took many fronts. It included efforts to educate the masses. It involved peaceful protest and encouraged people to free their minds from intoxicants. It also included armed struggle against the British Army.

To give an example from American History, the native people's struggle against their extermination at the hands of European settlers would have fit the definition. Just as one can make an argument for John Brown's raid at Harper's Ferry being part of the greater jihad against slavery, one that also included boycotts, speeches, protests, the underground railroad and so forth.

In modern times a perfect example would be the fight against ISIS. Their depravity and oppression is so great that it would make sense for all Muslim religious leaders to declare a jihad against them to liberate the people under their tyranny and end their attacks against the rest of the world. But that fight could not be won by arms alone. It's a jihad that would have to include political and economic reform, interfaith dialogue in the region, education and employment opportunities. In general, we've entered an era where the discussion of an outward jihad becomes problematic. It's all become so convoluted.

NOT A TAQWACORE BAND

JM: Any thoughts on Taqwacore and the films and books of Michael Muhammad Knight? Have these been an inspiration or do you view them as not-authentic Islamic punk?

NADER HARAM (Haram / I-SO): Michael Muhammad Knight sucks and has always sucked. He wrote some book romanticizing "Muslim punks" and made a bunch of money off of it, and then fucked off. He didn't interact much with me besides a few messages in 2015, and he made up this fictitious world he knows nothing about. He profited from it and never lived it. None of those bands besides The Kominas (who rock and I love) were ever in the punk scene in my world. It's absolutely non-authentic and should be disregarded. Also, I think he might be a white guy? Not sure on that. Anytime anyone has asked me about Taqwacore or if Haram is a Taqwacore band, I say I have nothing to do with that. What I do is different and you can't just slap a label like that on it. I refuse. He knows nothing about this life.

"AVRAHAM WAS A PUNK ROCKER"
JEWISH PUNK ROCK/*THE HEEBIE-JEEBIES* AT *CBGB'S*/*PUNK JEWS*/MOSHIACH OI!

With punk, I had the rebellion understanding that there is so much wrong in the world. But I never had the answer of what to do about it until I found Judaism.

—Yishai Romanoff (Moshiach Oi!)

No Holocaust, no punk.

—Steven Lee Beeber (*The Heebie-Jeebies at CBGB's: A Secret History of Jewish Punk*)

He felt that the Jews certainly had been persecuted and he had a lot of residual angst post-Holocaust; he felt that if people knew he was Jewish, he would be persecuted. That's part of the reason he changed his name from Bermowitz to Vega.

—Liz Lamere (Alan Vega (Suicide)'s widow / creative collaborator)

JM: In your 2006 book *The Heebie-Jeebies at CBGB's: A Secret History of Jewish Punk* you write that, "Punk rock has its origins in Manhattan's Lower East Side in the early 1970s—the apotheosis of a Jewish cultural tradition that found its ultimate expression in the generation born after the Holocaust." You highlight Jewish people who helped define the punk sound and feel like Lou Reed, Joey Ramone, The Dictators, Richard Hell, Malcolm McLaren, Lenny Kaye, Genia Raven, Chris Stein, Jonathan Richman and Helen Wheels and you write, "Punk reflects the whole Jewish history of oppression and uncertainty, flight and wandering, belonging and not belonging. Always being divided, being both in and out, good and bad, part and apart." Later in the book you write about the relevance of the Holocaust in punk: "No Holocaust, no punk." Tell me about this connection.

STEVEN LEE BEEBER (*The Heebie-Jeebies at CBGB's*): If you look at the generation that created punk rock, it's really the first one to come of age after the Holocaust. They grew up in the shadow of that horrible tragedy and had to deal with a world that was far from *The Wizard of Oz*. It was a very disillusioned world, not just for the punks. Lots of factors connect with other aspects of Jewish history and culture. One of them would be, "Why didn't the Jews fight back? Why did they go like lambs to the slaughter?" Which is not true. Lots of people fought back, and regardless, there weren't very many ways you could fight back. A lot of the guys who were growing up in the 60s were a little self-conscious about that, like Andy Chernoff, leader of The Dictators. He was not that connected to his Jewishness until Israel's victory in the Six-Day War, when it was suddenly cool to be Jewish. They were tough; he liked that.

If there's one thing people think of with Jews, it's an ironic sense of humor. There's a view of the world that it's not as it always appears, which is typical of a people who are on the outside and have a complicated relationship with the powers that be. There are lots of aspects of punk that seem to reflect parts of Jewish culture in that first incarnation. There was a real emphasis on the literary aspect of punk. Richard Hell was a poet before he led the Voidoids. Patti Smith was a poet. Tom Verlaine of Television, another poet. Allen Ginsberg performed with the Gluons on "Birdbrain" and the lyrics were very smart, funny and clever. The vast majority of the rock writers who championed punk at the beginning were Jewish. I had an interesting conversation with Richard Meltzer, considered the father of rock journalism, about how his grandfather used to go from town to town in America and challenge people to wrestling matches just to show them that a Jew could be tough. Dick Manitoba, lead singer from The Dictators, was a semi-professional wrestler and he and Meltzer were best friends.

> *Birdbrain is the ultimate product of capitalism / Birdbrain lends money to Developing Nation police-states thru the International Monetary Fund! / Birdbrain conceived the Final Solution to the Jewish Problem in Europe.*

—"Birdbrain" by Gluons with Allen Ginsburg (1981)

STEVEN LEE BEEBER (*The Heebie-Jeebies at CBGB's*): Hilly Kristal, the owner and creator of CBGB's, the club where punk started—his real name is *Hillel Kristal*. Hilly Kristal grew up on an agrarian socialist collective in upstate New York that was started by his great uncle and it was tied in with Zionism and the desire to get back to the land. Jews in Europe had been barred from owning land so it was this sort of spiritual connection to the soil and a romantic ideal, almost like the noble savage.

A lot of the punks came from that background. Chris Stein of Blondie; his father used to read all those magazines like *The Masses* and talked to Chris about it when he was a kid. Lenny Kaye was maybe not left to that degree, but very Democrat-FDR-leftist in his home. When he ended up in the Lower East Side where punk was percolating, he was there to go to grad school in history at NYU because he thought, "When the revolution comes, I'll have a little bit more under my belt." This was '68, '69, when a lot of people really thought there was going to be a revolution. An interesting aspect of early punk was the diverse cultures of New York City; a lot of Jewish and Italian immigrants came around the same time. If you look at punk, a lot of the first people were Italian or Jewish. On the Italian end there's Johnny Thunders.

EVAN KLEINMAN (*Punk Jews* documentary producer): My grandparents are Holocaust survivors. My father was born in a displaced persons camp after the Holocaust in Germany. The Holocaust is such a big part of me that when I started to read that book (*The Heebie-Jeebies at CBGB's*) a lot of things I'd been feeling started to make sense. If you grew up Jewish then you were raised with a certain Holocaust paranoia or anxiety. And I think that anxiety is probably best channeled through punk rock. My Jewish upbringing is what actually plunged me into punk rock when I was a teenager. I did play in bands and went on tour and that was a huge part of my life. I more or less abandoned my Jewish identity, and punk rock is what filled the void. NOFX had a song called "The Brews." One of their albums was *White Trash Two Heebs and a Bean* (1992). It was the first time I'd ever heard Judaism being put directly front and center in something that was totally not Jewish. They were deconstructing it and having fun with it. That was the first time I experienced punk and Judaism together.

> *Friday night we'll be drinking Manischewitz / Going out to terrorize the Goyim / Stomping shagitz, screwing shiksas / as long as we're back Saturday morning.*
>
> —from "The Brews" by NOFX (*Punk in Drublic*—1994)

JESSE ZOOK MANN (*Punk Jews* director): I had such a lack of religious upbringing that when I heard all of these anti-religious punk bands, I didn't know what the hell they were talking about! These people were very angry about very specific groups, especially Christianity. I did feel a little weird about wearing anti-Christian shirts and not really knowing very much about Christianity! But I probably learned more about religion listening to anti-religious bands than going to any kind of class.

LIZ LAMERE (Alan Vega (Suicide)'s widow / creative collaborator Alan Vega solo / solo recording artist / SSNUB / Backward Flying Indians): Alan (Vega) grew up in a traditional Jewish household in a part of Brooklyn with a lot of Italian Catholics and Jews. He saw the churches with statues of the saints, and the artistry of the stained-glass windows, and all of that was fascinating to him. He honored the traditions from Judaism. For instance, he lit candles on Yom Kippur. If you look at his light sculptures, there obviously is the cross, which to him was that universal symbol of infinity, where the dissecting lines will meet in infinity. He felt its power as one of the oldest symbols known to humanity. He felt that the Jews certainly had been persecuted and he had a lot of residual angst post-Holocaust; he felt that if people knew he was Jewish, he would be persecuted. That's part of the reason he changed his name from Bermowitz to Vega. He was an astrophysics major and really into astronomy, and he also chose Vega because of the star, Vega.

JM: You call yourself a cultural and religious Jew and I have the idea that Patti Smith enjoys a Buddhist path.

LENNY KAYE (Patti Smith Group): I do identify culturally because Judaism is not just a religion, it's also a people. It's like being Italian. A lot of Jewish identity comes from the food you eat and things like that. I can speak for Patti as well; we essentially believe in all religions because they all have great mythology. I feel really at home in the Jewish one because that's how I was brought up. But I love Buddhist culture, I love the calligraphy of Islam, I love the figure of Christ and his sacrifice. They're all the great tales of mankind and I don't think you can really say *one* is it. I'm American. That's where I happened to grow up. I might like Nigerian culture or wish I could visit India, but I'm not going to be *in* that culture. I feel like I'm *in* the Jewish culture. But that doesn't mean when I look at a beautiful piece of Hindu art, I don't appreciate the aesthetic and understanding that went into making it. There are a lot of Jews in punk rock, but certainly not the majority. Because Jews are musical, for a start. And if it starts in New York, there is a lot of Jewish culture there. I was just born too late to be a klezmer musician.

JEFFREY HYMAN (JOEY RAMONE)

CLAYSON BENALLY (Blackfire / Sihasin): It was so interesting connecting with Joey Ramone, who was born Jeffrey Hyman. He was from a Jewish family that was, like our family, Ashkenazi from Eastern Europe and Russia. After experiencing those atrocities firsthand, my grandfather—who was just a child when they fled—his view was, "How could there be a God after what I had witnessed?" He'd seen whole communities slaughtered by Russian soldiers and immigrated from Bialystock (Poland). We always identified Joey (Ramone) as one of our relatives, part of our true family. We looked up to him as Uncle Joey.

BERTA BENALLY (Blackfire manager / mother): Joey (Ramone) and I both had the same heritage. I even believe he might have been bar-mitzvahed! We had the same ancestry and he looked like my brother! My soul bro! After the Ramones broke up, Joey did his first solo show ever on the Navajo Nation at a festival that we put on. He saw beauty in so many things. He was ill at the time, diagnosed with lymphoma. C.J. (Ramone) was like, "You 'gotta meet my boss" and we became crazy friends. We argued a lot at the beginning and then he became my best friend. We could talk about anything under the sun, about religion and how nature was so critical. And how religions get so messed up because it's always about "My God is better than your God." It's just not healthy on this planet.

We both came from grandparents of immigrants to America that were fleeing for their lives from Russian pogroms, the massacres and murders. Look at what people had to go through, being persecuted continuously, and where are we at today? What the fuck has changed? I can't tolerate this. I want a better world!

Joey (Ramone) was so happy when we were recording the first Blackfire album. We did it in New York and he came down and told everybody he was our producer. I'm like, "You're not our producer." Don Fleming was our producer. I said, "Joe, you're our *spiritual producer*" and he loved that. He was very spiritual, very beautiful and he was a mensch!

REAL CHIVALRY OF SLAM DANCING

Joshua Safran is a lawyer, author and Jewish rabbi. Punk rock changed his life at a time when he most needed it. Safran writes in his autobiography *Free Spirit: Growing Up on the Road and Off the Grid* of the floating, hippie lifestyle that he had as a child. His upbringing also included sexual and physical abuse at the hands of his stepfather. Safran is now an advocate for survivors of child abuse.

JOSHUA SAFRAN (*Free Spirit: Growing Up on the Road and Off the Grid*): I was escaping from a very violent stepfather. I had a lot of anger and a lot of energy to go with that anger. It was undirected and chaotic. This man named Uncle Tony who was Mexican-American was the one person who had always been there for me when I was a kid and lived in the same commune that I was born in. His day job was as a janitor. He was a regular Gilman Street project guy, always going to Berkeley to listen to punk bands like Black Flag.

At one point he said to me, "I see you have a lot of energy and anger. You're now old enough and I'm going to take you with me and we're going to go to these shows." We would go into what is now called the mosh pit. At that time, we called it slam dancing! You're colliding with people in this chaotic and, in a sense, very angry energy. But actually, slam dancing happened in a very controlled manner. There was a real chivalry to it. You're colliding into the people next to you over and over. But if you went down, or if the person next to you went down, you would pick them back up again. Or if someone got hurt you would escort them out of the circle. Toward the middle of the circle it was more intense, and you could modulate toward the outside of the circle and later go back in. There was a real camaraderie and sense of brotherhood, and perhaps sisterhood, in the punk community.

Punk came at a very important time in my life. I shaved my head and was dressing in a lot of black clothing and skulls and I began skateboarding, too. It was an empowering and freeing experience. I got something out of my system and learned that there really was a model to be a man that was tough. My stepfather's obsession was on being physically powerful. In the punk community you could be that but it didn't mean beating defenseless women and children or being a tyrant.

JM: Have you heard of the orthodox Jewish punk band Moshiach Oi!? They were in a film called *Punk Jews*. There's also an excellent film by Liz Nord about Israeli punk bands titled *Jericho's Echo: Punk Rock in the Holy Land* (2004).

JOSHUA SAFRAN (*Free Spirit*): Not on my radar, but it is now.

JESSE ZOOK MANN (*Punk Jews* director): Moshiach Oi! draws interesting parallels between punk rock and Judaism. Even tracing it as far back to the story in the Bible of Abraham smashing idols and going against the mainstream practice of the day. Their view of the world is that people are robots and they're walking around on their phones and not really present. Yishai (Romanoff) says, "It's all about Hashem! People, wake up!" Hashem refers to God. He's trying to express the idea to wake up from the materialism and corruption that is so prevalent in the modern world, to see something more pure and inherently positive. A lot of people have accused Yishai of taking the prayer "Shemah Yisrael" and disrespecting it, being sacrilegious. People make comments like "Is this chillul hashem?" Is this disrespecting God's name? When people accuse them of that they're not looking outside of their mind to see what their real intentions are. And that's exactly what I think their music is meant to push you into.

YISHAI ROMANOFF (Moshiach Oi!): I wasn't religious at all. I was an atheist. I didn't identify as a Jew; it didn't have anything to do with my life at that time. I grew up orthodox going to private Jewish school and by the time I was fifteen I was not interested in religion at all. By high school I was totally an atheist and into punk rock, anarchy and drugs.

JM: So, your interest in punk came before Hassidic Judaism?

YISHAI ROMANOFF (Moshiach Oi!): Yes, way before. I didn't start getting interested in Judaism until 2006. I only became observant again in 2008. I started searching spiritually when I was nineteen after I had a spiritual experience on drugs. I was on mushrooms and I felt very strongly that there was a God. I went on a search for a couple of years and checked out Buddhism for a while. I ended up going to Israel on a free trip and that sparked my interest in Judaism again. I went back to Israel and connected with friends who had become religious. Little by little I got really into it and became observant again. I keep Sabbath, kosher and follow the laws of the Torah. It's the main focus of my life now. I was into punk and Buddhism and found *Dharma Punx* by Noah Levine and I was really into Buddhism for a year or two. I met Noah once when he spoke in Manhattan.

Punk rock was an important stepping stone for me on my spiritual journey and search for truth. Through punk rock I embraced individuality, questioning authority, having a defiant attitude toward the general society, and thinking for myself. We have a song called "Avraham Was a Punk Rocker." Avraham was the first Jew and grew up in a tyrannical society. They bowed down to statues and he smashed the idols and was taken before King Nimrod who told him, "You have to bow down before me or I'll kill you." He refused and got thrown into a fire! That is really punk rock! His whole life was punk, standing up for what he believed in and not backing down.

JM: How do the Jewish lifestyle and punk music support each other?

YISHAI ROMANOFF (Moshiach Oi!): Most punk rock is definitely not supportive of religious outlooks. Most of the music I was listening to—Leftöver Crack, Reagan Youth, Black Flag—they're all atheists. Those bands would not be supportive of a religious outlook. The way I came to punk rock was that I saw the world was so full of lies with people chasing after money. Punk rock was about being real.

The music was real and raw and wasn't about proving how good a musician you were. It was about being real and having a good time.

Black Flag was very sarcastic and I liked the way that they made fun of stuff that normal people do, like having TV parties and drinking beer. Punk rock saw the lies and how everyone's manipulating each other and putting on an act to make money and impress people. Punk rock got underneath all of that. With punk, I had the rebellion understanding that there is so much wrong in the world. But I never had the answer of what to do about it until I found Judaism. Yes, the world is screwed up and is full of lies. Everyone is chasing after money and vain desires. And in Judaism I learned that there is an answer; there is God in the world who is running the show and he has a mission and purpose for us. If we don't follow that mission and purpose, we get all screwed up and people start chasing after money and desires.

I see Judaism as being very punk rock. It is a rebellion. Judaism says that money means nothing. Having sex with lots of people means nothing. The only thing that matters is connecting to God and having peace. I see this as a rebellion against the vanity of the world. Real liberation comes through setting your mind free. Freedom is to know the truth and know what you need to do with your life. For me, that means following the teachings of our ancient tradition. Music is freedom because it rises above all words and ideas and communicates directly with the soul. When a person dances sincerely to music, he or she is allowing the feelings in their soul to guide the movements of the body. What could be more liberating than this?

JM: Are you interested in anarchism?

YISHAI ROMANOFF (Moshiach Oi!): I used to identify as an anarchist and I was a vegan for a while and involved in animal rights activism. These days, not so much. I'm more focused on spreading Rabbi Nachman in the world and connecting to God and spreading these ideas through music and literature. Political activism serves a purpose but what is going to bring ultimate change in the world is to draw people to God and help bring about the Messiah. That is what is going to fix the whole world. I'm more focused on the spiritual realm now.

JM: *The Heebie-Jeebies at CBGB's* by Steven Lee Beeber concludes that punk rock was started by mostly Jewish people like Lou Reed and band members from the Ramones, The Dictators, The Modern Lovers and producers like Malcolm McLaren and Bernie Rhodes. Beeber also writes this sentence: "No Holocaust, no punk." What do you think?

YISHAI ROMANOFF (Moshiach Oi!): I wasn't around when punk rock started. The people who started it were growing up right out of the ashes of the Holocaust.

I grew up in a different generation. But the statement "No Holocaust, no punk" doesn't register. I'd think, "What does the Holocaust have to do with punk rock?" When I was growing up the Holocaust was already history and didn't seem as real. For them it was a big part of their life and had a lot to do with what kind of people they became. I'm sure the Holocaust had an impact on lots of people but I don't know if it had as much as this guy says who wrote the book.

JM: Life in Israel is usually tense but the last three weeks there's been a major Israeli attack on Gaza. (July 2014) Are you interested in singing about Israel and Palestine?

YISHAI ROMANOFF (Moshiach Oi!): I don't involve politics in my music because I see it as a distraction. In Moshiach Oi! we have a clear focus on God and the Torah and spreading the light of Rabbi Nachman. The state of Israel is there but it's a whole other side of the spectrum. The main message for Moshiach Oi! is to bring the redemption closer.

The secular government in Israel doesn't mean much to me. I support the state of Israel but it's not the most relevant thing. It's not what is going to bring us security and safety. What will bring us ultimate security and safety is when the Messiah comes and gathers the exiles and brings us home. The people who run the state of Israel now are not religious and don't believe in the Torah. The politicians are liars. They're not so important to me and I'm not too interested in singing about politics. I believe in what I'm doing. If one day I woke up and I didn't believe in it anymore, I would stop doing it. I love punk rock and I love Torah and Rabbi Nachman.

PUNK IN THE PROMISED LAND
PUNK ROCK IN ISRAEL/WAR IN THE MIDDLE EAST

You declared a monopoly on suffering and built walls of hatred / We just built this country based on lies, on sealed circled sectors.

> —"Monopoly on Suffering" by Jarada
> (2023 album—*No Coexistence With . . .*)

Japan is sane, Jamaica is baked / Finland is sick and Israel is a disease.

> —"Sick State" By Tabarnak (2020 *Sharim Tabarnak*)

Put Jerusalem in Jordan / Give it to the Palestinians
—"Put Jerusalem in Jordan" by Marmara Streisand
> (*2014—Lullabies of Destruction*)

Don't wanna live in a trailer in the occupied territories / Or go to the market to harass Arabs.

> —"Rather Be a Punk Than a Dirty Settler"
> by Nekhei Naatza (1994)

In the 2007 film *Uncut from Israel* former Black Flag singer Henry Rollins tells an audience of young Israelis; "Kids keep dying and people keep getting blown up and it's awful, it's ghastly. You know this. I'm not saying it's your fault. All I'm saying is that if you do not stop it, all of you will have beautiful children—some of you have them already—and they will inherit the war you did not stop."

In an October 18, 2022 Bandcamp article titled "Nekhei Naatza: Israeli Punks Against the State," Yoni Kroll writes, "In some ways, not a lot has changed in Israel over the past three decades. The threat of regional war is still constant. Israel still occupies the West Bank and Gaza Strip—land that belongs to the people of Palestine. The Palestinian response to living under this military occupation continues, and violence turns to violence turns to violence. Since the first *Intifada*—Arabic for 'uprising'—started in 1987, more than 12,000 Palestinians and 1,500 Israelis have been killed, with many more thousands injured. In 2000 a literal wall was built by the Israeli government along the border, a move that has isolated the Palestinians even more."

On October 7, 2023, the violence increased once again when Hamas-led militants in Gaza attacked Israel, killing 1,200 and kidnapping 250. Israel's response has been a devastating attack on Gaza that to date (October 2024) has left almost 50,000 dead and another 100,000 wounded in what is widely described as a "genocide."

Since the 1980's many punk rock bands in Israel have sung out against militarism, religious extremism, and Israel's displacement and occupation of Palestinians. The 2004 documentary *Jericho's Echo: Punk in the Holy Land* by director Liz Nord is something of an Israeli version of Penelope Spheeris' 1981 classic *The Decline of Western Civilization. Jericho's Echo* features crucial interviews with Israeli punk bands plus concert footage. The film was advertised as, "Rebellious Israeli youth take up the arms of punk rock, loud guitars, and mohawks in the most politically charged area of the world." The highlighted bands are Useless ID, Chaos Rabak, Va'adat Kishut, Nikmat Olalim, Punkache, Kafa la Panim shel Limor Livnat, HaPussy shel Lussy and Retribution, the single band presented in the film that is pro-colonialist, advocating separation between Jews and Arabs. In *Jericho's Echo* a bandmember from Nikmat Olalim says, "People in Israel are against the occupation and we try to criticize it in songs," and a bandmember from HaPussy shel Lussy explains, "The people here have had enough with all the bombings that's going on around us."

JM: The Middle East, and Jerusalem in particular, is a center for Christians, Jews and Muslims. These world religions teach love and compassion and to fight injustice. They even teach us to be especially careful to respect people who have chosen a religious path different than our own. Yet, the wars and violence there seem endless. Any ideas about how this happens? How do people become extreme, fundamentalist?

ISHAY BERGER (Useless ID): I've always thought about this as a mix of a male ego problem going berserk with a dash of pure insanity backed up by business-political interests of those pulling the strings in the background. One thing that never changed for me was a "people are people" way of thinking. This extremism is pretty much one hundred percent nonsense and I never spend too much time analyzing the human mistake of religion and separation.

JM: I know that Useless ID has usually not had lyrics about Israeli militarism, Jewish extremism and the occupation of Palestine.

ISHAY BERGER (Useless ID): Useless ID always felt like it was *useless* to make it clear that we were against war and pushing religion on people. At some points we did address those issues, but to be honest, with punk it feels like preaching to the choir and I don't 'wanna hear thirty minutes of the same idea that I already agree on. So, we kind of have that as a guest theme, if you will. My other bands (Bo Labar, Tabarnak and Shesh Shesh Shesh) follow a similar route.

JM: Is it dangerous to be an Israeli band and sing about politics and religion?

ISHAY BERGER (Useless ID): It's not dangerous to sing about politics or religion for a band like us. Seems like the ones who *do* get in trouble for saying shit like that would be the old-school writers and intellectuals. Punk bands are sort of expected to do that and are pretty much ignored by the media anyway. Maybe that's another reason why we wouldn't.

JM: Have you had contact with Palestinian punk bands? I can't find any, past or present.

ISHAY BERGER (Useless ID): Been asked that before; wish I could say I did, but no.

HAMAS AND ISRAEL

JM: What are your feelings about the Hamas attack last October 7 (2023) and the ongoing war in Gaza by Israel?

ISHAY BERGER (Useless ID): Makes me sick, forever. October 7th was *beyond* insane and I am eternally devastated by the horrible atrocities done by Hamas on every single angle of the story. Every kill, rape, kidnap and person burned alive changed me forever. I feel like an alien in a world of violence and insanity. My views did not change but my eyes will never see the world in the same way they did until October 6th. The Gaza situation is so hard yet still going; it is a bit much for me to put it in words. I feel horrible about the regular, innocent, unlucky random people that are dying or suffering on every corner of this. I could have been born an hour away from where I am and live a life that is 100% pain and devastation. So, I cannot feel anything but sadness and sympathy for anyone in the picture.

JM: Do you feel compelled to make songs that talk about the current Gaza war?

ISHAY BERGER (Useless ID): No. People here live this on a daily basis and every little noise that may sound like an alarm going off will trigger each of us. People going to shows and listening to punk music did not come up with this situation. We didn't want it, no one asked our opinion about anything. What I can give to people is some rest and hope through raw, funny or angry music. But singing about the Gaza War is not something I feel like doing.

JM: How is it for you living in Israel now? In our previous interview (2016) you told me everyone you knew was trying to move away, many to Berlin. Are you thinking of this now?

ISHAY BERGER (Useless ID): It's scary, to be honest. The alarms, the threats, the unknown; it can get you down. I feel like I am taking a risk by staying here—but I do stay here. Just never been the type to relocate; good on those who did!

JM: Tell me about the ideas you were trying to get across with your band.

FEDERICO GOMEZ (Nekhei Naatza / Dir Yassin / Smartut Kahol Lavan): My brother Santiago and I are from Argentina and we were immigrants in Israel. (1984) And then we found out about this new music called punk. In Israel the punk music was very superficial and trend-oriented. What meant more to us was when we started to write to people everywhere around the world and we got all sorts of music, zines and information from international bands and writings about anarchism and animal rights. In the beginning, our band was protest music in general. But soon enough, it became more focused on specific issues.

ETAY LEVY (Nekhei Naatza): Anti-Zionism

FEDERICO GOMEZ (Nekhei Naatza / Dir Yassin): It wasn't exactly anti-Zionism. It was more against the military, against religion and about the role Judaism played in Israel's society. Of course, it was from the perspective of teenagers but it was still pretty radical compared to what was going on in Israel at the time, music-wise. In the beginning punk was a stand against mainstream society. The Intifada happened more or less at the same time I found out about punk. (1987) So, pretty soon they became connected in the sense that there were people fighting oppression and punk was the voice of the people that were oppressed. Not in the same sense, obviously. But it's a protest against the forces of authoritarian government like the army and the police. So, when we started the band in 1990, these things came together. It was obvious that we would start writing songs about, for example, the Intifada and the power of religion in Israel, and in the national identity of Israel.

JM: Did you feel like you were the only band singing about the occupation and being critical of extremist Judaism?

FEDERICO GOMEZ (Nekhei Naatza / Dir Yassin): There were a couple of bands. One band called Noon Mem was influential, though not musically. They were active in the second half of the 80s and split in 1990. They were pretty outspoken, but it was mostly focused on the military. They were singing against the occupation of the West Bank and Gaza. I don't think they were singing anything about Judaism.

ETAY LEVY (Nekhei Naatza): It's very frowned upon, saying anything negative about Judaism. No one really does it.

FEDERICO GOMEZ (Nekhei Naatza / Dir Yassin): There was another band that was connected to the punk scene, even though they play more industrial experimental music, called Duralex Sedlex. They have some songs that criticized religion and they were kind of big in the underground scene, which doesn't really mean a lot in Israel. We're talking about a couple of hundred people at best. They broke up around the time we started to get some traction with the band. So, we never played together. Duralex Sedlex were good musically and had some good lyrics, but they weren't exactly punk.

ETAY LEVY (Nekhei Naatza): To put it in perspective, our band was started when Federico was eighteen, and we were three years younger. We were teenagers and when we broke up, we were just mid-twenties. So, still very young and developing theories.

FEDERICO GOMEZ (Nekhei Naatza / Dir Yassin): We originally lived in a very small kibbutz. Santiago, me and two other guys that quit the band in 94 were living in the north of Israel very close to both the Lebanese and the Syrian borders. It's a rural area, no scene to speak about. The possibility of meeting people which will help you put your words into thoughts and offer some intellectual understanding was very limited. Musically, we were really good at overcoming this. And very soon, we were the people that knew the most about the punk scenes all over the world! Because we were super into it!

NEVER GO IN THE ARMY

JM: There's still so much war, police violence and poverty worldwide. If a punk band is not singing about these things, I sometimes wonder, "Why not?"

ETAY LEVY (Nekhei Naatza): Because it doesn't make money! Usually.

FEDERICO GOMEZ (Nekhei Naatza / Dir Yassin): There were two other members in the beginning of our band, and all of us had lived in other countries. We experienced different realities than Israel. Because of this, I think we were more open to criticize Israel and think about other possibilities. For most Israelis, it's obvious they're going to go to the army and be patriotic and Zionist. For me, it was very clear that I will *never* go to the army. And I think that made our group stick out in the scene because we wanted something completely different. For us it was never, "We'll do this for a couple of years, and then do something else." Political expression was something we wanted to attune in order to change society. We didn't think we were going to make a revolution, but we thought we can improve certain things; animal rights, for example. There's an expectation that people creating art are doing this with the idea of shaping society toward something better.

ETAY LEVY (Nekhei Naatza): And not falling into the trap of the Zionist Jewish nationalism. Not really Zionist . . . but the trap of the Israeli way of life where you're going to get drafted into the army and then anything that has to do with the arts just goes out the window. And once you get out, you're pretty much brainwashed and you don't go back to any scene and you just do what they tell you. That is most of the people in Israel to this day.

FEDERICO GOMEZ (Nekhei Naatza / Dir Yassin): I totally agree. Not going to the army is already taking a big political step in Israel. Most people go to the army; they don't question it. Some people don't go because of medical reasons or they just don't feel like it, but for us it was something very explicit and political. We rejected the idea of this country controlling and oppressing other people to the extent that Israel was, and is, oppressing Palestinians. Our music was not popular; we never wanted to be popular and there was never a chance it would be. It was something we did because it was a way of communicating with other people in Israel and abroad. We were expressing everything in a different way and aiming for different goals than most people we grew up with.

ETAY LEVY (Nekhei Naatza): I went and did the army. But I didn't do it for patriotic reasons; I had something else to prove. I wanted to see it on the inside and understand why kids are going in there and coming out brainwashed. I think I understood in the first ten minutes I was there! And then I was like, "Oh, shit! What did I do?" I came out and just went right back to doing DIY stuff, playing in the band. Even while I was in the army we still managed to practice and make records and go on tour.

Israel has changed a lot. I remember distinctly that during those days leading up to me going into the military, the Israeli army was still using rubber bullets.

Those days went out the window real quick. Rubber bullets changed into live ammunition. I realized they were using live ammunition even before they started talking about it in the news. They were covering it up. They were shooting people left and right and not revealing that, which is really fucked up. It just progressively got worse.

FEDERICO GOMEZ (Nekhei Naatza / Dir Yassin): It did get worse in Israel. My idea for a long time after Nekhei Naatza broke up was to continue and I was in two other bands that were also outspoken. (Dir Yassin / Smartut Kahol Lavan) Also, my views started to change because I got exposed to more people writing things critical of Zionism. The band I did afterwards (Dir Yassin) had lyrics that were much more clearly anti-Zionist than our band. And our band was very critical of Israel. It was a process. I started university and got exposed to more literature. Even in the 90s it's not like there was so much information. At least not before the Internet got more popular and cheaper.

JM: Etay, you mentioned how rubber bullets changed to live bullets. I'm picturing those bullets being aimed at Palestinians who were protesting against Israel's occupation.

ETAY LEVY (Nekhei Naatza): In a lot of cases, you don't really have to protest to get shot by the Israeli military. But yes, any form of opposition or you're just in the wrong place, wrong time, you can get shot. Even with rubber bullets you could lose your eye or get seriously hurt. But it very quickly escalated to live ammunition to where it's normalized. These days it's out in the open. (June, 2024) They'll shoot anybody. Literally anybody, including the hostages. Literally. That's what happens when you normalize violence on that scale.

ETAY LEVY (Nekhei Naatza): Zionism and religion and Israel kind of get rolled into one. We didn't specifically sing against Zionism, but we were outspoken against religion.

FEDERICO GOMEZ (Nekhei Naatza / Dir Yassin): I think it was an intuition we had. We couldn't quote a lot of political analysts or philosophers but we knew it was wrong. We knew how people were forced to see themselves as part of a nation that is a combination of nationalism and religion. We saw through that and later on we got wiser and got to read and experience more things. But, doing political actions in Palestine is something that started a little bit later, after Nekhei Naatza broke up and after Etay (Levy) already left for the United States. But we got more radical in the way we saw Israel, and the solution for the conflict with Palestinians and Israel's Arab neighbors. Nekhei Naatza was a process that helped us to develop those thoughts and meet people that think like us.

JM: Did you collaborate with Palestinian punks or activists? Was there communication across that border?

FEDERICO GOMEZ (Nekhaei Naatza / Dir Yassin): Activists, yeah. But later, not at the time. There were very few punks. We did have contact with Palestinians inside Israel from the Haifa area. They were involved in this band called Dictatorshit, which lasted only for some months.

ETAY LEVY (Nekhei Naatza): Oh, we played with them!

FEDERICO GOMEZ (Nekhei Naatza / Dir Yassin): People outside Israel that live in the West Bank or Gaza—Arab people—I don't know any that are into punk. I did know Palestinian activists when I was involved in activism when they were building the wall inside the West Bank (2002–2005). There was this band that played a concert there called Oi Vaavoi. They played for activists and just did a song or two and it was kind of weird. But I never met a punk from Palestine that lived in Palestine. I know Palestinian punks but they live in the diaspora; they are immigrants in other countries. I know many punks in Lebanon and Jordan.

Figure 21.1 Another controversial album cover from Israeli punk band Nekhei Naatza symbolizing the violence of settler colonialism and religious extremism in the Middle East. Contributed: Nekhei Naatza / Taklitim Holim.

There probably are punks in Palestine now but I haven't been living in Israel for more than twenty years.

ETAY LEVY (Nekhei Naatza): Living in Israel you don't really get to meet Palestinians, unless you're an activist or in the military. In the United States, most Palestinians I've met were into rap or metal and not hardcore punk. Even now, Palestinians get limited Internet access because Israel dictates everything.

OCTOBER 7, 2023—JUST A MASSACRE

JM: Things were already intense there and last year on October 7 (2023) Hamas killed 1,200 Israelis and took 250 hostages. Since then, Israel has been pummeling Gaza. About 40,000 Palestinians have been killed. Tell me your thoughts on what's happening there now.

ETAY LEVY (Nekhei Naatza): It's absolutely horrific. It's insane. It's not even a war. When they call it a war, I get mad because it's not a war. It's a massacre. It's genocide. That's exactly what's going on.

FEDERICO GOMEZ (Nekhei Naatza / Dir Yassin): Giving the beginning for this conflict as October 7 is problematic, because Israel has been bombing Gaza all the time, the past decades. It's just convenient for the Israeli authorities to frame their violence and destruction and death as some kind of act of defense. But the Palestinians have been suffering for decades; nonstop bombings, attacks. Gaza is basically a huge prison with very few possibilities. I refuse to say that this started now. Obviously, it's escalated but it's not a new conflict. It's the desperation of Palestinians. I think it's totally abhorrent to kill civilians. What Hamas did is horrific but Israel has been doing the same before October.

ETAY LEVY (Nekhei Naatza): I don't want to sound insensitive, but I wasn't totally surprised that it happened. I asked myself, "What took you so long?" Because, you treat people like shit for that long you're going to get bit at some point. And they got bit.

> *When will they blow up Tel Aviv's stock market? / When will they blow up the Sheraton?*
>
> —"Reconciliation with Hamas" by Nekhai Naatza (1994)

FEDERICO GOMEZ (Nekhei Naatza / Dir Yassin): We even had this song about Hamas on our record. We're trying to say that Hamas is not the main enemy. The enemy is the state of Israel and the people controlling that. I think we saw it coming. When we saw the oppression Palestinians were living with for decades, we knew that it's not going to be absorbed. It's going to create some kind of reaction. There have been Palestinian actions all the time, and Israel refused to acknowledge actions when they're peaceful. The last resort is to do something violent. It's horrific; the price is so many lives. 50,000 Palestinians or more. (June 2024) Inside Israel, most people approve the attack on Gaza. They think this price the Palestinians are paying now is okay. Even if you kill a kid, "He was going to become a terrorist. So, why not?" There are very sick ideas concerning what is legitimate.

ETAY LEVY (Nekhei Naatza): It always boils down to the same thing; racism. An Israeli life is more important than a Palestinian one. That's the way it's been.

FEDERICO GOMEZ (Nekhei Naatza / Dir Yassin): Palestinian people that are Israeli citizens are also getting killed. For Palestinians in the West Bank, it's also been nonstop attack and murders on a mass scale and confiscation of land, settlers going wild. There's extreme right-wing Jewish supremacists. In many places in the West Bank, the settlers control the army and they do whatever they want.

JM: I sometimes think about viewing Earth from outer space as if I'm an extraterrestrial studying human cultures and when I observe Arabs and Jews I might say, "Their foods, languages, beliefs and music are so similar they must be one group." They're living in the same area and yet they're killing each other all these years.

ETAY LEVY (Nekhei Naatza): It's crazy how similar we are! Each side has its own amount of pride of where things came from, and who invented what first. The eternal argument! It doesn't really matter. We're very, very similar!

FEDERICO GOMEZ (Nekhei Naatza / Dir Yassin): That's one of the things we started to dig into when we became older. An idea of how the country of Israel was created was that the Jewish people came to Palestine during the Ottoman Empire and the British Mandate, in the end of the nineteenth century and beginning of twentieth century, and that was the background before 1948. We were taught that Israel wanted to have peace with the Palestinians, to share and divide the country, and instead was attacked from all sides. But when you go back, you see very radical differences from what you've been taught. And the new discourse about this history was not popular, but it started to happen around the 90s. And now there's a very big backlash against people talking about the way Palestinians were treated and some are harassed for trying to convey this.

JM: Did your bands encounter police or government harassment or surveillance?

FEDERICO GOMEZ (Nekhei Naatza / Dir Yassin): Yes, we did. We were interrogated several times by both police and secret police. That happened after Israel's prime minister Rabin was assassinated in November 1995. After that, people were more interested in what we're doing. There was kind of a left-wing reaction to the murder and we were called to meet normal police in a strange place and it turned out to be secret police. This happened also with the bands I had afterwards. (Dir Yassin / Smartut Kahol Lavan) Also, police tried to infiltrate different anarchist organizations and animal rights groups. Probably they succeeded, I would say.

FEDERICO GOMEZ (Nekhei Naatza / Dir Yassin): The cover of our LP is a photo of Netanyahu *sieg heiling*. That's not a collage, it's a real photo. There was a big controversy when this photo happened two years ago. It was shown in an exhibition and there was a lot of discussions and debates. The photographer officially never gave us permission to use it but through a mutual friend, he said it was okay. He just doesn't want to be credited with the photo. Now, we've reissued the record and we didn't want to use that photo because of the problems it could bring for the record. It wasn't so important, to be honest. We just never thought Netanyahu will be such a key player for so long. The new cover; also people won't like it. I think it's as strong as the other cover.

JM: The new cover is sort of a menorah turned sideways and looks like a gun.

FEDERICO GOMEZ (Nekhei Naatza / Dir Yassin): Yeah, that's the one that just came out recently. It has an extensive biography of the band that we wrote together. (*From Nowhere to Nothing: Recordings 1994–97* by Nekhei Naatza released in 2022)

ZIONISM—BRINGING CIVILIZATION TO THE NATIVES KIND OF THING

JM: I was educated to understand that Zionism was a movement to create a safe place for Jewish people after the Nazi-perpetrated Holocaust. Many protests against Israel's current war on Gaza (2024) equate Zionism with colonialism and violence against Palestinians that has been part of Israel's history. But lots of Jewish people around the world understand anti-Zionism to mean anti-Jewish. Maybe there is a new, broader definition of Zionism that connects it to the militaristic government of Israel.

ETAY LEVY (Nekhai Naatza): New definition, old practices. This has been the case since the 1940s or before, with the treatment of Palestinians by the colonial powers. It's always been like this.

FEDERICO GOMEZ (Nekhei Naatza / Dir Yassin): I think that orchestrating a state which tries to be both democratic and Jewish is some kind of paradox that you cannot really overcome. Perhaps it's easy to say now, but I think they are incompatible. And people should know better than to try to do that. On the one side, I understand that after the Second World War there was such a huge crisis that people were just trying to stay alive. And there were very deep political, theological considerations. I know a lot of people that were Socialists but still Zionists. Obviously, I think there is a very big contradiction in that, but I understand why they ended up in Israel joining what became the IDF (Israeli Defense Forces) and protecting the land. It's not so strange. And you cannot go backward.

Obviously, there needs to be some kind of criticism toward the Israeli narrative or the Zionist narrative. It doesn't mean that every Jewish person that goes to Israel is a Zionist, but Zionism is colonialism. I cannot see how you can put it another way. Before the 40s, rich Jewish people were buying land and sending poor Jewish people to live in lands that were occupied, where Palestinian peasants had been kicked out of their land, because a rich person in Istanbul now owned their land. You cannot disconnect this history from a larger narrative that also encompasses nationalism and economic changes that were created in order to improve the conditions for some and not others. I understand why it came to be known as Zionism.

Israel was, from the beginning, a colonial project. If you read letters by the fathers of Zionism—for example Chaim Weizmann—they tried to convince the British that the Zionist project is a colonial project that goes hand in hand with what the British, French and other global powers were doing in other parts of the world at the time. Even then, it was a *bringing civilization to the natives* kind of thing. If you talk about the American genocide; not every European that came to North America had the intention of committing genocide. People came because they were persecuted. They were poor. There were other reasons many people came to what became the United States as it became a colonial power by taking over land of native people and dispossessing them of their means of living.

JM: Different groups had different intentions in creating Israel. I don't think the US government cared much about Jewish people. In some ways they directly helped Adolf Hitler. The US power structure wanted a stronghold in the Middle East.

FEDERICO GOMEZ (Nekhei Naatza / Dir Yassin): That's part of the of the very big picture.

ETAY LEVY (Nekhei Naatza): Definitely part of the big picture. One hundred percent.

WE COULD HAVE MADE A PUNK ROCK SONG

The Promised Band: The Story of the First All-Girl Band in Israel and Palestine is the 2016 documentary by Jen Heck which follows Heck and a small group of Israeli and Palestinian women who decide that becoming a band is the best way to defy political and cultural borders and Israel's separation wall. Their journey is profound and connecting and although the women do not play punk rock, the spirit of the film is DIY and anti-authoritarian. So much so that the online culture magazine Dazed called the film, "The first feminist punk band of Israel and Palestine." (Dominique Sisley—March 22, 2016)

JEN HECK (director *The Promised Band: The Story of the First All-Girl Band in Israel and Palestine*): We could have made a punk rock song, if anybody had been able to play anything! That was probably something that was said that ended up on the cutting room floor. If I went through the footage, there were probably lots of jokes about *how punk rock we were*. In terms of the way you describe punk as liberating or revolutionary—breaking the rules and how you look at authority— that's definitely apropos to what we did.

We oftentimes joked about it, because that's how you deal with stuff that stresses you out. But there were a few moments where we couldn't joke about it. There's a moment in the film when we get pulled over by the Palestinian Authority and it was scary. I thought I was going to go to jail. I didn't think we were going stay there forever but I thought we were going to be there overnight. Thankfully, that didn't happen. But those were the moments where it felt more like a defiance of authority than just how fun it might have looked in other moments. A lot of moments, it did feel fun and safe because we kept pushing and pushing. I felt a big responsibility because I was the person leading every- one and it couldn't have happened unless there was this neutral American. And you look at where things are now, which is an extreme because of the war that's going on. (Israel's War on Gaza—2024) But even before that, you wouldn't see people crossing over to Palestine.

JEN HECK (director *The Promised Band*): Something you see a lot in some extreme religious people—Christians, Jews, or Muslims—they're having a very literal interpretation of their spirituality. Jerusalem is a mecca of spirituality and the cross-section of those three major religions. As an outsider I see spirituality as a concept being thrown around a lot but as a true practice, I don't know. I think that's where this current conflict comes into play. (2024) Because people use religion—not necessarily spirituality—to create authority and enforce rules. And a lot of times the religion to an outsider just looks like a bunch of rules. And those rules really fall flat when it comes to going deeper into what spirituality is.

I think it's rooted in a fear; we want rules and structure because life is totally unpredictable and feeling out of control is scary. Maybe that's what religion does for people. But if you're really listening to what a religion is teaching, it requires you to be out of control with your emotions sometimes. It requires you to feel and you may feel something that you don't want to feel. So, it can be a real contradiction. In that regard, spirituality came into the movie in a lot of subtle and nuanced ways. The cross-section with punk rock is philosophical, not musical.

People involved in art and expression are more likely to try to understand spirituality, even if it fails. More than somebody who's blindly following a religion. But, we're a long way away from people understanding the nuances of that, probably because most people aren't leaders. They're followers. That's why religion is so powerful. It can sometimes be used for bad. Just like the people who flew planes into the World Trade Center said they did it for religion; but did they? Do you feel that's accurate? It was God saying, "Oh, good one. Very ingenious!" I don't think so! But, it's hard to argue with something that can't be proven because you can't literally point a camera at God and say, "So, was the World Trade Center your idea? Did you do that? Because you wanted the martyrs? How are they doing?" I mean, you could maybe explore that in a punk rock song!

JM: The Middle East is home to Islam, Judaism and Christianity. All three are based on teachings of kindness toward others, especially when others have chosen a different path. Yet, there has been constant warfare. Any thoughts on the current violence in Gaza/Israel?

GLENN WALLIS (Ruin): Can I quote two verses from the *Dhammapada* as an answer to this question? The Buddha says, "In the world, hostilities are *never* appeased by hostilities. But by the absence of hostilities are they appeased. This is an interminable truth. Some do not understand that we are perishing here. Those who understand this bring to rest their quarrels." This may sound naive but it gets to the heart of the matter. I agree; what would the world be like if people would just *live* the religious beliefs that they profess?

JEN HECK (director *The Promised Band*): What Hamas did in October was obviously amped up, times a thousand. It's like the playbook that keeps repeating. Part of the problem is that some people benefit from it. There's a leadership problem across the board, whether we're talking Israel or Palestine. Israel can't destroy all the Palestinians, because that would be genocide, and you can't come back from that. At the same time, I get why they don't trust Hamas; it's going to keep happening. So, what do you do? I do fear that the worst will happen before people realize, "Maybe we should have done this differently." I have a lot of empathy for people across both lines. I don't know what the solution is. We always joke—but it may be true—it's almost like you need to have women come in and take over, because you need such a bold moment of forgiveness. Because passing the ball back and forth is not going to ever change things.

YAOTL MAZAHUA (Iconoclast / Aztlan Underground aka Anahuak Underground): Palestinians are going through genocide in real time at the hands of settlers known as the state of Israel and the United States. Calling out Israel for its horrors is not about being antisemitic, it's anti-centralized power and empire. Since October 7, 2023 we're watching in real time what happened to indigenous people.

Indigenous people saw this contradiction when settlers arrived; preaching the prince of peace while murdering indigenous people in the name of God. While religion serves as a sanctuary for many, in the Middle East you have the complicating factor of a history of colonialism from the Ottoman to the British and French and this exacerbated the religious divisions caused by the dogma of Abrahamic religions. Christianity, Islam and Judaism all perpetuate blind obedience and foster judgment and persecution of "nonbelievers." Like the Discharge song "Religion Instigates" conveys; religion perpetuates and justifies war while hypocritically promoting peace. This is the reality of so-called Christian, Jewish, Islamic faiths all originating in the Middle East where the backdrop of geopolitical dominance exacerbates extremism and violence among each other.

GUDO WAFU NISHIJIMA (Zen teacher of *Hardcore Zen* author Brad Warner): In Israel there is such political fighting. The main cause may be difference of religion. If both sides insist on their religious standpoint, it is impossible for us to have the successful solution. When they want to solve the problem, they have to place the problem of religions aside and think about the real situation; their histories and what places the Palestinians live and what places the Jewish people live. Such real facts are the basis of solving the problem on the basis of justice. Such a realism is necessary to solve any kind of problem on Earth. Realistic thinking is important, and it is very important today because human beings worry that both idealistic spiritualism and materialistic monetarism are the cause of unhappy conditions in human societies. To solve those two contradictory fundamental philosophies, we have to enter into the area of action and realistic ideas.

ROB FISH (108): Religion has always carved itself a pretty tight niche. You mentioned that in the leftist community, spirituality and religion are a no-no. Historically there is a pretty good reason why. You don't have to look back a thousand years. Just look at current events today where religious ideas lead to the violence that we see today in the Middle East.

STEWART EBERSOLE (*Barred for Life*): Studying a lot of religious philosophies, I see that almost every single prophet has said the same thing; you need to will yourself to good. You need to know what good is because some people think that *bad* is *good*. Killing another person is bad. If you kill people in war that is bad. If you kill someone over a necklace that sucks. If you kill somebody because you don't know another way out of the relationship, that blows. Killing is stupid. One of the most frustrating things in our society is that you have people saying that abortion is bad, it's killing babies. But sending people to Iraq and having their legs blown off is okay because, "We need to civilize the barbarians." This is fucked up!

ED COLVER (punk photographer): Since I was a kid there's been pictures in the newspaper of war in the Middle East; Palestinian kids throwing rocks at Israeli tanks. And that's our money causing that shit! We're jeopardizing our national security to protect Israel? This is beyond reason. Did I vote to give money to Israel? Fuck no! Our government was taken over a long time ago by corporations and the supreme court opened the flood gates to allow them to do whatever they want.

RAY CAPPO (Youth of Today / Shelter): There's no way to find peace trying to side with either side. You have to look at it in a philosophical way. Just like in a marriage, if one person wants a divorce, it's going to happen. If one side wants to crush the other side, there will never be peace. Peace happens when one side starts to see the ideas of the other side, when you work with empathy. If world leaders can't work with empathy, they'll never have peace.

PAUL LANDERS (Feeling B / Die Firma / Rammstein): The war in the Middle East has nothing to do with religions. It shows really clearly how limited we humans really are.

EVAN KLEINMAN (*Punk Jews* producer): The Israeli-Palestinian conflict is very convoluted and complex. Jello Biafra went to Palestine and Israel (2011) and was supposed to play a show but ended up not because of pressure from certain BDS groups. (Boycott, Divest, Sanctions) He said he couldn't find any Palestinian punk rock bands.

YISHAI ROMANOFF (Moshiach Oi!) The true Torah of God has nothing to do with the politics that go on in Israel. I do believe that the land of Israel is the God-given land of the Jews. I reject the political establishment in Israel, including the Zionists who founded the state. They do not represent me, the Torah or the

Jewish people as a whole. They have their own agenda, and most of them are corrupt and compromised. I try to avoid political conversations about Israel, because most of the time people will only try to pull me into one or another side of a political dialectic that I want nothing to do with. I do believe in the right of the Jews to defend themselves and their land. However, the ones who are in control and leading Israel into these wars are corrupt and do not have our best interest in mind. I pray for the day when Moshiach (Jewish messiah) will come and remove them from their power, and lead the whole world to an era of true peace. I am pained by innocent lives lost on either side. Hashem should save us from wicked rulers who create these wars for their own gain.

DIRK MOLDT (*Kleine Prenzlauer Berg Geschichte* / Fatale) It's not religions. The violence is because people want more power and control. They all want to be chiefs. They want to be in control. They do not have a culture of speaking with each other. Some people—like Netanyahu—fear the end of the war because he has the impression that his leadership is over after the war, so he must hold onto this. It's just like Putin and Ukraine.

KYAW THU WIN (Rebel Riot): Many punk bands in England are active in this matter. (Gaza 2024) I think the whole world is crazy! Sometimes seeing news like that makes me feel like I don't have any feelings anymore. Burma also has civil wars every day. Violence, village-burnings, rapes and refugees from wars. Young people, women and children die every day because of fascist regimes. We are very disappointed. Authorities, terrorists are also completely incomprehensible. But I've found two things; things we can control and things we cannot control. That way, we don't spend time on things we can't control and instead work more on those things we can control. We do more people-to-people mutual aid direct actions. We start building small positive changes around us. That makes more sense to me.

KEN CHITWOOD (Dept. for the Study of Religion at Universität Bayreuth): It's impossible to think about violence in the Middle East, or in Sub-Saharan Africa or Southeast Asia or the list goes on, without thinking about resistance to colonial power and continuing privilege through neo-colonialism. Violence becomes one of the weapons of the weak and what some have deemed terrorism is also the weapon of the marginalized, of those without the resources of war. Although I'm a pacifist, I try to understand the violent resistance of others and why they feel they can justify their violence. Just like I tried to understand Christian Just War Theory, I try to understand violence of those who are not in power. Even if I myself reject violence as a means of approaching personal and political relationships.

22

PUNKS FOR PALESTINE
CONCERTS IN LOS ANGELES, CALIFORNIA—2023

With a heavy heart, we're calling on the Los Angeles punk community to take a stand. Witnessing multiple war crimes committed and the day-to-day updates on the civilians lives lost, Kristine, Juju and Jezel are organizing a benefit to raise awareness on our attempts to cease fire, aid Palestinian refugees and children, and stop military aggression. There will be a Palestinian vocalist highlighted in the band Inqirad as well as multiple Palestinian speakers to raise awareness.

—From 2023 press release by Kristine Nevrose, activist
and singer with Los Angeles punk band S.O.H.
(System of Hate) and other activists regarding the
November 5, 2023, Punks for Palestine concert

Punk rock musicians have a rich history of organizing concerts to raise awareness and funds to support social justice issues. In the 1970s, Rock Against Racism in the UK included massive marches and concerts with the Clash, Tom Robinson, Steel Pulse, Aswad, Gang of Four, The Au Pairs, X-Ray Spex, Buzzcocks, The Beat, The Fall and other bands. Punk bands have also donated album sales to organizations that address prison abolition, police brutality, militarism and capitalism. The international anarchist group Food Not Bombs has been connected to punk bands like Bad Brains, MDC, Fifteen, Rebel Riot and Good Riddance. In Washington, DC, Ian MacKaye and Positive Force organized anti-apartheid actions and Fugazi performed in front of the White House to oppose the 2003 US war on Iraq. In so-called Arizona (USA), Blackfire and other indigenous punk bands have helped build community centers and resist colonial resettlement. After Russia invaded Ukraine in 2022, Dave Dictor of MDC released two volumes of *Punk for Ukraine* with three hundred bands from thirty countries that benefit Doctors Without Borders.

After the October 7, 2023, Hamas surprise attack on Israel, the Israeli military responded with an assault that many feel was disproportionate and perhaps genocidal. About 1,200 Israelis were killed and 250 taken hostage on October 7, and to date (January 2025), about 45,000 Palestinians in Gaza have been killed and 100,000 wounded by Israeli forces, according to reports by the United Nations. Punks for Palestine concerts in Los Angeles, California, were quickly organized in an effort to stop the war and bring attention to the suffering of Palestinians.

PUNKS FOR PALESTINE—EXTINCTION

JM: Tell me about the Punks for Palestine concert in Los Angeles on November 5, 2023, just one month after the October 7th Hamas attack on Israel and Israel's military response.

ABDULLAH EL-KHATIB (Inqirad): The Punks for Palestine concert was definitely a step in the right direction for the scene. My friend Jezel told Kristine (Nevrose) of S.O.H. (System of Hate) about Inqirad and it just fit and we ended up raising a lot of funds. It felt liberating and I felt at home at the first concert. The support was phenomenal and I felt extremely welcome. Inqirad is the Arabic word for "Extinction" and I chose that name for our band to portray the struggle of my people and how Zionists and the Western world view us as subhuman and condone our extinction. It's important for me to express my Arabic tongue in my art and performance.

JM: Punk musicians have a long history of protesting racism, sexism, war and capitalism. Do you see the Punks for Palestine concerts as part of that lineage?

ABDULLAH EL-KHATIB (Inqirad): Of course! In essence all those issues exist in Palestine as well as the occupation of Palestine being its own topic. If you're fighting racism you have to fight for Palestine. At Inqirad's second show I talked about the struggles of my people. Most people didn't believe me when I was talking about how schools and hospitals are being bombed! As a Palestinian Arab the idea of Palestine never escapes you and you're taught about the resistance since birth.

JM: Were you already doing things related to Palestine before October 7, 2023?

KRISTINE NEVROSE (System of Hate): I'm obsessed with travel and in 2019 I went to Palestine. My whole world changed, just from being on the other side. I also met people in the punk scene in Israel and I was asking a lot of questions. I was very curious: "Why is there a wall?" and "What's going on here?" They all had the same answer: "Well, we feel safer." Their answers were very disappointing.

Also, me and my girlfriend went there together and she was born in Saudi Arabia. At the airport in Israel, I had never experienced such strange reactions. We got detained. They kept asking us about our religion and, "What are you planning on doing here?" It was three hours of being detained for no reason. I already felt prejudice. Then when we went to Palestine—because you have to cross the border to go to Bethlehem—it was a game changer. My life changed from seeing life there. I was crying the whole time thinking, "I can't believe this is what Palestine is."

We were taking pictures of the art and I remember going back to the airport in Israel, because you have to fly out of Tel Aviv. It was the worst; they broke my friend's camera. They were like, "Why do you have this image?" We had to dumb down the way we talked. We were like, "What? We didn't know! We just liked the bird!" It was a picture of a pigeon with a cross, like a target, and it said, "Free Palestine." We said, "We just thought it was a pretty bird." They threw away the camera! It was really bad. From there, I was more interested in traveling to places with different socio-economic classes. I recently went to the DMZ and saw a little bit of North Korea. I've been obsessed with other cultures and governments and how blessed, fortunate and privileged we are living here. (US)

JM: When the Berlin Wall came down in 1989 the cynical side of me thought, "Germany shouldn't destroy the wall; there will be another country that wants to build a wall soon enough and they should sell it to them." In 2002 Israel began building a wall to separate Palestinian people from the Jewish state of Israel. That wall is even taller and longer than the Berlin Wall.

KRISTINE NEVROSE (Systems of Hate): I've seen the Berlin Wall and the Israel wall is *way* bigger than the Berlin Wall! At the Berlin Wall you could see the other side by the naked eye versus with the wall in Palestine, you can't figure out what's on the other side. It's very tall. We had a driver (in Palestine) and he was around my age, mid-thirties. He was a musician, too. He told me, "You're so lucky. I've never played music outside of Palestine. I wouldn't even know how. Israel sees us as a big problem." He was so sweet.

I didn't know how intense the Israeli government was on them until we were driving around and I said, "Hey, let's go get some dessert." And he's like,

"Well, I don't have the Internet right now." And I was like, "What do you mean you don't have the Internet?" He said, "We have to go to a specific zone." I was like, "What does that mean?" I thought, "Oh my gosh, it's real intense here." We had to drive to a specific area called "a zone" where they had Internet.

He also told us they don't have enough water and only have specific food. I just never knew of this world! That's why I'm now so involved in Palestine, because I'm so obsessed with how governments are even allowed to do this. You see the IDF (Israeli Defense Forces) and they've got huge guns walking around and I can't imagine living in a community where there's just so much Big Brother going on. They're watching you doing everything. There's absolutely no freedom for Palestinians.

JM: Tell me about helping to organize Punks for Palestine concerts in Southern California.

KRISTINE NEVROSE (System of Hate): The first Punks for Palestine concert on November 5, 2023, happened at First Street Billiards (Los Angeles). It was so awesome! At first, we were like, "We don't have any money to throw a huge event like this." So, I messaged my friend Marco who owns that place and he was like, "I'm 'gonna donate some extra security and the sound guys. So, don't even worry about it." It was just open arms. He even donated money from the bar! We had to scramble everything very fast. I wanted our band to play so that we can get people going, even if we get hate. A lot of our songs are political and it wouldn't make sense to *not* play for something like this. A band called D.O.V.E. played and also a political-anarcho band called City Kings whose singer is Persian. We wanted to have Middle-Eastern folk and the main headliners were a Palestinian band called Inqirad. They weren't even active at the time, which is funny. My friend Abdullah (El-Khatib) is the singer and he said, "I don't know if we can play; we don't have a drummer." And I was like, "My boyfriend will play! He'll learn the songs. We have to get you out there so we can hear your experience as a Palestinian man."

JM: It seems like very few punk bands have been speaking out against the current war in Gaza that started eight months ago. (May 2024)

KRISTINE NEVROSE (System of Hate): It's been interesting. There's a lot of people who are silent and I'm disappointed, especially in the punk community. All we talk about is fighting all these rules and standing up for what's right. It is wild how there's not a lot of people putting in that effort. What we did for Punks for Palestine was beautiful. Once we saw what happened after October 7th we were like, "We need to do something quick!" In my very optimistic brain, I thought, "We need to help them *now* because it's going to be too late. We can't wait two months or six months. We need to do it now!" So, we scrambled and I messaged all the promoters in Los Angeles, "Please, let's organize something big."

I met some people who are in Palestine and asked, "What's the best organization to send money to?"—because you don't want to just trust the Red Cross. They said, "You have to choose ANERA." American Near East Refugee Aid. So, even if it doesn't get into Palestine, it still goes to refugees in the Middle East and that's what's going to happen when they're all displaced. We raised $10,000 from a small community that is mostly marginalized brown folk who are working class. It was so beautiful to see everyone work together. There were vendors making their own stuff and putting it in a raffle. Everyone just throwing in, it was really beautiful.

NO CARE

أنا زي الأسد ما عندي فريسى I'm like a lion, but I have no prey
عقلي سار قنبلة نووية My mind has become an atom bomb
مافي اهتمام مافي أهمية There is care there is no interest
بس هالجسد الي كلو ذرية Only this body full of atoms

—"No Care" by Inqirad (2021)

JM: Tell me about the song "No Care." An interesting line for me is, "You'll only grow if you are safe."

ABDULLAH EL-KHATIB (Inqirad): The song "No Care" was from one of the first poems I wrote some years ago in Arabic and it was my first time performing. I went to a poetry night and read it in Arabic. That line basically talks about the struggles my people's children have and how reduced our life spans are due to the conflict in Palestine. Life has always been a struggle in the occupied territory of Palestine even before October 7th. The conflict remains a huge issue in the Arabic dream. I don't view it as only a war, but it is also a genocide. (2024) It's an attempt to completely eradicate Palestinians. But the current international pro-Palestinian protests for humanity and the preservation of Palestine as a sovereign state make me hopeful that we will see a free Palestine in my lifetime.

I am a first-generation Arab-American. I was born in Massachusetts, but I was raised in Jordan. I'm half Jordanian and half Palestinian. My father and his father were born in Palestine and I'm from the city of Hebron. My dad was displaced in the war of 1967 along with my grandmother, grandfather and uncle. "Angel of Death" is a song about a hallucination I had as a kid. The words I'd hear from it growing up were very critical and brutal.

I'm unaware of any punk bands emerging from Palestine or Gaza although I believe they need it the most over there. The only interactions I had with Israeli punks were racist and genocidal. There does exist pro-Palestine Israeli punks but I had experiences with Zionist "antifa" that claim Palestinians are terrorists. One of them called me a "patriotic dog."

لما كنت صغير، لما كنت سبع اسنين When I was young, when I was 7 years old
ايجاني ملك الموت The Angel of Death came to me
قال إلي شو رح يسير في اسرائيل And told me what will happen in Israel
ما صدقته I didn't believe him
بس هو كان صحيح But he was right

—"Angel of Death" by Inqirad

ABDULLAH EL-KHATIB (Inqirad): Emotions brought up by this conflict are valid and are a very important part in harnessing the resistance. Having a calm mind is important in the face of the oppressor, but how can we have a calm mind when we are being displaced and slaughtered in a genocide? The anger in punk has always spoken to me; it's a very important part of my healing process and gives me room to express myself fully.

JM: It seems so strange that three major religions grounded in the Middle East—Islam, Judaism and Christianity—all preach love and kindness, yet the area is a warzone. Any thoughts on religion, extremism and violence?

ABDULLAH EL-KHATIB (Inqirad): It's wild because all three of those religions worship the same entity (Allah). I think it's a very shitty thing to use religion as an excuse for violence and war. Ever since the Abrahamic religions surfaced there has always been conflict and lots of bloodshed. It's not necessarily the religions themselves but how they are weaponized against those they were to protect. Organized religion has its drawbacks and I fully believe religion shouldn't have its effect on politics. I'm an apostate but I used to be very into Islam and went on pilgrimage to Mecca twice as a Muslim. Inqirad is anti-Islam, and I condemn Islam and my experience with it in my songs. Spirituality in the Arab and Muslim world is vital to its existence. I myself am an apostate and I lack the connection between punk and Islam. Spirituality is freeing and so is punk, so that's why they go hand in hand.

MUSIC SOOTHES MY SOUL

JM: Do you practice meditation, prayer or contemplation?

ABDULLAH EL-KHATIB (Inqirad): Out of the three, I practice contemplation. Music soothes my soul and it is its own experience. I use it as a way to express myself, especially through words. The idea of God serves its purpose in answering the unknown that every human being deals with and thinks about. In Gaza it has been helpful to give people something to hope for and a guarantee when they die as martyrs. I'm not spiritual, nor is Inqirad. In cases like Gaza, the people are connected with their belief in Allah and it has saved many lives from the troubles of the occupation.

JM: What's happening in Gaza is happening so many places where people have been displaced. People around the world are saying, "We want to live free and we don't want rules imposed on us." There was a genocide here in the United States and now there's discussions among indigenous people worldwide of, "How do we get land back?" We'll have to see what different strategies people use in different places.

KRISTINE NEVROSE (System of Hate): So many different practices. A lot of people are like, "Screw Thanksgiving!" The education that America has taught us is ingrained in us. For example, 9/11—as a kid, they're like, "Can you believe these terrorists did this? Now we're 'gonna go and kill them." And we're like, "Yeah!" Now I'm older and realize, "We were totally brainwashed into thinking that was okay for the US military to do that." I heard it was even worse in Iraq and Afghanistan (than the 2024 Israel/Gaza war) where they were going door to door. Nobody had that captured (on video) because nobody had that technology. Now we can see what's happening in Gaza. That's why I think there's going to be a change. I have big hopes that we are going to see a free Palestine in our generation.

KRISTINE NEVROSE (System of Hate): I got time to volunteer at the UCLA Gaza encampments and help people that were experiencing second-degree burns from the mace. That felt really good to help. That's more fulfilling than a bigger paycheck. What pissed me off is that a bunch of us healthcare providers got donations of Albuterol and Epinephrine, medications that run about $100 a pop. We had boxes and boxes but once the cops came in, they threw it all in the trash. The cops are aggressors; there's no other reason why they're there. But it was still a beautiful experience to see a community resist and build their camps. It was cool.

JM: After October 7th, the pro-Palestinian and anti-war movements gained momentum at universities across the world. In Los Angeles and here in Santa Cruz (California), there were student encampments and then the police came in. Have you been involved in the protests?

ETAY LEVY (Nekhei Naatza): Protests, yes. The UCLA thing? No. I'm kind of sad I wasn't there because it was kind of a riot on the part of the pro-Israeli supporters that came and started beating people with sticks. I would have loved to have been there. We're not involved in the shows but I've been to protests here in LA, definitely.

FEDERICO GOMEZ (Nekhei Naatza / Dir Yassin): I was so surprised to come into Los Angeles and see so many pro-Palestinian activists and graffiti. Same thing in Europe. I live in Sweden and I never saw so much support for the Palestinians as now.

JM: I've interviewed punk bands in Los Angeles who have organized Punks for Palestine concerts after October 7, 2023. Are there any concerts or events like this in Israel?

ISHAY BERGER (Useless ID): *Very* few. To be honest the amount of money that's being raised at these events is usually laughable—I would know after thirty years of playing and organizing shows here. While it is a cool cause and looks rad on paper, the actual result is close to nothing. I do know this runs deeper than money but at the same time, being a realist, it's probably more about *show the world and shock the local patriots* than about sending real help.

JM: Do you think there is an impulse for human beings to live free?

KRISTINE NEVROSE (System of Hate): Of course! Even when I was young, I felt this. My parents separated and my dad lived in the Philippines and my mom lived in America. My dad moved here when I was nine and told us, "We're in this religion now called Iglesia ni Cristo." I was like, "What?" It's this hardcore religious cult in the Philippines. When they were educating me on the different rules in this church I was like, "Absolutely not! I'm not going to follow this!" I was nine. At the same time, I didn't want to speak back because it was very hardcore. This religion is related to the government in the Philippines. It's a cult. Men and women sit separately, you couldn't say certain things and you couldn't date people outside of this cult. When I was twelve, I was like, "I'm getting the hell out of here." My mom said, "You're too young to be having this kind of idea." I said, "I think freedom is just instinctual." You can tell what feels right. That's why I'm really big on freedom and even religious freedom. Just because ideas are ingrained or you grew up in a specific religion doesn't mean you have to follow those rules. I think everyone has that instinct for freedom from the very beginning.

JM: Do you have any spiritual practices or are you more anti-religion?

KRISTINE NEVROSE: My religion is finding out who you are. Because after I got out of my cult with my family, I had to figure that out for myself. In my cult they were like, "This is the only religion that's going to heaven." Later, I went to different churches and realized, "Wait a minute! They all say the same thing!" My favorite change of life was when I went to India, to this place called the Golden Temple. I realized, "This temple feeds and shelters people for free. I'm confused!" I was in this religion where you just give money every Sunday and I've never seen a religion like the Sikh religion that gave back to the community directly. I got obsessed with this idea that people outside of a certain religion are going to hell, even indigenous folk. How are they going to hell? I'm like, "No way! It's not so black and white!" I'm more about spirituality and communicating with nature. I'm just about the sun and the moon and being one with Mother Earth.

"WHERE WERE YOU ON 9/11?"
HARAM

Figure 23.1 Nader Haram from New York–based band Haram on August 3, 2018, at Pickathon Music Festival in Happy Valley, Oregon. "Being spiritual is breaking away from the hive mentality of religion. I don't answer to anyone and I live on my own terms." Photo by Tojo Andrianarivo.

This is the first record that's made me cry.

—Ali Tadayon for MaximumRocknRoll
—August, 2019 review of EP by Haram titled
وين كنيت بي ٩ / ١١ ؟ Where Were You on 9/11?

Middle Easterners have never really found a place within the hardcore punk and metal communities to embrace their heritage. Unfortunately in a post-9/11 status quo, Middle Easterners have often found themselves hiding their ethnic background in the hopes of not being targeted for abuse and persecution. A friend of mine once remarked that "being Middle Eastern in the punk scene is a lonely existence."

—"The Struggle Goes on for Haram and Middle Easterners
in Punk" by James Khubiar
(CLRVYNT October 28, 2016)

Fifteen years ago today, we as New Yorkers were exposed to the darkness that already existed in this world. But we have grown and we are strong!

—Nader Haram at September 11, 2016 Haram concert
in Brooklyn

"Dead" is a word that describes a body which lacks mind and spirit. How can we consider Islām a vibrant, living religion if it stresses the rituals that we must partake, while neglecting our spiritual and intellectual existence? Perhaps it's time to revive them. Perhaps that will enable us to recognize God's beauty around us.

—*Being Muslim Today* by Saqib Iqbal Qureshi
(Rowman & Littlefield, 2024, page 106)

Nader Haram is the singer for New York hardcore punk band Haram. His parents both fled the 1980s civil war in Lebanon and moved to Yonkers, New York, where Nader was born. He was in the fifth grade when the 9/11 attacks happened at the World Trade Center, killing almost 3,000 people. That day he was singled out at his Catholic elementary school, taken to the principal's office and interrogated about his family, their travels to Lebanon and their Islamic religious practices. "Totally inappropriate questioning for a ten-year-old," he recalls.

Haram released their first EP titled *What Do You See?* in 2016 followed by *When You Have Won You Have Lost* (2017) and ٩/ ١١٩؟ وين كنيت بي *Where Were You on 9/11?* (2019). In 2016 the FBI and the New York Police Department investigated the band and interrogated Nader about the possibility of ties between the band's images and lyrics and the militant Islamic terrorist group ISIS. Nader later learned that an undercover police officer had attended Haram shows in New York City. Nader was also the singer for the band I-SO from 2021–2023.

FREEDOM IS NEARLY IMPOSSIBLE

JM: In what ways do punk rock and spirituality go together for you?

NADER HARAM (Haram / I-SO): I grew up Shia Muslim and was born to Lebanese immigrants. For me, being spiritual and religious feels more of an ingrained mentality that exists alongside punk in my identity. It's important to me to have hope, and for me hope is why we play punk. We hope and fight for a better world. We hope that there is more to life than being witnesses of violence and bloodshed in the world. It goes hand in hand.

JM: Do you view punk and Islam as both moving toward liberation and living free?

NADER HARAM (Haram / I-SO): I think truly being free in the year 2024—by my definition of freedom—is nearly impossible. We live in a society and country that systematically oppresses based on class, race and income. What is being free? I challenge people to answer that. My kind of freedom isn't achievable within these bounds. We won't see a world of general equality anytime soon. About ten years ago I decided to fight against that through music and lifestyle or die trying. I'll fight for a place for my own people through music and activism and my music is a threat in its own way. Singing in a foreign language already makes you a threat; singing in Arabic makes you dangerous. I like to double down on that and push the boundaries of expression and challenge audiences, authority and my peers in that way. Islam has had little progression and I also fight for a more accepting form of the faith. It's a beautiful set of beliefs but it's unfortunately plagued by archaic ideologies, those of which are shared by the other monotheistic religions.

JM: Punk rock can often be loud, intense and aggressive. Spirituality is often viewed as calm, compassionate and quiet. How do these realms go together?

NADER HARAM (Haram / I-SO): Being loud and aggressive gets you nowhere without purpose. You can't achieve purpose without being calm, and you can't achieve calm without being compassionate, accepting. I've lived through hell and without the people in my life that helped me get through it, I could not balance these two worlds. Aggression is rage but with spirituality you can control it and learn to express it in a meaningful way. That's what I do.

JM: You've said that Islamic prayer relaxes you. Do you think it's possible and helpful to be calm for the revolution?

NADER HARAM (Haram / I-SO): What revolution? I don't think we will get anywhere without violence, which I don't advocate for, but historically on this Earth real change has only been brought on with violence. Including the founding of the United States. Maybe more blood than has ever been spilled before. It's just the truth if you look at history. I don't think it's possible to be calm for a revolution.

JM: Do you practice a form of meditation, prayer or contemplation?

NADER HARAM (Haram / I-SO): Yeah, I pray in the Muslim tradition. We are supposed to pray five times a day but I usually just do it once at the end of the day. I don't really follow any of the rules; I just do what works for me in my life. It's ingrained in my lifestyle since I was a child. It helps me keep some sort of blind faith and hope that things will get better.

JM: Tell me why you left the Muslim faith as a kid. And how does Islam support your life, music and creativity now?

NADER HARAM (Haram / I-SO): Islam is such a limiting religion when put in the context of growing up in New York my whole life. I didn't have the same upbringing as everyone else. I was limited in what I can do, emotionally and physically. I hit a point in my young adulthood where I wanted to rebel and experience all the things I was kept from; drugs, sex and rock and roll. Eventually in my late twenties, I revisited the faith in a time of extreme hardship in my life. It was always there but I was so frustrated with it because of how much it ruined my childhood. Now I turned it into something I can express, and that's what I do in music. It's hard for most people to understand but my brand of music brought me close to those people who had the same experiences. Islam in my life now is on my terms, so a bastardization. Most Muslims would say it's the "Haram" way of practicing. Though I would reply that only Allah can judge me, and He knows why I do what I do.

SCREAM ABOUT IT

JM: You've said that you could've easily become a fundamentalist, but chose music and art instead. Tell me about that. And do you view music as a form of nonviolent action as opposed to violence?

NADER HARAM (Haram / I-SO): I talk about this subject a lot because for some reason people think that fundamentalists aren't human. Like they lose their humanity as soon as they become violent and kill. What led them to that? It's rage and frustration, loss of innocence, trauma, exposure to violence. The violent cycle. Western media just loves to demonize and profile. There's reasons why people become fundamentalist. They are wrong for it in the end, though I understand it. I was there and I say that often. I was filled with rage and sadness. I had no outlet and I was raised in a way in my environment in this country with bullying and racial abuse. I could have easily turned to violence to fill the void. Music can serve as an outlet and that's what I advocate for. Take all your emotions and scream about it, sing about it, dance. Others will come and talk to you; demand their attention through nonviolent means.

JM: It seems so strange that these three major religions—Islam, Judaism and Christianity—all preach love and kindness yet the Middle East is a war zone. Any thoughts on religion, extremism and violence?

NADER HARAM (Haram / I-SO): Religion can take over people's minds in a powerful way. It just completely turns people blind. They just see opposition. It's like a primitive form of a sports team rivalry. I don't fully understand it; it has always troubled me. Some people love to hate the differences between them. I stay away from organized religion.

HARAM ... IS HARAM

JM: Tell me about the name you chose for your band—Haram.

NADER HARAM (Haram / I-SO): Haram is the word for "forbidden" in Arabic. Haram in Islam is used as a label to forbid believers in doing certain things. For example, drinking alcohol is Haram, drugs are Haram. The easiest way to say this is everything about Haram. . . is Haram. And I realized that the first year we were a band, that performing music in this way, with me singing in Arabic in the way I do, is sacrilegious and threatening, taboo. Everything about it was Haram. So, it only made sense to call the band simply Haram.

JM: I think singing in Arabic was important for you when you played with Haram. And then singing in English felt more powerful and authentic in I-SO. Tell me about this change.

NADER HARAM (Haram / I-SO): I-SO in the time of this interview has stopped playing. (2024) We played for about two years from 2021–23 and wrote one record. I loved that band and everyone in it. It was the first time I sang in English. It took me out of this comfort zone that I felt I was in with singing in Arabic. I created a world that I got comfortable in. I really loved the challenge. I love challenging myself. I'm focused on Haram again now. I always tell people, if you want to know what the pandemic years were like for me mentally, listen to I-SO.

JM: What's the difference for you between spirituality and organized religion?

NADER HARAM (Haram / I-SO): Being spiritual is breaking away from the hive mentality of religion. I don't answer to anyone and I live on my own terms. I take and extract what I want from multiple faiths and live that way. It's a way out of the disturbing cultish way some religions operate. I don't want anything to do with that again.

WHERE WERE YOU ON 9/11?

JM: Tell me about your experience as a ten-year-old kid on 9/11 in NYC and being questioned by a school officer. And then much later naming a Haram album *Where Were You on 9/11?*

NADER HARAM (Haram / I-SO): I was in fifth grade when 9/11 happened. All I remember is the teacher telling me that the principal said that my mom was coming to get me and to wait in the office for her. I had no idea what was going on. When I got to the office there was an officer that taught us DARE classes and the principal standing there. The officer sat down and asked me what my parents did at home, if I was forced to pray at home, what we did when we visited Lebanon. Totally inappropriate questioning for a ten-year-old. I remember feeling so confused and troubled. It must have been around noon and my mother eventually picked me up and told me what was happening. That was the day I lost my innocence and became a troubled boy. It was the first time I felt anxiety in my life, worry, fear of authority. It set me up for who I am and what I do today. The album *Where Were You on 9/11?* is about that question. Everyone has a story from that day; it was a collective trauma we all share. And the record goes into that, and my story personally.

JM: Tell me about being questioned by NYPD and the Joint Terrorism Task Force regarding Haram. How did they treat you and what did they ask?

NADER HARAM (Haram / I-SO): They came to my house a few months after the Haram demo came out (2016). They called me and said they were at my parent's house which was the address on my license at the time. My parents had called me endlessly and I just had no idea what was happening. They asked if they could come meet me at my apartment. They pulled up; it was two of them. They said they were from the JTTF (Joint Terrorism Task Force) and had some questions and asked if they could come inside and I said, "Not without a warrant." So, we sat on the steps and talked. They seemed surprised that I wasn't a jihadi archetype looking person. They kept commenting on my tattoos and piercings. ISIS was the popular brand of jihadism at the time in the world so they had asked why the demo color was "ISIS colors" because the demo was in black and white. Why do I wear a headband with Arabic? If I believed in Islam and if I felt violent urges. They eventually left when I said, "I don't want to talk anymore without a lawyer." I didn't hear back from them. From my own legal work, I've learned there's a pretty big case file on me, which I don't care much about. They continue to harass me when they want.

JM: Were you influenced at all by Bad Brains and their ideas around Positive Mental Attitude (PMA)? Any influences from punks or bands that connect with spirituality?

NADER HARAM (Haram / I-SO): Not really. I love Bad Brains and all the old-school punk bands were a huge part of my upbringing. Bad Brains are kind of weird and homophobic now; the spirituality seems to have backfired into bigotry, which is sad. Their music is very influential and I hope they can change their current mentalities and be more accepting.

WAR IN GAZA—HELL ON EARTH

JM: What are your thoughts about the Israeli war in Gaza now and the possibilities of a free Palestine?

NADER HARAM (Haram / I-SO): The war in Gaza is hell on Earth. 40,000 plus people are dead, half of which are children. (June, 2024) I am gutted everyday and my life goal is to preach about their martyrdom. If there is anything to be punk for, to sing for, to be political for, to be radical for—this is the time. We will have a free Palestine in my lifetime. Fuck Israel and the IDF, and the United States for supporting the colonizing genocide-committing maniacs. They will pay in time. I'm happy for those on the right side of history!

JM: Are you connected with any protests against the Gaza war and "Punks for Palestine" events and concerts?

NADER HARAM (Haram / I-SO): Yes, of course. I can't speak on this much but yes, I am always involved in anything remotely radical, anarchist or punk, especially Arabic punk. You'll find me where those things are.

JM: Do you know any punk bands in Palestine or Israel? Or punk bands in Lebanon or other Muslim countries?

NADER HARAM (Haram / I-SO): I used to know about a band called Detox in Lebanon. And there was once a time where Haram was supposed to play a show in Israel with a band that had reached out. We have plans to go to the Middle East. You'll have to get back in touch with me! Until next time.

24

"LIFE IS A GIGANTIC MYSTERY"
IMPERMANENCE/DEATH/PARADOX/FORGIVENESS

Life is something deeper than our ability to conceive it.

—Mark Andersen (Positive Force DC)

Life is a gigantic mystery. We don't know where we came from, we don't know where we are and we're living on a rock that's orbiting around a ball of fire. I find that inconceivably bizarre!

—Glenn Branca (Theoretical Girls)

People can be out to get you and life can still be an opportunity. Know what I mean? The bear wants to eat you, but on the other hand it's beautiful to be in the woods.

—Peter Case (The Nerves / The Plimsouls)

MARK ANDERSEN (*Dance of Days* / Positive Force DC): The search for truth is one of my key concepts in terms of spirituality. Another is mystery because mystery is so much of what we encounter in the world. We find ourselves in what could be a great comedy or a great tragedy or some mix thereof. We know so little about what is ultimately true *and* we have to take a stand in each moment of our lives. The only way I can resolve that is to understand that this is a process. We take a stand or make a choice and then we reflect upon that choice out of the experience that ensues. Hopefully that will help us make a decision next time that is more in line not only with our values, but with *ultimate* values. I don't think truth measures one end of the spectrum and another end of the spectrum and then fits itself right in between those two extremes. Having said that, whenever you find a significant group of people holding a certain position, you can be certain there's something there that you need to reckon with. Striking the balance is always critical, to find what is truthful or authentic including in positions that you might not agree with. Truth is truth. It doesn't respect the ideological categories that humans construct.

GLENN BRANCA (Theoretical Girls): Life is a gigantic mystery. We don't know where we came from, we don't know where we are and we're living on a rock that's orbiting around a ball of fire. I find that inconceivably bizarre! I try not to think about it too much. When I was very young, I remember going to New Hampshire where the sky was absolutely dark and you could see the whole sky at night. It freaked me out! All of those stars and many of them aren't stars, they're galaxies. It was too much for me to handle. I admit I was stoned at the time, but still.

For any of us to think we can understand this is ridiculous. I believe that the world and reality are in a constant state of change. What may be true this minute may not be true the next minute. I don't believe in any kind of absolutism. What's true now may not be true the next time. If you look into the study of logic, it's a gigantic mess. Paradox is the real truth! Which means the real truth is that there is no truth! All I want to do, for the moment I'm here, is to be totally honest the best I can. Just to do something really interesting and exciting as good as I can possibly do it. That's all I imagine any of us can really do. Then of course, you've got politics and a world that is in a gigantic mess. We might as well be living in the dark ages. It's a horrible, disgusting, sickening place with evil people doing ugly things to other people! I feel embarrassed to have to be part of this world. But it's the only choice I've got! It's a lot of what my music's about; a shout-out. It's the way I feel. So many people are suffering—how can we tolerate that?

PETER CASE (The Nerves / The Plimsouls): I just had a heart operation (2009) I was in a situation where I had to really seriously think about my own death. All of these different things go by. I found it really useful to read William Blake right before I had this operation—*The Songs of Innocence*. The viewpoint is basically that the universe is a good place. You come down to thinking: "Is life evil? Is that the basic message here, that it's everyone for themselves and life is just brutal? Or is there some sort of caring concept in the universe?" You have to answer that for yourself. I think a lot of that has to do with what your experience has been. But also, your imagination. Because you can have a terrible experience and a great imagination and begin to sense that there's other things going on.

JM: I hope you're recovering well from the surgery and feeling healthy.

PETER CASE (The Nerves): Yeah, I'm doing great. It was a super trip, though. I had a couple of really dark nights. I felt like I'd been run over by a train. I faced death so close. I had this one procedure that went awry and I was about to have a major heart attack and they just happened to have a crew around that could take me in and do this really radical bypass surgery, on about twenty minutes' notice. When I came out of it, I was really beat up. I went through some real dark nights. It was good in a way because you see life as an incredible opportunity. People can be out to get you *and* life can *still* be an opportunity. Know what I mean? The bear wants to eat you, but on the other hand it's beautiful to be in the woods.

EVERYTHING IS THE GARDEN OF EDEN

PENNY RIMBAUD (Crass): After ten years of serious meditation practice, I'm beginning to feel like you're either in the material world or you're not. I visit it. I do whatever I can within it, which is never much fun, really, and then I get out of it, to where things have some intrinsic value. Of course, we're in the material world when we're doing something like this (interview) because it's the only thing available to us if we want to communicate. I increasingly believe that we can communicate much deeper in other ways. But that's another story altogether.

In a less developed and practiced way, that was the position I took within Crass. That was my role. We didn't assign roles, but as it progressed I could see the reflection of my own thinking coming through. We weren't just talking about external things. We were talking about deeper feelings, resonances and the culture of nature rather than the culture of materialism. It's a Taoist approach. I didn't know a great deal about Taoism back in the punk days but it was resonating because I've always loved nature. Nature is where I've wanted to be rather than at a party down the road. I'd prefer to sit in a tree for the night than be bored by someone talking about what's on television. Or second-hand ideas. You don't get second-hand ideas from an oak tree. You just get deep resonance. I'm only interested in the deep resonance. And in that we're all lovers and everything is the Garden of Eden.

JM: I enjoyed what you wrote about paradox in your book: "To me, the key to an authentic life is being able to live in the paradox, that rich, real, demanding and rewarding place. For example, I believe in the Situationist revolution of everyday life."

MARK ANDERSEN (*Dance of Days* / Positive Force DC): You could argue that there is a Marxist way of dealing with paradox. The different ideas and forces contend with one another and then what emerges out of them—the thesis versus the antithesis creating a synthesis—is stronger and more true. That's one of the ways changes happen in our world. I also think that's partly how we advance spiritually. Living with paradox is an essential reality that flows out of our encounter with mystery because whatever idea system we lean upon to try to find meaning and direction in our own lives, if we're honest we will notice how not everything in the world corresponds with our belief system. There are always places where something just doesn't fit or actually provides a very challenging counter-example. This is to say that life is something deeper than our ability to conceive it. It doesn't mean that you don't want to engage the question. As I just suggested, that's why we're alive. That's the essence of living; we're engaging the world and ourselves and challenging our truths and those of others.

Paradox is real. Everywhere you go you encounter it. Sometimes it's as obvious as someone who lives their life propounding one thing but actually doing something entirely different. I could mention names like Ted Haggard (former pastor—New Life Church) but that would be a little unfair. I could easily mention my own name. Or I could mention St. Paul from the Christian tradition. That's one of the things he writes in his epistles: "The thing that I despise is what I do."

JM: What about the paradox of connecting punk and spirituality?

MARK ANDERSEN (*Dance of Days* / Positive Force DC): Punk rock and spirituality—how could these things be connected? It does seem paradoxical. Certainly, a lot of what drew me to punk in the beginning was its brutally blasphemous tone. I literally remember causing my mom to cry because of some of the things I said. We were from a very deeply religious family and that roar of raw truth-telling, blasphemy or obscenity would seem to be the antithesis of the spirit, as I was taught what the spirit was. Patti Smith articulated this well in an interview where she was saying that blasphemy is actually a way of exploring the spiritual. You want to test the limits and challenge the accepted truths because it's part of the spiritual journey.

MATT CLEAVER (Stalin's War): Buddhism goes much further to finding truth. Even our best science is based upon what we can perceive of the natural world. We've evolved from single-celled organisms to having these five senses. Beyond that we have no conception of what the world is. Scientific analysis is based on one of our sensory perceptions. An example is astronomy; we know there is water on the third moon of Saturn because we see certain elements reflect a certain color of light and we use that to judge what's on that moon, but we can't see it firsthand. A big lesson I've gotten out of Buddhism is *what is real?* Without my perception of it, does this table really exist? That takes the question of reality much further. That's where a lot of spirituality comes in. One thing about Buddhism that I was really drawn to, is that it doesn't say you can't use logic or reasoning, it encourages you to question without end. Question absolutely everything!

JM: I heard you're Buddhist. The Dalai Lama was asked by scientists if Buddhism has any problem with the big bang theory of how the universe began and he said, "No problem, it just wasn't the *first* big bang."

ADELE WILSON (The Slits): It's not really possible for us to understand how many universes there are or how many big bangs there were or to really understand the concept of time, in terms of our lives. We can't even understand how brief our life is for that matter. So, using only our minds we can't really understand the universe or be enlightened. Our minds are limited but, because we're part of the universe, the whole of the universe also exists within us. Not just this universe, but all of them. We're connected and part of it.

JM: I know there was a period where you experienced paranoia and nightmares. How did you deal with the fear and how did this eventually change?

JOHNETTE NAPOLITANO (Concrete Blonde): That was a couple months before 9/11 and I maintain I felt that energy. I've researched that and a lot of people indeed felt that energy. Like when roaches run around before an earthquake. It was very bad, very dark, and when 9/11 happened I understood immediately *that* was what I had been feeling.

JM: It's so interesting to hear that the fear you experienced before 9/11 was a sort of pre-knowledge of events to come. Can you explain a little more about your experience?

JOHNETTE NAPOLITANO (Concrete Blonde): It's too long of a story but I'm no stranger to things like that. Upton Sinclair wrote a very good book called *Mental Radio* about telepathy and he conducted experiments with his wife. Albert Einstein wrote the foreword; he was very into it. I'm very aware that there is a lot going on we can't see and don't understand and I have complete faith in that. I think it's important to find where there *are* consistencies and points that connect between faiths. Too many things have happened to me that cannot be explained, so I have complete faith the universe knows what it's doing, even if we don't.

JM: You've said in some ways you're still paying for your past and you've tried to repair some of that. What has happened when you talk to people about the past?

JACK GRISHAM (TSOL / *A Principle of Recovery: An Unconventional Journey Through the Twelve Steps*): A lot of people don't care. They don't want to hear it. It's very important to learn how you face people you've harmed. You have to be very careful that you don't cause more damage by going back. There's a difference between paying back to serve *me* and paying back to serve *them*—two completely different things. What I've done is taken power from people and I need to give the power back the best way I can. Basically saying, "I wish I would've been a better friend to you. If there's anything I can ever do for you, please let me know." Not bringing up, "I didn't respect you." People don't want to be reminded they were disrespected, so it's a lot of work doing it right. A *lot* of work. Offering friendship to these people is huge.

JM: I'm guessing it takes internal effort of forgiving yourself for those acts in the past, too.

JACK GRISHAM (TSOL): Actually, forgiveness is something that's given and is never discussed; it's over when you say it's over. The beating that I gave myself was over when I was done beating myself. It was forgiven, it was done, it was a new life. So, there is no reason for forgiveness. It's almost like stepping into a different world. The thing was, having people forgive *me* was never a problem. I didn't care enough about *you* to worry about *you* forgiving *me*. Someone being mad at me never hurt me. I didn't give a fuck. But it was all of the hate and resentment that I felt for people that was important. That had to go. I didn't need to be forgiven. I needed to learn forgiveness, which is completely different.

JOHN DOE (X): As we get older, we see less of the differences between things and more of the common ground. Forgiving yourself and trying to experience whatever sadness you come across in your life—whether it's separating from your family or from a loved one—there is no timetable that you can impose. At the same time, the goal is to get through it, accept things and move forward. I guess that's what forgiving yourself is, for whatever you've done that you're not proud of. And forgiving other people for what they may have contributed. You can talk in very flowery terms about all of these great things you can do but putting it into practice is a lot harder. Forgiveness is important in going forward.

RAY CAPPO (Youth of Today / Shelter): Forgiveness is a big part of any spiritual tradition because we want to be forgiven for stuff we've done. We're very quick to note what people have done wrong to us but we're not quick to forgive others. That's the problem. So, in the same way God is forgiving, we also have to be God-like. We have to learn to unearth our resentment. You'll find this in the Eastern spiritual traditions, Christianity and in a twelve-step program. If I'm hanging on to anger or resentment it's ridiculous. Sometimes we resent people that are dead! You think you're punishing them? Who's getting punished? You are!

LIZ LAMERE (Alan Vega (Suicide)'s widow / creative collaborator Alan Vega solo / solo recording artist / SSNUB / Backward Flying Indians): Another constant theme in Alan's work is that there's this dichotomy between shining a light on the harsh realities of life, human nature and the universe and yet there's always this thread of hope. That hope always comes through his work. A lot of people misunderstood Alan and thought he was super doom and gloom, yet he was very enlightened, for lack of a better word. He saw the beauty in life, but he also didn't want to sugarcoat it. What bothered him was when he felt people were putting their head in the sand and not addressing very real issues. Particularly when Suicide was just starting during the Vietnam War, he felt very strongly it was not a righteous battle—not that any war is. War was his muse. He felt that war is not the way to resolve political conflict. We should be protecting our youth and helping them build their futures and not have the powers that be send these kids to get slaughtered. That really bothered him.

People would come in off the street looking to be entertained and he and Marty's whole ethos was, "We're not here to entertain you, we're trying to wake you up." The whole idea of Suicide was really a *societal suicide*. They said, "You're collectively anesthetizing yourself!" He saw a lot of his friends and fellow musicians doing heroin and basically killing themselves with drugs, rather than deal with reality. He was very fearless in facing reality. Not that he never did drugs himself. He experimented with LSD, but he never did it to escape or to destroy himself. It was always with a view toward further enlightenment.

ROB FISH (108): What in life isn't a contradiction? What relationship in our lives doesn't hold contradiction? *If there weren't contradictions, would there be meaningful relationships?* A lot of times I have to give classes or presentations at work. I'll tell people, "Think about the most dear relationship you have and the defining moment in that relationship." Generally, that defining moment comes from a negative experience. And what defines it as an important relationship isn't that it's always perfect without contradiction and bumpy roads. It's how we deal with those contradictions and difficult circumstance that makes one relationship deep and meaningful and another relationship casual or non-existent.

LIZ LAMERE (Alan Vega (Suicide)'s widow / creative collaborator Alan Vega solo / solo recording artist / SSNUB / Backward Flying Indians): Alan was very shy. Getting on stage to him was scary. He was a visual artist first but he was trying to push himself beyond the bounds. Alan was a seeker. He had this incredible, childlike ability to see things as if he's seeing them for the very first time with fresh eyes. I think he had to train himself to do that, right? Because our brains naturally go down the pathways they're used to and we have to consciously make decisions to open up other avenues. He was always challenging himself. Alan used to joke to me, "I'm like the research scientist in the basement." He wasn't doing it for fame and fortune, although he ended up being extremely influential across the board in any artistic, creative pursuit. A big part of that was because he was always throwing out the rulebook.

I went in the recording studio with him for thirty years and the mantra was, "I don't want to know about the manual." We were using all these effects machines that were relatively new and we were pushing buttons and turning knobs. Alan didn't want to find things that could be readily found by opening the manual. I think that's a good analogy for how he lived his life. He wanted to find things that hadn't been discovered before. I believe in the beyond that he is still doing that. It's going to sound crazy, but I still honestly get messages from him when I'm working on music that we recorded together, that I'm now co-producing with Jared Artaud. It's amazing.

Alan felt that there are no mistakes and no expectations and that's an incredibly freeing thing. If you think you don't know what you're doing, that's the best position to be in! Every moment is an opportunity to keep evolving, learning and growing. Every moment, we're living in a different world than we were living in five minutes ago, twenty years ago. Alan held the idea of constant evolution and not knowing. Ric Ocasek (The Cars) used to joke with Alan, "I want to be Alan Vega, free to do whatever I like." Alan would say, "Yeah, but it would be nice to have your money because then I'd be able to keep creating without worrying if I can pay the bills!"

GLENN BRANCA (Theoretical Girls): There is a hell of a lot about this life that we don't know and that we don't understand. I don't care how much the scientists have discovered—and believe me I'm very interested in mathematics and science—but for a scientist to think they've discovered something does not mean that they understand the nature of reality! That's ridiculous! All you have to do is look around and realize that this is beyond our understanding. I personally don't think that any of us have the right to try and tell anyone else what this reality is. I think it's either extremely complex or extremely simple and mundane. But I don't know which one it is, either way around.

JM: There's been a long-time battle between philosophies that focus on either *spiritual* or *material*. Some people believe the physical world is the real world, that we're subject to the forces around us and we don't have free will. This view holds that we are observers of the world and life is something that happens to us rather than something we help create. There's another view that says we create our own experiences through our thoughts and actions and that the physical stuff around us is part of that manifestation. Then there are spiritual philosophies that talk about doing away with all of the duality. What are your thoughts about these realms?

ARI UP (The Slits): (long pause) What are you? Virgo or what?

JM: (*laugh*) Leo.

ARI UP (The Slits): Leo, wow! I didn't expect that. (*laugh*) I think that scientists who say there is nothing spiritual, who say it's all a matter of fact, bang, bang, bang—that's over-the-top extreme. I think the people who are so-called spiritual or religious and think it's just totally about the maker and God; I think *they're* over the top because they're ignoring the science of the universe as well. The scientist ignores the spirit.

NADYA OSTROFF (The Slits / The Home Office): It's also the same when we meet people who think we shouldn't earn any money or have a place to stay that's clean and tidy. They think we should exist on some ethereal plane and just pack down like blow-up dolls! Pop up for gigs and then go down again! We have physical, emotional and spiritual needs that have to be met. The problem with being an artist is that some people think it's like a nunnery or priesthood where you have no material needs.

ARI UP (The Slits): Material needs! (Ari chants in unison with Nadya) Bumboclaat!

NADYA OSTROFF (The Slits / The Home Office): Pop stars get this thing of *I'm only material*. So, you're always walking a line. Always have to balance yourself every single moment of the day.

ARI UP (The Slits): Yin and Yang.

LIST OF INTERVIEWS

Ahrens, Silke (Kirche von Unten)—Email interview, 2024

Allen, Dave (Gang of Four)—In-person and phone interviews, 2003 and 2014

Alyokhina, Masha (Pussy Riot / *Riot Days*)—Skype interview, 2017

Andersen, Mark (Positive Force DC / *Dance of Days*)—Phone & Zoom interviews, 2010 and 2022

Anderson, Micah (Ta'leef Collective)—Phone interview, 2017

Asplund, Christian ("Sacred Music and The Punk Ethic")—Phone interview, 2017

Beeber, Steven Lee (*The Heebie-Jeebies at CBGB's: A Secret History of Jewish Punk*)—Phone Interview, 2010

Bastida, Ceci (Tijuana No!)—Zoom interview, 2022

Belli, Celine (Rotten Ruckus)—Facetime interview, 2024

Benally, Berta (Blackfire / Sihasin—manager) Zoom interview, 2024

Benally, Clayson (Blackfire / Sihasin) Phone interview, 2017 and Zoom 2024

Benally, Jeneda (Blackfire / Sihasin) Phone interview, 2017 and Zoom 2024

Benally, Klee (Blackfire) Phone interview, 2020

Bentley, Jay (Bad Religion) In-person interviews, 2000, 2003 and 2011

Berger, Ishay (Useless ID / Bo Labar / Tabarnak / Shesh Shesh Shesh)—Phone, 2016 and email, 2024

Biafra, Jello (Dead Kennedys / Guantanamo School of Medicine)—Phone interview, 2017

Bhikku, Ajahn Amaro (Buddhist monk, author and meditation teacher)—Zoom interview, 2024

Blush, Steven (*American Hardcore: A Tribal History*) Phone interview, 2020

Bonebrake, D.J. (X)—Phone interview, 2018

Bragg, Billy—Zoom interview, 2020

Branca, Glenn (Theoretical Girls)—Phone interview, 2009

Brannon, Brian (Jodie Foster's Army)—In-person interview, 2017

Burke, Clem (Blondie)—Zoom interview, 2020

Burnham, Hugo (Gang of Four)—In-person and phone interview, 2003 and 2014

Cappo, Ray (Shelter / Youth of Today)—Phone interview, 2007

Carlisle, Belinda (The Go-Go's / The Germs / Black Randy and The Metrosquad)—Phone interview, 2017

Casale, Gerald (Devo)—Zoom interview, 2023

Case, Peter (The Nerves / The Plimsouls)—Phone interview, 2008

Cervenka, Exene (X) Phone interview, 2008

Chancellor, Reid (*Hardcore Anxiety: A Graphic Guide to Punk Rock and Mental Health*)—Email interview, 2020

Chitwood, Ken (Dept. for the Study of Religion at Universität Bayreuth)—Zoom, 2024

Cleaver, Matt (Stalin's War)—Phone interview, 2007

Clements, Joe (Fury 66 / The Deathless)—In-person interview, 2017

Colver, Edward (punk photographer)—In-person interview, 2013

Cooper, Jordan (Revelation Records)—In-person interview, 2007

Corré, Joe ("Burn Punk London")—Phone interview, 2016

D., Chuck (Public Enemy / Prophets of Rage)—In-person interview, 2007

Dictor, Dave (Multi Death Corporation)—Phone interview, 2006

Dinsmore, Clifford (Bl'ast)—In-person interview, 2015

Doe, John (X)—Phone interviews, 2008 and 2009

Ebersole, Stewart (*Barred for Life*)—Phone interview, 2013

Eldred, Jake and Nick (Dun Bin Had) In-person interview, 2009 (Live on Free Radio Santa Cruz)

Elfman, Danny (Oingo Boingo)—Phone interview, 2019

El-Khatib, Abdullah (Inqirad)—Email interview, 2024

Fiebeler, Carsten (*OstPunk! Too Much Future*)—Email interview, 2024

Fish, Rob (108 / Resurrection / Judas Factor):—Phone interview, 2007

Fisher, Sarah (*Meditate & Destroy* film director)—Phone interview, 2006

Flouride, Klaus (Dead Kennedys)—Phone interview, 2010

Fowley, Kim (The Runaways, producer) Phone interview, 2010

Fox, Hardy (The Residents)—In-person interview, 2010

Fujiwara, Hidé (Ultra Bidé)—In-person interview, 2013 (Live on Free Radio Santa Cruz)

Gali, Morning Star (Indigenous Justice)—Zoom interview, 2024

Garcia, Camille Rose (The Real Minx)—Phone interview, 2007

Gill, Andy (Gang of Four)—In-person and phone interviews, 2003, 2015, 2016, 2017

Ginoli, Jon (Pansy Division / *Deflowered*)—Phone interview, 2009

Gomez, Federico (Nekhei Naatza / Dir Yassin)—Phone and email interviews, 2024

Gonzales, Michelle Cruz (Spitboy / *The Spitboy Rule: Tales of a Xicana in a Female Punk Band*)—Phone interview, 2016

Graffin, Greg (Bad Religion)—In-person and phone interviews, 2000, 2003, 2006, 2015, 2016

Grisham, Jack (TSOL)—In-person interview, 2007

Hannah, Chris (Propagandhi)—In-person and phone interviews, 2006 and 2013

Haram, Nader (Haram / I-SO)—Email interview, 2024

Harrison, Jerry (Talking Heads)—Phone interview, 2024

Hauswald, Harald (East Berlin culture/punk photographer)—Email interview, 2025

Heck, Jen (director *The Promised Band: The Story of the First All-Girl Band in Israel and Palestine*)—Zoom interview, 2024

Hitchcock, Robyn (The Soft Boys)—Zoom interview, 2023

Houston, Penelope (The Avengers)—Phone interview, 2010

Ignorant, Steve (Crass / Slice of Life)—Phone interview, 2019

J., David (Bauhaus)—Phone interview, 2003

Jarboe (Swans)—Phone interview, 2019

Jones, Preston (co-author w/ *Greg Graffin Is Belief in God Good, Bad or Irrelevant?*) Phone, 2010

Kanaan, Ramsey (AK Press / Political Asylum)—Phone interview, 2015

Kaye, Lenny (Patti Smith Group)—In-person interview, 2009

Kimball, Dan (The Elephant Boys / *Adventures in Churchland*)—In-person interview, 2013 (Live on Free Radio Santa Cruz)

King, Jon (Gang of Four)—Phone and Zoom interviews, 2015, 2021, 2022

Kirkwood, Cris (Meat Puppets)—Phone interview, 2009 (Live on Free Radio Santa Cruz)

Kleinman, Evan (producer *Punk Jews*)—Phone interview, 2013 (Live on Free Radio Santa Cruz)

Knight, Michael Muhammad (*The Taqwacores*)—Email interview, 2016

Koski, Darius (Swingin' Utters)—Phone interview, 2008

Kuhn, Gabriel (*Sober for the Revolution: Hardcore Punk, Straight Edge & Radical Politics*) Phone interview, 2013

Lamere, Liz (Alan Vega (Suicide)'s widow / creative collaborator Alan Vega solo / solo recording artist / SSNUB / Backward Flying Indians): Zoom, 2024

Landers, Paul (Feeling B / First Arsch / Die Firma / Rammstein)—Email interview, 2024

Langford, Jon (The Mekons)—Phone interview, 2016

Lee, Stan (The Dickies)—In-person interview, 2010

Lester, David (Mecca Normal / Horde of Two)—Zoom interview, 2021

Levine, Noah (*Dharma Punx* / The Deathless)—In-person and phone, 2003, 2011, 2018

Levy, Etay (Nekhei Naatza)—Phone and email interviews, 2024

Lindberg, Jim (Pennywise / *Punk Rock Dad: No Rules Just Real Life*)—Phone, 2007

Logan, Brad (Leftöver Crack)—In-person interview, 2016

Lucas, Dick (Subhumans / Citizenfish)—In-person interviews, 2008 and 2015

Lunch, Lydia (Teenage Jesus and The Jerks / Big Sexy Noise)—Phone interview, 2015

Lydon, John (Sex Pistols / Public Image Limited)—Phone interview, 2019

MacKaye, Ian (Minor Threat / Fugazi / Embrace / Positive Force DC)—Phone interview, 2006 (Live on Free Radio Santa Cruz)

Mann, Jesse Zook (director *Punk Jews*)—Phone interview, 2013 (Live on Free Radio Santa Cruz)

Manzarek, Ray (The Doors / X)—Phone interview, 2013

Marcus, Sara (*Girls to The Front: The True Story of the Riot Grrrl Revolution* / AKA Harlot Number One) Phone interview, 2018

Marić, Goran "Max" (Bjesove)—Snail mail interview, 2008

Martens, China (*The Future Generation*)—Phone interview, 2011

Martinez, Kristen (Observer Syndrome / Indigenous Punks Archive)—Zoom interview, 2024

Mazahua, Yaotl (Iconoclast / Aztlan Underground aka Anahuak Underground)—Email interview, 2024

McKee, DaN (*Anarchist, Athiest, Punk Rock Teacher*)—Email interview, 2024

McKee, Tim (How Punk Rock Saved My Life)—Phone interview, 2013

Meade, Michael ("A Song is a Road" / mythologist)—Phone interview, 2009

Moldt, Dirk (*Kleine Prenzlauer Berg Geschichte* / Fatale)—Email interview, 2024

Moon, H. Paul (*Hamac Caziim*, director)—Email interview, 2024

Moore, Thurston (Sonic Youth)—Phone interview, 2014

Morello, Tom (Rage Against the Machine / Prophets of Rage)—Phone interview, 2003

Morris, Keith (Black Flag / Circle Jerks / Off!)—In-person, 2011

Mothersbaugh, Mark (Devo)—Zoom interview, 2023

Murphy, Jason (Rebel Dharma)—In-person interview, 2008

Muttaqi, Sean (Vegan Reich)—Email interview, 2016

Napolitano, Johnette (Concrete Blonde)—Email interview, 2007

Nawrocki, Norman (Rhythm Activism)—Phone interview, 2012 (Live on Free Radio Santa Cruz)

Ness, Mike (Social Distortion)—Phone interview, 2008

Nevrose, Kristine (System of Hate)—Zoom interview, 2024

Nigh, Adam (Craig's Brother / Too Bad Eugene)—Phone interview, 2010

Nishijima, Gudo Wafu (Zen teacher of *Hardcore Zen* author Brad Warner)—In-person, 2005

Numan, Gary (Tubeway Army)—Zoom interview, 2021

Ostroff, Nadya (The Slits / The Home Office)—In-person interview, 2006

Ott, Jeff (Fifteen)—Phone interview, 2018

Pankonin, Key (Die Firma / Ichfunktion)—Email interview, 2024

Pattex, Patti (Cut My Skin)—Email interview, 2024

Powers, Kid Congo (The Gun Club / The Cramps / Nick Cave and The Bad Seeds) Zoom interview, 2022

Pundik, Jordan (New Found Glory)—Phone interview, 2014

Ramone, C. J. (The Ramones)—Phone interview, 2018

Rankin, Russ (Good Riddance)—In-person and phone interviews, 2006 (Live at Free Radio Santa Cruz) and 2020

Ray, Amy (Indigo Girls / Daemon Records)—In-person and phone interviews, 2003 and 2015

Redondo, Don (Jodie Foster's Army)—In-person interview, 2017

Reed, Tait (Junk Sick Dawn / Noise Clinic / Power Strip)—In-person, 2013 (Live at Free Radio Santa Cruz)

Reeder, Mark (The Frantic Elevators / Die Unbekannten / *B Movie: Lust & Sound in West Berlin 1979-1989*) Email interview, 2018

Reyes, Ron (Black Flag / Piggy)—In-person interview, 2015

Richman, Jonathan (Modern Lovers)—In-person interview, 2008

Robb, John (The Membranes / *Punk Rock: An Oral History*) Zoom interview, 2023

Romanoff, Yishai (Moshiach Oi!)—Email interview, 2014

H.R. Human Rights (Bad Brains)—In-person interview, 2010

Rimbaud, Penny (Crass)—Zoom interviews, 2020 and 2021

Rottstock, Wenke (Kirche von Unten)—Email interview, 2024

Safran, Joshua (*Free Spirit: Growing Up On the Road and Off The Grid*)—Phone interview, 2014 (Live on Free Radio Santa Cruz)

Sane, Justin (Anti-Flag)—Phone interview, 2010

Satrapi, Marjane (*Persepolis*)—FaceTime interview, 2019

Schamal, Mita (Namenlos)—Email and Zoom interviews, 2019 and 2024

Speiche (Gesellschaftliches Fehlverhalten / KvU)—Email interview, 2024

Spheeris, Penelope (*The Decline of Western Civilization / Wayne's World*)—Phone interview, 2007

Spooner, James (Afro-Punk / *The High Desert: Black. Punk. Nowhere*)—Phone interview, 2009

Stand, Mike (The Altar Boys)—Zoom interview, 2024

Stockberger, John (Sense Field)—Phone interview, 2017

Stern, Eddie (Lou Reed's yoga/meditation teacher / Chop Shop)—Zoom interview, 2024

Stewart, Francis (*Punk is My Religion*)—Email interview, 2024

Strom, Moana (Stalin's War)—Phone interview, 2007

Talen, Reverend Billy (The Church of Stop Shopping)—Phone, 2010 (Live on Free Radio Santa Cruz)

Taylor, Joseph Ojo (Undercover)—Phone interview, 2015

Thomas, David (Rocket From the Tombs / Pere Ubu) Phone interview, 2006

Thu Win, Kyaw (Rebel Riot)—Email interviews, 2018 and 2024

Trynka, Paul (*Iggy Pop: Open Up and Bleed*)—Phone interview, 2009

Up, Ari (The Slits)—In-person interview, 2006

Vanderpol, Rikki (Dying for It)—Phone interview, 2018

Voglibonze (Buddhadatta)—Email interview, 2024

Wakeling, Dave (English Beat)—In-person interview, 2007

Wallis, Glenn (Ruin / *An Anarchist's Manifesto*)—Email interviews, 2024

Warner, Brad (*Hardcore Zen* / Zero Defects)—In-person interview, 2007 (Live on Free Radio Santa Cruz)

Wickersham, Jonny (Social Distortion)—Phone interview, 2011

Wild, Chuck (Missing Persons)—Phone interview, 2013

Williamson, James (Iggy and The Stooges)—In-person and phone interviews, 2007 and 2013

Wilson, Adele (The Slits)—In-person interview, 2006

Woods, Lesley (Au Pairs)—FaceTime interview, 2024

Wei, Wu (SMZB)—Email interview, 2021

Zickler, Jörg "Jolly" (Kirche von Unten)—Email interview, 2024

Zoom, Billy (X)—Phone interview, 2008

BIBLIOGRAPHY

BOOKS, FILMS AND ARTICLES

Aardsma Benton, Ruth A. "Punks in the Church: The Relationship Between the Punk Subculture and Church in East Germany." Master's Thesis 2018—Western Michigan University.

Abraham, Ibraham. *Christian Punk: Identity and Performance*. London & New York: Bloomsbury Academic, January 23, 2020.

Anderson, Mark and Mark Jenkins. *Dance of Days: Two Decades of Punk in the Nation's Capital*. New York: Akashic Books, 2001.

Asplund, Christian. "Sacred Music & the Punk Rock Ethic—Faith in Works Lecture Series." Utah: Brigham Young University, December 13, 2017.

Beeber, Steven Lee. *The Heebie-Jeebies at CBGB'S: A Secret History of Jewish Punk*. Chicago: Chicago Review Press, 2006.

Bergland, Jeff, Jan Johnson, and Kimberli Lee, eds. *Indigenous Pop: Native American Music from Jazz to Hip Hop*. Tucson: University of Arizona Press, 2016.

Biel, Joe. *Beyond the Music: How Punks are Saving the World with DIY Ethics, Skills and Values*. Portland: Cantankerous Titles, 2012.

Blumenthal, Sara. "War and Peace: Interview with Moana Strom and Matt Cleaver of Stalin's War." *Mandala Magazine*, 27, June-July, 2006.

Blush, Steven. *American Hardcore: A Tribal History*. Los Angeles: Steven Blush & Feral House, 2001.

Boatwright, Angela. *Los Punks: We Are All We Have*. Los Angeles, 2016.

Boelke, Michael and Henryk Gericke. *Too Much Future: Punk in the DDR*, Berlin, Verbrecher, 2007.

Brannon, Bella. "Keith Morris—A Jewish Perspective from the Punk Rock Legend." *HáAm UCLA's Jewish Newsmagazine*, December 18, 2022.

Brannon, Bella. "Rocking it from the Casbah to CBGB's: How Jews Pioneered Punk Rock." *HáAm UCLA's Jewish Newsmagazine*, December 8, 2021.

Case, Peter. *As Far As You Can Get Without A Passport*. Atlanta, For Now Press, 2006.

Cave, Nick and Sean O'Hagan. *Faith, Hope and Carnage*. New York: Farrar, Straus and Giroux, 2022.

Chancellor, Reid. *Hardcore Anxiety: A Graphic Guide to Punk Rock and Mental Health*. Portland, Oregon: Microcosm, 2019.

Chen, Miguel. *I Wanna Be Well: How a Punk Found Peace and You Can Too*. Massachusetts: Wisdom Publications, 2018.

Cogan, Brian. *The Encyclopedia of Punk*. New York: Sterling Publishing, 2006.

Collin, Matthew. *Guerilla Radio: Rock 'N' Roll Radio and Serbia's Underground Resistance*. New York: Thunder's Mouth Press / Nation Book, 2001.

D'Ambrosio, Antonino. *Let Fury Have the Hour: Joe Strummer, Punk and the Movement that Shook the World*. New York: Nation Books, 2004.

de Segovia, José "Lutheran Dissidence in East Berlin—Hans Simon was the Lutheran Pastor of Zionskirche. He wore a turtleneck jumper and always had a pipe in his hand. The Stasi spied on his every move." *Evangelicalfocus.com*, January 22, 2024. https://evangelicalfocus.com/between-the-lines/25093/lutheran-dissidence-in-east-berlin

Dictor, Dave. *Memoirs From A Damaged Civilization: Stories of Punk, Fear and Redemption*. San Francisco: Manic D Press, 2016.

Doe, John. *Under The Big Black Sun: A Personal History of L.A. Punk*. Boston, MA: Da Capo Press, 2016.

Federal Agency for Civic Education. "Church from Below" Jugend Opposition in der DDR. https://www.jugendopposition.de/node/145405?guid=205

Fiebeler, Carsten. *OstPunk! Too Much Future*, documentary film, Berlin, Germany, 2006.

Flanagan, Harley. *Hard-Core: Life of My Own*. Port Towsend, WA: Feral House, 2016.

Flea. *Acid for the Children: A Memoir*. New York: Grand Central Publishing, 2019.

Frias, Fernando. *Ya no estoy aqui ("I'm No Longer Here")*, Mexico, 2019.

Gessen, Masha. *Words Will Break Cement: The Passion of Pussy Riot*. New York: Riverhead Books, 2014.

Gimarc, George. *Punk Diary: 1970–1979*. New York: St. Martins Press, 1994.

Ginoli, Jon. *Deflowered: My Life in Pansy Division*. San Francisco: Cleis Press, 2009.

Glasper, Ian. *The Day The Country Died: The History of Anarcho Punk 1980–1984*. Oakland: PM Press, 2014.

Gonzales, Michelle Cruz. *The Spitboy Rules: Tales of a Xicana in a Female Punk Band*. Oakland, CA: PM Press, 2016.

Gordon, Arvan. "Kirche von Unten and other Basis Groups in the GDR 1987–88." biblicalstudies.org, https://biblicalstudies.org.uk/pdf/rcl/17-2_127.pdf

Graffin, Greg. *Population Wars: A New Perspective on Competition and Coexistence*. New York: St. Martin's Griffin, 2015.

Graffin, Greg and Steve Olson. *Anarchy Evolution: Faith, Science and Bad Religion in a World Without God*. New York: Harper Perennial, 2010.

Grisham, Jack. *A Principle of Recovery: An Unconventional Journey through The Twelve Steps*. Huntington Beach, CA: Grisham, 2015.

Hartmann, Andreas. *My Buddha is Punk*. Documentary film—2015.

Hayton, Jeff. *Culture from the Slums: Punk Rock in East and West Germany*. Oxford: Oxford University Press, 2022.

Hell, Richard. *I Dreamed I Was A Very Clean Tramp*. Harper-Collins, 2013.

Hey Wild Crew. *Macehualopunks*. Mexico, 2022.

Hockenos, Paul. "Anarchy is Possible, Mr. Neighbor—Punks, Freethinkers and Anarchists in the GDR Fought to Change Socialism. You Hardly Read Anything about Them in History Books." November 8, 2017, TAZ.

Hockenos, Paul. *Berlin Calling: A Story of Anarchy, Music, the Wall, and the Birth of the New Berlin*. New York: The New Press, 2017.

Jensen, Keith Lowell. *Punching Nazis and Other Good Ideas*. New York: Skyhorse Publishing, 2018.

Jones, Preston. *Is Belief in God Good, Bad or Irrelevant?* Illinois: Intervaristy Press, 2006.

Joseph, John. *The Evolution of a Cro-Magnon*. PunkHouse, 2007.

Joseph, John. *Meat is For Pussies*. Harper, 2014.

Knight, Michael Muhamad. *Muhammad: Forty Introductions*. Soft Skull Press, 2019.

Knight, Michael Muhamad. *The Taqwacores*. Soft Skull Press, 2009.

Kuhn, Gabriel. *Sober Living For The Revolution*. Oakland: PM Press, 2010.

Lamere, Liz. *Infinite Dreams: The Life of Alan Vega*. Lanham, Maryland: Backbeat, 2024.

Letts, Don. *Punk Attitude*. Fremantle Media, 2005.

Levine, Noah. *Dharma Punx: A Memoir*. Harper Collins, 2003.

Lipp, Florian. *Punk und New Wave em letzten Jahrzehnt der DDR*. Waxmann Verlag GmbH, 2021.

Manzoor, Nida. *We Are Lady Parts*. UK, Working Title Television, 2021–2024.

Marcus, Greil. *Lipstick Traces*. Cambridge, MA: Harvard University Press, 1989.

Martens, China. *The Future Generation: The Zine-Book for Subculture Parents, Kids, Friends and Others*. Baltimore: Atomic Book Company, 2007.

McNeill, Legs and Gillian McCain. *Please Kill Me: The Uncensored Oral History of Punk*. New York: Grove Press, 1996.

Mohr, Tim. *Burning Down the Haus: Punk Rock, Revolution, and the Fall of the Berlin Wall*. Algonquin Books of Chapel Hill, 2019.

Moon, H. Paul. *Hamas Caziim: An Indigenous Punk Documentary*, Zen Violence Films, New York, 2011.

Morris, Keith. *My Damage*. Philadelphia: De Capo Press, 2016.

New Breed Films. *We Must Bleed: The Germs Documentary*, 2023.

Nilson, Tyler and Michael Schwartz. *Los Frikis,* New Slate Ventures, 2024.

Noebel, David A. *Rhythm, Riots and Revolution* Tulsa, Oklahoma: Christian Crusade Publications, 1966.

Peterson, Brian. *Burning Fight: The Nineties Hardcore Revolution in Ethics, Politics, Spirit and Sound.* Huntington Beach: Revelation Records, 2009.

Pop, Iggy. *I Need More*. Los Angeles, 1997.

Reeder, Mark. *B Movie: Lust and Sound in West-Berlin 1979–1989*. Germany, 2015.

Robb, John. *Punk Rock: An Oral History*. Oakland, CA: PM Press, 2006.

Rollins, Henry. *Occupants*. Chicago: Chicago Review Press, 2011.

Rombes, Nicholas. *A Cultural Dictionary of Punk: 1974–1982*. New York: Continuum Books, 2009.

Sorrondeguy, Martin. *Beyond the Screams / Mas Alla de Los Gritos: A U.S. Latino Hardcore Punk Documentary*. Lengua Armada, 1999.

Spooner, James. *The High Desert: Black. Punk. Nowhere*. Harper, 2022.

Stern, Eddie. *One Small Thing: A New Look at the Science of Yoga and How it Can Transform Your Life*. New York: North Point Press, 2020.

Stewart, Francis. *Punk is My Religion: Straight Edge Punk and 'Religious' Identity*. Oxfordshire: Routledge, 2017.

Terry, Chris L. and James Spooner. *Black Punk Now*. New York: Soft Skull, 2023.

Trynka, Paul. *Iggy Pop: Open Up and Bleed: A Biography*. New York City: Crown Archetype, 2011.

Rundfunk Berlin-Brandenburg. *Nazis in der DDR der Fall Zionskirche*. Germany, 2007.

Vale, V. "Search and Destroy: The Authoritative Guide to Punk Culture" (Complete Reprint of Issues #1–6 and #7–11) San Francisco: V/Search Publications, 1996.

Valentino, Bianca. *Conversations with Punx: A Spiritual Dialogue*. Australia: House of B, 2011.

Warner, Brad. *Hardcore Zen*. Massachusetts: Wisdom Publications, 2003.

Wright, Robin. *Rock The Casbah: Rage and Rebellion Across the Islamic World*. New York: Simon & Schuster, 2011.

INDEX

Page references for photographs are italicized